DATE DUE

NOV 2 9 1993	DEC 0 9 1999	
DEC 0 1 1993	MAR 0 9 2000	
JUN 1 9 1995	APR 3 - 2000	
NOV 0 9 1995	1 0 APR 2002	
	NOV. 1 3 2003	
DEC 0 1 1995	- 9 DEC 2003	
RECEIVED NOV 2 0 1995		
DEC 0 5 1997		

PERSUADERS

PERSUADERS

Influence Peddling, Lobbying and Political Corruption
in Canada

Paul Malvern

 Methuen

Toronto   New York   London   Sydney   Auckland

Canadian Cataloguing in Publication Data

Malvern, Paul.
    Persuaders: influence peddling, lobbying and political corruption in Canada

ISBN 0-458-99500-2

1. Lobbying — Canada.   2. Pressure groups — Canada.   3. Corruption (in politics) — Canada. I. Title.

JL148.5.M34 1985   322.4'3'0971   C85-099555-8

Printed and bound in Canada by John Deyell Company

1 2 3 4   85   89 88 87 86

CONTENTS

1

Introduction

One of the supposed payoffs from being a writer is the promotional tour which accompanies the release of your book. I say "supposed" for this pleasure tends to be more pleasant in anticipation and reflection than it is at the time. In reality, it is a sort of exercise in advanced forms of sado-masochism. The sadistic part involves boring some poor interviewer with your views (always passionately held, of course) on topics about which he or she could do very nicely without hearing. Still, a job is a job, particularly in these hard times, and most interviewers do their job with skill and care, and try, usually successfully, to seem interested. My heart goes out to them at such times. The masochistic part lies in the inner turmoil and anxiety which the poor writer must endure doing six or seven interviews a day, each in a different city, wondering each time how big an idiot he has just made of himself. There are moments, however, when the chemistry between writer and interviewer is right and the interview becomes not only a genuine pleasure but also a learning experience for both.

Such a situation occurred on the first day of the promotional tour to publicize my book, *Fighting Back*. On this occasion I had the distinct delight of lunching with and being interviewed by an extremely attractive woman who was one of the business reporters for the *Ottawa Citizen*. She was forthright from the very beginning. Her first question was, in effect, what was in it for me? What kind of person writes a book trashing Revenue Canada, that most feared Canadian institution? What was my problem?

I replied that I had come from a little village in the country and that country people believed in justice and expected politicians and the political system to operate the way they were supposed to, the way they claimed to. She looked astounded and asked me if I didn't think that naive. I had to admit that from a big city perspective it was the height of naivete. But the majority of the country still lives in places whose names are not Toronto, Montreal, Ottawa or Vancouver, and I believe

1

that the majority of Canadians does not share that fashionable cynicism so *au courant* in the major cities.

I have been grateful to that woman ever since, for she helped me to understand something important about myself. Ever since I was a child I wondered what could be the matter with me, and now I knew. All that time I had expected things to be the way that I was told they were. The problem was that I could not help but notice that despite all the talk about fine tailoring it seemed that the emperor did not actually have any clothes on. I occasionally pointed this out to people around me. They did not seem pleased. I learned that it is best for children (and later adults) to keep quiet about the numerous discrepancies between what our betters tell us and what really is. Nevertheless, I have never given up on the idea that if we are told by our betters that the world is a certain way and that they act in a certain noble way, then they will actually act that way.

This book is intended to show that the political system and the actors therein do not operate at all as we are told they do. What is passed off as truth in our schools, by our politicians and by the media is as far from truth as anything can be. The picture which develops may not seem a pleasant one for most; it was not a pleasant one for me to discover and accept either. Still, I suspect that my vision of what is really going on in Canada may not come as a complete surprise to readers, most of whom have probably thought at one time or other that the government was not listening to them or was not concerned with their needs. After all, wasn't that the reason for the big landslide in the 1984 Canadian general election? But it doesn't seem to matter whether we vote the rascals out or not. Things always stay the same. During the 1984 election one disgruntled man remarked, "It doesn't matter who gets elected. We still end up with a government." My sentiments entirely.

If you have felt that no one was listening to your needs, then I suggest just one thing — perhaps it is because the government is too busy listening to the loud and influential voices of a favoured few, so busy it doesn't have either the time or the money for your problems. In other words, there are rich and powerful people and groups that are going behind our backs to get those "goodies" from government that are by rights ours. You think not? Read on and find out how it really is. And pour yourself a stiff one. You'll need it.

One last thing. For those of you who are either unemployed or think that you too would like to be rich and powerful I have included a section on how you too can get in on the graft.

PART I

THE SETTING OF THE GAME

Like everything else in life, the exercise of influence can be seen as simply a behavioural game. It exists in a setting, is based on certain rules and has a goal or goals. In the next three chapters we'll look at the historical, structural and behavioural setting of this game. If it seems a bit general, don't worry; later chapters will fill out the details nicely.

2

Lobbying, Influence Peddling and Corruption: A Great Canadian Tradition

In the nineteenth century French novelist and social critic Emile Zola noted that behind every fortune is a crime. With apologies to Monsieur Zola, we might add with equal truth that behind every nation is a lie, or rather a complex of coherent lies, that becomes the "national dream" or official ideology, the cement which holds the nation with its many diverse and often conflicting interests together. It is the stuff of nationhood, a nation's reason to exist. Without it workers would not accept restrictions on their salaries. Without it soldiers would not throw away their lives on faraway battlefields. Without it voters would not continue to believe that the sole purpose of politicians is to further the interests of their constituents. It is this myth which is preached every day as absolute truth from every pulpit, schoolroom, radio and television set in the country. It is very powerful and it is believed.

The strength of this myth may be seen from the shocked reaction at the obscenely hasty patronage appointments following the retirement of Pierre Trudeau. Why were Canadians so shocked? This sort of graft is as Canadian as the beaver, the maple leaf, McDonald's hamburgers and U.S. television programs. The history of corruption, graft and influence peddling is there for all to see. Since few attempts have been made to suppress the details, the question is, why do so few people seem to know about it? The answer is that the process of propagating the national myth has been fabulously successful. Despite all the evidence to the contrary, the Canadian people really do believe that they are governed by politicians who have their best interests at heart. Canadians really do view their state as neutral and concerned with some vague and never defined idea called the "national interest" or the "common good."

People should not have been surprised at the two hundred odd (and I do mean odd!) Liberal Party cronies who have been allowed to swill at the public trough — many for the rest of their lives — thanks to the largesse of the Prime Minister. For it is not "peace, order and good government" which has been the tradition of Canadian government, but rather a slightly different triad — patronage, undue influence and influence peddling.

The practice of influence peddling is as old as the nation itself. Much of the early history of the area which we now call Canada was concerned with the fur trade. Very early on, the two great imperial powers which have moulded our history — England and France — discovered that enormous wealth could be garnered by harvesting the vast numbers of pelts from fur-bearing animals in the new land. This was an age of mercantilism, and government felt no compunction whatsoever about interfering and guiding economic forces. Indeed it often took a very active role in many of the leading commercial ventures. Almost from the beginning, both governments granted charters to monopolies. Companies granted these charters had a virtual licence to print money. Do not imagine for a moment that the grants resulted from some sort of seventeenth-century tender system that balanced off qualifications and ability to do the job against the larger national interest and the impact on the native peoples and the environment. Nothing of the sort. There were no impact studies; no Royal Commissions as we know them. Rather, the only studies and hearings were intimate chats to determine how the person of the King, his family and lackeys might benefit from this rape of the New World. The bribes, the secret entreaties and lobbying that went on to gain these charters would cause modern-day influence peddlers to turn green with envy. These people were good — very good — at the business of bringing undue influence to bear on matters of state. They played a hard game indeed, for the stakes were enormous.

Canada Before the Conquest
The current practice of ministers of state being hard pressed to resist using their insider information to make tidy sums for themselves, their friends and favourite constituents and businesses finds its roots in this period. One of the first companies in New France to engage in the fur trade was Champlain's, founded in 1614. Its monopoly was abolished in 1620. The next year William De Caen and his nephew, merchants of Rouen, obtained a charter, soon absorbed Champlain's company, and for a while carried on business without any competition. Pretty dull so

far, but it gets better. In 1627 they began to experience some stiff competition from a company whose major stockholders were rich Parisians. Not unexpectedly, these gentlemen sought to gain the monopoly for themselves. The fact that this newcomer, the Company of New France, was granted a fifteen-year monopoly plus ownership of the entire St. Lawrence should not come as a great surprise since the company's founder was none other than Cardinal Richelieu, the power behind the French throne. It is hard to compete with influence like that.

The trade in beaver pelts seems to have been not unlike our present-day drug trade. The sums involved were enormous, and large amounts of money could be made very quickly. This fast money drew the most unscrupulous elements in society and soon found its way as bribes and gifts to public officials. As influence peddling and lobbying techniques of today go, it was a primitive means for influencing government decisions, yet it had one major virtue — it worked.

Like the present-day drug kings, the individuals who were engaged in the fur trade were ruthless. They would do anything to hold onto and increase the profits of their businesses. One of the slimiest tricks of the trade was to give the Indians alcohol. Once they were well and truly drunk, the traders would then steal their furs. The price was certainly right and the strategy had the virtue of being simple. Better yet (or worse yet, from the point of view of the Indians) it worked. In fact it worked too well.

Initially the more responsible elements of society (white society, that is) were truly horrified by the abuses of the trade. On April 17, 1664, the Sovereign Council issued a decree prohibiting bartering or giving intoxicating beverages to Indians. The Church added its voice to the condemnation of these practices. In 1669 Mother Mary of the Incarnation wrote, "What does the most harm here is the traffic in wine and brandy. We preach against those who give these liquors to the savages, and yet many reconcile their consciences to the permission of this thing. They go into the woods and carry drinks to the savages in order to get their furs for nothing when they are drunk. Immorality, theft, and murder ensue. . . ."[1] Now, when Mother Mary said "immorality," she wasn't kidding. We are not talking here about putting a lampshade on your head and dancing on the table. The Marquis de Demonville wrote in January 1690 to the Marquis de Seignelay, the King's Minister at Versailles, "There is no crime they do not commit in their excesses. A mother throws her child in the fire;

noses are bitten off; this is a frequent occurrence."[2] The good Mother was correct. This was immorality.

Eventually, the moral response began to waver. The 1664 decree of the Supreme Council was rescinded in 1668 when the same Supreme Council made it lawful for all Frenchmen inhabiting Canada to sell and deliver liquor to the Indians. There was just too much money in the trade, and the traders were able to influence the loftiest and most respected elements of society and government. Even the Church was corrupted. Governor Frontenac, writing to Colbert, the Minister of Finance under Louis XIV, said of the Jesuits that "they think as much of the conversion of Beaver as of souls; for the majority of their missions are pure mockeries. . . ."[3] Then the flood gates broke. Government officials went from being the object of bribes and gifts to actually being involved in the trade illegally themselves. A commission of twenty prominent men was set up to investigate the widespread corruption, but the commission's findings were later discounted when it became clear that most or all of its members were involved in the trade in one way or other themselves.

The fur trade was not the only source of influence peddling and corruption in New France. Land too proved to be a great temptation. One of the most effective lobbyists in New France was the Church. It is estimated that the Church was granted about one–fourth of the approximately 8 million acres which was given away by the State up to the Conquest in 1759. With such an enormous source of wealth plus that garnered from the fur trade, the Church went from the role of major lobbyist to that of almost a State unto itself. Indeed, dispatches of officials to France began to mention with resentment the Church's new attitude. Finally, the Church began to see itself as no longer subject to the authority of the civil judicial authorities. This is, of course, a rather magnificent example of what can happen when one interest group gets too much of its own way for too long a period of time.

The Church should not be held completely responsible for the abuses of influence peddling that occurred during this period. Others, including the military, found the temptation too great to resist as well. It was easy for the rich and powerful interests to get their way, because these interests had easy access to the innermost centres of decision making and state power and were extremely effective at presenting their cases. The same elements are present in Canadian society today, with the difference being one of degree. What is clear is that the free play which influence peddlers and "lobbyists" enjoyed and the internal decay which resulted played no small part in softening up French Canada for the British conquest.

British Rule After the Conquest

With French rule in Canada involving enormous corruption, both public and private, it seemed as if any other regime would be an improvement. Those that thought this were sadly mistaken. With the coming of British rule, a new period of corruption and influence peddling was dawning.

Even before the conquest the record of influence peddling among the British was a sad one. The founding of the Hudson Bay Company, that great symbol of native "Canadian" capitalism, must have been one of the greatest *tours de force* in the history of lobbying. The charter granted by Charles II in 1670 provided the company with enormous powers and privileges, including an exclusive and perpetual monopoly of the commerce in all of the waters "in whatsoever latitude they shall be, that lie within the entrance of the streights commonly called Hudson's Streights, together with all the lands, countries, and territories upon the coasts and confines of the seas, streights, bays, lakes, rivers, creeks, and sounds aforesaid, which are not now actually possessed by any of our subjects, or by the subjects of any other Christian prince or State."[4] In addition to the purely commercial advantages, there were other privileges granted which meant that the Hudson Bay Company was able to function virtually as a state in its own right. In return for this the Company was obliged to pay two elks and two black beavers whenever and as often as Charles or his successors entered the Company's territories. Not a bad deal on the Company's part and not that bad for Charles either since he really did not have any right to the territories he ceded. The real fun began, however, with the conquest. Up to then British activities had been limited by the French, but with the French defeat the British were really able to show their genius for exploitation.

Following the conquest, the emphasis in corruption and influence peddling began to shift further away from the fur trade and move towards obtaining large tracts of land. One of the first acts of the new British administration in Canada was to create a new land-owning class. The advantages were obvious. First of all, these people would have a vested interest in the survival of British power in Canada (Stalin used a technique similar to this in the 1930s to consolidate his hold over the Soviet Union), and second, it was a means by which the new rulers could enrich themselves as the officials ensured that they, their friends and relatives were early recipients of many of the best grants. However, they would also be able to enrich themselves as a result of bribes from others receiving land and by fraudulently skimming off some of the State's revenues from the sale and granting of lands. This is exactly what happened.

One of the first acts of the new British Administration was to abolish the old seigneurial system. This was a pity in one way for there were some features of the old system that were positive, one of the best being that under French law any person who applied in good faith could obtain land from government officials. The abuses which occurred were a result of evasion of the law rather than a result of the law. In any case, the seigneurial system of land grants was abolished in 1763. It was replaced in 1791 by a system of so-called free grants and free tenure. The word "free" is a complete misnomer. In fact, this system resulted in perhaps even worse abuses than had occurred under the old system. J.C. Langelier, in his list of lands granted between 1763 and 1890, notes that the system gave rise to "the plague of large landowners which has so greatly hindered the settlement and material advancement of the Province."[5] Apparently this system was replete with abuses. Individuals would make deals with Provincial officials, obtain whole townships and close it to settlers. This happened in a large portion of the Eastern Townships.

Langelier goes on to describe how the system really worked: "A person wishing to thus take possession of a portion of the public domain, first came to an understanding with the members of the Executive Council and the person occupying the highest positions, to secure their concurrence and that of the Governor. He afterwards came to an understanding with a certain number of individuals, picked up at hap-hazard, to get them to sign a petition to the Governor, praying for the granting of land he desired. To compensate them for this accommodating act on their part, he paid his associates a nominal sum generally a guinea, in consideration of which they at once transferred their shares to him as soon as the letters patent were issued."[6] Not only were members of the government aware of this, they took part in it from time to time: "These frauds were committed with the knowledge of the Executive Council, several of whose members used this means to obtain large grants of public lands."[7]

This practice proved to be so lucrative to government officials that they resisted all efforts to eliminate it by those members of the ruling elite who might be of a more public-spirited nature. In Lower Canada, Governor Prescott attempted to stop the waste of public lands, but his actions brought down the hatred of the Executive Council upon him. Judge Osgoode (think of Osgoode Hall, that bastion of legal education in Ontario), who was head of the Executive Council at the time, was able to secure Prescott's recall. Thus was virtue rewarded. His successor proved to be more to the liking of the Council in that he permitted continued plundering of Crown lands.

But let's not forget our friends in the fur trade. They were able to take time out from their activities in stealing from the Indians to get their share of the goodies back home. It would seem the North West Company either had powerful influence over or controlled the new governor, Sir Robert Shore Milnes, and the Executive Council. Indeed, some of the more powerful members of the Executive Council were principals in the North West Company. Needless to say, they were among the leading recipients of the booty. Interestingly enough the list contains names of people whose descendants are among the leading figures in Canadian society.

Let us not for a moment suppose that this influence peddling, graft and corruption was peculiar to Quebec. Judge Thorpe, writing on December 1, 1806 from York (now Toronto) to Sir George Shee, complained of a "shopkeeper aristocracy" which had curried favour with past lieutenant governors and now surrounded the new one. According to Thorpe, their influence stretched from Halifax to Detroit and their object was to "get as many dollars as you can for [from] the Governor by land."[8] Once they had fed at the trough their family and friends were next. They were given huge tracts of land for whatever price they cared to pay. This system of "set your own price" was not known for resulting in overpayments. The price was always right.

Judge Thorpe's campaign against this "shopkeeper aristocracy"[9] provides us with a wonderful glimpse into the lobbying and influence peddling practices of the time. According to Thorpe, public lands were a major temptation and often were bartered openly in situations that stank of corruption of public officials. Public money was often missing under such circumstances that only the embezzlement of public funds could reasonably explain. There was an all-powerful clique which set itself up as final arbiter of what was good and bad and had the power to enforce its demands. Thorpe was carried forward by a popular swell of support for his campaign to expose and end these abuses. He was elected by this groundswell of supporters to the Ontario House of Assembly. Unfortunately he had by this time acquired many powerful enemies. Certainly, his charge that many of the members of the Assembly had been bribed by grants of public land won him few friends among fellow members. Judge Thorpe was finally rewarded for his efforts by being dismissed from public office.

One of the greatest lobbies of the day was of course the so-called Family Compact. This group differed somewhat depending on the part of the country. In most of the country it seems to have been a "party" made up of the elite of the country. It counted among its members the courts, the highest segments of the Anglican Church and a good portion of the legal profession (plus ça change, plus c'est la même chose). Lord Durham, in his Report on the affairs of British North America, states: "by grant or purchase they have acquired nearly the whole of the waste lands of the Province; they are all-powerful in the chartered banks, and till lately, shared among themselves almost exclusively all offices of trust and profit." [10] In Nova Scotia "The Family Compact" seems to have actually had something of a family character to it. Two families made up five members of the Executive Council of that province and until 1837 five members were co-partners in one banking house. [11]

Apparently, the graft of officials knew no bounds in this period. Vast grants of land had been set aside as a reward to loyal supporters of the British Crown during the American Revolution who came to be known as the United Empire Loyalists. Many of these people found that their immediate need to stay alive was such that they were forced to sell these grants just to stay alive. As might be expected, there was a line-up of public officials only too happy to exploit these newly arrived citizens. And exploit them they did. Most of the land granted to Loyalists and their children was ultimately bought by speculating government officials for ridiculously low prices. It is estimated that the price for 200 acres of land varied from a gallon of rum to six pounds, with the first sum more often the price than the second. I should point out that when I speak of officials I am not referring to petty officials or functionaries. The highest officials in the land were involved in this scam. Lord Durham cites in his report the names of Mr. Hamilton, a member of the Legislative Council (100,000 acres), Chief Justices Emslie and Powell and Solicitor-General Grey (20,000 to 50,000 acres). In addition, members of the legislative and executive councils and the House of Assembly were listed as very large purchasers. It's good to see the warm welcome which our "betters" of the time extended to their newly arrived friends and allies. Never had loyalty to the Crown been better rewarded!

As noted before, a good portion of the members of the Family Compact was made up of members of the Church of England. This connection was to prove invaluable for the Church in its new home. Soon members and high church officials were able to join their lay brothers and sisters at the public trough. Some of the oinks emanating from this feeding frenzy began to take on a certain ecclesiastical flavour. The Clergy Reserves had arrived.

About 3 million acres were granted for the support of Protestant clergy. The original impetus for this had been the desire on the part of the Church of England to be placed on an equal footing with the Roman Catholic Church. After all, the Church of Rome had had its time at the trough before the Conquest, so why shouldn't the Church of England have its time now? The Anglican Bishop of Quebec writing to Lieutenant-Governor Milnes in 1803 complained that: "Compared to the respectable Establishments, the substantial Revenues, and the intensive power and privileges of the Church of Rome, the Church of England sinks into a merely tolerated Sect; possessing at the moment not one Shilling of Revenue which it can properly call its own. . . ."[12] Sad, isn't it? Don't worry though, because help had already appeared on the horizon, even before the Archbishop's epistle. The clergy reserves, as they were called, had been established by an act in 1791 which directed that whenever the government made a grant of land it must set aside a tract of land equal to one-seventh of the land that had been granted. As if this were not enough, various frauds and irregularities occurred which meant that the clergy of Upper Canada received one-sixth of the land granted instead of the one-seventh originally intended. Indeed, in some cases the clergy received lands that should have gone to the public. Gustavus Myers in his study *A History of Canadian Wealth* asserts that not only were the clergy aware of these frauds perpetrated for their benefit but that highly placed churchmen such as Bishop Mountain of Quebec and Bishop Strachan of Toronto obtained land individually. According to Myers, "There is not a scrap of evidence that the clergy ever called attention to the excess land that they thus fraudulently or erroneously acquired or sought to restore it. . . ."[13] As always, having friends in high places paid off.

The Golden Age of Influence Peddling

The rebellions of 1837 represented the end of a sort of quasi-feudalism in Canadian history even though both had in fact failed. Up until this point wealth had come largely from land in one form or other. Originally, it was the forest fur trade that held out the greatest promise for quick fortunes, with influence peddling and corruption centred on obtaining charters and bribing officials so as to avoid various laws designed to prevent the worst excesses of this trade. This was a game that could be played only by a few very rich and powerful people. The group that it sought to influence or corrupt was also very small since power had been tightly centralized in the hands of a lucky few. There were no media and very few governmental reviews and checks and balances to interfere with the "under the table" deals that went on. In fact, many of these fraudulent deals were barely concealed since there was no need to keep them from the public view. After all, the views, feelings and wishes of the mass of people were of no consequence. As the economy became more concerned with agriculture and as the holding of power became somewhat more decentralized (not much, but a little) the game became a little different. Now one was occupied with obtaining fraudulent land grants or benefiting from the frauds of others as with the churches. Bribes still worked and government officials still wanted to get in on the corruption themselves.

However, by the early to mid–nineteenth century, one was beginning to see the emergence of pesky newspaper people and worse yet, even reformers. One now had to exercise a little caution. Still, there was only so much money that could be made since agriculture was essentially a labour intensive activity. The beginning of the capitalist phase in Canadian history in the mid–nineteenth century augured a new era. Now one could become filthy rich through influence peddling, whether the influence peddler was a government official or entrepreneur. The game was beginning to get more sophisticated and more difficult but it was also more fun. This was the golden age of influence peddling — the age of the coming of the railroads.

While this was the high point in influence peddling, it was the low point of public morality. While public officials had been vilely corrupt in the past, their duplicity had been tempered by their small numbers. The number of elected officials had increased, but unfortunately their greed had not diminished. The result in terms of the public purse was devastating.

Toward the middle of the nineteenth century it became clear that there was a dramatic need for a major network of railways in Canada. Part of that need came from the type of economy which Canada (or what was to become Canada) possessed. Essentially, the country represented a resource hinterland for its imperial mistress, then Great Britain, later the United States. It was imperative to get the products of the hinterland — timber, minerals, furs, fish, agricultural products — on their way to the cities of the East, notably Montreal, and abroad. In addition — and here it is difficult to assess the importance as a factor —

there were political considerations which involved tying this widely dispersed land together.

While it was clear that the building of railroads was necessary, it was not clear where the capital for such a mammoth project would come from. Eventually, government volunteered. The influence peddlers and corrupt politicians could not believe their luck.

Usually when we think of influence peddling and corruption, we imagine a situation where outside interests are so intent upon achieving their ends that they start to bend the rules to get politicians, judges and civil servants to do what they want, offering various carrots or sticks. Still, the politicians and government officials are here, the lobbyists there. But with the railroad scandals, a large number of the people who were to issue charters and make the laws that would set up the government financing for companies that would do the work on building the railways happened also to be principals in the companies seeking the money. Many of those who benefited financially were not just ordinary Members of Parliament; rather, some were among the foremost members — party leaders, Cabinet Ministers, even Prime Ministers.

The amazing thing about this period in Canadian history is just how open and well known influence peddling was. Speaking of the behaviour of members during debates, Lord Sydenham wrote in 1840, "But when it came to their own affairs, above all, to money matters, there was a scene of confusion and riot of which no one in England can have any idea. Every man proposes a vote for his own job; and bills are introduced without notice, and carried through *all* their stages in a quarter of an hour!"[14]

One of the more candid parliamentarians and promoters of railroads must surely be Sir Allan M. MacNab, famous for his statement that railroads were his politics. And so they were. The promoters of the London and Gore Railroad Company were headed by MacNab, and when the line developed later into the Great Western Railway, MacNab was its president. In his parallel career MacNab was also a member of Parliament, later Speaker of Parliament, a knight, Prime Minister in 1854 and finally he was raised to a baronetcy in 1856. He was also Chairman of the Legislative Assembly Standing Committee on Railways for a number of years. Probably just a coincidence.

MacNab was of course just the tip of the iceberg. Other famous promoters in the Parliament of the time were George E. Cartier, and even John A. Macdonald, who saw dual service at one time or other as a parliamentarian and railway promoter. There were others, many others, some members of the Canadian parliament and cabinet, others holding office in provincial assemblies or at the municipal level.

This was only part of the situation, however. Obviously not every member was a lobbyist for the railways or a stockholder in railway companies. Very few, however, did not have some monetary benefit to be gained. Some were large landholders whose land would rise in value as a result of the coming developments; some were suppliers of goods and services that would be sold to various railway companies once development and construction began. Almost all stood to gain something. Almost all did gain something.

One of my favourite scandals involved Sir Francis Hincks and the Grand Trunk. In 1850, Parliament passed an act which contained a conditional provision that the Grand Trunk Railway could be constructed as a public work by the Canadian government in conjunction with various municipalities. This was a clear statement that private enterprise was not needed for this project. Why was this clause never carried out? The answer lies in the person of Sir Francis Hincks. In his capacity as Inspector General or Finance Minister, Hincks was sent as an envoy to England to negotiate with the British government. He did not insist upon final inclusion of the clause mentioned above; rather, he turned over the contract for building the railway to the British contracting firm of Peto, Brassey, Betts and Jackson. Originally this was put down to the belief that Hincks had bowed to pressure from the British government, but the picture took on a different complexion when it became known that this company had given Hincks £50,000 of paid-up company stock. This revelation caused such a stir among the general public that the Upper House of Parliament was compelled to strike an investigating committee. The problem with this committee was that the investigators were men who had received "gifts" from mysterious donors just as Hincks had. Despite extremely damning evidence against him and a very weak explanation from Hincks himself that he had merely been holding the stock in trust in case some parties in Canada might be interested in buying the company's stock in the future, Hincks was exonerated.

Anyone who thought that the scandals involving the railways would subside as the industry matured was to be sorely disappointed. If anything, the scandals got worse and the sums got bigger. Ultimately they were to encompass one of Canada's foremost companies and force the resignation of Canada's first Prime Minister.

The formation of the CPR had not been easy. A number of companies were competing for the business of building a railway coast to coast.

The government was reluctant to deal with any of the competitors and made it clear that no government money would flow until the companies were amalgamated. There was, of course, reluctance on the part of some of the companies to do this. No one wants half a loaf when they think they can have the whole thing. It was Sir Hugh Allan who ultimately settled matters. His campaign consisted of two thrusts. He engaged in a bribery scheme of truly heroic proportions to ensure that government was "properly fixed" and, this out of the way, brought about an amalgamation of companies that led to the formation of the CPR. On February 5, 1873, the Governor General signed the charter for the company and the CPR pledged itself to build the railway within ten years from July 20, 1871. In return, it was to receive a land grant of 50 million acres and the subsidy of $30 million payable from time to time. The company was allowed capital of $10 million — not bad for people just starting out in business. How could a fledgling company start out in such handsome style? How indeed!

On April 2, 1873, Lucius S. Huntington rose in the House of Commons and in effect accused the Prime Minister, Sir John A. Macdonald, of having sold the charter for the CPR in return for a large amount of money to be used for securing re-election. As it turned out, he was correct.

Under pressure Macdonald agreed to a parliamentary committee which would investigate the charge. Things went along well for a time; no results were forthcoming. Unfortunately for Macdonald, Huntington suddenly published a series of letters and telegrams from Sir Hugh Allan of an extremely damning nature. Apparently, Allan had worked overtime on influencing public opinion, pressuring the government and bribing government officials. In one of his letters, he wrote: "But even in that view, means must be taken to influence the public, and I employed several young French lawyers to write it up for their own newspapers. I subscribed a controlling interest in the stock, and proceeded to subsidize the newspapers themselves, both editors and proprietors. I went to the country through which the road would pass, and called on many of the inhabitants. I visited the priests and made friends of them, and I employed agents to go among the principal people and talk it up. I then began to hold public meetings, and attended to them myself, making frequent speeches in French to them, showing them where their true interest lay. The scheme at once became popular, and I formed a Committee to influence the members of the Legislature. . . ."[15]

All this work succeeded magnificently. Of course the government was not slow in asking for favours either. Sir George E. Cartier wrote the following letter to Allan on July 30, 1872: "The friends of the Government will expect to be assisted with funds in the pending elections, and any amount which you or your Company shall advance for that purpose shall be recouped to you. A memorandum of immediate requirements is below." The memo went as follows:

NOW WANTED.[16]

Sir John A. Macdonald	$25,000
Hon. Mr. Langevin	15,000
Sir G.E.C.	20,000
Sir J.A. (add'l)	10,000
Hon. Mr. Langevin	100,000
Sir G.E.C. (add'l)	30,000

As a result of this new information, a Royal Commission was appointed. It started work with a vengeance. The testimony of both Allan and Macdonald was highly damaging and incriminating. Macdonald's own testimony indicated that he had engaged in selling charters along with Allan in order to receive money for election purposes and Allan stated that he had spent about $350,000 in bribes and other expenses to promote the CPR deal. Sir John A. Macdonald was forced to resign.

What followed this grand period of railway building may be described as being more of the same, although there was less entertainment value to be had in the early wild and woolly times. One character does stand out — William Lyon Mackenzie King. King was personally about as drab a character as you could imagine, but even he was involved in the mud of influence peddling. Up until King, most of the slime involved indigenous Canadians trying to influence their politicians. King had an embarrassment of riches. Not only did he have native Canadian lobbyists vying for his attentions and plying him with gifts of money, he was courted by the Rockefeller family throughout his administration. King had started off his career as a union buster for the Rockefeller family, and just prior to the entry of the United States in the First World War he was employed to "bring labour peace to the mines of Colorado." What this means is that he was involved in suppressing existing unions and replacing them with company unions. His performance pleased the Rockefellers enormously and his personal contacts with the family continued for the rest of his life. The

Rockefellers were generous too. John D. Rockefeller, Jr. gave King a gift of $100,000 in 1948.

After his death, most Canadians were astonished to discover that King had been quite a wealthy man despite the fact that he had never had any income (so it seemed) other than his salary. The answer lay in the many gifts he received. A fund of $225,000 was collected for him by Peter Larkin in order to allow him to live in a manner appropriate to the owner of Laurier House, and he was left $50,000 in 1944 upon the death of Sir William Mulock. There were corporate gifts as well. Says Larry Zolf about King and patronage, "In the early 1930s the Beauharnois power company through its campaign slush fund virtually corrupted prime minister King . . ."[17] The aftermath of the incident was a scandal which killed one senator and forced two others to resign.

Of course, no look at lobbying, influence peddling and political corruption in Canadian history would be complete without mention of Maurice Duplessis and his Union Nationale which ruled Quebec for most of the period from 1936 to the early 1960s. While there were abuses of power in Ottawa during the King era, Duplessis's reign was one long abuse of power. It was institutionalized graft at its very worst. No feature of the system went untouched — elections, tendering of government business, appointments to government jobs and the administration of justice. No institution, no matter how respectable, was free from corruption. Of course, business at all levels was involved, but what was surprising was the involvement of the police, the courts and even the Church.

Elections during the Duplessis era were a joke. Votes were bought, ballot boxes stuffed, and voters' lists tampered with. Sometimes these corrupt practices were covert. Just as frequently they were open.

Still the real manipulation took place through the corruption of institutions by Duplessis. Large sectors of the trade union movement were corrupted by the government's rather magnificent but tightly controlled program of dispensing patronage jobs and business was an integral part of the system. It was well known that no contract of any significance would be won without a "contribution" to the Union Nationale. In some cases a kickback to the party was built into each contract, and a percentage would be "kicked back" to the civil servant who let out the contract, who would in turn give the lion's share to the Party, keeping a modest portion for himself. Newspapers were also corrupted, with those supporting the UN assured of large government contracts and those who were opposed getting nothing.

The Church was extremely vulnerable because of the heavy cash requirements needed to fund its work in education, hospitals and social services. The cost of a parish hall or program was often a sermon by the priest in support of the Union Nationale in the upcoming election. Even school commissions were corrupt. Duplessis once stated bluntly, "It is our principle — and I'm not hiding it — that when there are two school commissions asking for grants and one is friendly, take care of our friends first; when there is enough to take care of opponents we do so generously without political considerations." This policy applied to all aspects of government and community life. Duplessis made this clear in a statement in 1952: "I warned you in 1948 not to elect the Liberal candidate. You did not listen to me. Unhappily your county did not obtain the subsidies, the grants which could have made you happier. I hope that you have learned your lesson and will vote against the Liberal candidate this time."[18]

That is enough of the past. Let's look at how these great Canadian traditions unfold in today's society.

3

The Real World of Politics: The Federal and Provincial Settings

All of us as school children are exposed to an idealized and fairy tale–like view of how the Canadian political system works. It is said to be made up of institutions that function well and whose sole purpose is to serve the needs of the nation. It is a landscape peopled by civil servants who work hard, politicians who are intelligent and public-spirited, and a citizenry that is well-informed and bases its vote on the issues of the day. One day's perusal of the media gives the lie to this view. Nevertheless, this view is part of the official ideology of the nation and as such has power, so it serves as a useful backdrop for a study on how the political system actually operates.

According to the official view, Parliament is supreme. Elections are contested by the political parties on the basis of the issues of the day and give a meaningful choice to the electorate. The parties take their ideas from the people and, once the winner has been proclaimed, the policies espoused by the winner become public policy. Individual MPs give voice to their constituents' wishes. The Prime Minister is a member of Parliament like the others, but is *primus inter pares*, which is to say, first among equals. He is guided in his policies by his cabinet and by the views of MPs. Bills passed by the Lower House go to the Senate for approval and may be vetoed on occasion if they seem especially ill-considered. The senators are ladies and gentlemen of unusual qualifications who have achieved the status of elder statesmen and stateswomen. Senators serve one other important function: they represent various regional and minority interests and thus give a balanced and compassionate understanding that might otherwise not exist. Once a bill has passed the House of Commons and Senate, it becomes law and is administered by the civil service, which is non–partisan and acts in a fair and unbiased manner. On occasion Parliament and the civil service may seek advice from various interest groups or individuals with special knowledge. The influence of these individuals and groups is not undue. Politicians and civil servants balance off the wishes and needs of these groups and individuals against the greater good of the national interest.

Sounds good, doesn't it? Well, it's true that there are elections, there is a building called the House of Commons, there is a Senate Chamber — that great Canadian monument to the concept of the resurrection of the dead. There are civil servants — millions of them, it seems, and all of them at lunch or on course. There are lobbyists and representatives of special interests. The rest of this view is wishful thinking at best and propaganda at worst. The question then is, what is the real nature of Canadian politics? The answer is not a pleasant one.

First of all, let's forget about elections. One of the most important truths about the Canadian political parties is that they are virtually the same. A poll conducted during the last federal election showed that 49 percent of those interviewed could not identify any difference between the two major parties. As for the NDP, which touts itself as a real alternative, it is in fact little more than the left wing of the Liberal Party. The ease with which NDP stalwarts like former Governor General Ed Schreyer can mingle in the establishment once blessed by the major party in power tells the electorate just how little difference there is between this "socialist" party and the two major political parties.

Of course, none of this really matters much anyway. Individual MPs have no independence once elected and have virtually no influence. This is particularly true of backbenchers of the party in power, who must submit to tight party discipline. Former Prime Minister Trudeau, speaking no doubt of the doubtful qualifications of ordinary MPs, is reputed to have remarked that MPs were nobodies twenty minutes from Parliament Hill. James Gillies and Jean Pigott, in a recent paper on the legislative process, remarked that in fact the reverse is the case: "It is on Parliament Hill, when assessed in terms of impact on policy formation, that MPs are nobodies. Parliament does not have significant input in policy formation — and Canadians do not have the type of responsible government that in many cases they think they have and in most cases expect to have.[1]

One of the most telling pieces of evidence for this decline in the importance of Parliament and MPs is that fewer and fewer lobbyists ever take the time to lobby MPs. It just is not worth their time or energy. Robert Presthus in his book on elite accommodation in Canada questioned lobbyists as to where they go to influence government and contrasted this with the situation in the United States:

Target of Interest Group	Canada	U.S.
Bureaucracy	40%	21%
Cabinet and executive assistants	24	7
Legislators and leg. committees	27	59
Judiciary	3	3
Other	6	9
Total	100%	100%

Source: Robert Presthus, *Elite Accommodation in Canadian Politics* (New York: Cambridge University Press, 1973), p. 255. Reproduced by permission.

Quite simply, MPs in Canada just don't have what it takes anymore. More and more power has been transferred away from Parliament to the Cabinet, Prime Minister, the upper levels of the civil service and to newly aggrandized bodies like the Prime Minister's Office and the Privy Council. More and more it seems that control by the people is becoming increasingly tenuous. In fact, such control is largely imaginary.

Worse yet, these targeted bodies are becoming less responsible and more undemocratic. The cabinet has gone from a body operating in a very personal way to a highly bureaucratic one. The process of formalization begun under Pearson found its ultimate expression under Trudeau when everything was considered by a committee before it could come to cabinet. The result, as we all know, has been the increase in importance of such bodies as the PMO and the Privy Council cited above.

The civil service has seen a similar trend toward increased power and decreased control by unelected officials. In a recent interview with George Bain of the *Vancouver Sun* on the television talk show *Realities*, host Robert Fulford noted that many upper level civil servants were becoming public celebrities in their own right and were expressing contempt for their Ministers because of their supposed lack of knowledge and competence. So much for control of the civil service.

The Senate has come into a discredit which surpasses even that which it enjoyed in the past, a truly remarkable feat. The appointments in the last days of the Trudeau administration were notable for a lack of ability and credibility. In addition to the usual list of party hacks were such worthies as Ann Cools, famous for her part in trashing the computer centre at the then Sir George Williams University.

Much of the activity in the Senate seems to be centred on touting for the financial and economic establishment of the nation. The good news is that this is not a new phenomenon. It has been the stalking horse for the rich and powerful for a very long time and this takes us to the matter of influence peddling and lobbying. By this time it should not come as too great a shock to realize that the death of Parliament and the power of elected officials has been accompanied by a dramatic increase in the number and power of a great army of lobbyists and influence peddlers. In the arena of policy making, the election and ballot box have been replaced by the backroom boys and girls, the greased palm and the deal made behind the backs of the public. It is not a pleasant realization.

Lobbying and Influence Peddling

First, a little about the terms we will be using. The terms "interest group," "pressure group," "lobby," "lobbying" and "influence peddling" are by no means exact terms. In ordinary usage "interest group," "pressure group" and "lobby" have come to mean very much the same thing. By and large, all of these refer to a group of individuals bound together to exert pressure upon government so as to achieve a common goal and acquire a common benefit. The choice of which term you use seems to depend pretty much upon how nice you feel toward the world on a given day. "Interest group" seems the nicest or at least the most value free. "Pressure group" seems a bit worse, carrying the sense of pressing someone to do something against their will. "Lobby" somehow seems to have en even worse connotation, probably because it has an American ring to it. We Canadians will watch American TV, listen to American music, read American books and slavishly follow American mores, but God help anyone who accuses us of being like the Americans. So it is with lobbying.

Influence peddling, however, is the worst of the lot. It carries with it the quality of selling connections or influence for filthy lucre. What could be cruder or nastier? Of course the joke here is that that is virtually what every lobby, interest group, pressure group or whatever is ultimately up to. They have access to influence, whether through the media, the ballot box or economic sanctions, and they try to get a bigger piece of the pie for themselves or their constituency. No matter how idealistic the group is, it all comes down to money at some point or other. Influence peddling does have the meaning in some people's eyes of government officials illegally using insider information and contacts to further their interests or those of their friends, relatives or some business associates. Of course, the conflict of interest rules are so weak and so foggy that it is virtually impossible to obtain convictions, and whenever anyone does seem to get caught with his or her pants down, a Commons committee just relaxes the guidelines or rules. Then again, some people see it in terms of outsiders seeking to exert *undue* influence — whatever that is — on public officials to get their way with the public purse. How that differs from lobbying is beyond me; perhaps there is an implication of bribes in some people's minds. Of course all lobbies try this in a slightly subtler form, usually involving promises of votes or future positions on boards of directors or jobs or plants for constituents. With this in mind it strikes me that the term influence peddling often comes down to lobbying that the person using the term disagrees with, or some sort of grab at the public purse of which the speaker or writer is not a beneficiary. It is "bad lobbying." It is what someone else does.

Whatever we call it, it is increasingly important in the Canadian political scene, accompanying the decline in the importance of Parliament. Lobbying is now a very big business. In May 1980, it was estimated by the *Ottawa Journal* that trade and professional associations alone numbered 300 and that they employed over 2,000 people and spent more than $122 million per year.[2] That, of course, represents only a portion of what is out there. There are many large lobbies in Ottawa that are neither trade nor professional associations. In addition, there are many lobbies that purposely have their head offices in other cities, since lobbies with offices in Ottawa tend over time to take on the perspective of the government. Also there are many lobbies at the provincial or municipal levels. While there is no estimate of the total spent, a half billion dollars per year does not seem unrealistic. If it is correct, that's a lot of money. It is a lot of influence too.

It should be noted that this is one "industry" that is almost completely unregulated. The late Walter Baker, then Opposition House Leader, tried to introduce a private member's bill in 1978 to regulate lobbies. Bill C-22 called "for the registration of lobbyists, and a declaration by them stating in whose interests they are working."[3] It failed to pass, as do virtually all private member's bills. The other major attempt at some form of regulation came in 1983 with the unanimous passing of Bill C-169, the Elections Expenses Act, which came into effect in January 1984. This bill stemmed partly from the advice of the Chief Electoral Officer who, in his report to Parliament in 1983, noted the growing power of special interest groups during elections: "These people have spent unlimited sums of money to promote or oppose a particular candidate or registered party, sums which they do not have to account for in terms of sources or amount."[4]

The part of the act that caused some members of the public to claim a threat to the freedom of speech was its provision which stated that no one except a candidate or party could incur expenses for the "purpose of promoting or opposing directly and during an election, a particular registered party, or the election of a particular candidate . . ." between the date of the election writ and election day.[5] There was a side to this that made some sense. One argument was that it is not fair to ask parties to restrict their spending at election time and then allow pressure groups to engage in unlimited spending. Others alleged the possibility of deceit on the part of political parties. After all, what was to prevent party workers from circumventing the existing electoral law by setting up the XYZ pressure group whose real purpose was to promote a certain candidate's election? They would have unrestricted use of funds for promotion and advertising. There was, however, a more sinister side. There was a great deal of gossip, at the time and since, to the effect that this was in fact an attempt to muzzle the Right. Apparently, many politicians had been frightened by the successes of right-wing groups in the United States such as the Moral Majority and the National Conservative Political Action Committee, both of which had considerable success in helping elect conservative candidates and defeating liberal ones. So successful were they that even a very high-profile candidate such as Senator George McGovern was knocked out of office by these lobbyists. Many knowledgeable observers felt that the legislation was really aimed at pro-life groups and the National Citizens' Coalition. Certainly these two groups believed this to be the case and used their resources to challenge the bill. In the end it was the National Citizens' Coalition which challenged it in an Alberta court. On June 26, 1984, Mr. Justice Donald Medhurst of the Alberta Court of Queen's Bench ruled the law unconstitutional in that it violated the right to freedom of expression provision of the Charter of Rights. Justice Minister Donald Johnson declared that the government would not appeal.

One of the major problems in the real world of Canadian politics is the temptation of politicians and civil servants to use inside information and influence to benefit themselves, their relatives and friends, in other words to act as influence peddlers. And while there have been few attempts to regulate the activities of lobbyists, there has been a *show* of effort to curb this worst form of influence peddling which results from conflict of interest. But it has been nothing more than a show and contains no real substance.

Types of Lobbies

There are many different types of lobbies, and with the change in the Canadian political system outlined earlier, there has been a dramatic increase in the number and impact of interest groups, lobbies and influence peddlers. With this increase in importance, there has been a new interest in these groups by political scientists. One element in this study has been an attempt to classify the groups according to their characteristics or activities.

One of the major ways of splitting these groups up is to divide them into economic and non-economic ones. Presumably the economic ones would include such groups as agriculture, labour and business groups. This classification is useless for a couple of major reasons. One is that it doesn't really tell us anything important about either group and the other is that it ignores the fact that even if a group is in the supposedly "non-economic" camp, its demands are almost certainly of an economic nature or involve a demand for money. Thus, it is almost impossible to differentiate the two types. Fortunately, there are other ways of looking at the problem.

One way is to set up a continuum with completely self-interested groups on one end and completely altruistic ones on the other end. The world being what it is, self-interested interest groups tend to be the larger sub-division. It comes as no surprise to realize that their demands tend to be of an economic nature and are very much in the direct self-interest of the lobbyists or influence peddlers. The motto of these groups and individuals can be neatly summed up in one word — *gimme*. The other type, the promotional groups, tend to be interested in doing things for the larger good of the community. An example would be the John Howard Society, which is dedicated to improving the lot of prisoners in prisons and, once they are released, in society.

Another way of looking at interest groups is to place them on a continuum with issue-oriented groups on one end and institutionalized groups on the other end. This typology is a good one because it tells us a lot about how long these people are likely to be with us and whether they are likely to pull any punches. For instance, issue-oriented groups are quite informal and are likely to be around only as long as their cause is. There is a tendency in these groups toward fanaticism and extreme action. They *believe* and thus feel that virtually anything they might care to do is justified because their hearts are pure and their cause is GOOD. Government hates to deal with these people because they are so unpredictable and have demands that are not amenable to compromise. There is another reason though seldom stated — these people often *are* in fact pure and good and tend to generate large amounts of guilt and self-examination in politicians and upper level civil servants — people not famous for either goodness or purity. Contact with such purists causes hands to tremble at payday. This is unpleasant and therefore contact with these monsters of virtue is kept to a minimum.

The institutionalized lobbies are government's cup of tea. These lobbies tend to be long lasting and highly bureaucratic. Members are quite well disciplined and will do whatever their leaders tell them to do. The leaders themselves are a jolly lot by the standards of the politicians and civil servants and are usually well paid. They are politicians themselves, after a fashion. They are as much concerned with advancing themselves and keeping things under control as they are in aggressively promoting the interests of their members. They pull their punches and can be counted upon to avoid actions that would embarrass anyone. In short they are just as slimy and corrupted as the civil servants and politicians they deal with on a daily basis. They are always welcome.

Yet another way of looking at pressure groups is to see if they are autonomous, that is, if they set themselves up and are independent of government, or if they are what is known as *reverse* interest groups. Now the term "reverse interest group" is a masterpiece of euphemism. It really tells us nothing at all, does it? Not surprising really, when you realize that reverse interest groups are agents or mouthpieces of the government. They are funded by government, probably could not exist without government assistance, and ultimately pay back government with interest. Their purpose is to tell the government what it wants to hear. If an opinion is not being expressed which the government wishes expressed, it simply sets up a group to voice that opinion and lobby it to do what it wants to do anyway. Voila! Instant public opinion. It's a case of as much democracy as you can buy. There are other reasons of course, most relating to social control and making the job of administration easier.

Another function of the reverse interest group is that its leaders communicate the message of government and try to create enthusiasm for government policies. Voila! Instant support for new legislation. Yet another function is that the group keeps the population and social change under the thumb of government. If government didn't step in from the start and provide its own leadership and world view for such groups, they might eventually develop their own indigenous leaders and the habit of thinking for themselves. God only knows what would happen then. They might even, God forbid, take actions that might be embarrassing or threatening to the continued rule of the powers that be. They might represent a real threat to the status quo.

A good example of this phenomenon is the rapid rise and fall of Maude Barlow. By her own declaration she is a "professional feminist." Originally, she had been pretty small stuff — doing some work with the Ontario Police College on sexual stereotyping. Some time later she became President of the Canadian Coalition Against Media Pornography. She had a bit of luck in her career. Just after the introduction of Pay TV, the First Choice network announced its intention to finance and broadcast Playboy soft-core porn in Canada. These shows tended to be pretty tame stuff, but this did not deter Maude Barlow. She saw her issue and ran with it. She became an instant celebrity. Her nation-wide campaign for legislation to control pornography caught the attention of the Liberal powers that be and they saw their opportunity just as Barlow had a few short months before. She was approached by Tom Axworthy, no stranger to making deals behind closed doors.

Barlow was made advisor on women's issues to the Prime Minister. It was a great deal. Not only did she become a national celebrity, but she also received a salary of $54,000. From the Liberals' point of view it was a dream come true. They now had their very own "women's movement leader" on the payroll, someone who could give the movement some of their slant and who could be counted upon to sell the government's policies.

In a feature article on Barlow entitled *Trudeau's fighter eyeing role as MP* in the *Toronto Star*, March 29, 1984, Barlow gushed about the glorious Liberal government and how sensitive it was to women: "Women need a party in power that is sensitive to them and their problems, a party philosophically able to help women," she says. "I took this job because I think this is the party that can and would [help women]."[6] You can't buy political advertising this good. Still, there was some indication that she realized some of what might really be going on. The journalist, Jackie Smith, says, "The hardest part of her job has been to be a women's advocate, while not being an apologist for the party."[7] Says Barlow herself, "Nobody's paying me to cause trouble."[8] That kind of says it all.

Finally, there is a continuum between active and categoric lobbies. While these terms may sound like a sociologist's nightmare, they are simple to comprehend. This continuum assumes that there are latent groups in society that become active only if there is an urgent matter of interest that comes up. Otherwise they are members of the group simply because they are part of some category such as members of a particular religion. A recent example might be Sikhs who on a day-to-day basis are involved in the day-to-day business of existence. However, when an incident such as the seizure by force by the Indian Army in 1984 happens, their group feeling is enhanced and their participation may become more active.

Pressure Points, Resources and Styles

The nature of the lobbyists and lobbies determines what their resources will be, what access points they will have in the decision-making process and ultimately what style of lobbying they will use. It is an axiom of lobbying and influencing that you have to start from an honest appraisal of who you are and what resources you possess. Obviously, the resources of the Canadian Manufacturers' Association will have a vastly different resource base from that of the Black Women's Caucus. The first will be rich in money and have well-trained and full time professional staff, the latter will be poor in money but rich in numbers of highly motivated people. One should not assume that the former type of organization will automatically win all the battles. The latter type, if it uses the resources at its disposal well, can expect to win a surprising number of clashes with the "big boys." Just as the nature of the group and its resources determine the style of the lobby, so too these factors will determine in large measure what access or pressure points will be at its disposal. Obviously, members of the elite will have the easiest access to the innermost levels of political decision making. It is their state and their government after all. "Relief," to paraphrase the commercial, "is just a telephone call away." For the rest of us, more difficult and less ladylike or gentlemanly paths await, and the openings and access points available will be less frequent and less sensitive.

A final point is that of whose interests are served by lobbying and influence peddling. At first this seems ridiculous. After all, if an organization is going to take the time, trouble and expense of setting up a full-time lobbying organization in Ottawa, Toronto or Regina, it must ultimately get its interests put forward and met or none at all.

Right? Wrong! Interestingly enough, the real interests that are being met are those of the leaders, the permanent staff and the government. For many leaders, perhaps unconsciously for all leaders, the real agenda is their own personal agenda. The interest group then becomes a vehicle for private ambition or for settling scores from the almost buried past. Who can say that the courageous fighter for the rights of automobile workers isn't at some level using that fight to propel himself into a lucrative sinecure ten years out? Who can say that that feminist leader who wakes up fighting every morning isn't still secretly fighting back at the editor who never recognized the value of her writing? Who can say that the hard-hitting lobbyist for small business and a more laissez-faire society isn't really fishing for a top government job ten years on so that he may become head of the regulators? No one can say it because it happens every day. Similarly, it is often the case that lobbyists will start out forming a relationship with bureaucrats fully expecting to manipulate the pants off government with the final result that it is the civil servants who end up doing the manipulating.

Allied with the question of whose good is sought is the question of what objective is sought. In addition to the usual reasons which flow from influencing government policy, such as more money for the group and changes in legislation or the economic or regulatory climate, there are other less tangible benefits. One of the most common goods sought by the leaders and permanent staffs is the maintenance of their control over the membership at large and even just keeping their jobs. Studies have shown that many leaders are prepared to sacrifice the needs or demands of their members so as to acquire recognition as the legitimate voice of the group by the government. In less genteel circles this is known as selling out. Quebec writers such as Pierre Vallières have introduced us to a similar phenomenon in their world — the "roi nègre" or simply the "vendu(e)." It occurs everywhere, always, and knows no colour, sex or language. It is, after all, human.

Last and certainly not least, there is the government's interest. Groups that take the government's money soon find their task more and more that of apologist for and transmission belt of the government. For many it is a wicked dilemma. If you don't take its money, you won't exist to get your message across. If you do, you end up as a mouthpiece for the government. It's a tough life.

Corruption

The Canadian political system is much like an iceberg in that about seven-eighths of its true nature lies hidden from view. The graft and corruption which runs through our history seems to have been glossed over or purposely omitted. The reasons for this vary though one cannot rule out purposeful omission and falsification in the case of government and the educational system. As we shall see later, there are a number of factors that impede its search for truth. With historians — probably the most honest of the group — it is almost certainly a case of point of view. Still, the reality of past corruption is there to see for those who wish to acknowledge the truth. The unhappy truth is that this tradition continues.

One of the most pitiful examples of self-delusion by Canadians is their insistence that corruption in government is a feature of other people's political systems but not theirs. A recent example of this was the federal Task Force on Conflict of Interest report entitled *Ethical Conduct in the Public Sector*. This study was the result of the scandal which surrounded the apparent conflict of interest involving former cabinet minister Alastair Gillespie. In chapter one of the report, the authors state that "in comparison with certain other countries, where the political system is grounded on forms and practices of systemic corruption in government, Canada appears almost squeaky clean."[9] This is what I call the "Bongo-Bongo theory of corruption," which states that corruption is something that happens in faraway countries in the Third World. It happens in El Salvador and Zaire, but never in Canada. But it does happen here. It is systemic in as much as it is an integral and key part of the political system. It is just that we do not call it corruption. In fact it is not really called anything since it is not talked about very much — if at all.

Actually, there are two types of corruption in the Canadian political system: "good" corruption and "bad" corruption. "Good" corruption is made up of those practices which are integral to the operation of the political system and to keeping the existing elite in power. It includes such things as political patronage and party machines. "Bad" corruption consists of those practices that are conducted on a freelance basis by individuals who see their opportunity to make some quick money and take it. This is frowned upon by the powers that be since it discredits the system and gives the public a hint at the rot which exists everywhere below the surface of respectability. It is "bad" because it threatens the stability of the system and the continued holding of power by the elite. Such "bad" corruption is usually covered up — for the sake of public confidence, of course — then if the attempt at whitewashing fails, harsher means are used. The offender will be thrown to the wolves for the good of the larger whole.

Just before the federal election of 1984 there was an incredible furor over the huge number of patronage appointments made by Prime Minister Trudeau just before stepping down and by his successor John Turner, under duress, of course. About two hundred and fifty Liberal Party hacks were sent to their rewards: the Senate; judgeships; ambassadorships and directorships of crown corporations. You name it, they got it. Somehow the outrage that arose seemed to come from a belief that this was a sort of crime against the political system and a remarkable event. The truth is that it was by no means remarkable. It was not a betrayal of the way the system works — it is the way the system works all the time.

Patronage is the heart of the party system in Canada. It is because of this system that the Progressive Conservative and Liberal Parties are able to hold a monopoly over power as they do and one reason for the NDP's inability to threaten their stranglehold on power.

Here's how the system works. To gain power, political parties need two things: money and people. With money you buy all sorts of valuable things like advertising, signs, space in halls, organizers and staff. In an extreme pinch you can even buy votes. People do two things for you. They vote for you and they can work for you to help persuade others to vote for you. The question is, how can you get these important resources? The answer often involves patronage.

It is probably true that the mass of voters are pretty much uninterested in politics and political ideas. By and large, sincere appeals to their public-spiritedness get you nowhere. Look at the NDP and the fringe parties of the left and the right! What does seem to work is giving favours: "You scratch my back and I'll scratch yours." The party in power has an enormous advantage over opposition parties. It can give out well paying government jobs, bestow honours, award large contracts, alter legislation or create new legislation — all of which could be extremely helpful to various businesses or groups in society. Patronage, then, is the system whereby governments hand out these goodies, not on the basis of need or talent, but rather on the basis of who is a political friend or contributor. It is not good for the country, but it is very good indeed for the parties and their friends.

Examples abound. One of the most effective political machines in the country was that of John Munro, Liberal MP, Cabinet Minister and would-be Prime Minister. Some years back, Munro was mentioned in some wiretap tapes in the possession of the RCMP. To clear his name he released many of his files to the press so that he might be found innocent in the eyes of ordinary citizens. This turned out not to be such a good idea since reporters were able to find numerous examples of patronage. Michael Lypka, for example, a member of Munro's finance committee, gave $500; he was reappointed director of the CBC. W.J. Cheeseman, president of Westinghouse Canada Limited, was made a member of the Science Council and the Defence Research Board; Westinghouse had donated $2,500 to Munro's 1972 campaign. John G. Langs was one of the most prominent fund raisers for the Liberal Party and was also generous to Munro at election time, giving $4,500 to Munro's 1972 campaign. His law firm was also generous; there was an entry in the firm's books for a donation of $7,500. Mr. Langs was appointed director of the Bank of Canada.[10] Good things just naturally seemed to happen to those connected with Munro.

These examples are not exceptions to the system. Everyone does it and feels no guilt about it. Munro summed up the general feeling of politicians on this phenomenon when he said in a July 2, 1974 interview with the *Globe and Mail*, "Of course there's patronage, and you know it, and everyone knows it. . . . Is it wrong to favour a past political supporter over some one else if the two have equal ability? Of course it isn't."[11] The Trudeau appointments at the end of his "reign" indicate that political loyalty and past services are often more important than ability for the job.

Power Brokers
There exists a group of extremely influential individuals whose major talent seems to be the ability to pick up a telephone and call rich and powerful individuals in government, business, labour, sports, crime, you name it, and get what they or their friends want. Almost always these people have power positions within the two major parties. In such cases, their power flows from being able to deliver either money or supporters when called upon to do so. At the same time, their influence cuts horizontally as well across party, occupational, ethnic and class groups. Their stock in trade is trading favours. Unlike the traditional party machine boss who often trades patronage like jobs or contracts at the bottom for money, these individuals are above all this. They wouldn't dream of asking you for anything at the time in return

for a favour. It is just helping out a friend. However, a few months later, they might call up and ask you to buy a few tables at a fund-raising dinner for someone you have never heard of before. You will buy these tables of tickets cheerfully and ask if there is anything else you can do to help. Many of these very powerful individuals are bagmen and lawyers. In a sense their business is renting out their personal power and influence to those with money to spend, but who have had no interest in gaining personal power, and as such are in a bit of a bind at the time.

The Media

The institution which is supposedly given the sacred task of routing out corruption in the political system — the free press — is actually part of the problem. Usually, it takes the form of either planting or killing stories, depending on what the powers that be might wish at the time. As a group, journalists are probably no worse than anyone else and as such often chaff at commands from editors to kill stories. As a result, many tales of these things abound. For good reading in this area, I heartily recommend either Walter Stewart's book *Canadian Newspapers: The Inside Story* (the article on the *Toronto Star* is unusually entertaining) or the portion of *Their Town: The Mafia, the Media and the Party Machine* which deals with the *Hamilton Spectator*. The point of all of this is that stories do get changed and reworked to satisfy rich and powerful interests. Newspapers also will write stories to satisfy the political needs of those in power. An example of this was the choice of Georges Vanier for Governor General. To help then Prime Minister John Diefenbaker, John Bassett arranged for a cover story in *Weekend Magazine* saying what a great choice he would be for the post.[12]

Those activities outlined above are forms of political corruption, but they are "nice" ones. They are forms of behaviour and activities which the powers that be see as valuable and "good." They are "good" because they perpetuate the elite's rule. Now for the "bad" forms.

Believe it or not election rigging and ballot box stuffing still goes on. Not often, but it does happen. The most common circumstances involve hard fought elections where the result is likely to be very close and the stakes are high. The election for the leader of the federal Progressive Conservative Party saw a number of practices that were remarkably close to election rigging. It was reported in the press that supporters of Brian Mulroney had gone to hostels and given money to residents to join the party so as to be able to vote for Mulroney delegates. Not to be outdone, there were numerous examples of this by

Liberal Party hopefuls trying to get nominated to run as Liberal candidates in the 1984 federal election. In one particularly shocking case, hopeful Tony Iannou showed up a few minutes before the closing time for new members with bags containing new memberships, all supporters of his candidacy. An appeal revealed that about half of these were bogus since the people either had not paid for the memberships themselves or did not exist. Iannou lost. The winner, June Rowlands, was morally outraged, although she shouldn't have been since she had been parachuted into the riding by the highest levels of the party and had no real connection with it. The candidates with real credentials as members of the riding were bulldozed by head office money and outside organizers. So much for democracy.

But let's move on to the frauds. As with the Mulroney example cited above, it is important to find people who are really down on their luck and will do anything for money. One of the groups often used for election fraud purposes are "winos." In the first scam you get together a bunch of people and pay them so much for voting. Person number one is given a piece of paper resembling a folded ballot. This he puts in his pocket. Upon entering the polling booth he takes out the folded piece of paper and puts the real ballot in his pocket. He comes out of the polling booth and puts the look-alike "ballot" in the ballot box. Upon leaving the polling station he gives the real ballot to the political "organizer" and gets his money. The "organizer" puts an "X" in the appropriate box and gives it to person number two who gets a ballot from the polling officer and in the polling booth makes the switch as before. The polling clerk gets the ballot filled in by the "organizer" and the "voter" walks out with a clean ballot, gives it to the "organizer" and gets his money. And on and on it goes.

Another fraud involves voting in place of people who are away on holiday or unlikely to vote. There are two parts to this one. The first one involves a situation where the "organizer" knows that someone will not be voting because he or she is on holiday or will be away on business or something of that sort. Someone will then claim on election day to be that person and vote under their name. In some cases it has happened that dead people have been enumerated and someone claims to be that person on election day. The second fraud is a bit more daring. In this case one of the scrutineers will be in on the scam. About an hour or a half hour before the polls close, the scrutineer will pass on a list of those who have not voted yet. The "organizer" quickly attempts to discover if they are likely to vote. If they are unlikely to do so, someone else will vote for them.

Without doubt one of the most common "aberrations" from the democratic norm is conflict of interest. It happens at all levels and is so common that I seriously wonder if it is all that unusual or "abnormal." This problem is one of the few areas where there has been even a show at limiting or stopping influence peddling. Probably that is because it is so damaging to the reputation of the Canadian political system. Even long-suffering and patient Canadians have a limit, and conflict of interest seems to represent that limit of tolerance.

As mentioned before, the "Gillespie affair" occasioned a Royal Commission, ostensibly to study the whole problem of ethics. Many suggested that the real reason was to sweep under the rug the allegation that a former minister of the Crown had breached conflict of interest guidelines. While the Royal Commission report was pretty much a washout in terms of censuring the guilty or suggesting any remedies, it did represent quite a good synopsis of what conflict of interest is and how various jurisdictions have tried to limit it. One of its contributions was to list those practices which it saw as "unethical" behaviour by public servants and office holders. There are nine forms of such conduct:

1. self-dealing by a public office holder.
2. assistance by public office holders to private parties dealing with the government.
3. discretionary transfer of economic value (translation: money) to a public office holder from a private source.
4. post employment assistance by former public office holders to private parties dealing with the government.
5. private gain derived from information acquired in an official capacity.
6. private use of government property.
7. partisan political activity by a non-elected public office holder.
8. criticism of government policy.
9. conduct unbecoming to one's public position.[13]

This is all sanitized and fuzzified so that the unwashed masses such as you and I will not understand a word of it and will go away no better off than we were before. Good news though. A translation does exist. Mine:

1. Don't make business deals that involve your ministry. If you do, don't get caught.
2. Don't lobby *openly* for every business that approaches you.

3. Don't accept bribes.
4. Wait a decent period before going to businesses with your inside knowledge and contacts following your defeat or resignation.
5. Don't use insider information to make yourself rich while in office.
6. Don't use government planes to holiday with your mistress.
7. Civil servants would be foolish to try to get their ministers defeated in elections even if they are right about the ministry being incompetent.
8. Don't bitch to the media about the ministry you are working for while you are still taking their money.
9. Don't pinch your secretary's behind unless she says it's OK.

In all fairness to politicians, it is almost understandable that so many politicians should fall victim to the temptations of office. After all, there are so many temptors and temptations. But enough of the theory! Let's have a look at specific instances of influence peddling and how the rich and powerful are involved in going behind your back to get their way with your money.

4

Municipal Politics: Earth Mother or Money Machine

Everyone knows that old saw that you can't fight city hall. This, like so many gems of folk wisdom from the past, is pure nonsense. City hall's resistance to influence peddling and lobbying is virtually non-existent. If you ever wanted an easy level of government to penetrate and control, this would have to be it.

City politics is a sieve which lets every influence peddler and lobbyist through to the very heart of the decision-making process. Do you want a job for your brother-in-law the loser? Do you want an exception made to the official plan — just for you? Consider it done. But why? Why is it so easy? There are two major reasons: accessibility and money.

The key to re-election is being accessible to the people you represent. In fact, the very grass-roots quality of municipal politics makes accessibility to politicians simple. If citizens want to contact their alderman, reeve, city councillor or other representative, it is as easy as dialling the telephone. Unlike the federal and provincial levels where there are hordes of people on the government payroll whose sole job is to keep citizens away and where the place of work and usual residence of the elected officials is often in another city, municipal politicians have none of this to protect them. Your representative lives very close to you and his or her number is in the telephone book. You want him? You've got him. Any hour of the night or day. Unfortunately for politicians, this accessibility, which means always being on call and having your ear bent continually by the greedy, the self-interested and the crazy, is critical to electoral survival.

The other factor is money. If accessibility and responsiveness are the left foot of municipal politics, money is the right. Money for posters, money for advertising, money for renting halls, and so on. No money, no election success. It is as simple as that. Still, consider the situation of the city politician. By and large, municipal politicians have limited resources. To get elected in a large Canadian city requires on average an outlay of between $20,000 and $30,000. A junior alderman usually makes a salary of about $30,000 if he's lucky. The question is, where is the money to come from? Occasionally, very occasionally, political parties will sponsor candidates; however, sponsorship does not mean that the party will pitch in financially in a big way. They might give some, but never more than a portion. Almost always the candidate has to find the largest share himself, even with party sponsorship — a rare event at best. The other part of this is warm bodies to canvas, man telephones and do the thousand and one organizational tasks involved in a campaign. No one has that many friends.

The other aspect to the effect of money in laying a municipal politician open to influence peddling is that there is a lot of money around. Money for bribes, money for gifts — money which could flow from politicians using their positions to aid deals that would profit them personally. The temptation can prove too much.

City Hall: What's It All About?

As with most things, the role and functions of city hall look very different depending on who you are and what your situation is. To the little guy, city hall is a highly personal entity. It is an enormous pest when it demands the payment of taxes or when it passes by-laws we do not like, but most times, it has a quality not unlike that of a great Earth Mother. It shelters us, regulates our lives at a very mundane level (usually in a benevolent manner) and provides any number of useful services to us which make life in a highly complex urban environment bearable. To others, particularly those in the property industry, it is more impersonal; it is a money machine.

By and large, it is very difficult to get particularly worked up about the influencing peddling that goes on at this level. Usually it is just a case of a taxpayer trying to get someone in city government to use his or her influence to help the taxpayer get his problem solved. It might be a restaurateur who cannot get a liquor licence or a small business person who cannot get proper customer parking facilities. It might deal with traffic flow or the siting of group homes in the community, police protection, snow removal, garbage collection and so on. The list is endless.

Basically, what is involved is an alderman acting as an expeditor. For example, for builders the issuance of building permits is critical and, unfortunately, one of their biggest headaches. The process of getting a permit involves a lot of bureaucratic manoeuvring and lots of red tape. Too often there seem to be a lot of "catch 22s." The process works something like this:

1. Before you can get a building permit, you need a demolition permit.
2. Before you can get a demolition permit, you need a building permit.
3. Before you can get a building permit, you have to have had an on-site inspection and an approval of plans.

It's not really a big deal. It's just that it takes a lot of time and effort to wrestle the bureaucrats to the ground. A few friends in high places can help because they collapse the time frame. Aldermen are particularly helpful in this because they are highly influential with city hall employees. What they might do is to speak with the building commissioner and say something like: "I'd like you to meet Mr. So-And-So. He has a problem. Now I wouldn't dream of asking you to do anything illegal or contrary to instructions. Still, I wonder if we couldn't find some way of making this whole thing go faster and still stay on side." Magically, it does.

At a more personal level, there is the matter of "on-street" parking permits. Parking, as all of us who live in large cities know, is a source of irritation and expense. Getting a permit to allow you to park overnight in the street is not impossible, it just takes a lot of time and effort. It could take three weeks to arrange. Also, all the permits for your street might have been issued already and all you can get is permission to park a few streets away. Enter the friendly politician. As a real life example, Ms. X lives on Y Street. She just moved there recently from another neighbourhood and has a boyfriend who intends to visit her a lot and overnight. She has no problem getting a parking permit since she lives on that street. The only problem is "when" since the clerks are overworked. She risks getting a lot of expensive parking tickets until she can get her permit. Her boyfriend is another story. Since he lives elsewhere, he is not entitled to a permit under any circumstances. What these two young lovers did was to call their local alderman who called the nice man in the licence office to explain his interest in the matter and in a few minutes the clerk called the woman to tell her that she could pick up the two permits in two hours.

Obviously, the politicians don't do this for the good of their health. Each alderman keeps a card file containing the names of all those whom he or she has helped. At election time, the people who received the help will be asked to help the alderman with his or her re-election. It may involve a campaign contribution, help in canvassing or just taking a sign. Still, the favour will be called.

As I said before, it is very difficult to feel particularly incensed about this sort of influence. If anything, it is a case of bending a few rules to make the system more sensitive to individual circumstances. This form of influence humanizes what might otherwise be a very inhuman bureaucratic system. But other forms of influence peddling have a more sinister quality.

In case you did not know it, the "big boys and girls" represent the property industry. You and I might personalize city hall, but these people do not. To them city hall is a money machine and municipal politics is money and property values, no more, no less. The really sad thing is that these folks with their somewhat jaundiced view of politics come out on top almost all the time.

From the perspective of this group, the activities of city hall fall into two categories only:

1. Servicing urban property. This means providing the services and facilities that make the difference between a piece of ground and a usable piece of urban real estate for housing, commerce, factories, dump sites and so on. There's no end to the services required; traffic, public transportation, public health, garbage collection, etc.

2. Regulating urban property. This involves controlling virtually every detail, no matter how seemingly insignificant, of land and property use. Such regulation might include such things as what building can be erected, how big, what it can be used for and building standards. City planning, zoning by-laws and construction standards fall into this category.

The important thing to realize is that everything that city hall does affects land values. That in turn affects the profits of those companies in the property industry. All developers follow developments at city hall with enormous interest, but the very rich and the very smart ones do not wait for changes to happen and then react to them. Rather, they take an active role and make change happen through their influence peddling and lobbying.

City hall is involved in regulating all aspects of the property industry. An idea of just how pervasive it is can be seen from the table on page 42.

WHO DOES WHAT:
SERVICING AND REGULATING THE PROPERTY INDUSTRY AT CITY HALL

	Toronto (City of)	Winnipeg	Vancouver
Departments Servicing Urban Property	Fire Public health Public works Parks & recreation	Fire Police Works	Fire Health Police Engineering (Board of Parks)
Departments Regulating Property	(City Planning Board) Development Buildings	Environment	Planning Building Electrical
Internal Housekeeping Departments	City clerk Finance Personnel Legal Audit Purchasing & supply Real estate Property Surveyor	City clerk Finance	City clerk Finance Law
Other Departments			Social services Family & children's court Civil Defence Museum Auditorium

The departments categories for Toronto are those of the City of Toronto. A number of city government functions, like police, are carried on by the second-tier city government, Metro Toronto.

In a few cases, city government boards with independent staffs have been included in the list in order to cover essential functions. These are listed in brackets.

Source: James Lorimer, *A Citizen's Guide to City Politics* (Toronto: James Lorimer & Company, 1972), p. 4. Reproduced by permission.

The Property Industry

Well, what is this property industry that seems to be connected so closely with and have so much influence over municipal governments all across the country? Basically, it encompasses all the businesses and professionals that are involved in providing accommodation. This means all types of buildings: offices, stories, factories, industrial parks, shopping centres and so on. Usually this industry is thought of in rather narrow terms as just being developers and builders. In fact it is quite a bit larger than this and includes such groups as lawyers, real estate agencies, speculators, insurance companies and banks. We could even expand the definition to include all those companies that are primarily involved in providing goods and services to the businesses, companies and professionals listed above. The table on page 44 gives an idea of just what groups and individuals make up this industry.

My definition of the composition of the property industry may at first seem overly detailed, but it is critical to our understanding of how influence peddling works at the municipal level. The reason is that many people who actually have a vested interest in the prosperity of this industry declare themselves as neutral and are thus flying under false colours. To underestimate the size of the industry is to underestimate the sinister nature of the industry's influence buying and lobbying.

While all of these companies and individuals are players in the influence peddling game, the really key players are the developers. They are the ones that put together the elements for the deals and projects that all other members of the industry will plug into and benefit from later. Without the developers there would be no property industry as we know it. What developers do is spot a hole or an unfulfilled need in the accommodation market and then put together all of the elements which will be necessary for completion of the project. Such elements might include land, building designs, professional services (lawyers, architects, engineers, etc.) capital and, last but not least, political influence for gaining approvals and exemptions. It is the developer who will deliver the politicians and bureaucrats.

It seems like a huge task, and it is. To accomplish it the developers have huge resources of money, political contacts, expertise and favours owed to them. But this is only part of the story. Big as they are, these development firms are often just parts of even bigger corporations. CEMP and Fairview (now part of Cadillac-Fairview) were set up by the Bronfman family. Genstar was founded by the vast Belgian

Composition of the Property Industry

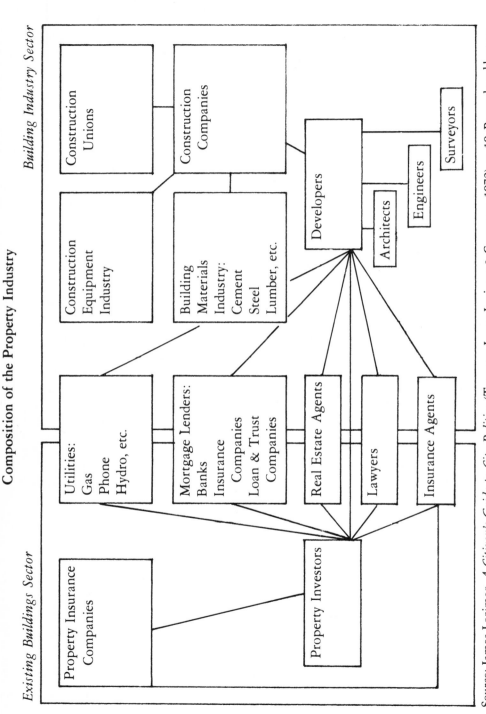

Building Industry Sector

Existing Buildings Sector

Source: James Lorimer, *A Citizen's Guide to City Politics* (Toronto: James Lorimer & Company, 1972), p. 19. Reproduced by permission.

multinational, Société Générale, which owns about one-fifth of all the industry in Belgium and has connections with the Rothschilds and Rockefellers. It tends to play hardball. One of its more celebrated involvements was in the mineral-rich Zairan province of Katanga where it is reputed to have instigated the uprising by secessionist elements. The uprising failed but resulted in thousands of dead and the mysterious death of Dag Hammarsjkold, Secretary-General of the United Nations. There are other big backers as well. Trizec was founded by William Zeckendorf and the British firms Second Covent Garden Property and Eagle Star Insurance. Marathon Realty is the Canadian Pacific Railway's land development subsidiary. The point is this: The developers have *vast* resources to draw on. When you take on a developer, you really have a tiger by the tail. One last thing about the developers per se. There is another reason that they should be so good at influencing government; they have had so much experience in doing it.

The connection between the development industry and government goes right back to the founding of the industry. In fact, the development industry was a conscious creation of federal government policy following the Second World War. Once having created this Frankenstein, government has made sure that this, its unnatural spawn, thrived. Changes to the Income Tax Act in 1972 consciously benefited large developers at the expense of smaller operators and builders. The result has been an ever-increasing concentration of all the best land in Canada in the hands of the few largest developers. Clearly, government — if not God — is on their side.

If these people are so active in lobbying and influencing government on an ongoing basis, they must have some political goals, but they are not exactly the same as yours and mine. Their major goals are:

1. The protection and maximization of property values. Simply put, this means that you shouldn't look for an easing up in property costs or rent increases next year. The "big boys" are lobbying all levels of government for policies that will ensure that property never drops in price. If their lobbying succeeds — and it almost always has so far — this means that housing costs will never go down. Their right hand slaps the politician's back while their left rifles the wallet of the same citizens the politician claims to represent. To support this strategic goal they have the following short-term tactics:

a. Make sure that the supply of land for new building is very tightly regulated. This leads to a perennial shortage of such land and prices stay high.

b. Ensure that once high prices are achieved, they are never allowed to drop. A drop in land prices would inevitably lead to a drop in profits. To developers a falling profit is like someone stealing from the collection plate at church. It just cannot be allowed to happen.

c. Restrict innovation and new techniques. This is a shocker, isn't it? You would think that people in the property industry would love innovation since it would lead to lower costs, but lower costs will ultimately lead to lower prices and, as we saw in points "a" and "b," this will just not do.

d. Promote civic growth and expansion in general. This explains that dreadful boosterism that seems to eternally emanate from city hall. Boosterism is really just propaganda for developers. Booming business conditions mean higher demand for housing, industry and accommodation. And that means higher land prices.

e. Keep property taxes at the lowest possible level while still maintaining those services which support high property values. You can always tell what city services support high land prices by watching the voting records of politicians owned by the developers. Sewers and road repairs get their votes. Welfare, daycare and libraries are, in the view of developers, manifestations of the devil himself.

f. Improve public services to privately held land.

2. Maximize new construction. To ensure this, the property industry lobbies municipal governments to:

a. Encourage and promote new development and redevelopment. Goodbye nasty old historic buildings, welcome boring, tasteless, but profitable highrises.

b. Designate more and more land for reuse and high density development.

c. Ensure that development and growth happens in the municipality's jurisdiction. This is a matter of "beggar your neighbour."

d. Make sure that the cost of public works and services needed for development will be borne by all taxpayers and not just the developers. This is a neat scam. This means that taxpayers are picking up some of the developers' costs of doing business.

3. Keep the property industry in the hands of the property industry itself. No doubt government would probably do all of the things that the developers and other members of the property industry are presently involved in. No doubt that would mean lower housing costs for taxpayers. But how could the developers make obscene profits if this happened? How indeed? The result is that the members of the property industry pour their mighty resources into maintaining the political status quo. The politicians they buy may not always be intelligent, they may not always be honest, but, once bought, they almost always vote the right way.

Fair enough. Let's assume for the moment that you and I are filthy rich developers. We know our strategy and we know where we have to go to get it fulfilled. That's where city hall comes in. Below are some of the sure-fire techniques that are used every day to use city hall to get money out of your pocket and into the coffers and balance sheets of enormously rich property industry companies. Think about this next February as you struggle through the snow-clogged streets of Yorkton, Montreal, Scarborough or Prince Rupert. Be comforted that your money is paying for the tan that some developer will be getting in Cozumel at the very same moment.

Game Plan #1: Get Elected

Have you ever wondered why so many of the representatives on your city council seem to be in positions that relate to the property industry? There are lawyers. There are owners of construction companies. There are insurance brokers. There may even be a few honest-to-goodness developers (former ones, since they would never dream of harbouring a conflict of interest). It's coincidence, of course. And the Easter Bunny and Santa Claus really do exist.

Not everyone who runs for public office is wholly motivated by civic spiritedness. Many business people, especially those that have some connection, however tenuous, to the property interest, enter municipal politics with the single-minded intention of improving the health of their businesses. Once elected, they retain their businesses and jobs and keep an eagle eye open for opportunities.

Almost all business people find a stint in city hall improves their prospects enormously. Lawyers are very big winners; they find that their time in city politics acts as a crash course in the real world of real estate law. This experience plus their almost constant contact with developers ensures that they will graduate later on to the high-paying world of lawyer to the development industry. The retainers are extremely generous and the checks never bounce. You can't lose.

A fine example of this from Toronto is Karl Jaffary, who was elected to city council as part of the reform group so prominent in the late sixties and early seventies, was highly placed in the National Executive of the NDP, and acted nobly and honourably in defence of the little guy against the developers. Still, time passes and one must be practical. He no longer is on council. Instead he acts as legal counsel for some of the biggest developers in the country.

Insurance agents sound safe, don't they? In fact, they do pretty well on council too. They meet lots of people who own or are building new apartment or office buildings and who have been known to remember the kindness of insurance agent councillors who cast favourable votes by taking out insurance policies with these very same political friends. Real estate agents use their time on council to gain important inside information about the local real estate market.

One of the problems these people have again and again is conflict of interest. They are, of course, obliged by law to declare such conflicts of interest. Sometimes they do. Sometimes they don't. A good example comes from the "Toronto the Good" of 1971. In that year two developers, Cadillac Development and Greenwin Developments, were trying to get city hall approval for a high-rise development in what is now known as the St. James Town area in the centre of the city. The local ward alderman, Mr. Ben Grys, strongly supported a rezoning request at the city's planning board and then went on to promote it at city hall. It turned out that Grys had a connection with the development that he had neglected to mention. Reform alderman John Sewell revealed that Grys's wife had owned two houses in the redevelopment area. These houses had been sold to Cadillac and Greenwin at the same time as Grys had been fighting for the rezoning application at city hall. Grys's wife held two mortgages totalling $125,000 which might never have been collected had the rezoning not gone through. What was really curious was the refusal of council to censure Grys. On February 3, 1972, it voted 9 to 7 against a request that it ask Mr. Grys to resign. It was even more curious since Grys had by this time changed his story and had admitted a conflict of interest in this matter. Sewell and fellow reform alderman Karl Jaffary took the matter to court where the judge ruled that Grys had indeed been in violation of the conflict of interest provisions of Ontario's Municipal Act. The act, unhappily, did not provide for removing anyone from office because of such a violation so Grys stayed on, although he was later turfed out by the voters. There was a happy ending to all of this, though, for he soon made his way back to council. All was forgiven.

Edmonton was the site for something rather like this, maybe even worse. I realize this story is a little bit dated, but it is so delicious that I just cannot resist recounting it. William Hawrelak, mayor of Edmonton up to 1959, was enormously popular. His success as a vote getter was without equal. He was even considered for a cabinet position by the federal Liberals, but unfortunately, they lost to the Conservatives before this dream could become a reality. Hawrelak's approach to personal profit from office followed what is a classic pattern among civic officials. He bought land at a cheap price and transferred ownership to a company which he secretly owned — Metropolitan Investments. Then the real fun began. He used his influence as mayor to get the land rezoned for such purposes as gas stations, motels and shopping centres. As if this was not enough, it was revealed in a judicial inquiry held later on that he accepted 340 shares in Alberta Gas Trunk Inc. from the Imperial Bank, the bank that handled the city's money. Commenting on this transaction, Justice Porter, who chaired an inquiry, noted that "there was quick and ready profit." Hawrelak accepted 300 shares at $150 per share from Trans-Canada Pipeline, which led to what Justice Porter described as "a certain and immediate profit."[1] While mayor, he was also on the payroll of Loblaws at $20,000 a year. Loblaws at the time was trying to get a particular warehouse site, and the mayor, of course, got it for them.

Upon the release of Mr. Justice Porter's report, the city sued Hawrelak for recovery of $226,000. In a speech to council, Hawrelak announced that he felt compelled to resign, yet his tone indicated no sense of remorse or any recognition of wrongdoing. Indeed, he criticized the report and rejected "the principle . . . which seems to flow from this report that a person, upon accepting public office, must relinquish and avoid all private business ties."[2] He settled the suit by payment of $100,000 and $4,359 in court costs. Just as with the Grys case, voters apparently decided that there was nothing wrong and re-elected Hawrelak as mayor in October 1963 with an eight thousand vote majority over his only opponent.

The real and most long-lasting benefit from the point of view of the property industry comes from having people on council who share the industry's views and who are prepared to advance the political pro-

OCCUPATION OF RECENT EDMONTON MUNICIPAL CANDIDATES BY PERCENTAGE

Occupation in election year	1974 Candidate	Elected	1977 Candidate	Elected	1980 Candidate	Elected
Law	7.5	15.4	—	—	—	—
Business	35.8	46.2	50.0	46.2	37.5	53.9
Professions	18.9	30.8	15.8	30.8	18.7	15.4
Teachers	9.4	—	5.3	7.7	10.4	—
Other White-Collar	13.2	7.7	13.2	15.4	14.5	7.7
Blue-Collar	7.5	—	15.8	—	14.5	7.7
Others	7.5	—	—	—	4.1	15.4
Number	53	13*	38	13	48	13

*Council included twelve aldermen and the mayor.

Source: James Lightbody, "Edmonton" in Warren Magnusson and Andrew Sanston, *City Politics in Canada* (Toronto: University of Toronto Press, 1983), p. 272. © University of Toronto Press 1983. Reproduced by permission.

gram of the industry. What the industry seeks is an automatic majority on council for its policies when important (that is, property-related) issues appear on the agenda.

Actually, there are a number of ways in which this automatic majority can come to pass. One way is for members or representatives of the industry to run for election. This strategy has been used very successfully. James Lorimer was able to show quite convincingly that the city councils of Vancouver, Winnipeg and Toronto in the early seventies were controlled by members of the property industry. Of course, it is not necessary for council members or aldermen to actually be members of the property industry to represent the industry's needs in municipal government. Often it is merely necessary to be of a high enough class position that you share the proper middle-class or business values. In such situations representatives may find themselves voting more or less constantly with the business and property industry representatives on council, board of control or other municipal governing body. Certainly, municipal politics is very much a middle-class game.

From the preceding table we can see that for the decade commencing 1974, 87 percent of the successful Edmonton candidates were professionals (including teachers or business people). The question is whether this heavy middle-class representation translates into political behaviour among municipal politicians. If we are to judge from the next table, it would seem that this is mainly correct, although there are some signs of a weakening in the trend.

States and affiliations on Edmonton city council* 1971-80

Year	CGA[t]	URGE	EVA	Independents Conservative	Progressive
1971	8	0	0	3	2
1974	8	2	1	1	1
1977	7	3	0	1	2
1980	6	4	1	1	1

*Council included twelve aldermen and the mayor.
[t]An official slate was designated by the CGA only in 1977, but those incumbents, plus others with previous attachments or strong linkages, have been listed for the other years.

(continued)

Year	Total Conservative
1971	11
1974	9
1977	8
1980	7

Source: James Lightbody, "Edmonton" in Warren Magnusson and Andrew Sanston, *City Politics in Canada* (Toronto: University of Toronto Press, 1983), p. 271. © University of Toronto Press 1983. Reproduced by permission.

By way of explanation, CGA (Civic Government Association) is the small "c" conservative group which traditionally represented business and property industry interests. URGE is the Urban Reform Group of Edmonton, which is not necessarily against development, but seeks more citizen participation and more cautious development. Even this reform group is far from radical. Donald Higgins in his status report in 1981 of citizen groups across the country had the following to say: "So much depends on the *context* of the particular city. For example, it struck me that the four fairly clear progressives on Edmonton's city council . . . would in the context of Toronto's city council most likely be of the soft-middle variety."[3] The only really anti-establishment group is EVA, the Edmonton Voters' Association, which was formed to represent the Edmonton and District Labour Council. As can be seen, the EVA has not been notably successful. Clearly, representing middle class interests, whether of the "quiche" or "meat and potatoes" variety, pays off at the polls.

This is just the tip of the iceberg. Business and property industry-oriented coalitions have been quite successful in other cities. The Non-Partisan Association (NPA) in Vancouver, the Independent Citizen Election Committee (ICEC) in Winnipeg and Mayor Drapeau's Civic Party in Montreal all represent coalitions representing business and development industry points of view that have held on to power for very long periods indeed.

The ICEC in Winnipeg is a particularly striking example. Formed in 1971 following the reorganization of local government in Winnipeg, the ICEC has had as its goal the contesting of Unicity elections. In this it is the latest embodiment of a tradition of municipal coalitions with an anti-socialist bias which have consistently aided business and the property industry on the political front. A number of politicians saw the reorganization of local government in Winnipeg in the early seventies as a heaven sent opportunity for a turn to the Left. How wrong they were!

With its electoral support in the suburban middle and upper-middle-class wards, ICEC easily dominated the first three Unicity elections in 1971, 1974 and 1977. It thus also dominated all of the most important committees as well.

Speaking of the success of this coalition of prosperous and business-oriented citizens, one observer had the following to say: "[The ICEC and its precursors] have been enormously successful, never losing control of Winnipeg City Council for the past 57 years."[4] During this time the ICEC and its predecessors have consistently pursued the interests of business and development although not necessarily declaring themselves as such. As two Winnipeg political observers put it: "The group's (ICEC) obeisance to business and development interests is camouflaged as simply prudent, efficient municipal administration."[5]

To achieve their goal of control over city government the development industry is prepared to put its money where its mouth is. Priority targets for this money are candidates from the property industry, but there are others. An obvious choice would be politicians affiliated with either the Liberal or Conservative Parties and of a sympathetic turn of mind. Curiously enough, some of this money has on occasion gone to NDP and reform politicians who are quite antagonistic to the development industry. That seems strange, yet it makes some sense after some reflection. Some developers have a long time horizon when looking at the political scene. Their reasoning is that even radicals mellow with time.

Toronto and Montreal were famous for the rabid quality of their reform politicians a few years ago. In Toronto, the names of David Crombie, Karl Jaffary and John Sewell were synonymous with a vigorous, often bitter, opposition to developers, and in Montreal Nick Auf der Maur was the scourge of the "fat cats." And now look at them. Crombie is a Conservative Cabinet minister, Auf der Maur ran as a Tory in the 1984 federal election, Jaffary is a lawyer for developers and Sewell, after a stint as mayor, is a columnist for the *Globe and Mail*, Canada's foremost small "c" conservative newspaper. The reasoning of many developers is that if this group could mellow, why not others? Why not indeed? And on this assumption developers' money finds its way on occasion into the war chests of radicals and reformers.

Game Plan #2: Lobby Those In Power
Trying to influence elections and thus control councils are just part of the tactics of development industry and other business interests. Much

of their activity takes place as lobbyists between elections.

One of the best examples of this took place in Toronto in 1984 and involved a proposed Scotia Bank plaza and tower. In this case the developer was Campeau, its major client the Bank of Nova Scotia. Both these organizations are not without considerable political clout. The problem with this development was that what Campeau and the Bank proposed to do would violate the city's official plan. Nevertheless, the city decided to allow the development despite the opposition. This was not too surprising. John Sewell told me in an interview that Campeau had placed one of their Vice Presidents, Walter Jensen, in Toronto City Hall for a year with the task of lobbying officials and bureaucrats concerning the development. (Interestingly enough, Jensen has since gone on to become Massey-Ferguson's new "development officer.") Massey-Ferguson is preparing the development package for its 10 hectare site south of Adelaide Street in downtown Toronto. Not inappropriately, the article in the *Globe and Mail* which heralded this new post was entitled "Lobbyist spells grief for council"!

Apparently, Jensen did a good job, but just when it seemed as if the development would be approved, a group made up of three NDP aldermen and Downtown Action, a five-member "leftist" citizens' group, stated its opposition to the plan and announced that it would fight it at the Ontario Municipal Board. Actually, this group was quite clever in its approach. First of all, Downtown Action was incorporated so the members would be safe from being sued if the action failed. (Developers' lawyers often sue people who unsuccessfully oppose developments. This is meant to discourage other civic-minded citizens who might be tempted to challenge the status quo in the future.) Second, they knew that this could tie up the development for as much as six months and cost Campeau millions. The result was that Campeau and the opposition struck a deal by which the group would stop their opposition in return for a donation of $2 million to the co-op housing movement in Toronto. The reaction of Mayor Art Eggleton and other aldermen was negative and bitter. Of course, they had been stung by the fact that these NDP aldermen and this left-leaning group had been able to wring concessions out of Campeau that they had not. What was even more interesting ultimately was the revelation that this practice of developers buying exemptions to official city plans was not uncommon. This was not the first time in Canadian municipal history it had happened, it just involved the largest amount of money.

Another incident concerned the efforts of Westcliff Management Ltd. to build a regional shopping centre in Fredericton, New Brunswick in the late seventies and early eighties. The problem here was that while Fredericton's city council was interested in attracting more commercial development, its planning policies could not allow such development in a peripheral location without significant modifications or amendments being made to the approved plan. In November 1978, Westcliff submitted just such a proposal. As a result of pressure from shopping centre developers, city council rejected the recommendations of its Planning Advisory Committee by passing a motion that malls could locate anywhere in the city subject to normal planning controls. This was not the end of the matter, however. Opposition to the development grew and in response to pressure from citizen groups council defeated a motion that would have amended the official plan and allowed the mall development. Instead, council invited proposals that would mesh with the existing official plan. It received such a submission in November 1979. This is when the developer really turned on the pressure. Westcliff responded with letters of commitment from Simpsons-Sears, The Bay and Eaton's. This pressure worked. City council voted to reconsider the Westcliff proposal even though it was to look at the details of the proposal that meshed with the official plan the next day. Over the next few months council made it clear that it was secretly well disposed to the Westcliff proposal — no matter what the official plan, the Planning Committee and citizens' groups might say. On April 14, 1980 council approved the Westcliff proposal.

A good illustration of how lobbying can influence even those councils dominated by those opposed to developers took place in Ottawa. Since the 1978 municipal elections, Ottawa politics has been dominated by council members representing what is known as "residential" or "consumption" interests. What these interests promote are the preservation of residential communities, public transportation, social housing, better social services and better recreational facilities. This is a far cry from the program of the development industry, but developers still get their way. In Ottawa, groups such as the Board of Trade and the Commercial and Industrial Development Corporation of Ottawa-Carleton exert enormous influence, and they are by no means the only organs of business influence. The Rideau Centre redevelopment scheme is a good illustration of just how potent this political pressure can be. Originally the municipal government was against the scheme, but the combination of an economic slump and lobbying by business interests turned this opposition into enthusiasm. Much of the lobbying centred around the claim that such a development would stimulate the building and tourist industries and that if the development were not pursued, the tourist dollars would flow to Hull instead. (God forbid!) In time this lobbying resulted in Ottawa council ignoring many of the same citizen groups that had put the reform councillors in office in the first place.

Other Corporate Groups

Thus far, I have spoken largely about developers as players in the influence game, but these are by no means the only representatives of business lobbying at the municipal level. For instance, every city has a chamber of commerce, board of trade or similar organization. One advantage these groups have over others is continuity over time. They also have access to detailed information which impresses elected officials and bureaucrats. Furthermore, given the background and experience of most elected officials, there is an affinity between politicians and corporate lobbyists which translates into easy access and influence. One final advantage these business groups have over citizens' groups is their unified structures and ideologies.

In addition to corporate groups organized at the local level, there are a number of organizations at the national level which have enormous influence over what ultimately happens at the municipal level. One such group is the Urban Development Institute (UDI), a national organization with provincial branches. Established in 1957, its membership is composed of companies and individuals engaged in the real estate and development industry. Typical members would be mortgage companies, land and property developers, property owners and managers, engineers, architects, lawyers and planning consultants. The financial power of those represented is enormous.

The UDI has a professional staff and the resources to act as a very effective lobby. In the mid and late 70s, for instance, it made use of a political consulting firm in Ottawa. Also it has from time to time mounted impressive public relations campaigns. One such campaign involved its attack on rent controls in Ontario and British Columbia. Finally, a significant part of its effort has involved active participation in disputes at the local level. For instance, its lawyers represented it at the Ontario Municipal Board's hearings concerning the City of Toronto's "45 foot" by-law. It has been involved in the campaign against restrictions put on "adults only" buildings by a City of Toronto by-law and it acted before Nova Scotia's Planning Appeal Board over the city's attempt to protect views from the Citadel.

The Housing and Urban Development Association of Canada (HUDAC) also has provincial branches. Its members, however, are mainly residential builders. The two major thrusts of HUDAC have been to push for an increased supply of mortgage money for residential construction and to try and improve the image of builders in Canada.

Because of the overlapping memberships and boards of directors, these organizations find it easy to form coalitions with each other and with other corporate lobby groups. This results in enormous political clout. A typical example would be the hearings on Toronto's "45 foot" by-law mentioned earlier. Objections were registered at the Ontario Municipal Board by UDI, HUDAC, plus connected industry organizations such as the Canadian Institute of Public Real Estate Companies, the Ontario Association of Architects, the Toronto Redevelopment Advisory Council, the Toronto Building Trades Council and the Toronto Construction Association.

These corporate lobbies, with their tremendous financial resources, can buy the services of the very best lawyers. In one case a developer's lawyers successfully argued that the Ontario Municipal Board could not allow unincorporated ratepayers' groups to appear before the Board, thereby crippling much of its opposition. The experience and research capability of these lobbies result in technical information which is invaluable to officials and gives the lobbyists credibility and influence. Then there is the matter of exchanges of personnel between the lobbies and government. William Teron, for example, was originally a major Ottawa developer, became president of the Central Mortgage and Housing Corporation (CMHC) in 1973 and in late 1975 was appointed deputy minister of Urban Affairs in Ottawa. A similar case saw an Atlantic regional director of CMHC moving to manage a development company in Alberta. The corporate lobbyists, then, with their substantial organizational and financial bases are thus able to move from the local, to the provincial, to the federal level with great ease as the need or opportunity arises. The result is enormous influence.

The White Hats: Citizens' Groups

The last ten to fifteen years have seen a major increase in the number and influence of citizens' groups at the local level, reflected in the composition of city councils and boards. Their growth represented the first cracks in the structure of developers and business control of local government.

The styles and goals of these citizens' groups are far from monolithic. Chief among the "old style" groups are the ratepayers' associations active in every community. Ratepayers' associations are essentially reactive and usually have the following goals:

1. To protect homeowners from higher municipal taxes.
2. To defend the neighbourhood from rezoning and intrusions which they perceive to be undesirable.
3. To secure more services and improvement projects for the neighbourhood.

Traditionally, these groups have avoided the pressure tactics which are the stock in trade of the newer style groups. Rather, they have relied on a commonality of interest with councillors. Until recently these groups have been very successful. The problem is that, as the composition of councils has changed and the process of democratization has proceeded, these groups have found their tactics less successful and have been forced to transform themselves into "new style" community groups or become irrelevant.

The 1960s represented a watershed in the history of interest groups and lobbying at the municipal level. Whereas the "old style" ratepayers' organizations were restricted to homeowners, relied on contacts on council and were reactive in nature, the new "community associations" or "neighbourhood groups" were highly democratic and included both property owners and tenants. Other interesting features have been their orientation and tactics. The "new style" groups tend to initiate discussion of issues instead of just react to them. Essentially, they see themselves as advocates who present citizen demands to city officials — and "demands" is an appropriate word. These groups do not go hat in hand as supplicants to government. They tend to be quite strident. Most of all they adore the media and use it extensively and effectively. Picketing, circulating petitions, street theatre and angry confrontations with city officials make these groups the darlings of municipal reporters in search of stories in an otherwise dreary news landscape. The largest cities — Toronto, Montreal and Vancouver — seem to provide the most active and entertaining examples of these groups in action.

One of the most successful groups has been the Toronto Island Residents' Association which has thwarted efforts by city hall officials to evict them. These people played the media like a musical instrument. One of their media events involved hiring professional actors who, with local residents, dressed up in costumes and staged a mock "invasion" of the island by the sheriff. They even turned on the air raid sirens — great for a radio backdrop. The event was held at a time when they knew that the media would have very few good stories to cover, so they got good coverage. The impact on municipal politicians was enormous.

One of the problems such groups experience is that they are organized on a sectoral rather than city-wide basis. Two difficulties arise here. One is that their concerns are focused on just one part of the city, making their base of support somewhat narrow. The other flows from this narrow focus of interest and support — the possibility of a conflict between groups. There is only so much money, and if one neighbourhood group gets goodies, this might mean that during times of restraint other neighbourhood groups would lose out. There is also the possibility of municipal politicians, bureaucrats and developers setting these groups against each other. From time to time such groups have tried to deal with this problem by creating umbrella organiza-tions, but such coalitions have not been notably successful or durable.

A type of lobbying that has been notable for its success is that which is based on a specific issue. Some of the best known involve pollution or transportation. One of these was the battle by a group with the initials SSSOCCC (Stop Spadina Save Our City Co-ordination Committee) to stop the Spadina Expressway in Toronto. This battle raged from March of 1962 when Metro Toronto Council approved about $74 million (a lot in those days!) for the expressway's construction. It was finally stopped by Premier Davis in 1971 just before the provincial election when, in effect, he overturned a decision by the Ontario Municipal Board, which was a remarkable event then. By this time the city had already spent almost $70 million on construction. Similar actions by citizens' groups have taken place in Vancouver with the question of a third crossing over Burrard Inlet and the East End Expressway and in Halifax with the regional garbage dump and the Quinpool Road development. The Burrard Inlet conflict was particu-larly fascinating because it revealed the true feelings of many municipal officials to these groups. During a public meeting on March 15, 1972, Vancouver mayor Tom Campbell complained that the crossing was in danger of being sabotaged by "Maoists, communists, pinkos, left-wingers and hamburgers."

There is one difference of critical importance between the "old style" and "new style" citizens' groups that has not been mentioned so far. Unlike the ratepayers, new style groups often try to change the decision-making process itself. As such, there is on occasion a revolutionary potential inherent in these groups — a potential that has not been lost on left wing groups. (Chapter 5 deals with just such a radical civic group, the Montreal Citizens' Movement.)

Perhaps the major ongoing problem experienced by "new style" groups is the difficulty they have in establishing their legitimacy in the eyes of civic officials. As we shall see again and again, the perceived legitimacy of interest groups at all levels of the political system largely determines how much influence and success they are likely to have in lobbying government. Certainly, the "new style" groups have a major disadvantage right from the start. The ratepayers' associations have little difficulty in establishing their legitimacy; their claim buttressed by their owning property. This is something politicians can understand since most of them own property too. The "new style" groups are more difficult to assess, particularly since many members are tenants. Worse yet, their high-pressure tactics predispose many politicians to see them as illegitimate, especially since they often challenge the right of elected officials to speak on behalf of citizens on every issue. In turn, many politicians claim that the citizens' groups are little more than malcontents and radicals unrepresentative of the public they claim as theirs.

Finally, there is the problem which goes along with "single issue" orientation. The problem is, what happens when the issue is resolved? The group must collapse if it is unable to find a new issue with great public appeal, so the landscape of municipal politics is littered with the corpses of lobbies that die sudden deaths upon the successful conclusion of their efforts. The leaders of many lobby groups, especially those hoping to use them as vehicles for political careers, fear success as much as their opponents.

Bureaucrats

Bureaucrats have a powerful stake in the cut and slash of interest group politics at the municipal level. Initially, bureaucrats were resentful of the demands made by these groups. It seemed a usurping of their authority and their "right to rule." An example of how this translates into dealings with interest groups is that of a meeting between the then Metro Toronto Parks Commissioner Tommy Thompson and a Toronto Island residents' group resisting eviction. Thompson was an unusual public servant. He had a charming and likeable image and was fond of talking with the media about how he relaxed by making jams and jellies. He was like a favourite uncle to the city of Toronto. It was with this background that citizen group members were shocked during the course of a meeting called to demand improvements in transportation services. As one of the members of the group tells the story: "When the chairman and speakers requested improvements in transportation services, Thompson lost patience, became offended, and accused the residents of vandalizing the freight wagons, wrecking the waiting shed and generally showing disrespect for park property. We were 'you people.' It was a revelation to see his authoritarian, patronizing side in contrast to his public image. Many members . . . reacted angrily to the unjust accusation of vandalism, but others were intimidated and made pathetic attempts to flatter the commissioner out of his bad temper."[6]

This is probably not one of the smartest ways of dealing with such a confrontation. It is, however, quite human and understandable. There are other municipal bureaucrats who are, shall we say, more "sophisticated." Instead of feeling threatened they see the personal advantages of encouraging, manipulating and using the operation of the lobbying system at city hall. There was a minor scandal in October 1984 when it was learned that many Toronto bureaucrats had charge accounts with the finest restaurants in the city, paid for by already overburdened taxpayers. Said city auditor Jacob Rabinowitz: "Eating at restaurants such as Barberian's (an extremely fine and extremely expensive steakhouse) is the 'day to day' lifestyle of senior bureaucrats."[7] It was revealed that most of the meals involved negotiations and meetings with developers. If there were no lobbying, there would be no meals at Winston's.

Actually, this is small potatoes compared to the games played by many top-level bureaucrats, some of whom have encouraged the growth in size, numbers and aggressiveness of citizen groups. There are two major reasons for this encouragement. First of all, increased demand on services from city hall means more employees and hence more power and higher salaries for the top-level bureaucrats whose departments experience this growth. Thus bureaucrats often have a vested interest in the success of those lobbying them. Second, some bureaucrats use lobby groups to support their internal political battles. If you can encourage a number of large and aggressive citizen or business groups to demand what is in fact your position, you have acquired a major advantage over your bureaucrat rivals. This was attested to by Susan Fish (whose community activities helped pave her way to council, then to a provincial government cabinet position) who explained that the apparent support for the citizen participation movement by Metropolitan Toronto planners was largely a tool they used to build up their power base to help them in their struggles with other departments and some members of council.[8]

PART II

THE IDEOLOGICAL LOBBIES

There is an Arab poem which begins: "What is life? It is merely a castle in the air."

In this section we will look at those lobbies which not only build castles in the air, but also try to move into them. One dreams of a golden future where there will be no war, poverty, pollution or racism. Another dreams of a golden past where all was good and beautiful and safe and tries to make this imagined past our future. Yet another dreams of a golden future where there will be no gender. Two things are common to all of these dreams: they are primarily concerned with ideology, that is, a closed, self-justifying system of ideas which attempts to mould reality in the ideology's image; and they insist upon everyone else believing as they do, because they consider themselves to be right.

5

The Holier Than Thou Left

It is probably impossible to come up with a crisp, concise and all-encompassing definition of just what constitutes "the Left" in Canada. This is probably because of the variety of groups and points of view that have come together under this ideological banner. Among the groups which like to view themselves as "left-wing" or "progressive," are the usual communist, socialist, anarchist and trade union groups, as well as other groups not traditionally part of "the Movement." These might include some environmental, feminist, media, multicultural, nationalist and community action or social work groups. The trouble with this latter category is the inconsistency of the groups. It is difficult to get a really good ideological fix on them. Sometimes they use a left-wing, Marxist or radical analysis; sometimes they do not. Some of their members are hard-core leftists; some are not. Perhaps all we can say for sure is that, by and large, the non-traditional "left-wing" groups share some memberships and some goals with the traditional left-wing groups. What it all comes down to is that this somewhat amorphous group which I am calling the Left is made up of people and groups who share the following ideas and goals to a greater or lesser extent:

1. Opposition to the establishment. This varies in intensity but has at its core the conviction that what has gone before and what exists now is either misguided or absolutely wrong. Usually this takes on the quality of a moral critique. Often it has the quality of a "holier-than-thou" stance. This opposition to the "establishment" is often paradoxical — and even humorous at times — since many groups are funded by and have members from the very establishment which they oppose.

2. A belief in progress and the perfectibility of man and society. This takes many forms but ultimately is centred around the march of mankind under the guidance of and pressure from

"progressive" forces to some golden future for humanity in which there is no want, racism, war, gender differences, etc., etc.

3. A belief in the efficacy and positive role of government in redressing grievances and in bringing about this "better world."

This is, very crudely, the setting and direction of "the Left." So let's have a look at the practices and progress of this parade of pressure groups in their march to "a better tomorrow."

Strategy and Tactics

The Left has two strategies. The first is the reformist strategy which views the march toward the future as possible through incremental change. In other words, the "system" can be reformed. To this purpose some left-wing groups, in fact the great majority of them, attempt to lobby the existing government to change policies to reflect the groups' conception of what is right, or to replace the ruling party with their own choice, usually the NDP. Either way, such groups see the government and "system" as useful tools to achieve socialism, communism, syndicalism, anarchism, feminism, the "conserver society," the "New Jerusalem" or whatever other goal they might have. This class of groups is the home of would-be left-wing lobbyists. After all, if the government is not benign, or at least neutral, why lobby it?

There is another class of leftists made up of those who view the government as a tool of the real powerhouse of society, the rich. To these leftists, reform and lobbying are useless since "the system" is hopelessly flawed. Only complete revolutionary change can make things right. They lobby government too, but their ultimate demand is that the government dissolve itself and let them rule. Thus far, politicians have not appeared willing to accede to their request that they step down.

Because the groups vary so much in terms of goals and values, it is not surprising that the tactics they employ vary as well. Still, as a rough generalization, the tactics seem to fall into two broad categories: The election of a left-wing government, which as noted usually means electing the NDP and pressuring the government through a variety of measures to enact legislation and regulations which will be "progressive," which in left-wing jargon means "something they approve of." This lobbying or pressuring has been elevated to the status of a fine art by the Left, so much so that even though the number of dedicated and self-identifying leftists in Canada is small, the Left has been very successful in persuading the government that the left-wing view is the "voice of the people." Good examples of this lie in the born-again feminism of most levels of government, the abolition of capital punishment and some of the abuses inherent in some human rights legislation, like the assumption of guilt until proven innocent. This lobbying approach has involved the use of single-issue lobby groups to fight specific lobbying battles, the formation of coalitions bringing these groups together for actions of mutual benefit and more ideologically-oriented multi-issue lobby groups like "progressive" trade unions, "progressive" church groups and left-wing think tanks.

The lobbying approach developed by the Left is elegant, flexible and has worked like a charm. Essentially it contains these components:

1. The use of single-issue lobby groups to fight for specific causes. Usually these organizations have broadly-based memberships whose diversity and seemingly non-partisan nature makes them more credible to politicians in office, usually Conservative and Liberal Party members not given to dispensing political goodies and favours to NDP or Communist organizations. The trick is that these organizations are often far from non-partisan since frequently they seem to have left-wingers in leadership positions. If the groups do not start out with a left-wing outlook or set of demands, they often end up that way as a result of the hidden agenda of their left-wing leaders.

   Their lobbying techniques may involve:

   a) *Direct action.* The techniques may be innocuous, as in handing out leaflets, picketing or holding demonstrations, but as the level of ideological commitment rises, the intensity of the direct action may escalate. More intensive techniques may involve occupying offices, invading factories or plant grounds and other acts of civil disobedience. A recent example occurred when demonstrators "invaded" the grounds of the Litton Industries plant in North Toronto (Litton, you will recall, manufactures Cruise missile guidance components.) Another action involved an "invasion" of an Ontario Hydro generating station by members of the ecology movement, the high point of which came when activists climbed a smoke-stack and stayed there for a day or two. At the high end of the direct action scale were the activities of the West Coast group called Direct Action. Among their acts were the destruction of B.C. Hydro power lines and finally the bombing of the Litton

Systems plant mentioned previously, which resulted in some serious injuries of plant workers.

In terms of directly influencing government, such actions have little effect. If anything, these techniques betray the groups' powerlessness. If they had any real power and access they would be employing the quiet, behind the scenes techniques employed by the real heavy hitters in the influence industry. Government dislikes confrontation and conflict, so these tactics seem to stiffen the resistance of government to their demands, no matter how great the support for the demands might be. Even a mass demonstration like the 100,000 person rally on Parliament Hill by trade unionists and supporters protesting wage and price controls had no effect on government policy.

Where direct action techniques do work is in getting media attention for causes. A flashy bit of street theatre ensures extensive media coverage which can give credibility and imply a strength and public support such groups may not really possess. Still, the illusion is there and illusion is what the media and the political system are all about. It is possible, therefore, that these actions do work in an indirect fashion. The demonstrations manipulate the media which then manipulate the government.

b) *Litigation.* The Canadian political system is famous for its legalism and its domination by lawyers. The new constitution and Charter of Rights make the courts even more important in the determining of public policy. A number of advocacy groups have made effective use of this feature of the system over the past few years, based on the assumption that if you cannot beat them in the legislatures, you can always try the courts. Women's groups have found this an extremely fruitful path to lobbying success. A case in point are the efforts of Dr. Henry Morgentaler to set up freestanding abortion clinics across the country. From a strictly legal point of view he is guilty. Pro-choice groups do not have the political clout or the preponderant support of the public to change the law, yet Morgentaler has been able to continue his work simply because no court will convict him. Legal challenges by women's groups in other areas have probably resulted in social change which is much faster than might have been the case were they to rely simply on lobbying legislators. A good example is the Quebec feminist group Action Travail des Femmes which succeeded in getting a Canadian Human Rights Commission tribunal to direct Canadian National Railways to allocate one job in four to women in its St. Lawrence region, which makes up all of Quebec and part of eastern Ontario, until thirteen percent of blue-collar positions are held by women. Is it good law? Of course not, but it certainly is an example of excellent lobbying.

Such use of litigation is by no means restricted to feminist lobby groups. Some of the other advocacy groups engaged in using this approach are the National Anti-Poverty Organization, the Canadian Civil Liberties Association, the Consumers Association of Canada (admittedly, anything but a left-wing group), the Public Interest Advocacy Centre, the Advocacy Resources Centre for the Handicapped, the Canadian Environmental Law Association and the Canadian Environmental Law Research Foundation.

c) *Direct Lobbying.* This involves the traditional techniques of getting sympathetic opposition politicians to ask embarrassing questions of the government during question period, holding meetings with government MPs, civil servants and cabinet ministers (if you have the clout, which most do not), submitting briefs to government commissions, testifying at hearings and so on. Sadly for these groups, they seldom have the heavy political clout which comes either from money or from being clearly able to influence large numbers of voters. As a result they are often forced to use the more dramatic but less effective tools which make up direct action lobbying. Probably the only groups in the advocacy area that seem to have had any consistent success in direct lobbying are some of the very large feminist groups. This success reflects the fact that their activity is less a case of lobbying by the oppressed than of one part of the elite speaking to another.

d) *Lobbying the Media.* We have looked at a portion of this under "direct action" above. Like street theatre, dramatic and shocking reports make great copy. There are some advocacy groups that are remarkably good at fighting the "battle of the statistics" through the media. A good example involves the question of how far women's wages lag behind those of men. Various women's groups delight in telling us that women earn only about 60 percent of what men do. Any group or person who comes up with another figure is likely to be either attacked vigorously and discredited or ignored. A 1984 report by the federal Ministry of Labour reported that the wage lag was less than that normally touted; the report and its authors were savaged. In fact, if one looks at the wages of men and women in their late teens to thirties the wage gap is very slight. Why are we never told this? The reason is that too many government departments, politicians, media people and lobbies have a vested interest in telling us that an enormous gap exists. The politicians have a "cause" upon which to campaign for the votes of women, bureaucrats can advance their careers and engage in empire building based on programs to redress this "glaring inequity" and it all makes good copy for the media. Another war of the statistics and a source of shocking reports is "the poverty line," which goes up and down like a yo-yo depending on who is drawing it.

Single-Issue Groups

From the point of view of the Left, single-issue groups that claim to be mainstream and independent and which lobby for specific "progressive" measures present a number of advantages and opportunities.

The issue orientation of the groups attracts a large number of people from the wider population, from which two benefits follow. One is the possibility of introducing these people to left-wing ideas and ultimately to recruit them for the partisan Left; the other is that the more broadly-based membership of these groups makes them more palatable to politicians in power. In many cases, the leadership of these groups is left-wing and thus is able to turn the groups toward supporting positions that might not be the case were there more centrist leaders.

This situation of left-wing leadership and broadly-based membership can happen in two ways. The first occurs when left-wingers form an organization whose demands are so clearly just that the group acquires a mass following. The more common technique is where an existing group is taken over by left-wingers and used for purposes not originally intended. This is "the virus ploy."

Let your mind go back to your high school biology for a moment. There we all learned about how a virus spends its time. First the virus enters a healthy cell and takes over the part of the cell that controls the workings of the cell. It rearranges the genetic code in the cell so that it begins to see its work as using itself and its resources for producing other viruses. After a time all that is left of the cell is millions of viruses and the cell membrane. At this point the cell membrane ruptures, releasing these new viruses to enter new cells.

This is also how the Left works. Left-wing organizations take over the leadership positions, alter the goals of the organization, persuade activists from the group of the justice and correctness of their policies, recruit these people for their left-wing party organization and off they all go to enter other groups. Part of the reason that left-wingers are so successful at taking over these groups has to do with the intelligence, hard work and dedication of these people. Let's face it, most of us are lazy. We have our own problems and we have to be very dedicated indeed to do the work necessary to make a lobby group work after a hard day at the office, factory or farm. Leftist activists are different. They have a powerful ideological motivation. They work hard and have a great deal of self-discipline and dedication. All of this contrasts with the relative apathy of the wider membership of groups. The result is inevitable. Viruses take over cells. Leftists take over advocacy and social justice groups.

All the major left-wing parties (like the NDP, Communist Party of Canada, Communist Party of Canada (Marxist–Leninist), the Canadian Party of Labour, various Trotskyist groups, etc.) engage in this "virus ploy." My favourite example involves the Marxist–Leninist penetration of the Montreal Citizens' Movement (MCM) in the 1970s.

Radical politics in Montreal often resembles a cross between pre-revolutionary Moscow and a circus. Scores of tiny and extremely radical left-wing and nationalist groups plot the overthrow of the State in coffee houses and cafes. Community groups, nationalist groups, trade unions and student groups all have a radical cast unknown in English Canada. It is all very charming and romantic. The trouble is that all this idealism, dreaming and romanticism leads to incredible factionalism and internecine warfare among left-wing groups. A historian's comment on seventeenth-century Polish politics — "anarchy tempered by civil war" — is an apt description of Montreal radical politics in the 1970s and 1980s. Still, there are times when the Left seems to regain its sanity and develops some measure of mutual tolerance and self-control. Coupled with a reasonable platform and series of demands, it then represents a real threat to the powers that be. The Front d'action politique (FRAP), a coalition of trade unionists, community groups and student radicals in the late 1960s and early 1970s, was very successful in lobbying for social change at the municipal level. Unfortunately, it had bad friends. Mayor Drapeau was able to destroy it by a smear in the municipal elections which followed the October Crisis by suggesting a link between the FRAP and FLQ. Probably there was some small overlap of membership, but this was almost certainly of little consequence. Nevertheless, the smear worked. FRAP was destroyed. It did live on in a way though. Segments of FRAP went on to take part in the founding of the Montreal Citizens' Movement in 1974. The death of FRAP was due to murder. MCM was to die of a "viral infection."

The MCM started off as an alliance of left-wing and nationalist (Quebec nationalist, that is) groups. The NDP, Communist Party of Canada, Parti Québecois, and community organization activists all contributed to its formation, and while part of the core of this group was made up of leftovers from FRAP, there were new people who were drawn by the promise of municipal reform and the election of a city government more in tune with the needs of ordinary Montrealers.

MCM was definitely a healthy organism. In 1974, MCM sent eighteen out of fifty-two city councillors to city hall. Now, anyone who has ever had influenza will attest to the fact that viruses seem to be drawn to healthy organisms like sharks to blood. So it is with political viruses. The Marxist–Leninists (especially the CPC–ML) saw this sign of robust good health on the Left and made a concerted effort to invade the body, take it over and use it for its own purposes. Its strategy vis-à-vis MCM was to launch heavy attacks on its policies and its leaders and to try and bore away from within it and take it over.

These things it did with devastating effect. Quebec activist Jean Guy Lagüe had the following observations concerning the Marxist–Leninists' tactics: "All the interventions and manoeuvres of the M–L (Marxist–Leninist) group finally coverge in the same direction: the hegemony of *one* organization and one ideology over all militant progressive forces [radicalese which means the Marxist–Leninists take over the left-wingers' organizations]. The M–L sympathizers, themselves only intermediaries transmitting absolute orders, are found in command positions within the groups and only rarely participate in material tasks of implementation, except such tasks as may ensure their control of the organization . . . This is undoubtedly the most serious setback citizens' groups have suffered in years. . . ."[1]

These Marxist-Leninists proceeded to very methodically penetrate and take over the organizations making up MCM and when they succeeded the groups lost their vitality and became little more than mouthpieces for the Marxist-Leninists' propaganda. One example was the takeover of the Centre de formation populaire (People's Training

Centre) in 1976. From that time on, the only information tools were to be study groups for *In Struggle* and *The Forge*, two Party newspapers. This experience was replicated whenever the "viral infection" succeeded. Food cooperatives, day-care centres and tenants' associations were affected as well. With these attacks on member organizations, their subversion and increasingly extreme positions and demands, the MCM started to decline. In the election of 1978, MCM candidates won only a few seats. In 1982, MCM merged with the hitherto rival group MAG (Municipal Action Group). That's enough background. Let's have a look now at some of the more prominent left-wing single-issue groups.

Feminist Groups

Probably no movement has given the Left more problem ideologically than the feminist movement. While socialist thinkers like Engels, Marx and Lenin dealt to some extent with the "woman question" and while the socialist and especially communist movements have included the liberation of women in their platforms, there are clearly problems with the equality of the sexes in communist countries. A quick look at the names making up the top Soviet leadership suffices to show how far that society has yet to go on this issue. In spite of the rhetoric, equality of the sexes has also been just a sideshow for the Canadian Left. Doubtless, this low priority resulted in part from the perceived self-interest of the male-dominated trade union movement, the major resource for the Left for activists and money. The Left is now made up almost exclusively of born-again feminists. (Those who aren't feminists are keeping their views to themselves.) Partly this is the result of the feminization of the workplace which presents organizing opportunities for a trade union movement threatened by layoffs and the erosion of its traditional male support in primary industries. Women are simply too important a potential source of union dues to ignore. The second reason stems from the success of feminist lobbies in pressuring both government and the traditionally male-dominated leaderships of the NDP and the unions. The Left found itself profoundly embarrassed at being left behind the federal government in responding to this new social reality. Furthermore, there are more and more women activists in the bastions of the traditional Left which are demanding that the NDP and the unions lobby on behalf of feminist concerns. This lobbying has resulted in a rethinking of the concepts of social and economic justice. When it lobbies government, the Left almost always makes certain that it covers the "women's point of view."

One would expect that independent left-wing feminist lobbies would be unnecessary. But the Left has had a blind spot to the suffering of women until recently, and many left-wing women found it necessary to carry on the fight for their rights elsewhere. Indeed, much of the initial passion for a revived feminist movement came not from the traditional Left but rather from an alliance of left-wing and lesbian women working on their own, an alliance in the midst of being cursed by its own success. As with so many left-wing causes, the left-wing feminist groups are discovering that as they become successful in wresting concessions and reforms from government, they begin to lose mass support. After all, most people, men and women, are usually only concerned with fine-tuning the system and making it more sensitive to *their* needs. Few of us wake up in the morning thinking of how we can turn society on its head. There has been a shift in the leadership of the women's movement from leftists with dreams of a bright revolutionary future, to more right-wing leaders more concerned with women of a certain class (bright, young, well-educated and upwardly mobile.)

Evidence of this shift to the right can be seen in the increasing tendency towards women's organizations which are bureaucratic rather than grassroots, led by members or would-be members of the elite, rather than those from more humble circumstances, and in the issues given priority. A strange alliance which would have been inconceivable before is that between feminists and the Right which seeks tougher laws and stricter enforcement of laws to suppress pornography. More important is the increasing importance placed by feminist lobbies on assuring easy access by women to the top jobs in business and government. The class basis of this is obvious. Removing impediments to women becoming Supreme Court Justices or corporate presidents means nothing to single mothers on welfare. In short, the left-wingers who were so key in the resuscitation of feminism are losing control to the "new women," the beneficiaries and defenders of the capitalism they seek to destroy.

Peace Groups
If women's groups on the Left have been the most successful single-issue group, the various peace and disarmament groups are the second most successful, not necessarily in lobbying government but in lobbying

the people. This sector of lobbying activity — as with most sectors on the Left — is a virtual circus. There are hundreds, perhaps thousands, of groups across the country dedicated to disarmament and an end to the arms race. The tactics used have been essentially those of direct action — demonstrations, petitions, attempts at disrupting cruise missile testing in the Northwest Territories and the Prairies (one group tried to bring a missile down with a fishing net and balloons), peace camps, and caravans — as well as the blowing up of a portion of the Litton plant by an admittedly tiny and extremist group.

While there has not been any practical response on the part of governments to this movement (unless you count the Trudeau farces of his peace mission and the setting up of a Peace Institute), this lobbying which clearly represents a groundswell of popular support has definitely caught the attention of politicians who plan on seeking re-election. When former Defence Minister Coates told the media that no one paid any attention to protesters, Prime Minister Mulroney was quick to contradict him in public. A sign of just how powerful these peace lobbies have become is the fact that the government feels obliged to perpetrate shams such as the Trudeau ploy. The hope of government is that it can buy off the public cheaply, leaving the lobbies without a constituency. The current disarray of the peace movement indicates that the government may be right.

Anti-Poverty and Social Policy Groups

These groups deal essentially with society, its organization, the redistribution of incomes and the social safety net. They are, in brief, advocacy groups that lobby and sponsor litigation in the "public interest," which is usually meant to be the interest of the poor and underprivileged. Think of them as social workers and do-gooders with lawyers, government grants and the sympathetic ear of the media and you have a good grasp of how they work. Basically their work is organized around:

1. Lobbying government directly. This lobbying may take the form of putting pressure on elected officials and bureaucrats or testifying before Commons and Senate committees and regulatory bodies.
2. Preparing reports, position papers or press releases. These may be directed at government or the media. Whatever the target, the goal is the same. They attempt to document a particular position and provide some sort of intellectual framework for a change in

government policy. The really successful studies are those whose key statistics are accepted at face value and quoted again and again later by government reports and media accounts. Good examples of this sort of war of the statistics involve such things as how many people should be classed as poor or how to interpret the workforce figures in Statistics Canada reports.

3. Making direct appeals to the media. This has the major goal of changing public opinion, thereby changing government opinions. Usually these appeals are centred around specific events like the appearance of a new set of statistics, a major government study or some pending legislation. The trick in all of this is to try to generate enough media attention and public support in the form of letters to the editor and letters and telephone calls to MPs' offices to sugget massive public support. Occasionally, such direct appeals do actually strike a resonant chord in the public. In such a case the lobby may conduct a poll which, if favourable, will be sent to government and released to the media for publication and broadcast.

4. Litigation. This technique has yielded great benefits, but the problems traditionally have been finances and skilled legal counsel. Actually, they are the same problem. While some lawyers are idealistic and prepared to donate some of their time and expertise, ultimately there is a limit to the ability of people to give of themselves. When all is said and done, the following equation determines these groups' ability to use litigation to further their causes: "No money equals no access to justice." This is hard to accept initially, but it does have a certain simplicity and a rough truth. Most advocacy groups have found remedies to the problem of funding. One solution is direct government funding. The National Anti-Poverty Organization (NAPO) relies on this approach. Indeed, its whole budget comes from government. The advantage is that the cheques come on time and never bounce. With this money NAPO can maintain an office, lobby and initiate litigation, although there is always the danger of political interference by the government. More common is the situation of funding from various levels of government as well as private sources. The problem of manipulation by the funders still exists, but there is the possibility of maintaining some semblance of independence. If worse comes to worst the advocacy group in question can always try to play the funding bodies off against each other. A good example is the Public Interest Advocacy Centre

(PIAC), which provides advocacy services for other advocacy groups. Its major clients are NAPO, the Consumers' Association of Canada, some native groups such as the Inuit Tapirisat of Canada and some environmental groups (e.g., Canadian Arctic Resources Committee). PIAC has chosen the regulatory process as its area of concentration and represents and researches the cases of its clients before these bodies. It also provides legal training to these groups so that they can do the same for themselves in time. The criteria which PIAC uses for selecting cases are: the group or individual concerned must be unable to get legal help elsewhere; and the case must have broader significance than just for the individual or group concerned. Once PIAC accepts a case it takes responsibility for the entire course of the action. It may involve just the tribunal level, in which case appearances are made by one or two counsel, or it may involve appeals to the Federal Court of Appeal or Supreme Court of Canada. In such cases well known and high-powered lawyers will argue the case.

The PIAC gets its funding from a variety of sources, the majority coming from the federal department of Consumer and Corporate Affairs (about $250,000). The rest is from such groups as the Donner Canadian Foundation, the Law School Training Program and the Ontario Ministry of the Environment. This funding has traditionally been project related, i.e., when a project is finished, so is the funding.

There is one group, and a small one at that, which supports itself through private funds alone. The Canadian Civil Liberties Association (CCLA) has taken this path to avoid any possible interference or manipulation from government. It is a difficult path indeed. Its money comes exclusively from contributions from members and other private individuals. As you can imagine, the good folks at the CCLA live close to the ground. Nevertheless, it has played a powerful role in helping those with just causes who would otherwise never be heard. The group's influence has been enormous. The CCLA is involved extensively in various forms of aiding litigation by advocacy groups. One role is that of friend of the court in litigation where it is not the initiator. In some cases it is an intervener; it is "the client." In such cases the CCLA is usually represented by a staff lawyer or member prepared to donate his or her services. In other cases it may provide the advocacy group with a lawyer but not become involved itself.

Multi-Issue Groups

Multi-issue groups are more ideological than the single-issue ones. What motivates them is their world view, from which everything else flows: the stands they take, the tactics they use and the demands they make. The highest-profile examples are the liberal churches, trade unions and political parties.

The Churches

Religion is undoubtedly the most enduring form of ideology on the planet. Churches (synagogues, temples, mosques, etc.) are essentially vehicles for the teaching and perpetuation of an ideology. The link between church and state, religion and politics, has existed through time and Canadian churches and church people are on the leading edge of the ideological lobbying activities of both the Left and Right.

In Canada the more liberal denominations — the United Church, the Unitarians, the Anglican Church, Reform Judaism and even the Roman Catholic Church on some issues — are actively involved in lobbying for a number of liberal or left-wing causes. These involve such things as disarmament, ecology, feminism, redistribution of wealth and so on. Wherever there are demonstrators or protestors, the liberal clergy are there. The reasons for this presence are many. One revolves around the quest for moral and ethical perfection that lies at the heart of all religion. Part of this is the desire of clergy to see "good" and "justice" prevail. There is, as well, a similar world-view between the clergy and the Left. Both are highly moralistic (this is the case with the Right as well) and basically they speak the same language.

There are the reasons which are less noble. The flip-flop of the churches on the question of feminism is fascinating. How, one may ask, can the same institutions go from a two to three thousand year history of unquestioning support for the "oppression" of women to an unquestioning support for feminism? Is it a new moral awareness? Or is it a realization that a large and growing proportion of their active membership is female and that if they don't pander to feminism they are lost? What about war and peace? The same churches that blessed armies going into battle now demonstrate against militarism. What about homosexuality, abortion, the right of the rich to retain their wealth? Is the change in political stances a case of high moral motives or is it the crassest form of institutional and personal self-interest? Doubtless it is a mixture of the two. In any case the presence of the liberal churches in left-wing lobbying is highly visible.

There are many single issue church lobby groups, and one area in which such lobbying is common is international relations. The liberal churches have many groups that try to influence government policy vis-à-vis right-wing or racist regimes abroad, like South Africa and South and Central American countries. Sometimes this lobbying takes the form of demanding that the government press these foreign governments to liberalize and extend human rights. On other occasions the church groups demand an end to Canadian business investment in countries like South Africa. (This is, of course, playing tough. If all foreign investment were withdrawn, civil war and revolution would be the probable result, the South African government being what it is.) At the extreme, some groups have support for national liberation and guerrilla movements in the Third World as their goal. In this the liberal church groups have the example of the World Council of Churches which has frequently railed against imperialism (U.S. imperialism only, of course) and has occasionally provided financial aid to guerrilla movements.

The churches are active on the home front too, with lobbying taking the form of sponsoring colloquia, letter-writing campaigns to government officials, picketing and demonstrations, preparing briefs for presentation to government committees and the release of studies and position papers to the media. A good example was the Canadian Conference of Catholic Bishops' December 31, 1982 "New Year's Statement," which entailed a scathing attack on the government's economic policy and Canadian capitalism. It was a sort of "communism with a Roman collar." Not that they did not hit the mark at times. It was just a surprise to see princes of the Church — that same church which has for centuries supported every corrupt dictator in the "Christian world" — condemning an economic and political order which they and their predecessors have had such an important role in creating in the first place. How the world changes!

The leading light in the "gang of eight" was Victoria Bishop Remigio Joseph De Roo, chairman of the Bishops' social affairs commission. De Roo is that strangest of beasts, the establishment radical. As a bishop of the Roman Catholic church he finds himself in the Canadian ideological elite. Still, he is a radical who calls for more power for unions, less dependence on the U.S. military industrial complex and a new economic order in which the poor and "solidarity coalitions" would play a major role. De Roo's position as a bishop and establishment figure gives him obvious lobbying advantages. He has the power, credibility and financial resources which come from being a highly placed Church official, and his standing guarantees him access to major government and business figures. They call him back when he leaves a telephone message. Not many left-wing lobbyists can claim this.

The churches do not always act on their own. Sometimes church people and clergy work in other lobbies as individuals. The problem here is that they occasionally cannot pick and choose what they are supporting. A priest or nun's support for most feminist lobby groups would place them in the awkward position of being seen to support abortion since that is the position of most of these groups. This has happened to the Anglican Church, which is presently an organizational member of the National Action Committee on the Status of Women (NAC) and as such is committed to support NAC's lobbying efforts on behalf of abortion on demand. The funny part is that the church's official policy is opposed to this demand. The other — and extremely common — tactic is to form coalitions with other groups. Liberal church groups have been one of the keystones of left-wing coalitions. The great advantage of church groups is that they bring powerful resources with them — money, large numbers of people, powerful economic and political connections and, most importantly, respectability. It is easy to attack or ridicule trade unionists, communists and students, but it's very difficult to attack ministers, priests, nuns and rabbis.

This is, of course, the hypocrisy of the clergy who play at revolution. It is as if they tell their opponents that they cannot hit them below their belts and then wear their belts on their heads. In a sense, they lack the integrity of all other political players. The other lobbyists — leftists, rightists, business lobbyists, feminists, ethnic lobbyists and so on — all take the blows as well as dish them out. The clergy alone retain and use a privileged position. It's the perfect game. They get the thrill of playing without the dangers and risks inherent in the game.

Trade Unions

The Canadian trade union movement has lobbied on behalf of a large number of "progressive" causes from its inception. Those causes which it supports, and those it does not, represent a curious mixture of leftist idealism and hard-nosed self-interest.

If government refuses to listen to trade union lobbyists as it frequently does, it is not the fault of these lobbyists. The unions have developed an extremely sophisticated lobbying strategy. A major component is active financial and political support for the NDP. The theory is that once the NDP is in power it will back the trade unions with "progressive" and pro-union legislation and regulations. We have no way of knowing how this would work federally since the NDP has never formed a federal government. It has, of course, won frequently at the provincial level, but the size of the payoff has varied considerably with the province, the point in time and the personalities involved.

Even if the NDP doesn't win, the unions find their support pays big dividends, including a big say in what the official policy and agenda of the NDP will be. It was the international union bosses who had the most to lose by the presence of the Waffle, that marvellous mixture of mild Marxism and extreme nationalism that spiced up an otherwise bland NDP in the early 1970s. They feared its nationalistic and socialist agitation would shake their control over the Canadian union movement. As a result they used their clout to persuade the NDP leadership that a purge was in order. A purge did indeed follow.

There are a number of ways in which an opposition NDP can help their trade union allies in lobbying government. NDP members can help by embarrassing the government with questions planted by union lobbyists, through their presence on Commons Committees plus the informal contacts they possess with MPs of other parties.

Another component of union strategy is campaigning on specific issues. Basically, what this comes down to is a lobbying blitz. Such a campaign can happen in response to some crisis or a specific piece of legislation (wage and price controls would be a good example) or as a result of input from members at annual conventions. The Canadian Labour Congress (CLC) and provincial labour federations hold annual conventions at which delegates initiate and vote on policy recommendations and union leaders pick two or three as the subject of major lobbying campaigns for that year. This is quite a clever approach. If the unions campaigned on all the resolutions passed, their resources would be stretched so thin that none of their campaigns would succeed. By concentrating their resources on a very few issues, their lobbying efforts have an excellent chance of having real impact should the government be predisposed to listen and act.

When the trade union movement puts on a major push it pulls out all the stops. Such a blitz might involve the following:

1. Meetings with elected officials at federal, provincial and municipal levels. Usually the way this works is that the federation will hold a two or three day conference in Ottawa or a provincial capital. The first day will bring the participants up to speed on an issue and fire up the troops. On the second day the partici-

pants will go out in groups of three to meet with legislators. Sometimes these groups will hit all MPs and cabinet ministers from one region; other times they will hit all of the members of one party's caucus. Since they outnumber the MPs, they have a certain psychological advantage right away. There is strength in numbers. What they do is simple. They outline their point of view and ask point-blank what the MP's party is prepared to do about the situation. If the MP says that the party is against the union position but he or she is secretly for it, the lobbyists ask directly what the MP is prepared to do about it. After all of the meetings have been conducted, all of the conference partici- pants cum lobbyists get together for a debriefing which results in a report and a follow-up press conference to announce the results.

2. Meetings with civil servants.
3. Letter writing campaigns. Letters are sent en masse to news- papers, MPs elected officials at the municipal and provincial level and civil servants.
4. The commissioning of polls. Good results get trumpeted to the media; bad results get buried.
5. Demonstrations. The demonstration on Parliament Hill to protest the imposition of wage and price controls had 100,000 participants.
6. Planting stories with sympathetic journalists.
7. Placing advertisements in the media. In early 1985, the union movement tried to place a series of ads with radio stations in Ontario asking consumers to boycott Eaton's. I say "tried" because all but two stations refused the ads. The stations said this was for "legal reasons," but never stated what they were. Union officials gave me the example of Standard Broadcasting, owned by Conrad Black and Associates. Black is a director of Eaton's. Pure coincidence, of course. The Ontario Federation of Labour is considering action against the stations with the adver- tising council, press council and the CRTC. One ploy will be to oppose the stations' licence renewals.
8. Annual meetings with the Prime Minister and Cabinet or Pre- mier and Cabinet at the provincial level. Union lobbyists say these meetings are little more than speeches to the deaf and accomplish very little.
9. Commissions studying specific problems which travel across the country hearing testimony from individuals and groups

affected by social and economic problems. Most of those who testify or submit are shills. Still, what the heck! It makes great media.

10. The building of "broadly-based" coalitions. One such coalition organized around interest rates brought together farm, church and labour groups. My all-time favorite was something called "The People's Response to the Planned Depression." It's sort of catchy.

The above is just a partial list, but it gives some of the favourite tactics used by unionists in lobbying. The important thing is that the labour movement has become increasingly sophisticated in its use of these techniques. There is more professionalism in lobbying today; we are beginning to see great flexibility in the application of influence. CLC Political Education Director Pat Kerwin told me that the trade union campaign against wage and price controls represented a turning point in the movement's lobbying strategy. Up until and including this campaign, lobbyists used what he calls the "cap in hand" technique. The unions would usually respond to government initiatives or crises and essentially go to government begging for mercy. The ineffectiveness of union efforts to combat the wage and price freeze campaign showed how inadequate this technique was. The government's poll showed that the public was solidly behind controls, so it felt no need to fold the program in response to union lobbying. With the new stress on proactive campaigns, the unions decide where and when a battle will be fought.

In addition to this new stance there is a new experimental approach. If one technique is not working, union lobbyists are now happy to try others. A good example is the campaign on interest rate policies. The usual direct approaches to government were not working since the government was determined to stay the course. Instead of continuing to beat their heads against the wall as they would have done previously, the unions changed tactics and began to buy advertising time on television in the hope of influencing public opinion. This worked much better, bringing indirect pressure on the government.

There have been a number of union lobbying victories. Usually these have involved fairly technical matters like labour code amendments to parts four and five of the Health and Safety Act. At the provincial level, success has been even greater. For instance, the Ontario Federation of Labour has had considerable success in persuading the government of its point of view on strikebreaking and compulsory union dues. But at the federal level the results in terms of affecting general social and economic policy have been poor. Union lobbyists say that the problem is that past federal governments have had such a very different philosophical orientation from the unions that the government hears the demands but either simply disagrees or lacks the political will to do anything.

Another problem for the unions is getting their message out. We have already seen the difficulty the OFL had in placing advertisements on radio stations in Ontario. This is part of a larger problem. In many cases the media, with the exception of the slightly left of centre government-owned media, is antagonistic to unions. Owners are happy to play the role of "friend of the oppressed" as long as it doesn't affect business costs. Feminism, bilingualism, multiculturalism, disarmament and native rights are wonderful and easy to support. They do not cost the owners a cent. Unions are a different matter. They raise labour costs. Therefore, from the point of view of media owners the union struggle has nothing to do with the social justice. Instead it is a danger to democracy. (It is fascinating, isn't it? Morality seems to correlate strongly with financial self-interest.) Another problem is that most union demands involve matters that simply do not have the flair and sensationalism of which the media is so fond. No sparkle, no sex and no violence means no media coverage.

Another major lobbying disadvantage is that unions organize ordinary people who do not have a lot of money or high socio-economic status. They are not members of the elite. The elite cannot or will not empathize with these people. Furthermore, union leaders and lobbyists come from fairly proletarian backgrounds themselves. They do not have the social contacts and easy social bearing that other more advantaged lobby leaders have. Unlike business leaders, for example, they are not likely to run into cabinet ministers, high-level mandarins or Supreme Court judges at the club or at cocktail parties. They cannot have those informal little chats that are so effective at resolving "misunderstandings." The lobbyists and those they represent do not look, sound, act or live like those they lobby. Therefore, they lose.

Coalition Building
So far we have looked at left-wing lobby groups concerned with single issues and ideologically motivated multi-issue groups. By themselves they have some success. The real key to lobbying success for the Left, though, is coalition building.

Coalition building involves the creation of a common front by a number of groups to lobby for a special issue of interest to all of them. It is by no means a new tactic for the Left. It has been used throughout this century. Sometimes it has been an informal network of people with similar ideas, at other times it is a more formal system as with the Solidarity Coalition in British Columbia. What distinguishes coalition building by the Left now from that of the past is the size, sophistication and success of recent efforts.

The absolute size of the militant Left is not all that great. In small and medium-sized cities the Left is lucky if it can count its activists in the hundreds. In the largest metropolitan communities like Montreal, Toronto and Vancouver, the number of letter writers, demonstrators, spokespeople, people who phone open-line radio shows and so on is usually in the region of a few thousand, yet their influence is enormous. The reason is organization.

One factor is the existence of networks called by their detractors "Dial-a-demo." What this entails is a list of names of people who can be called upon often at a few hours notice to come out to virtually any action of a left-wing nature — demonstrations, boycotts, letter writing, calling MPs and provincial legislators, attending court trials, lobbying government officials, etc. Indeed, there are cases where people have gone to demonstrations without knowing the reason for the demonstration. I know a Toronto woman who is plugged into the Gay, Feminist and Socialist "Dial-a-demo" telephone networks. She received an urgent call one winter day in 1981 to attend a demonstration at the provincial parliament buildings. She neglected to ask the purpose of the demonstration but was certain that it must be an eminently just cause. When she got there she discovered that they were protesting the slaughter of seals in Newfoundland. She looked down in horror to see that she was wearing seal skin boots.

While the process of formal coalition building goes back to earlier in this century, the real golden age of formal coalition building started about fifteen years ago. Probably the beginning of the modern phase took place in Quebec in the late sixties and early seventies. This grew out of a coincidence of two growing forces in the province, nationalism and the trade union movement. The first major success was the Front Commun, which saw the major unions and union federations unite in what was essentially a general strike. In addition to the usual job actions, demonstrations and manifestos, this coalition undertook some real militant acts. Some radio stations were taken over by commando-like squads of militants, one city was taken over and stores in another were forced to stay shut for days. Probably the greatest victory of this coalition was the election of the Parti Québécois. After all, lobbying of small "c" conservative governments can only get you so far; the best solution is to have your own government. To "progressive" forces and interest groups, this is like being locked up in a candy store. How can the government say "no"? Indeed, this is just what happened in the early stages of the PQ government. The government paid off virtually all the groups that had combined to put it in office. There were "French language only" laws for nationalist groups, big wage increases and pro-labour legislation for trade unionists, women's rights and anti-racism legislation, funding for left-wing community groups and patronage goodies for people whose ideological perspectives would have made them pariahs anywhere else in the country. The coalition had worked like a charm.

Another major coalition building exercise took place in British Columbia in 1983. This was a classic. The catalyst was the early legislation and first budget of Premier Bill Bennett which contained a number of measures aimed at a rollback of the extensive social welfare system put together by successive NDP governments. There was something for everyone — promises to cut civil service jobs by one-quarter, spending cuts in education and social programs, a threat to scrap the provincial human rights commission and an end to rent controls. The clumsiness and insensitivity of the government made coalition building easy.

Operation Solidarity was made up of hundreds of citizen, community, church, women's, teachers', students', ethnic and tenant groups plus the labour movement. In an unusual show of labour solidarity, the operation included virtually the entire spectrum of organized workers — private and public sector workers and affiliates and non-affiliates of the British Columbia Federation of Labour. This represented real money and real numbers, about 500,000 people. Very quickly there were branches of Operation Solidarity in towns and cities all over the province. During the summer and fall of 1983, the coalition mounted increasingly effective demonstrations of opposition to the government. In July and August the labour movement produced demonstrations of 25,000 at the legislature in Victoria and 45,000 at the sports stadium in Vancouver. September and October saw a petition campaign and other political protests. On October 15, 60,000 people marched around the Social Credit convention at the Hotel Vancouver. On November 1, strikes began with the B.C. Government Employees Union (BCGEU) withdrawing all except essential services.

Following this, 90 percent of B.C. teachers went out on a job action. The following day a majority of school principals did the same. The threat of a general strike loomed.

It was the threat of a general strike that ultimately defeated the Operation Solidarity. The non-union elements might complain of form in the previously solid front. The threat frightened the top union leaders almost as much as it did the government, for it brought with it the danger of a situation which was totally unpredictable. One result from such a strike might have been the development of a new and more radical leadership which threatened that thing dearest to most trade union leaders — their control over their organizations. Better that Solidarity lose its struggle than that they should lose their jobs! It was this danger that set the stage for the meeting between the Premier and the International Woodworkers of America (IWA) boss, Jack Munro. What resulted was an informal agreement that allowed industrial workers and teachers to go back to work. The government and the BCGEU reached agreement on a contract. The end was in sight for Operation Solidarity. The non-union elements might complain of having been left in the lurch, but with the powerful union groups gone they were lost.

This example is particularly good because it shows how these coalitions come together, how they operate and the problems involved in keeping them together. The original force for the creation of the coalition was a perceived common threat and there was a more or less left-wing ideology that acted as an organizational cement that held these groups together. What is really interesting is that self-interest was ultimately more important than the shared ideologies. The initial cracks in the facade of unity were the results of the trade union leaders seeing a threat to *their* self-interest, and not necessarily that of the unions they led. Finally, when many of the unions got most of what they wanted they were prepared to abandon the others in the coalition.

This was by no means the end of the matter though. This had been an important educational experience for many of those involved. The Bennett government has grown shrewder. It now attacks one opposition group at a time rather than taking all of them on. The union movement, especially the more radical elements, learned that the existing leadership was never likely to carry through on radical confrontational politics and lobbying. In late 1984 there was what amounted to a purge of the more conservative leaders in the B.C. Federation of Labour. The BCGEU, the 50,000 member public service union and its allies, took over control of the Federation from more conservative private-sector unions like the IWA. Jack Munro, the author of the agreement that killed the Solidarity Coalition as a mass movement, was purged from the executive of the Federation. He and other purged officials were replaced largely by former Operation Solidarity militants seeking a more aggressive approach to altering government social policies.

There was one final result. Various attempts have been made to set up Solidarity type coalitions in other provinces and at the national level. The Social Planning Council of Metro Toronto, for example, spearheaded an attempt to form such a coalition in Ontario. Furthermore, there was a conscious effort by the Solidarity Coalition of British Columbia to export its goals and techniques to other provinces. In late September 1984, this coalition sponsored a national conference on coalition building in Vancouver. The conference speakers are listed in the table below.

Speaker	*Organization*	*Topic*
Normand Caron	Quebec Federation of Labour	Financing Coalitions
Chaviva Hosek	National Action Committee on the Status of Women	Lobbying
Ed Finn	CUPE	Media
Larry Kuehn	B.C. Teachers' Federation	Political Strikes
James Sparks	Operation Dismantle	Protests and Demonstrations
Peter Warrian	Ontario Public Service Union	Choosing Winning Issues
Wilson Head	National Black Coalition	What happens when the Government won't listen?

Yet a country-wide network of left-wing coalitions remains at the talking stage only. What would be required to make the dream a reality would be a federal government bent on some sort of authoritarian approach to restraint. This, as we all know, is not the Mulroney style. His attachment to government by poll and consensus means such a network of coalitions is almost certain to stay just a dream for a long time.

Government and the Left: A Special Relationship

One of the great joys of being a left-wing activist is the thrill that comes from being a rebel defying authority. The inner picture of the world borne by almost every left-winger is of himself or herself standing, courageous and defiant, in the face of a government and elite bent upon crushing the Truth and defeating efforts to build a new tomorrow. Probably there was a certain truth to this picture up until the mid-sixties. During the depression it was completely correct. However, with the passing of years, especially the Trudeau years, this picture has come to be less a real picture and more a case of wishful thinking. The fact is that there has been a major shift to the Left of government and the elite over the last twenty years. The result has been a sort of paternalistic attitude by government (especially the federal government) toward left-wingers and left-wing lobby groups. Probably this is due to the fact that the leading lights of the Trudeau government were individuals who had cut their political teeth on "progressive" politics in a radicalized Quebec or were specialists in buying the English-Canadian electorate with its own money through a whole series of "progressive" projects. Even the Tories have their former radicals and Red Tories. The Crombies, Flora Macdonalds and Walter Macleans of the PCs owe much to their slightly left of centre stances.

There is, then, a certain nostalgic fondness for these latter-day radicals, the left-wing lobbyists. The feeling of many establishment politicians seems to be: "They are young. They are impatient. I was once myself. Doubtless, with time and life experience they will become older and wiser as I am." The result is a sort of special relationship between government and left-wing lobbyists. There are other reasons too. Government officials are isolated from those they govern. The left-wing groups are usually the loudest and best organized voices, especially in matters of social policy. Politicians may be forgiven for sometimes confusing the loudest voice for the people's voice. Another reason is that politicians are human. They want to be on the side of the angels. They want to do "good things." This desire makes them fall easy prey to the demands of groups who almost always couch their demands in moral terms. Throw a few liberal clergymen into the lobbies and politicians see themselves heaven bound. All they have to do is accede to the left-wing lobbies' demands and they are halfway there.

There is another side to this relationship. The Left likes government. The more there is, the better left-wing groups like it. As we shall see in the next chapter the Right often has a pathological dislike of government. What this means is first, that the Left is more likely to work on and with government and second, once there, it will find fewer problems in working within the system. It is not just a case of lobbying government. The early sixties and seventies saw significant numbers of young people of varying shades of red and pink enter government in the hopes of using the levers of power to help bring about social change. They are still there and are now in positions of authority. Their dreams and their will to fight are a little threadbare but, like Pavlov's dogs, they still salivate (and dispense money) when lobbyists provide the correct political stimulus. They are pushovers.

Now, the above may seem a little far-fetched, but ask yourself this. How many left-wing, feminist, advocacy and labour groups get funded? The answer is "very many." In fact, some are exclusively funded by government and as such are reverse interest groups. Now, ask yourself this, how many right-wing groups (leaving aside the ethnic associations) are funded by government? In the case of the federal government the answer is virtually none.

Obviously, this is just the tip of the iceberg. There are many liberal church groups that are putting forward left-wing demands. It is impossible to determine what proportion of those funds are used for lobbying as a "progressive" lobby and what proportion goes to legitimate church/synagogue/temple activities. The same goes for trade unions, ecology groups and so on. The important thing is how many groups opposing them get funded? In the sexual area the main anti-feminist or pro-life groups like In Search of Justice, REAL Women and Campaign Life get exactly zero from the public coffers. It is interesting to compare this with the $11 million that went to various women's groups from the federal government in fiscal year (FY) 1983–84. Probably a coincidence. Similarly, it is difficult to think of any right-wing group concerned with social or economic policy that has received any money from the government. The Fraser Institute, Canadians for Foreign Aid Reform, The National Citizens' Coalition, Ken Campbell's Christian Renaissance Canada and the Jewish Defence League might as well not apply for government grants.

In some cases the entrance of left-wingers into government departments has been so significant that the departments become little more than left-wing lobbies and instruments financed by the taxpayer. This is by no means the case in every department or ministry of government. Obviously the Ministries of Finance and National Revenue are unlikely ever to have a high proportion of left-wingers in their ranks, but there are some areas that seem to be little more than job creation programs for the Left. Departments and crown corporations in broadcasting and the arts are ever popular. The most heavily left-dominated bodies, though, are in the areas of foreign aid and international development.

The most obvious example of a government agency that has been taken over by the Left is CUSO. Some may argue that CUSO is not a government body. It is classed as a non-government organization but this is a mere facade. In FY 1983–84, $15.4 million of its $18.5 million came from the federal government (CIDA). That amounts to a whopping 83 percent. To my mind that makes it a government body, no matter what the organizational charts and annual reports might say. The majority of CUSO's work consists of sending Canadians abroad to help in the development of the Third World. The effects of these programs vary. Most are beneficial, the rest are at least not harmful. But not all of CUSO's work is innocuous. There seems to be a tendency for CUSO people in Canada and occasionally in Third World countries to get carried away with ideological zeal, and when that happens real problems crop up.

The radicalization of CUSO staff members in Canada is a problem which resembles the "chicken and egg" question. Is it a case of left-wingers being drawn to CUSO in inordinate numbers because of their concern for social and economic justice? Is it a case of people sent to Third World countries being radicalized by the horrible inequities and human suffering which they witness? Is it a case of left-wing staffers in CUSO hiring friends and acquaintances who just happen to be left-wing as well? Is it a case of being a little piece of the student radical movement of the late sixties which has been preserved by government funding to present? Whatever the reasons, the headquarters staff of CUSO tend to be more or less uniformly left-of-centre.

This left-wing political perspective has had some fascinating effects. One has been conflict between headquarters staff and staff in the field who do not share a left-wing or revolutionary perspective. One returned CUSO volunteer, Reg Kendall, a successful poultry farmer from Thamesford, Ontario, who was stationed in New Guinea asserted that CUSO supervisors were more concerned with filling out reports that looked good than in dealing with reality. He spoke of incompetence: "I went to Yangoru to teach welding only to find that there was no power. So, how the hell can you teach welding with no power?"[2] His most serious charge, though, was that CUSO was toying with the idea of providing the West Papua Liberation Front with aid and money.

Actually, CUSO has dabbled in revolutionary and guerrilla struggles through its aid and its funding of various projects conducted by revolutionary movements in the Third World. Its present cause célèbre is Southern Africa. Two groups that have benefited from CUSO largesse are the South West African Peoples' Organization (SWAPO) and the African National Congress (ANC), both fighting guerrilla wars in Namibia and South Africa. Some fascinating reading material is the CUSO pamphlet produced in co-operation with OXFAM Canada entitled, *Brochure of ANC (SA) Projects: Canadians Express Solidarity with the South African People's Struggle for Freedom.* In response, CUSO has replied that it only funds humanitarian projects. One wonders, though, just how scrupulous hard pressed guerrilla organizations would be in using this money solely on humanitarian projects.

This suspicion about the non-political and non-military quality of the CUSO presence abroad has occurred to some foreign governments as well. Madagascar, for instance, expelled SUCO, the Quebec variant of CUSO, for subversive activities, and following the election of Prime Minister Edward Seaga, Jamaican police raided the CUSO offices in that country in a search for guns. The *Canadian Tribune*, the Canadian Communist Party's official newspaper, claimed that police roughed up Canadian Jamaican staff.

CUSO is by no means involved just in development overseas. It is active in lobbying in Canada for increased public support for foreign aid and for liberation movements in the Third World. This lobbying activity involves the following:

1. Financial and other support for groups lobbying on behalf of increased foreign aid and support for liberation movements. Below are some examples:

Date	Amount of Funding	Agency	Purpose
1975	$2,000	CUSO	Grant to Task force on the Churches and Corporate Responsibility (TCCR). This group lobbies government and corporations against investment in South Africa, Guatemala and Chile.

(continued)

1977	Travel and Living Expenses	CUSO	Brought in South Sahara guerrilla fighters on a speaking tour of Canada to lecture against Morocco.
1979	$2,500	CUSO	To finance Canadian speaking tour of two Patriotic Front members seeking funds and support.
1983	$2,000	CUSO	To the International Defence and Aid Fund for Southern Africa for a program to promote an anti-South Africa view of life in Southern Africa.

CUSO is not alone in these activities. The main funding body of CUSO, the Canadian International Development Agency (CIDA), gives money to a number of NGOs which are very clearly involved in lobbying for changes in Canadian foreign policy toward right-wing regimes in Southern Africa and Latin America. CIDA gave IDAFSA, mentioned earlier, $9,000 in 1982–83 and $220,000 in 1983–84. A similar group, the Victoria International Development Education Association (VIDEA) which apparently decorated its Victoria office with posters in support of guerrilla movements in Central America and whose "development education programs" feature strongly anti-American political messages received $30,000 in 1981–82, $38,680 in 1982–83 and $50,155 in 1983–84. In both the case of Ottawa-based IDAFSA and Victoria-based VIDEA the money given to these organizations was for development education. This was originally intended to be educational materials concerning development problems. What it deteriorates into all too often is anti-American propaganda and pleas for the general public to pressure governments to provide more funds to organizations like CUSO and CIDA. This investment in lobby groups, if successful, will result in larger budgets for CIDA and CUSO. It is an indirect way of lobbying one's political masters for more money and power.

2. Lobbying government and business either by itself or in conjunction with other lobby groups for changes in foreign policy and investment policies abroad (e.g., South Africa, Chile) and for increased foreign aid budgets.

In the foreign policy area CUSO has put its resources very heavily behind groups trying to oust South Africa from Namibia and to overthrow the South African regime itself. For instance, CUSO/SUCO produced a twenty-eight page attack on Israel and South Africa entitled *Zionism and Apartheid*. The Jewish community was not amused. While it was in the mood, SUCO continued the attack on Israel with a book entitled *International Solidarity*, which supported the PLO. Still, attacks on Israel are just a side show. The real lobbying thrust involves support for revolutionary movements in Southern Africa and South and Central America. CUSO has urged the government to squeeze South Africa. At its General Meeting, December 5 and 6, 1981, CUSO issued a demand that, "the Canadian government pressure Canadian-based multi-national corporations to withdraw operations from South Africa and Namibia,"[3] and at the same meeting urged the government to support the call for international economic sanctions against South Africa in the UN and to extend diplomatic and material support to SWAPO in an effort to achieve Namibian independence. CUSO has had a close association with OXFAM Canada and the Toronto Committee for the Liberation of Southern Africa (TCLSAC) in trying to lobby the Canadian government and people for support for the liberation movement in Southern Africa and a hobbling of the present regime in South Africa. This support involved the participation of CUSO financially and as a participant in or organizer of conferences on the future of the region and the struggle against South Africa.

According to Ian Smilie, former executive director of CUSO, development education "has become for CUSO and for many other NGOs an important part of our raison d'être."[4] The most important CUSO programs have been The National Campaign to End Bank Loans to South Africa, The People's Food Commission and support for the campaign against baby formula use in the Third World.

6

The Holy Terrors of the Right

The problem of defining the Right is similar to that of defining the Left. Like the Left, the Right does not constitute just one group or one guiding ideology. Rather, it is made up of a large number of groups and individuals with widely divergent views, aims and backgrounds. There is no one set of ideas. As with the Left, probably the best we can do with the Right is to try and develop some general idea of those beliefs which seem to make up the core of most groups and then note differences when they arise. Essentially, the major common attitudes and beliefs are:

1. *A certain suspicion of government intervention in the economy and society.* The Canadian Right seeks a return to something resembling free market capitalism and individualism in the political and social realms.
2. *Anti-establishmentarianism.* The Right views the Canadian elite or establishment as being either social-democratic or small "l" liberal. It views this elite as being responsible for the present collectivist or statist organization of the economy and society with its heavy government intervention.
3. *The ultimate imperfectibility of man and society.* Human beings are, in this view, imperfect and are likely to stay that way no matter how society or the economy is organized. The best that anyone can hope for is some minimum restraints to avoid the Hobbesian state of nature which would be "nasty, cruel, brutish and short."

Throughout this chapter I will try to avoid the use of the words "conservative" and "liberal" as much as possible. This is because of the degradation of the terms as a result of popular use. At present most Canadians use the term conservative to mean someone who opposes collectivism, socialism, social welfare or other forms of state intervention. According to this view, conservatives represent the last vestiges of individualism and free enterprise. By this same popular wis-

94

dom "liberalism" is essentially collectivist, mildly anti-business and pro–state intervention. The problem is that these popular definitions confound any sort of political, economic or social meaning since they are almost the reverse of what is understood in most political, social and economic theories or philosophies. In its original and proper meaning, the term conservative refers to a political philosophy which embraces a collectivist view of the world and which approves of state intervention in society and the economy, although not of the same sort as the Left would like to see. True conservative thinkers have often been inimical to free market capitalism and a laissez faire approach to society. On the other hand liberalism — that philosophical and ideological offshoot of the work of John Locke — is the ideological foundation of capitalism and individualism and eschews most government intervention in society and the economy.

In Canada one sees a remarkable coincidence of conservatives and socialists when it comes to economic and social policy and the role of the state. A good example of this coincidence is the often aggressive policies of the Conservative Party in creating and fostering the existence of state-owned enterprises like Ontario Hydro and the CBC. As such, the Conservative Party is often far from being right-wing in the sense of encouraging less government intervention or more individual enterprise. The Liberal Party is far from being "liberal" since it has for some time now pursued a highly collectivist, interventionist and, during the Trudeau years, a somewhat social-democratic philosophy and set of policies. The result is that the Liberal Party is in fact not "liberal." The Conservatives may be conservative, but they are often far from being right-wing. Confusing? Not really. All I can say is that where possible I will try to avoid using such terms and instead talk about "social-democratic," "welfarist," "collectivist," "interventionist" and so on. When I slip up or when there is no alternative to using the terms "liberal" and "conservative," I will be using them in the popular sense rather than the more precise philosophical sense.

Pet Peeves of the Right

In some sense it is possible to differentiate the Left and Right by saying that people on the Left tend to have a romantic image of some perfect future they are trying to build while the Right is preoccupied with some romantic image of the past which it is trying to re-create.

It is not always easy to develop a clear picture of what sort of society the Right is for. It is an easier task to identify those things which it is against. Some of the major preoccupations of most right-wingers are:

1. government intervention in the economy.
2. decline in law and order (capital punishment figures large in the scheme of things for many right-wingers).
3. a perceived decline in moral standards. (The decline of the importance of organized religion and the increased incidence of open homosexuality and abortion are seen as sure signs of such a decay.)
4. the strength of the national defence force.
5. fiscal responsibility.
6. the strength of the trade union movement.
7. high taxes.
8. universal social programs.
9. perceived abuses in human rights commissions and legislation.
10. reductions in individual liberty.
11. immigration.
12. the integrity and strength of the family.

If you find yourself in agreement with some of these points, don't be overly concerned. This does not mean that you are a latent fanatical right-winger. The fact is that most of these are reasonable concerns shared by large portions of the population. This is obviously just a partial list. Some right-wing groups would add to it, some would subtract. Still it does give us a rough idea of what we are dealing with.

Curiously enough, the Right, until recently, could count Pierre Trudeau and his captive Liberal Party among their closest friends. The reason lies in Trudeau's pushing the Party from a fairly right of centre, establishment and business oriented position to one very close to that of the many West European social democratic parties. His policies on such issues as metrification, capital punishment and other law and order issues, women's rights, relations with the United States and the Western Alliance, bilingualism, multiculturalism, Western Canada, energy and many, many other issues has won the Right more converts than it ever could have by its own efforts. Many rightists were known to have wept when it was announced that Trudeau would be going. A great but inadvertent recruiter for right-wing causes had passed from the scene.

There had been just too much change in too short a period of time, and people wanted the security that a vaguely remembered but seemingly rosy past offered. With the insensitivity and arrogance of the Trudeau technocracy, the groups on the Right were able to mobilize discontent around specific issues. Once it had the public listening to it on these issues, it was well on its way to converting the public to its wider critique and goals.

Single Issue Lobbying

The government has made the job of the Right quite easy by taking a very doctrinaire approach to social policy and by excluding views held by significant portions of the Canadian public from the start because it considered these opinions to be totally wrong or illegitimate. People — decent people to whom one listens anyway — just shouldn't think that way. Or so reasoned the federal government. Be it the use of Imperial measure, bringing back the noose or a more "conservative" view of family and sexual matters, the federal government had its mind made up and was determined not to listen to opposing points of view. It wasn't listening. But the Right was.

Metrification

How this could have been turned into a national issue in the first place is beyond me. Still, the federal government managed to make it just that. The reasonable approach would probably have been to selectively convert to metric, though I personally fail to understand how people buying hamburger or milk in kilos and litres helps Canada to compete in the world market which was after all the reasoning behind the conversion program in the first place. Nevertheless, the technocrats in Ottawa had determined that everything must change, no matter how the country might feel about it. The government knew best. This arrogance was transmitted to the public quickly.

The leadership for the anti-Metric movement came from two major sources — the Conservative Party and a lobby group called Measure Canadian, headed by president Gill Cyr. At times the Tories played a direct role in lobbying against the metric policy, quite apart from their usual ploys at question time in Parliament. One of the most dramatic moves occurred when thirty-seven Conservative MPs operated a gasoline station outside Ottawa called the Freedom to Measure station serving up gasoline in gallons. They were daring the federal government to charge them. (Charges were laid eventually, but against two Toronto service station owners who were made the goats of government fiat.) Measure Canadian used an advertising campaign on TV to try to influence voters to vote against the Liberals who were determined to hang tough on metrification, and for the Tories, who had supported them so consistently. In the end the Tories won the election and paid back the anti-metric lobby for its help. The new Tory government declared that henceforth it would be possible to use Imperial measure for a large number of goods. The metric lobby had won. So had the Right. It had won some converts and support for its favourite political party.

Law and Order

Law and order is an issue which the Right consistently champions. But it has had little success in actually getting the government to listen to its demands for the use of a heavier hand in dealing with criminals, heavier sentences and conditions for parole once they are convicted, and a return to capital punishment. Its success has been considerable in getting its point of view across to the public, however, since there is considerable evidence of an ever increasing proportion of Canadians who support a return to capital punishment. Indeed, this probably explains the reluctance of either the previous Liberal federal government or the present Conservative one to the idea of a referendum to settle the question.

Some of the most vocal groups demanding such measures are police associations. Every year there is a litany of demands from the association of chiefs of police and unions representing prison guards and other correctional officers demanding such measures, yet each year the government rejects the demands. Still, the general public is listening. There were two events in 1984 which aided these law and order lobbies enormously. One was the election of the federal Conservatives since a number of Tory MPs have been vociferous proponents of tougher treatment of criminals and the return to capital punishment. The various lobbies could now be sure that their arguments would be presented to the very heart of power. The other event was the sudden increase in the number of police murders. It looked for a time as if the criminal element in society had discovered a new fad. What these events did was encourage and mobilize public support with one result being the National March for Law and Order Reform held in Ottawa in November 1984. This march was made primarily by police, prison guards, relatives and right-wing supporters. By Ottawa standards it was not a huge event; there were only about 1,500 marchers who bore one petition with 3,000 names and another petition from a group called Victims of Violence with 9,000 signatures. The numbers did not scare the politicians. What did scare them was the ugly mood of the officers and the fact that the police wore their uniforms. This carried the veiled threat of a coup, in the politicians' minds.

One can see the beginning of an overlapping membership of leaders and members between the marchers and other right-wing supported organizations. Many of the Tory MPs who supported the march and cause were active in the groups lobbying government for the repeal of metric legislation. One of the speakers at the march, Peterborough MP Bill Domm, had been very active in the movement against metric measurement, and Rev. Kenneth Campbell of the Renaissance Organization, a right-wing religious group active in a number of political causes, was a speaker at a debate in Toronto on the question of capital punishment. He spoke in favour of it, of course. The Right wins when it supports such a movement, whether the movement is successful or not. By showing its support, especially in the face of scorn and attack by "respectable" bodies such as the more liberal churches and the media, the Right assures itself of supporters for some future date when it will have to call political debts.

Taxation
Taxation is probably the most powerful symbol of the organizational weakness of lobbies on the Right. This issue has been effectively used by the Right in the United States (viz. the tax revolt in California under the banner of Proposition 13 which rolled back public spending in that state). It is curious that the Right has been notably unsuccessful in exploiting and organizing taxpayer rage toward inequities in the tax system and wasteful government spending. Some groups have emerged to fight against government fiscal and taxation policies, but these have by and large been merely the expression of short-term rage following some unusually onerous or unfair addition to taxes. Usually these movements die out after a frenetic spasm of activity. Two groups whose purpose is to fight the somewhat arbitrary behaviour of the federal government in this area and the extremely arbitrary actions of Revenue Canada, CATS (Citizens Against Tax Squandering) and CASE (Canadians for a Sensible Economy), have had virtually no impact.

Immigration
A good many of those on the Right perceive enormous dangers in an open door immigration policy, especially as it pertains to immigrants from the Third World. In this they probably express the reservations felt by many Canadians. It is never spoken, but it is always there. The only difference between the Right and ordinary citizens is that the Right does not worry about being labelled as racist, whereas this potential charge is usually enough to silence most others.

One right-wing lobby group in this area is C-FAR (Citizens for Foreign Aid Reform). Actually, C-FAR is interested in much more than just the question of foreign aid. It is also concerned with the spread of Communism, race, left-wing religious groups, Third World politics and immigration from the Third World. This group, headed by Paul Fromm, operates out of a suburban Toronto post office box. Fromm is a study in himself. In 1968 he founded the Edmund Burke Society, a sort of cerebral right-wing group, in conjunction with Don Andrews. This connection with Andrews dogged him ever after. Andrews transformed the Edmund Burke Society into the Western Guard, which was not cerebral at all. Rather, it was a sort of racist and fascist group that often saw its members involved in violent encounters with left-wing and ethnic organizations. Andrews was sentenced to a brief jail term in 1978 and forbidden to associate with the Western Guard. His response was to form the Nationalist Party of Canada and to attempt to form a merger with the Ku Klux Klan. In 1981, when Fromm became treasurer of the PC Metro Toronto organization, his past association, combined with some unfortunate remarks on his part concerning race and immigration, led to his being dumped from the post in the same year.

C-FAR functions largely as an educational lobby group. Through its newsletter, pamphlets in its "Canadian Issues Series" and forums it attempts to educate the public concerning issues it feels strongly about. Its pamphlet series has dealt with such issues as sociobiology, CUSO and radicalism, the left-wing danger from the World Council of Churches, overpopulation, foreign aid and Third World immigration. Its "Alternate Forum" has dealt with such subjects as the operation of the KGB in Western societies and flaws in CUSO's programs overseas. In addition the organization submitted a brief to the Royal Commission on Participation of Visible Minorities in Canadian Society. To say that the Commission was not well disposed to the brief would be a gross understatement.

To date, C-FAR has not had any visible impact. This is not to say that right-wing lobbies are never successful in this area. One group that has had a notable lobbying success is the National Citizens' Coalition which we will study in some detail later on. This group was largely successful in closing the doors to the flood of "boat people" from Indochina. Using information from a former immigration official, Kim Abbott, the Coalition sponsored two full-page advertisements in August and September 1979 which accused the government of poor planning and alleged that each "boat person" "will sponsor at least

15 of their relatives, on average, and this will lead to at least 750,000 people in Canada in the not too distant future."[1] The 15 to 1 ratio was labelled as nonsense by the Minister of Employment and Immigration Ron Atkey who claimed the advertisement "smacked of racism." Editorial writers and liberal spokespeople across the country condemned The Coalition and its campaign. The only people who supported the Coalition were ordinary people. A poll showed that 63.6 percent of Canadians thought the government's ceiling of 50,000 "boat people" was too high. Soon after the public attack of the policy by the Coalition, the government announced major reductions in the sponsorship program. The Coalition might not have won kudos from the more liberal elements in society, but it had been successful in its lobbying activity.

Right-to-Life

Without doubt the most successful right-wing lobby, both in terms of its influence upon the political system and its ability to mobilize large numbers of people, has been the anti-abortion or "right-to-life" movement. Part of this success has been the result of the legitimacy which clings to the group as a result of its association with the Catholic Church. Part, but not all. What really sets this group apart from other right-wing groups is its organizational finesse. We will look at this group later; suffice to say that it is remarkable among right-wing groups on account of its support among many mainstream segments of the population.

Foreign Policy

Since the Vietnam War, the Right has had an ever-decreasing influence on the agenda setting and determination of Canadian foreign policy. It is as if events of the sixties and seventies completely discredited anything the Right might have to say on the subject. This trend is beginning to change, although very slowly. An indication of that change is that many voices in support of a more right-wing agenda are coming from prominent Canadians. One such voice is that of Peter C. Newman, famous Canadian writer and darling of the Canadian elite. His book *The True North: Not Strong, Not Free* was an offshoot of his work on the subject of foreign policy and military spending for the Business Council on National Issues, the lobby for very big business in Canada. Now this is really a joke in as much as it represents the ultimate in self-interest on the part of big business. It is, after all, these very big businesses, represented by the Council, which would benefit from any increased government spending to revamp the Canadian military. Of course, it is not just this group. There is a bevy of lobbyists for big business and the military industry, including virtually all U.S. companies or their subsidiaries. After all, what is the point of having an empire if you can't make it pay?

And it isn't just big business that is busy lobbying for a more hawkish foreign policy and military stance. There are some pure right-wing groups that are out there beating the bushes for a holy war against communism and getting tough with the Third World. Apart from C-FAR, there is the Peace Through Strength coalition, basically an umbrella organization for a number of groups which believe that disarmament is undesirable if it means a surrender to communism. To these groups the surest way to peace and an enduring halt to military accommodation with the Soviet Union is to build up Western military might and to face up to what they perceive as the aggressive and imperialistic nature of the Soviet Union.

Support for the coalition has a definite ethnic quality to it. Many supporters are people from Eastern Europe or South East Asia. (This is amusing, since these are the same boat people who the National Citizens' Coalition was attempting to keep out on the grounds that there would be many communists among them.) This support is understandable because people from these regions have suffered from the revolutions, the civil wars, massacres and repression which accompanied the takeover of power by the communist movements in these countries. Their charges and fears as to the nature of communism may seem simplistic to native born or liberally-minded Canadians, but they at least have some first-hand basis for their views. This hatred of communism born out of first hand experience brings with it such passions that it is often difficult to control them at demonstrations. One Peace Through Strength activist told me that some of the Indo-Chinese members have gotten into trouble with the police at demonstrations because their emotional scars are so fresh. This sensitivity sometimes translates into attacks on counter-demonstrations.

One of the major groups which is part of the coalition is the Canadian Anti-Soviet Action Committee (CASAC) headed by Geza Matrai. Matrai is a fascinating character. He came to Canada after the Hungarian revolution of 1956 and is something of an institution on the Right. He has been active in many key right-wing organizations and a measure of his success as an organizer is the virulence with which he is attacked by the Left. One pamphlet by a group called the Committee to Defend Anti-Fascist Unionists had the following uncomplimentary things to say about Matrai and his organization: "The KKK and Nazis have found fertile ground on the fringes of the new Cold War. It is no accident that William John Beatty, ex-fuhrer [sic] of the Canadian Nazi Party, together with former members of the white-supremacist Western Guard like Geza Matrai and Paul Fromm [remember him from C-FAR?] resurface today as the Canadian Anti-Soviet Action Committee. The fascists are the domestic shock troops of the drive to ignite the entire earth in thermonuclear war against the Soviet Union. CASAC, the Nazis, Richardson, the Klan are targeting us and ours for union-busting, race-terror and genocide." That's what I like — a nice, objective, well thought out political statement.

Of course, Matrai has done some things which annoyed both the Left and the Canadian political elite. One of his most famous stunts involved what amounted to the mugging of the then Soviet Premier Kosygin in 1974 during his tour of Canada. If you will remember, Prime Minister Trudeau was caught up in the glow of détente then and developed a small crush on the Soviet Union. In this spirit he welcomed Kosygin to Canada. This tour was like a red flag (literally) to a bull as far as the East European community in Canada was concerned. Matrai took it upon himself to point out to the Canadian people and the world that all was not forgiven as far as the "workers' paradise" was concerned. He jumped Kosygin and wrestled him to the ground. For this he was awarded a few months in jail. In an interview with Matrai in late 1984, he informed me that his life was in danger while in custody. Apparently, he had made a statement a short time earlier as a Social Credit candidate in which he stated a Party policy which was that drug dealers who were found guilty of peddling more than once should be executed. While Matrai was in custody the *Toronto Star* did a report which included a section on his background, part of which quoted this very statement. Unfortunately for Matrai, the majority of his fellow prisoners were drug dealers. They were not amused. There were numerous threats against him and on one occasion a prisoner threw a large basin of boiling water into his cell. It missed.

I have to confess that my exposure to individuals on the Right had been rather limited until I began researching this book. My idea of what these people were like was gleaned from the media — authoritarian and evil. Matrai was a bit of an eye-opener. I first had contact with him as a result of a television interview in 1984, and having read some of the Left's comments on him I was expecting the worst. Instead what I discovered was a soft-spoken, articulate and thoughtful individual around forty. He is now a student at the University of Toronto in political science (so what else is new?) and supports himself as a hair-dresser on the side. Whoever thought of hairdressers as right-wing?

Matrai's group, CASAC, is certainly a busy one. It sponsors speakers and forums, one of its most famous being a speech at the University of Toronto by retired U.S. Army General John K. Singlaub. Singlaub is also an interesting character. A former commander of U.S. forces in Korea, he was fired by former President Jimmy Carter. This is some-thing he is enormously proud of. He is presently President of the World Anti-Communist League and goes about the world preaching the need to roll back the red peril and support freedom fighters in anti-communist struggles such as in Afghanistan. Clearly, he is bad news for liberals and left-wingers with heart conditions. Another activity of CASAC has been an attempt to create a boycott of Lada automobiles and other Soviet products. Finally there are the inevitable demonstrations as occasion requires, and letters to the editor. These are busy boys and girls.

Probably the real motherlode of right-wing influence on foreign policy has to be the East European ethnic organizations. One of the amusing aspects of multiculturalism à la Pierre Elliott Trudeau was that his government through its multicultural programs was forced to fund the very anti-Communist and highly nationalistic organizations which it loathed so very much philosophically. Even more amusing was the fact that virtually none of the members of these groups were ever likely to vote for the Liberal Party. The Conservatives certainly, the NDP maybe, but the Liberals almost never.

Governments are usually assailed by demands from these groups that the Canadian government single-handedly rewrite the history of Eastern and Central Europe and roll back Communism.

The Canadian government has yet to approach the Soviet govern-ment about the possibility of detaching any of the Baltic States or the Ukraine from the Soviet Union, but still the lobbying goes on. One of the groups used by these ethnic lobbies has been the East European Progressive Conservative Association. This tack has paid off. At least they now have a friend at the highest levels of government. This friend is Michael Wilson, the present Minister of Finance, who has been one of the key figures in this organization. This is not too surprising considering the size of the East European communities in the west end of Toronto where Wilson has his riding. One of the major demands of this group is the strengthening of the Canadian armed forces, as well as the little matter of the breakup of the Soviet empire. Wilson had the following remarks to make at the founding meeting of the organization: "Let us not forget that whenever we demonstrate any weakness, be it economic, military or political, we are robbing those peoples living in Latvia, Lithuania, Estonia, the Ukraine, Poland, Hungary and Czechoslovakia of the hope and inspiration they need to sustain their continuing fight for freedom . . . We are the voice of these captive people."[2]

Religious Fundamentalism

There is a sense among most in the Right that somehow our society is not what it used to be morally or ethically. Nowhere is this point of view more passionately held than among the more conservative religious groups. Until recently these groups have been demoralized by the many social changes that have taken place, but there is now a new sense of confidence. Instead of stepping aside and letting the more liberal groups and forces have full play they are fighting back and making their power felt.

Protestant Fundamentalism

Whenever anyone thinks about "fundamentalism" or "Moral Majority" it is almost always Protestant fundamentalist groups that come to mind. This is probably the most powerful proof of the high visibility and influence of these groups, not in the eyes of government perhaps but at least in the eyes of the public. These groups have been extremely active in lobbying against what they would term "moral decay," the signs of which are easy to identify — abortion, pornography, homosexuality, the rise in the divorce rate, drugs, promiscuity, etc. For a long time this lobbying activity was laughable. Many groups acted in a reactive or ad hoc basis and they often lobbied for things that just did not have much popular appeal either because they were essentially U.S. issues exported to Canada (like prayers in the schools) or because they reflected how badly the groups had been left behind by society at large. A good example of the latter are the many attempts by "holier-than-thou" community members to ban books like Salinger's *Catcher in the Rye* or Margaret Laurence's *The Diviners*. The charges of obscenity and blasphemy that accompany these campaigns have an anachronistic ring to them and they succeed only in eliciting yawns from the general public and a sickening wave of self-righteousness from liberals in the media and artistic community. Recently, though, the Protestant fundamentalist groups have become better organized and follow much more successful lobbying tactics and strategies.

Probably the most successful lobby group in this area is that of

Kenneth Campbell, a Baptist minister located in Milton, not far from that latter-day Babylon, Toronto. Campbell has been successful in setting up something called the Renaissance International. Actually he heads what amounts to a number of organizations: Renaissance Canada; Renaissance Ontario; Moderate Majority and Teens for Tomorrow. Under the Renaissance banner he has campaigned against books he considers obscene or blasphemous in schools, homosexuality and aspects of the proposals made to provide public funding to Catholic high schools. In 1981, Renaissance was even involved in lobbying against Trudeau's efforts at repatriating the constitution. More recently Campbell has formed a political wing called Solidarity which he has used to campaign across the country against abortion and metric measure and for capital punishment and more government accountability.

Campbell has been more or less badly treated by the media. Usually the tone of articles I have ever read about him seem to suggest he is either mad or a joke. In a series of articles on the Right, Val Sears of the *Toronto Star* engaged in a little bit of gratuitous pettiness by referring to Campbell as "very junior-grade Falwell,"[3] after Jerry Falwell, the Leader of the Moral Majority in the U.S. This sort of cheap shot was not surprising. Sears, after all, is a long-time left-winger, an NDP supporter and father of the head of the Socialist International. Also, relations between Campbell and the *Star* have been difficult almost from the beginning, largely because of the ideological chasm which divides the two. The *Star* refused one of his advertisements, although you have a little sympathy for the newspaper when you realize that the title of his ad was to be: "How the Church should Respond to Gospel Perverts," the "perverts" being the members of the United Church committee who had recommended the ordination of homosexuals. What was worse was that he wanted to run it on the church page. That's really asking for trouble.

If the media have found Campbell funny, especially in the early stages of his organization's history, there is some sign that they and some of the more liberal groups in society are beginning to find the joke a little less amusing. The fact is that his group has had considerable success in countering the growing political power of the homosexual community in Toronto. Until Campbell entered the fray, the various gay lobbies, teamed up with some politicians on the Left, seemed unbeatable. Also, his base of support is just too big, is growing too quickly, and is too well organized for politicians to ignore completely. In March 1984, a *Toronto Star* article discussed the 60,000 name Renaissance mailing list which Campbell had to influence the selection of the Progressive Conservative leadership convention.[4] In December 1984, Val Sears claimed that the Renaissance mailing list was 150,000.[5] Could it actually be that Renaissance had grown 150 percent in one year? Apparently, it had. In any case, no government can long afford to ignore the views of a man who is able to persuade 150,000 adults to pay to read his political opinions.

Campbell seems to be reaching out to form alliances with other right-wing single issue lobby groups. In 1984 he spoke out in favour of the testing of cruise missiles and at rallies in favour of capital punishment. Clearly Campbell's influence and his lobby groups are likely to grow in the future, especially given the conservative trend which seems to be growing in Canada.

Catholic Fundamentalism

Generally, the Roman Catholic Church and its many sub-groups have followed essentially centrist or left-wing paths. There is one group, though, that seems to take an extremely right-wing line — the Pilgrims of St. Michael. This group is made up of fragments from the White Berets of the recent past who were somewhat famous (or infamous, depending on your point of view) for some of their right-wing positions and antics. About their only manifestation is their paper called *Michael Fighting*, a little gem which is like a bit of the Middle Ages brought forward to our century. The tone of religious obscurantism and fanaticism makes it a poor pick-me-up. One copy decried the "horrors" of compulsory education where, according to this paper, children are being taught sexology, blasphemy, concubinage, nudism, communism and rape. School must have changed since I attended.

Jewish Fundamentalism

Pressure by religious fundamentalists on the polity has not been uncommon in Christian societies throughout history, but this sort of fanatical religious activity aimed at government has not been a feature of Judaism. Regrettably, this is no longer the case. The Jewish Defence League has come to Canada.

I have a great deal of sympathy for the members and supporters of this group. I have chatted with Meir Halevi, the leader of this group, and found him to be a decent sort of person. The problem with his group, however, is that it is based on a fear that seems to be completely out of control — a fear which seems to deform the personalities of those who are its unhappy victims. The fear of another holocaust like that of Nazi Germany gives rise to this group's major lobby technique — the threat of violence, albeit violence of a defensive nature.

One of the major problems the group has is developing support for its activities and its claim to speak for the Jewish community in Canada. By and large there does not seem to be a groundswell of support for it among Canadian Jews. There are a number of reasons for this. One involves the success which establishment-oriented groups like the Canadian Jewish Congress have had in lobbying government at all levels for the supression of racism and hate-mongering. Clearly it is difficult for the JDL to claim that representatives of the Canadian Jewish community are not being heard by government.* In other words, this success in influencing government ensures that the JDL will never represent a very significant proportion of the Canadian Jewish community. Another reason is the basic decency of Canadian Jews. There is a real sense of embarrassment at the antics and extremist statements of JDL leaders. The JDL represents a threat to the leadership of the Jewish community and an ever-present source of aggravation to non-Jews. As such it contains the potential for a backlash and increased anti-Semitism. These two threats do not make the JDL one of the most popular groups in the Canadian Jewish mainstream. Nevertheless, the JDL does have a constituency and a growing one at that.

There are three main vehicles the JDL has used consistently and successfully in building its base of support. One is the media. As we have seen with both the Left and right-wing groups, the media eschews mainstream and reasonable groups for more extremist ones simply because the extreme ones make for better copy or ratings. This is an area where the JDL shines. Its thinly veiled threats of violence and its scare stories of neo-Nazis under every bed make for great shows. The payoff for the JDL is increased visibility and credibility. The assumption of many is that the JDL must be representative and powerful. If not, why would the media ask them their opinions? Another vehicle for building support has been the use of direct action and street theatre techniques like boycotts, picketing, marches and occasionally violence. The JDL has on occasion used these techniques to communicate to some that the establishment organizations have failed them and that only

---

*For a description of the lobbying activities of the Jewish Canadian Congress see Chapter 8.

the JDL is their friend and protector. The final technique is the use of meetings open to the public.

Everyone should attend a JDL open forum at one time or other. They are masterpieces in the technique of manipulating fearful people. I attended one at a Toronto synagogue in late 1984. The forum dealt with "The New Anti-Semitism" and drew a very mixed group of about two hundred people. Based on the questions which followed the speeches and pep talks, I assumed that the attendees were by and large neither crackpots nor fanatics. They were fearful, though. Very fearful. There is an authoritarian quality to these get togethers, with JDL marshalls —burly, clean-cut lads — stationed at strategic places throughout the hall to provide security for the audience. There was something insidious about this show. It inculcated a real feeling of security and, I think, a feeling of dependency on the part of the audience toward the JDL. I felt for the first time that I was really safe from the evil gentiles — and I'm not even Jewish.

That feeling of being protected laid the groundwork for what was to follow. The main speaker was a middle-aged Jewish-American woman who had been with the JDL in the U.S. and is now head of the Museum of the Potential Holocaust in Israel. Her talk initially dealt with what she perceived as the rising tide of anti-Semitism in Canada and elsewhere in the world. She discussed some of the racist and far-right groups (virtually all of her examples came from the U.S.) which were threatening to destroy the Jews. Afterward, she developed an analysis for why there might be such a revival of anti-Semitism in North America. She concluded by saying that a rerun of Nazi Germany was certain in Canada and the U.S. Her solution was for Canadian Jews to employ defensive violence when necessary and to flee to Israel, the only safe place in her opinion, as soon as possible.

The problem was not the analysis but rather the recommendations. Much of her analysis had a factual ring to it. After all, there probably is a slight revival of anti-Semitic feeling. And, I suppose, if the situation were as critical as she suggested, her recommendations would probably be reasonable. The problem was the tone and motivation of the whole thing. What she described was a country where almost everyone who was not Jewish was an anti-Semite. Worse yet, the speaker coined a phrase for the occasion, "Jew hatred," which has a nasty Nazi quality to it. She was careful to make the distinction between anti-Semitism and Jew hatred. Anti-Semitism was, she told us, a case of gentiles not wanting to live next door to Jews or join the same service clubs as Jews, but this was old hat. Jew hatred, however, which involves a desire to kill all Jews, is what gentiles (myself included, presumably) really seek. A sort of Canadian holocaust. It was the global nature of her accusation which made me begin to slump in my chair.

The scary thing about the meeting was that the tone of fear seemed almost magically to have transformed into anger and hatred. It wasn't a case of the audience screaming for blood, but the speaker seemed to be drawing on a bottomless pool of anger. She followed her attack on "goyim" with an attack on reform Jews ("wishy-washy"), then went on to rhapsodize on the subject of violence. She related with some apparent satisfaction that: "The JDL in New York broke Nazi heads with hatchets and I mean hatchets." To her mind violence was a necessary tool at times: "Violence is awful but sometimes it's necessary. How necessary depends on the situation." She also attempted to justify the use of violence on the basis of the Old Testament: "Our whole Bible is full of violence. And why? Because we have to survive ... There is good violence and bad violence." Her speech ended with a combination of Jewish fundamentalist theology and Israeli nationalism which was used to buttress her plea that Canadian Jews resist while still here and return to Israel quickly.

There has been little attempt on the part of the JDL to ensure that demonstrations stay strictly non–violent. There have been numerous picket line fights with racist or far-right demonstrators. They have not perhaps been all that common, but they have made the point. Those who take a diametrically opposed stance (like Nazis, racists and ultra-rightwingers) have come to expect the worst in confrontations with this group. An example was the trial of Ernst Zundel in late 1984 and early 1985. Zundel was charged with making claims about the Holocaust which were untrue and which were intended to incite hatred. He and his supporters wore bullet-proof vests and hard-hats when entering and leaving the court room, supposedly to protect them from potential violence from the JDL and other groups.

To date, most of the JDL's activity has been directed either toward building support for its ideas and actions among the Jewish community or "confronting" those it sees as enemies. It has had little experience in lobbying government, although there was a recent exception in late 1984 when the JDL attempted to get the federal government to lift its ban on the entry of Israeli Rabbi Meir Kahane into Canada. Kahane is the worldwide "father figure" of the JDL, both here and abroad, who has a reputation for inciting violence and racial hatred. In fact, he has even been denounced by prominent Israelis as dangerous because of his provocative actions toward Arab communities in Israel and his comments which seem to suggest that Arabs as a group are not completely human. This lobbying failed to get the entry ban lifted. There are rumours that many members of the mainstream Jewish lobby groups pressured the government to resist the JDL's pressure, fearing that he would incite racist feeling while here.

Coalition Building

As noted in the chapter on the Left, what has given left-wing groups real political clout is their success in building coalitions of groups around some issue which they deem of real significance. This lesson has not been lost on the Right. They have begun their own attempts at similar coalition building. We have already seen some of these coalitions in action — The Peace Through Strength coalition, whose main participants are the Canadian Anti-Soviet Action Committee (CASAC), fundamentalist Christians (e.g., the Toronto Alliance of Christian Laymen) and members of the East European and Indo-Chinese communities and the Rev. Kenneth Campbell's Renaissance group of organizations.

Campbell's is just one example of the rebirth of an organizationally and politically effective coalition of right-wing single issue groups with some notable successes. The opposition movement to the liberalization of the abortion laws is essentially a coalition of groups such as the formal right-to-life lobbies, religious groups such as the Roman Catholic Church and many conservative Protestant churches and other of the more conservative groups in society. Given the strength of the feminist lobbies there is little doubt that there would now be abortion on demand throughout Canada without the active opposition of this coalition. Metrification is also an area of at least partial success. And finally, the whole question of law and order is an area where pressure from right-wing coalitions are likely to see substantial victories in the future.

Multi-Issue Groups

So far we have looked at groups that are largely concerned with a single issue but which find themselves coming together from time to time with ideologically compatible groups in "common-cause" coalitions. Their raison d'être, however, remains a practical struggle for the resolution of one problem rather than a wide-ranging reordering of all aspects of society. Still, there are some multi-issue groups involved in trying to reorder society according to their ideological perspective.

The National Citizens' Coalition

The NCC has been the "bad boy" of Canadian politics right from its founding in 1973 as a non-profit, non-partisan organization. There is nothing particularly cerebral about this bunch. They are doers, pure and simple, who leave the philosophizing to others. But they really know how to get the goat of the liberal/social democratic elite in Canada. Every time they take out another full page ad in a national newspaper or launch one more right-wing crusade, the politicians, civil servants, media people, liberals and social democrats howl in righteous indignation and rage. Some of their campaigns are a bit ill-considered, but I still figure that anything that causes the above "fat cats" to howl cannot be all that bad.

Essentially, what the NCC does is to say in public what a very large proportion of the population thinks, but is too timid to say itself. So far the Coalition has railed against the soft lives and indexed pensions of bureaucrats and civil servants, an "open door" policy toward the "boat people," wasteful government spending, forced unionization and bureaucratic bungling. Some of the issues it promotes are balanced government budgets, selling Crown Corporations and entrenching property rights in the constitution.

Some of the "feedback" which the Coalition gets from the media and government is the charge of bigotry. During the NCC's campaign against high levels of immigration from Indo-China, editorial writers attacked the Coalition's stand bitterly. The *Toronto Star* called the Coalition's thinking "small-minded and mean" and "callous and indifferent." A similar view by government officials has been fairly consistent no matter which party is in power. A recent example of this bipartisan approach to trashing the group took place at a Commons committee hearing on privileges and elections in December 1984. Liberal John Nunziata and PC Gilbert Chartrand both took it upon themselves to use the hearing as an opportunity for attacking the Coalition. Nunziata said, "I'm going out of this meeting convinced that the organization is a fraud. I think the organization is being used by individuals or corporations to further their own political beliefs, and I think it's very dangerous for our democratic process."[6] Not to be outdone by his Liberal colleague, Chartrand took the occasion to express the fear that the Coalition might be a front for people with dangerous intentions. He said that the Coalition drew to mind another coalition, the FLQ. Well, what can you expect when you criticize the high salaries of MPs?

The NCC has about 30,000 members and is an exclusively English Canadian phenomenon, unknown in Quebec, with offices in Toronto, Calgary and Vancouver. In addition to testifying at Commons Committee hearings, the Coalition uses radio, television, newspaper advertisements and direct mail in an attempt to influence public opinion and, through it, politicians. This direct approach is a testament to the unwillingness of government to deal with the group as it would with most other lobby groups. Nevertheless, the government's unwillingness has not neutralized the Coalition. In fact, it has been extremely successful in many of its campaigns. Perhaps the most important victory was its overturning of the amendment to the Election Expenses Act which sought to forbid advertisements during elections of the very sort which the NCC had used with such powerful effect. Clearly the measure was aimed directly at the NCC. The Coalition campaign which followed resulted in a ruling by the Alberta Supreme Court against the constitutionality of the amendment.

The Fraser Institute

One of the traditional weaknesses of the Right is that it represents two constituencies which government has found easy to ignore: the well-to-do who refuse to take their place in the statist and essentially liberal elite consensus, and the middle class, especially those in the small business sector. Often the lobbying which passes for right-wing is as much as anything a sort of primal scream from sectors of a middle class which finds itself increasingly alienated from a government which seems intent on its destruction. Government has not been overly sympathetic or attentive to the efforts of these lobby groups because:

1. They represent groups outside of the coalition which the Liberal Party of Canada sought to build over the Trudeau era. It remains to be seen if the Mulroney government will draw these groups into its "golden circle."
2. Their demands are antagonistic to the thrust of social, political and economic development which has been pursued over the last two decades. The present thrust is toward building a corporate state with increasing government regulation and ownership of the economy. The right-wing lobby groups possess an individualistic philosophy and oppose government intervention in the economy and society.
3. The "primal scream" quality of these groups makes it difficult for government to understand exactly what is being demanded of it

and how it should respond. The Left is better able to articulate its demands in terms of policy recommendations and so has had better success.

4. The lack of a solid and convincing ideological framework and critique has made the Right appear illegitimate. This lack of a philosophical rationalization has made it easy for government to dismiss the complaints and demands of right-wing lobbies as reactionary drivel and the ravings of bigots, racists and "crackpots."

The success and importance of the Fraser Institute lies in the fact that it provides an ideological and intellectual framework for the Right in Canada. The government may not appreciate the lobbying positions of the Institute or its critique of government policy, but the one thing government cannot say is that the Institute's positions are either poorly thought out or inarticulate. Other right-wing groups seem to possess a sort of brutishness, all passion and action and very little subtlety. The Institute is more cerebral and good humoured. There is a certain elegance to it.

The Fraser Institute was founded in Vancouver by Michael Walker, a professional economist and former economic model builder for the federal government. The Institute has succeeded in its role as a right-wing think tank. As of its tenth anniversary in 1984 it had twenty-five books in print, weekly radio talk spots, a syndicated newspaper column, a best-selling board game, two new subsidiary offices in Toronto and Ottawa and a budget of $900,000.

The important thing to realize about the Institute is that it is by no means either fly-by-night or made up of crackpots. It is financed largely by contributions from some of the leading corporations in the country and its board of directors represents some of the most wealthy, powerful and well respected people in the land.

The greatest influence of the Institute derives from its role in public education. Clearly, its aim is to bring about a long-term shift in values and attitudes rather than to lobby against specific legislation or matters before government. In this there is some evidence of success. Supporters of the Solidarity Coalition in British Columbia charge Walker with being the intellectual *eminence grise* behind Premier Bill Bennett and his government's austerity program. Understandably, Walker declines this "compliment." Nevertheless, the Institute is effective in reaching the public. As of mid-1984, the Institute had received 50,000 column inches of press commentary since its founding in 1975. A good portion of the credit for this lies in the effectiveness of Walker in dealing with the media. Anyone who has ever read some of his articles or seen him on television will vouch for him as an articulate and humorous spokesman. This sense of humour has resulted in some rather bizarre incidents. On one occasion hostile NDPers and Operation Solidarity supporters arrived at the Vancouver office intending to occupy it. Walker was warned in advance by the media. When the would-be occupiers arrived, they were greeted by a banner welcoming them to the Institute, coffee, a book stand, membership application forms and the offer of guided tours.

Actually, the Institute needs to be witty and effective with the media because not all of its ideas are popular with the public. Some of its least popular positions have involved opposition to rent controls, minimum wage laws, wage and price controls, tariff barriers and medicare. On the other hand, its opposition to bureaucratic bungling, wasteful government spending and high taxes put it on the side of the angels.

In addition to these largely economic questions the Institute has started to make forays into the social sphere as well. As we saw in the last chapter, one of the major groups in the left-wing coalitions are the churches. The Institute has begun to try and cut away some of this support for the Left by the founding of the Centre for the Study of Economics and Religion under the direction of Walter Block. Probably because of the threat which this represents to the support for the Left, the centre is making many leftists see red. One of its activities involves organizing forums. Two such forums took place in Regina in late 1983 and dealt with theology, economics and Third World politics. One was paid for by the Liberty Fund Inc., a U.S. right-wing organization. This intrusion into their "turf" was resented enormously by both left-wing groups and some church officials. Some officials in the Roman Catholic church and United Church boycotted the two events and finally encouraged (or forced) a number of theologians and economists to pull out.

The Unrespectable Right

So far we have looked at what I call "the respectable Right." Sure, some of them are a little ham-fisted or a little reactionary, but they do not suggest violence. There is a tiny lunatic fringe, however. And these guys don't fool around.

There has been a frequent attempt by some media people and many of the Left to lump all of those on the Right into the same basket. Thus, business liberals and philosophical conservatives often find themselves accused openly or by inference of racism or Nazi-like activities. As we have seen, this charge is usually unfair, although it must be admitted that such smears are rather effective in neutralizing many conservatives. Usually, this is just a matter of mental sloppiness, but occasionally it may be a conscious act.

The "unrespectable Right" is that collection of people and groups promoting racism, authoritarianism and militarism which has existed in various guises throughout Canada's history. For instance the Canadian Ku Klux Klan was born in the 1920s. The 1930s saw a flourishing of fascist groups and groups sympathetic to Nazism. Such groups included the Quebec Parti Nationale Sociale Chrétien, led by Adrien Arcand, the Swastika Clubs in Ontario, the Canadian Nationalist Party in Manitoba and the Canadian Union of Fascists. It was these very lobbies that represented a major factor in Prime Minister Mackenzie King's decision to close Canada to European Jews seeking to flee the Nazi Holocaust.

The 1970s and early 1980s saw a major revival of this section of the far Right. Immigration from Third World countries and major social change caused something resembling trauma among some elements of the majority white population. The accompanying sense of insecurity and threat left these people vulnerable to propaganda from far-Right and racist groups.

Probably the most visible manifestations of the "born again" unrespectable Right was the Ku Klux Klan in the late seventies and early eighties. The sad fact is that this revival would have been impossible without the active complicity of some opportunistic media people. The media faithfully recorded virtually every Klan event, broadcast portions of Klan statements and gave Klan leaders a platform from which to proselytize. With the media attention accorded the Klan, some closet racists were drawn out of the political woodwork and rallied to the cause. What started as a bad political joke perpetrated by a few misfits began to appear as a serious political and social threat. Speaking of the role of the media in this growth of the organization, Klan leader Alexander McQuirter said, "The news media really blew it up and did all our work for us."

This revival of the Klan was accompanied by a growth in and new openness of other far Right and racist organizations. In many cases informal alliances were formed between the Klan and these groups and what followed was not pleasant. People started getting hurt, often badly.

The influence strategy of these groups was to make a direct appeal to those people who felt threatened by recent major social changes. In a sense it is understandable that the media would get hooked by the Klan and similar groups. Their actions made exciting news stories, their demonstrations had lots of colour and sound. There were costumes, there was drama. There was almost always violence. Their other actions — beatings, the pitched battles with leftists and anti-racist demonstrators, the racist graffiti in public places, the outrageous public utterances — made great thirty-second clips for the six o'clock news. Ratings grew. So did racism. Usually this media complicity was unconscious, but not always. The worst case of conscious complicity with the Klan involved the attempted Klan takeover of the Caribbean island of Dominica in 1982. The Canadians who were part of this conspiracy occasionally used the facilities of Toronto radio station CFTR for this project. Amazingly, the station had been informed of this plot early on in the planning and did not inform police. Rather the station decided to keep quiet about the plot in the hopes of a "scoop" when the invasion took place. One of the conspirators sent a telegram to her co-conspirators via CFTR. When the plot was finally smashed by police and the role of CFTR became public, one reporter and the news director left the station. No further action was taken by the government against the station. The effect was, however, different for the Klan, for the trials that followed were the beginning of the end. The ultra-Right had been beaten back once again.

7

Combat in the Erogenous Zone: Sexual Politics

So far I haven't really given you much of an opportunity to get into the great game played by so many with such profitable results. Let's face it, most examples discussed so far have required too much from the average would-be opportunist. I assume that most readers are neither land developers nor tavern owners, which rules out most of the really good action in the municipal area. Terror from the Right and self-righteousness from the Left require that you believe in some fairly strange concepts such as racial superiority, unbridled capitalism, sexual abstinence, the unidimensionality of the working class or the ultimate goodness and constant idealism of Soviet foreign policy. That's asking too much. Besides, membership in either group means that you will be pretty much a social outcast with all except those inhabiting the extreme fringes of society. People will avoid you at parties. Your telephone calls will never be returned. Worst of all, there are virtually no material benefits from this sort of activity.

Do not despair! Here's an easy field. It is easy to get into and pays extremely well. The Senate, Royal Commissions at hundreds of dollars a day, patronage jobs in Crown Corporations, national fame, all of these may be yours. The only entrance requirement for this area of influence peddling is that you possess genitalia.

Unfortunately, there is a tiny catch. You cannot be a heterosexual male. Gay men can play, and some have done pretty well. But the best category of all is that of woman, lesbian or straight. Both are equally good.

There is one other catch. You have to be prepared to "play hard ball." This game is so tough that players often apologize for hitting above the belt. You are probably a little doubtful that it is quite so nasty as I claim, so try this on for size. Here's a sample of the rhetoric you will be expected to employ. The following is an exerpt from a letter to the editor in the August/September 1984 issue of the *Canadian Forum*. The letter says in part that, "males should be ashamed not only of possessing phalluses, but also of the crass propensity to actually thrust with them, a violent act of such blatancy that, to use Gloria Steinem's phrase, 'little murders' are constantly taking place in the bedrooms of the nation."[1] Now, the important thing about this letter is that it didn't appear in some radical lesbian magazine. *Canadian Forum* is an "ever-so-fashionable" leftist magazine. It is, by the standards of most magazines in the world of sexual politics, a pussy cat. The really hard-nosed ones get nasty.

The good news is that once you have passed these first two hurdles you can be assured that you will find something to suit your tastes, style and needs. There is something here for everyone.

One of the really fascinating things about sexual politics is the incredibly moralistic tone which permeates this interest group behaviour. Everything is phrased in absolutes. There are no greys. Everything is completely black or completely white, completely good or completely evil. There is a theological quality to it all. You are on the side of the angels and your opponents are on the side of the devil. Below is a list of the possible theological categories available, based on my reading of the media and government ukazes:

1. The angels. These are the feminists, individuals on the side of goodness and light and the betterment of "personkind." God, a woman, will be on your side no matter what you are required to do to further your personal, career and organizational goals. Should you choose to place yourself on the side of the angels, you will find many important allies who will support and finance you and who will help you in your lobbying efforts. Your reward for doing God's work will be on earth as well as in heaven. Earthly rewards include top jobs in industry and soft jobs in government.

2. The devils. These are the traditionalists. They are counter-revolutionaries who worship a false (male) god. The traditionalists wish to cast "personkind" back into the darkness which existed prior to the dawning of the feminist era. The main sources of succour and aid for the angels — government and the media —have turned their faces from these evil creatures and damn them at every turn.

3. The rebel angels. These are the homosexuals. For the moment these are allied with the angels. Considering that they are men,

they are unexpectedly good people since they are almost exclusively pro-feminist. They worship not only the one true god,
but occasionally mortal men as well.

Having laid out the theological landscape in this realm let's examine
how the various lobbyists operate.

The Feminist Lobby

Conflict between men and women for dominance — the celebrated
"war of the sexes" — is as old as humanity itself. The co-founder of
Marxism, Friedrich Engels, wrote in his seminal work, *The Origin of
Family, Private Property and the State*, that the first class conflict was
between men and women. Usually, as is endlessly pointed out by
feminists, the rulers have been men and the ruled, women. Byzantium
and Ancient Egypt provide us with examples of periods and regimes
within the Western tradition with matriarchical characteristics. But
whatever the organization, tension between men and women has been
constant.

There were periods of agitation by women in the nineteenth and
early twentieth centuries but the real fun never really got going in a
serious way until the mid to late 1960s. A major catalyst for the rebirth
of feminism in North America was the student radical and black
liberation movements which began in the U.S. and spread north.
Women, quite rightly, felt that their role in "the movement" should be
more than just serving coffee, doughnuts and dope to their men at
demonstrations. It seemed that for all the radical jargon of the time
their lives were little different from those of their mothers which they
detested. Probably even more important were the development of
more reliable birth control techniques and the relaxation of laws
governing abortion. Women, it seemed, were no longer victims of
their biological destiny.

Another factor, and I suspect the most important one, took place in
the economy. The 1960s were a time of unbounded economic growth
and prosperity in North America. As the economies of both Canada
and the United States grew, there was a demand for new workers to fill
the new places that were being created every day. At about the same
time men began to become disillusioned by their traditional role as
providers and industrial drones. Many concluded that there must be
more to life than playing one's part in the "rat race." Men began to
drop out of the corporate environment or at the very least began to be
less enthusiastic cogs in the corporate wheel. The dilemma of North

American corporate capitalism was how to provide a new source of well-educated, well-trained and enthusiastic workers, scientists and technicians and managers. Immigration was a partial solution and was used as such. The problem was, however, that these newcomers brought cultural baggage with them that often took years to overcome or assimilate. This was a "quick fix" at the working class and agricultural levels but of only limited help at the skilled, professional and managerial levels. The answer to these labour shortages was a virtually untapped pool of talent and labour. Women were perfect. Large numbers of them were well educated and they were enthusiastic. While decades of experience in business had taken much of the bloom off the corporate rose for men, women were a different matter. The monetary and psychological rewards of the workplace made the job of homemaking in suburbia seem like torture and oppression by comparison.

Yes, this possibility of women entering the workplace had business in a reverie. From the corporate point of view this was great. Women were bright, well educated, and had exactly the same cultural background (or so it seemed at the time) as their male counterparts. You could plug them right in without any problems. Better than that, many managers counted on the continuation of lower rates of pay for women, as had always been the case. Teamed up with this was the traditional passivity of women. The result was a sort of corporate wet dream. Women in the workplace translated into larger corporate profits.

Curiously enough, even bad times played their part in accelerating this trend. In the seventies there was a contraction in the labour market. The rate of growth in employment started to slip badly, but expectations continued to grow in spite of this. The result was that women did not leave the labour market as had always happened before. There were other reasons too. The financial obligations which families had made during the good times continued no matter what the state of the economy. Large mortgages taken out during earlier and better times still had to be honoured. Other large credit purchases still carried large monthly payments. To meet these payments wives' incomes became a necessity rather than a matter of choice. The only alternative would have been for families to accept a lower standard of living. North Americans, dedicated materialists that they are, steadfastly resisted such a suggestion. As a result women have become a major and permanent feature of the workplace and economy in Canada.

It is this background which leads us to an understanding of the beginnings of the feminist lobby in this country.

On the face of it, the structure and organization of the lobby (or movement, depending on your perspective) is the ultimate in democracy and grass roots participation. A huge number of single-issue and locally-based groups abound, reflecting a dizzying number of viewpoints and interests. In theory, the views of these groups' members are transmitted to government and become input to the policy-making process by the following paths:

1. The direct lobbying of grass-roots and single-issue groups working independently or in coalitions with other groups.
2. The lobbying of women working within non-feminist groups such as labour unions, teachers' federations, political parties and so on. The purpose of this lobbying is to ensure that these non-feminist groups become lobbyists for feminist interests.
3. Through the National Action Committee on the Status of Women. This large bureaucratic organization, ostensibly independent of government, lobbies media and government at the national level.
4. Through the Canadian Advisory Council on the Status of Women. This group is totally financed by the federal government and is an integral part of the government machinery. It often acts more as a tool for government control of the movement than as an agent of social change. Provincial Status of Women Councils act in a similar fashion.
5. Federal and provincial Status of Women Ministers. The intention here is to provide direct access to the very heart of cabinet decision making.

It sounds impressive, and it is. Let's look at how it works.

Grass-Roots and Single-Issue Lobby Groups

There are hundreds of grass-roots groups, maybe thousands. Most cities with a population of more than 50,000 have their own "status of women" group. Such groups tend to be highly ideological and definitely have a multi-issue orientation. If any issue has a feminist orientation, these groups support it.

There are single-issue groups at the grass-roots level too. These tackle virtually every issue concerning women's lives. They may champion the rights of lesbians, they may have an ethnic orientation, they may represent a business or profession, they may be in support of some special problem like rape or abortion. If there is a cause, there is almost certainly a group fighting the good fight.

Of course, it is not just a case of these groups trying to improve the lot of women. Many of them have staked out for themselves the goal of perfecting men as well. It is always gratifying, from a man's point of view, to realize there are a large number of groups dedicated to saving men from their vices. For those men with a weakness for drink, there is the Women's Christian Temperance Union, that leftover from an earlier feminist movement. The new feminist movement seems headed in a similar direction, with groups dedicated to saving men from the horrors of striptease, "girlie" magazines and porno movies. There are groups to keep men from family violence (women, apparently, are never violent). There are any number of groups dedicated to stopping men from making passes at their secretaries, pinching bottoms and making lewd suggestions to ladies in the street. The intent is to provide external controls on the beastliness lying in all men which men cannot or will not control themselves.

Because these groups are so different from each other in structure, memberships and goals, it is not surprising that they possess vastly different resources. For most, people represent the most important resource. Interestingly enough, the memberships are often quite small, yet they exercise enormous influence. The explanation lies in the dedication and motivation of their members. They believe one hundred percent with a great moral certainty, which is a mighty advantage over the rest of us in this age of uncertainty and self-doubt.

Possessing dedicated members is not enough, however. In a capitalist society like Canada, money is one of the most valuable and sought after political resources that any group can have and this often represents a problem. There are a number of sources of money available to women's (that is, feminist women's) groups. The first and greatest is surely good old Mother Government. The federal government is an unusually large contributor to feminist coffers. The Secretary of State alone earmarked $11.4 million in 1984 for the promotion of women's rights in Canada — almost three times as much as the $4.4 million which the federal government devoted to this purpose the year before. This is only a part of it. Other departments like Employment and Immigration, Justice and Health and Welfare ladle out funds to various women's groups as part of other programs. With all this money one would think that the grass-roots organizations would be well-financed and rolling in money. As we shall see later, however, the lion's share goes to the big bureaucratic women's lobbies or grass-roots organizations which are often little more than government tools. The funding for the genuine grass-roots organizations is either non–existent or set up in such a way as to ensure that they wither on the vine.

There are other sources of course. One is other, socially conscious groups such as the more liberal churches and trade unions. Another is the pocket books of well-to-do women. Contrary to popular media belief, not all women are impoverished, single mothers eking out a bare existence on pitiful welfare checks. There are women — heiresses, professional and business women — who contribute to the work of their feminist sisters. One example is Nancy Jackman, the feminist scion of the Jackman family which controls billions of dollars of assets and which, through its lean management of many companies, contributes to the unhappiness of many Canadian women. According to the feature stories which have appeared on Nancy Jackman, she has two great passions: the Anglican Church, and lobbying for women's rights. She is one of the leading lights behind the Legal Education and Action Fund (LEAF), a group founded in October 1984 which has set itself the mission of testing the equality provisions of the Charter of Rights and Freedoms which came into effect in April 1985. This group has set itself a funding target of $10 million. My guess is that it will not have any difficulties in meeting its objective. You can bet that the Rosedale and Mount Royal set will open their hearts and bank accounts to the cause of social justice à la Jackman.

Of course, not every group is lucky enough to have a Nancy Jackman behind it. For most, it is a horrible day-to-day struggle just to survive. Still there are avenues open to help them, especially in the area of litigation. Many women litigants have used legal aid programs to pay bills resulting from their actions. And there are other bodies which help or take on such cases and in some cases prosecute them themselves. Unions often take on cases involving women's rights issues as they pertain to collective agreements, and the Canadian Civil Liberties Association (CCLA) also acts on behalf of women and women's organizations on occasion.

Tactics and Techniques
These groups use a vast array of direct lobbying techniques. Some of the more popular ones are:

1. Blitzing politicians. Often this takes the form of bombarding politicians with letters and telephone calls to protest or promote policies.
2. Blitzing the media. This takes the form of flooding newspapers and magazines with letters to the editor or calls to open-line radio

shows. Even if the group is tiny, this technique can give the impression of widespread support. Sometimes this takes the form of taking over meetings. One of my favourite examples took place at a meeting in Toronto in 1984 to protest pornography. This meeting brought together a wide range of community groups, groups that in some cases could agree on nothing other than their opposition to pornography. As a consequence it was decided that no reference would be made to other feminist issues such as abortion and homosexuality so as not to break up the united front. This was quite wise since there were groups such as the Salvation Army present, groups not usually thought of as hard core feminists. Toward the end of the meeting about eight women took over the stage, unfurled banners supporting lesbianism and abortion on demand and harangued the audience on these topics for a fairly lengthy period. The media, of course, loved it. The flash bulbs popped and the microphones recorded every word. The demonstrators loved it. After all, you couldn't get the media to cover a press conference on lesbian rights if you begged them. The demonstrators had all the media they could wish for. Unfortunately, some of the other participants at the meeting were less than happy. The Salvation Army members who attended were surprised the next day to see that the Army had finally come out of the closet.

3. Blitzing bureaucrats. This is like shooting fish in a barrel. Bureaucrats are such timid creatures that all activists have to do is to send them a few harsh letters or say a few harsh things in the media and the bureaucrats give these distaff lobbyists whatever their hearts desire. A good example is the Museum of Man in Ottawa. Apparently, some feminist groups complained about the word "Man." At the time of writing, museum officials were scurrying about looking for a new name that would see this "offensive" word expunged. Two things were remarkable about this incident. First of all, the numbers of protesters who precipitated this incident was tiny. Museum official Faye Kent was quoted as saying that she had received "about fifteen or twenty letters." Imagine! Only fifteen or twenty letters were necessary to force the change of an institution's name and the expenditure of hundreds of thousands of dollars for new stationery, signs, promotional material and advertising. The amusing part is that the fifteen or twenty people who wrote the letters probably knew each other. The second remarkable part of this is that such

silliness is far from an isolated event. This nonsense is part of a policy of excising this most hated word wherever it might occur. For example, the federal employment department's Manpower Consultative Service has become the Industrial Adjustment Service for just this reason. Sadly, this is not a joke. By the time our bureaucrats are finished "courageously" combatting "sexism" in the language, the tab will be in the millions. The tragedy is that real women's concerns like shelters for battered wives, better health care, daycare and job retraining could have used this money to better effect. The bureaucrats and lobbyists will go home with a nice, warm feeling. The women they claim to be helping will go home bruised and hungry.

4. Blitzing government hearings. Have a look at the back of a report from almost any government commission, task force or study. There you will find a list of the groups and individuals that prepared submissions or testified before hearing members. The list is like a catalogue of feminist organizations in Canada: Lethbridge Status of Women's Council, Moose Jaw Status of Women Council, Tuktoyaktuk Status of Women Council etc. And on and on it goes. Since they all share virtually the same ideology, they all sing the same song. And there are so many of them! What are the commissioners to assume? It must be the voice of the people. And so it is, sometimes. Unfortunately, sometimes it is not; it just seems that way.

5. Rigging government commissions from within. Anyone who thinks that government commissions, task forces, studies, etc. are objective and made up of members who are fair, unbiased and independent, is a good candidate for either an intelligence test or psychiatric care. They are quite simply rigged. The members tend to be either party hacks or people whose biases are so well known that their findings can be guessed with certainty in advance. The last thing any government wants is a commission report which will come up with findings at variance with government policy or which might embarass the party in power. This is as true in the area of sexual politics and lobbying as it is elsewhere. A good example of such a study was that conducted by the CRTC to study what to do about sexism in the media. Its report was entitled *Images of Women in the Media.* Not surprisingly it found the most horrible sexism prevalent in the media and recommended draconian rules and massive government intervention to counteract this "crime." I say "not surprisingly" because the issue

was never in question. First of all, the commission memb
was stacked in favour of feminists. Second, the terms of refe
virtually dictated the findings which emerged. Third, a large
number of the groups which testified were feminist lobby groups.
The hearings were stacked, and they were meant to be stacked.
The reason was that the CRTC had a strong vested interest in the
commission finding as it did since the only possible outcome of
such findings and recommendations would be an increase in the
powers of the CRTC and its members. What bureaucrat would not
rejoice at this turn of events?

Women Working Within Other Organizations

Women working in single-issue or grass-roots organizations made no
bones about their identity. They were women's organizations and that
was that, and the need for them could be explained by the fact that
there was a certain amount of truth to the argument that women and
their concerns were low priorities in Canadian society and the groups
that make it up. Churches, unions, professional organizations and
other organized groups just couldn't be bothered to take up the cause of
women's rights. There was another reason too. Feminism was not seen
as a legitimate viewpoint. This is difficult to imagine now that it is
given an approval and attention that sometimes resembles idolatry.
Nevertheless, up until a few years ago, many government and media
voices regaled the public (and a very receptive public at that!) with
scorn for feminist notions and demands. It is amusing to note the same
media and government types now fighting among themselves to kiss
the hem of visiting feminist big shots and to be the first to express
their concurrence no matter how absurd the claim or demand. Times
change with fascinating results. One of the major results of this change
in attitude (or at the very least change in outward behaviour) has been
a rush by other organizations to jump on the feminist bandwagon.

Unions

Of all the institutions in society one of the most sexist up until recently
has been the union movement. Let's face it, unions have been very
much men's clubs for the proletariat. The executives have been almost
exclusively male and the demands have been those of the male membership. Unions have been only too happy to accept a continuation of
discrimination against women in the marketplace, both in wage rates
and in hiring. After all, it fit into the closed shop mentality that is so
much a part of unionism in North America. Acceptance of inequality

meant that male union members could represent a labour aristocracy. Unionized men thus would ride on the backs of their sisters outside the golden inner circle of unionism.

Now unions loudly trumpet their commitment to women's issues. Abortion on demand, free day care, homemakers' pensions, even affirmative action hiring at the expense of men, are all born-again key principles of unionism. Now when unions and the NDP lobby government, they lobby for feminism at the same time. What could have brought on this conversion? The answer lies not in morality, but rather in the rather knotty question of how a union movement survives declining memberships and workforce changes.

Consider the following statistics:

- Union membership is declining as part of a long-range trend.
- There has been a permanent reduction in the number of jobs available in the heavy manufacturing and resource extraction industries, industries which are male-dominated. At the same time, the service sector — an area of female strength — is growing rapidly.
- Labour force participation for women over twenty-five increased between 1981 and 1984 from 48.1 percent to 50.3 percent. At the same time it dropped for men.
- Between 1962 and 1981 the female labour force grew by 169 percent. During the same period the male labour force increased only 46.4 percent.
- During the same period the number of female union members increased by almost 300 percent, while male union membership increased by only 72.5 percent.

Faced with these facts what would you do? Exactly! Unions are falling over themselves in their drive to lobby on behalf of "women's issues." So great is the rush that the CLC decided that it just couldn't wait for women to be elected to executive posts. At its convention in March 1984 it set up six posts just for women. Some time later a major union official was quoted as saying that affirmative action in the workplace was critical even if it meant that men presently on the job would have to be laid off. Whatever happened to the good old days when unions fought to keep people from being laid off? Clearly, unions are not sentimental. If you lose the battle of demographics, you lose the union movement's support.

The Churches

The conversion that is even more remarkable than that of the union movement is that of the churches. This one is just too much fun to gloss over because, as noted before, over the last couple of thousand years the Christian Church has been one of the most enthusiastic supporters of traditional family structures and sexual roles, which makes mincemeat of any claims by churches that their role is one of acting as a moral critic of centuries of abuse. After all, if there was indeed oppression, then they must have been among the worst oppressors. The truth is that the leaderships of the various sects that make up organized Christianity always like to rap themselves in the mantle of morality and ethical integrity when they are actually involved in shoring up attendance and financial support. This matter of changing sexual roles and mores is just one example of a long and somewhat dishonourable tradition that goes back two millenia.

The extent to which the churches have tried, somewhat belatedly, to ride on the coattails of what they perceive as the rising feminist tide, can be seen by their public pronouncements both to the outside world and internally. In fairness, this is almost exclusively restricted to the more liberal Protestant churches like the United Church and the Anglican Church and the more liberal elements in the Roman Catholic Church (probably a very small minority of Catholics). A glance through the *United Church Observer* makes one think that one has accidentally picked up a publication of the National Action Committee on the Status of Women. In addition to the usual articles condemning U.S. foreign policy and supporting national liberation movements, there are an equal number of articles calling upon the faithful to shun the sin of traditional family organization and walk on the paths of righteousness as revealed by the holy scripture revealed by feminist saints over the last two decades.

Of course, this beating of breasts and wearing of sackcloth is not reserved for internal publications only. On many occasions I have been amused to read in the media articles about the evils of institutionalized sexism in the church and, best of all, the rampant nature of sexual harassment among the clergy. A two-year study by a committee of the United Church released in mid-1984 claimed that one-third of the women who work or study full-time with that denomination have experienced sexual harassment. How exciting! The mind swims with visions of a church absolutely rotten with randy ministers pinching nubile bottoms and showing innocent young women the naughty parts from Second Kings and Deuteronomy. Can this actually be an under-handed and sneaky way of enticing more men into the church?

Even that bastion of conservatism, the Catholic Church, is creaking and groaning under assaults from liberals and feminists in its midst. A group of thirty Montreal women held a press conference in August 1984 to say that the Pope is the head of a "misogynist and patriarchal" institution and that the Canadian government should not spend any taxpayers' money on the Pope's visit. This group claimed to represent organizers from community centres, women's groups and unions. The reaction, as you can imagine, was a little less than warm. The govern-ment did fund the Pope's visit, thus proving itself irrevocably sexist, and about the only thanks that these intrepid souls got for their efforts were "hate letters" from women in the Church. Well, never mind, the struggle continues. After the Pope's visit, a committee submitted a report to Roman Catholic bishops recommending a larger role for women in the Church and an end to sexist language. Cardinal Carter was fit to be tied. He was reported as having claimed the document was "negative to the point of being abusive."[2] In addition Carter had the following objections to the committee and its report: "It is open to doubt as to whether the committee really represents the majority of Catholic women in Canada. . . .[3] It seems well established that not only was the committee selected with only one viewpoint in mind, dissent-ing voices not being encouraged, in fact, they were pretty much gagged."[4] Old habits die hard.

The "Others"

There are literally hundreds of other organizations that are being used in the same way as the unions and churches. Usually, the organizations that come to serve this lobbying purpose have a large percentage of women in their membership. The best examples are in the areas of education, social work, groups with a left-wing orientation, the media and artistic groups. At times it seems as if these groups are virtual mouthpieces for the feminist movement at government hearings and in media pronouncements. Over the last year or two, for example, many organizations having nothing to do with feminism have joined the chorus of voices demanding greater censorship, especially of materials with a sexual or violent nature.

Particularly fascinating are groups in the area of education and entertainment, which one would normally suspect of having a bias in favour of freedom of speech and thought. A very nasty conflict broke out in ACTRA, the group representing actors, actresses and media performers. If ever there was a group that should oppose censorship this is it. Nevertheless, ACTRA was for a brief period taken over by a feminist faction which lobbied for a ban on union members' participation in performances which these feminist members viewed as pornographic. The takeover trammelled under foot virtually all the existing democratic features of policy formation in the organization. Part of the process involved one or two meetings with a carefully selected sample of the membership attending. Furthermore, at least one of the meetings purposely excluded any men just in case. This was one of those delicious examples of the standard operating behaviour by ideologues, namely, that discrimination and arbitrary use of power are evil until they are in your benefit. These actions were later repudiated by the rank and file members. Still, for a while, the radicals had their way.

By and large, the taking over of unrelated organizations or organizing within so as to make your message its message. has been an extremely successful form of lobbying, one of the major benefits being that it gives the impression, whether correct or not, that there is widespread support for the feminist point of view.

This type of lobbying has had a number of successes, which flow from the nature of the lobby groups. They are small and involve a lot of face to face interaction with those lobbied. The groups have an ad hoc quality which, combined with the small membership makes them flexible in tactics and response, at least as flexible as any ideology will allow. They often have real roots in society which means that their internal organization is often highly democratic and members have a level of commitment and enthusiasm that gives them an influence that far outstrips their numbers. As the expression goes, "Faith can move mountains." As it does sometimes.

These very strengths, however, are in fact profound weaknesses. Research studies such as Robert Presthus's book, *Elite Accommodation in Canadian Politics*, indicate that other factors besides being democratic and having a pure heart and a just cause are important for success in lobbying. Indeed, these studies indicate that government does not like dealing with democratic mass organizations made up of highly motivated and committed individuals. All that purity upsets upper level civil servants and politicians, and all that democracy and grassroots involvement means that the leaders are harder to corrupt and manipulate. Governments like to deal with groups like the government — distant from those governed, highly bureaucratic and led by people whose primary preoccupation is their own careers for which they will happily sacrifice the wishes of their members if it comes to that. And that brings us to the rest of the feminist lobby.

Personally, I have the greatest admiration and respect for those women's groups that are democratic, straightforward, honest in as much as they tell you who they are and what they are after, and have little in mind except the betterment of women as they understand it. Sure, there might be a bit of careerism among some of these women, but it is bound to be extremely limited. What most face is hard work, a constant uphill fight and lots of very negative feedback from the male half of the world and probably from a good portion of the female half as well. These are the idealists.

From now on we are going to look at a world that is much fuzzier. There's very little that is black or white here. Rather, motives and goals in the groups and leaders that follow are problematic. Whose interests and whose view of the world are uppermost? The members'? The leaders'? Some other organization's? The government's? It is often unclear and varies from lobby to lobby. If we are to believe the media, it would seem that the feminist lobby has made enormous gains for women as a whole. At the same time, a journalist on the national desk of one of the country's largest newspapers told me that he thought the greatest achievement of the women's lobby in Canada had been in advancing the careers and interests of the women who lead it. Who's right? Let's have a look at the more organized lobbies for the answer.

The National Action Committee on the Status of Women
If there is one group that comes close to being *the* feminist lobby in Canada, it is definitely NAC. Its origins are particularly interesting since they shed a great deal of light on the whole question of the influence government is able to exercise on feminist lobby groups in its position as the primary contributor of funds.

NAC really took off as a group in 1981 during the height of the debate and lobbying which ultimately resulted in the framing of the new Canadian constitution and Charter of Rights. During this debate, many feminists felt that the special needs and concerns of women were not being addressed. At this point, the Canadian Advisory Council on the Status of Women (CACSW) was the major body for co-ordinating the effort of feminist lobbies to make their presence felt in the debate, and under its aegis some of the groups most involved in lobbying had organized a conference on women and the constitution. Lloyd Axworthy, the Minister Responsible for the Status of Women, asked (demanded?) that Doris Anderson, then President of CACSW, cancel the conference for the time being since it might embarrass the then Liberal government in power. Anderson was horrified at this clear interference in the independence of her organization and resigned in protest. Axworthy was mystified at her apparently bizarre behaviour. After all, what was the problem? Wasn't she a long time Liberal Party stalwart? Didn't her appointment largely stem from the Party rewarding one of its faithful for past services? The Party had fulfilled its part of the bargain, why couldn't Anderson fulfill her obligation? And besides, he, Axworthy, was paying the bills. That gave him the right to give orders that would be obeyed, didn't it? In Axworthy's eyes Anderson had simply not understood the nature of her position or the function of her organization.

Anderson was not a person to suffer in silence. She did a number of things designed to embarrass the government and to hobble its policies on women's rights. She called news conferences and summoned up help from friends in the media to humiliate both Axworthy and the government. Finally, when she could not get her way with the directors of her organization, she left CACSW and took her ample political resources — and bitterness toward the government and CACSW — to NAC.

What followed was not pretty. NAC became a vehicle for what amounted to a campaign to destroy any credibility CACSW might have had up until that time. In a very real sense, NAC blacklisted CACSW. This body found it increasingly difficult to get well qualified women to join CACSW. The confrontational stance hurt NAC as well. The Quebec group, La Fédération des Femmes du Quebec, withdrew from NAC for eighteen months due largely to NAC's cold (and sometimes hot) war with the government and CACSW.

NAC is remarkable organizationally. It claims to be a democratic organization representing the wishes of all women in Canada, which is quite a claim. The really noteworthy thing about it is that membership is by other organizations only. Individual memberships do not exist. At present it consists of over 360 women's organizations representing three million Canadian women members; these groups cover a wide spectrum of viewpoints and interest. According to NAC, the only requirement for membership is that groups seeking admittance be committed to the betterment of Canadian women. In fact, NAC is not as tolerant of varying opinions as this would suggest. Take the abortion question. Reproductive choice (support for abortion on demand) is critical to NAC's philosophy. Chaviva Hosek, present head of NAC, said in March 12, 1984 interview that NAC "would not feel comfortable" with a group that actively opposes freedom of choice.[5]

So how representative is NAC? This is a difficult question. On the face of it, it is highly representative. It encompasses not only the usual collection of feminist organizations of varying stripes, but also more mainstream organizations. For instance, one does not normally think of member organizations like the United Church, Progressive Conservative Women's National Caucus or the Imperial Order of the Daughters of the Empire (IODE) as being cells of raving feminists, yet they are members of NAC. Still, in spite of this variety there is a unanimity of opinion on questions of policy that is contrary to what one might expect.

A good part of this unanimity seems to be the result of NAC's bureaucratic quality. Since its members are other organizations rather than individuals, those policies that emanate from NAC are often an expression of the views of those organizations' leaders rather than those of the general memberships. Another part of this is that many of NAC's policies seem not to have been reviewed recently; they are often a matter almost of traditions. A good example is, again, abortion.

NAC has taken a very clear and aggressive position in favour of abortion on demand. At a meeting in March 1984 between the then Minister of Justice Mark MacGuigan, then Opposition Leader Brian Mulroney and NAC representatives, the two politicians were booed and hissed when they refused to knuckle under to pressure on this issue. Norma Scarborough, head of the Canadian Abortion Rights Action League (CARAL) reportedly yelled: "You don't have a right to force your opinion on the women of this country. The women of this country want the right to make decisions for themselves when faced with an unwanted pregnancy."[6] Now this is fascinating because NAC is clearly claiming to speak for Canadian women on this issue and yet many of its member organizations are on record as opposing abortion on demand. Ann McCartney, the IODE president, was quoted as saying, "We are right now reviewing our position (on membership in NAC). It's the abortion issue that caused the problem . . . I really don't feel that I can speak for 14,000 or 15,000 members on an issue like that." She went on to add that since the IODE had joined, there had never been a vote on the issue within NAC. "We never had a say,"[7] she said. It is reasonable to ask, if the president of this organization does not feel capable of representing her members on this issue, what gives NAC leaders the right to claim to speak for them? The Anglican Church's "wish" for abortion on demand is also being communicated to the Government of Canada by NAC. This is curious since it went on record as being opposed to just that.

There are a number of features of NAC which make its policies seem more a reflection of its leaders than those of the three million people it claims to represent. One is its regional character. In an important sense it is a Toronto organization. All of its leaders have come from the Toronto area and its office is in Toronto. This Toronto bias has raised doubts in some minds as to its ability to speak for women across the country. NAC is aware of this problem. Just prior to leaving office in 1984, President Doris Anderson said, "It (NAC) will never be accepted while it remains in Toronto."[8] She was speaking specifically of NAC's difficulties in its relations with women in Quebec, but one can see the applicability of this remark to the other regions as well.

Whatever one may think about how representative the organization is and how it develops policies, it must be admitted that once it does formulate demands, it has been extremely successful at lobbying government. Some of the more notable successes are:

1. Gaining access to government policy makers at all levels. NAC has been unusually successful at getting a sympathetic hearing from the highest levels of government. NAC officials regularly meet with the Prime Minister and the leaders of the two opposition parties. Part of the explanation for this ease of access comes from the fact that many members of NAC are members or "soon-to-be-members" of the elite themselves. Take Doris Anderson for instance, who in many ways has epitomized the organization. From time to time she has attempted to claim membership in the ranks of the dispossessed masses, but she is anything but that. She is a member of the elite, whether she will admit it or not. She is to be found in the *Canadian Who's Who* and in *Debrett's Illustrated Guide to the Canadian Establishment*, she is a long time Liberal Party member who during the Trudeau years was appointed president of The Canadian Advisory Board on the Status of Women in thanks for service to the Party, she was editor of *Chatelaine* for two decades and she is an Officer of the Order of Canada. She is or was active on the boards of the Ontario Press Council, the Civil Liberties Association, the Toronto Free

Theatre and the Roland Michener Foundation. And on and on and on. What all of this adds up to is a background that very much resembles that of other members of the elite. She looks like them, she talks like them, she goes to the same parties and has the same political convictions they do. In brief, those who hold real political clout in this country would find it fairly easy to do business with her.

The same is more or less true of other past and present presidents of NAC. Laura Sabia is a long time Ontario Progressive Conservative stalwart. The PCs owe her. Lynn MacDonald, former NAC president and a supposed defender of the oppressed in the guise of being a federal NDP member, is the scion of a B.C. family that is anything but working class. Before her ascension into the heavens of federal politics she taught sociology at the University of Toronto. Senator Lorna Marsden is another University of Toronto sociology professor. Other NAC presidents have drawn their sustenance from this university. Former president Kay Macpherson is married to C.B. Macpherson, professor of Political Economy. Chaviva Hosek, the current president, is an English professor there. These are no members of the oppressed. They are not involved in scrambling for a meal as they might sometimes like to claim, for the benefit of public sympathy. They are people with all the advantages of life, "cadillac feminists" in the words of Lloyd Axworthy. If this represents some sort of revolutionary or radical force, it is clear that it is a palace revolt.

2. Being viewed by the government as the one legitimate voice of all women in Canada. This is critical. In fact it is the most important victory that any lobby group can make. A number of benefits flow from such a victory. First of all, it gives you access to significant government funding. (In FY 1983–84 NAC got $185,000 from the federal government; in FY 1984–85 the figure became $300,000.) Another benefit is that once the government gives its stamp of approval, virtually every other sector of society (like the media) plus other groups in your lobby area will likely see you as *the* voice as well. When you talk, everyone will listen and many will believe.

How NAC managed to gain this legitimacy in government eyes is highly indicative of how the Canadian political system works generally and how lobbies gain this government stamp of approval. Basically it resulted from four factors. First, its leaders enjoy high socio-economic status (SES). They are in the main either members of the elite or people from professional and other well placed groups in society. The one president who came from an apparently working class background, Grace Hartman, was the former president of CUPE, one of Canada's largest unions. Presidents of large unions are about as typical of their members as Conrad Black is of his employees. Second, the structure of NAC is very similar to the governments it lobbies. It is big, bureaucratic and distant from its members. There is virtually no questioning of policy and no fear of pesky rank and file members seeking policy reviews. Government only has to deal with a few people and it knows that if it strikes a deal the deal stays struck. NAC will sell it to women and lobby them on behalf of the accommodation. The resulting enthusiasm for government policies may well translate into votes in the next election. Third, the style of NAC is similar to that of the government — behind the scenes and consultative. Government detests such popular manifestations as demonstrations and sit-ins. The only direct action NAC leaders will undertake is bargaining and negotiating in oak-lined offices or press conferences under hot television lights. A tough fight for NAC leaders takes place in the Parliamentary Restaurant contending with fork-wielding Cabinet Ministers rather than on picket lines against club-wielding police. Finally, the goals of NAC leaders are remarkably similar to those of people on the government side. While leaders are doubtless fighting for the rights of women, they are human beings with personal needs and ambitions that may or may not coincide with those of the women they represent. These are not self-denying Jacobins and puritans; the joys of fine restaurants, the feel of silk dresses and the exhilaration of the national limelight are not unknown. These and other such joys are ones which they would very much like to continue to experience. Careerism and its corrupting and moderating requirements are not unknown either. Bureaucrats and politicians love working with people like these, for they are rather like themselves.

3. Being viewed as the legitimate voice of *all* women by the media. The media are not all that bright and cannot understand that women are actually people and thus capable of having individual wants, needs and ideas. Instead they have come to the conclusion that there is just one set of ideas held by all women and have concluded that NAC is the one legitimate voice. The implications

of this conclusion cannot be underestimated. NAC gets constant and unquestioning transmissions of its ideas and opinions as if they were fact. The end result is that what starts out as mere opinions by NAC leaders ends up as societal orthodoxy. In many areas NAC seems to have virtually a monopoly over the expression of public opinion on social issues.

4. NAC has been extremely successful in manipulating politicians. Part of this success stems from its skillful manipulation of the media, which can make politicians' lives extremely unpleasant. Lloyd Axworthy and the officials at CACSW have been the victims of what can best be described as media smearing as a result of displeasure by a few NAC leaders. Other examples of turning the thumbscrews could be observed during the 1984 federal election campaign. Here NAC was unusually effective in bending politicians' arms behind their backs. There was the little matter of the 30,000 kits that NAC made up and sent out which told women how they could twist the arms of politicians at campaign meetings, and, best of all, was the televised debate for the three party leaders which consisted of them being quizzed on "women's issues" at a media event exclusively organized and run by NAC.

There was something extremely sinister about this. What we saw was a meeting that consisted exclusively of testing political leaders on their concurrence with the policies of one lobby group. One wonders what the reaction of the media would have been if this event had been organized by the Canadian Chamber of Commerce or the Council of Muslim Communities of Canada. Almost certainly it would have condemned this as interference in the democratic process and the holding up to ransom of the political system by some special interest group. This was not the reaction of the media, however. Rather, it was extolled as a victory for democracy. (Sometimes I think that they should close down the bar of the National Press Club forever. Some formerly fine minds have clearly turned to mush.) As sinister as this event was, the danger was lessened by two factors. One was the unremitting tedium of the event; letters to the editor complained of this one for days. The other was that the women from NAC had underestimated the degree to which politicians will lie, and make promises — only to break them after the election. If we were to believe Messrs. Turner, Mulroney and Broadbent, we would have to conclude that the entire Canadian treasury would be turned over to representatives of NAC's choosing and that the only policies that would ever be made would be female supremacist ones. This has not happened.

Status of Women Councils: Their Master's Voice
Let's face it. Be they the Canadian Advisory Council on the Status of Women (CACSW), the Provincial Councils or municipal ones — these bodies are the creations and, more or less, the puppets of government. They are funded by government and are filled with party hacks and patronage appointments. Worse yet, it shows.

CACSW is mistrusted by many hard-core feminists. This mistrust flows from the organization's close connection with government. It is totally funded by the Secretary of State (its budget in the period ending March 31, 1984, was $2,188,000) and reports to the Minister Responsible for the Status of Women. One view might be that this close relationship would be good for the cause of women since it provides women with access to the highest levels of government. Instead, NAC and its supporters accuse the organization of being just a tool of government, trying to sell the government of the day's policies to women. This indignation is a little amusing when you realize that very few women's groups which call themselves independent of government would exist were it not for government funding. The government, by this argument, bought a $185,000 piece of NAC during this same period.

There have been examples of blatant political interference. The aforementioned tiff between Anderson and Axworthy during the constitutional debate was really only the tip of the iceberg. This dynamic duo rubbed each other the wrong way very early on. Soon after Anderson took over as president of CACSW she decided to try and streamline operations. One of her first acts was to get rid of a staff member in the Winnipeg office. Very shortly thereafter she got a telephone call from an irate Liberal MP, one Lloyd Axworthy. He demanded to know why she had gotten rid of one of his most loyal campaign workers and demanded she get her job back. Anderson's problems really began with a vengeance when Axworthy was re-elected in the next general election and was appointed Minister of Employment and Immigration. He requested and got the new portfolio of Minister Responsible for the Status of Women. He was now Anderson's boss. More manipulation of CACSW by Axworthy was to follow.

Provincial status of women councils are far from clean as well. Officially these councils have the following general goals: to advise the government on women's issues; to conduct research on various issues of concern to women; to lobby government on behalf of women and their concerns which fall under provincial jurisdiction and to inform the public of issues and policy alternatives of interest to women.

In fact, provincial governments have secret agendas and unstated reasons for supporting these bodies which are perhaps more important from the governments' point of view. They are: to provide a source of patronage appointments for women belonging to the ruling party; to co-opt and neutralize those women who might prove embarrassing to the government if left out in the cold; to give the appearance of change and to communicate the government's ideas to the population and to sell its policies to the community.

One way provincial governments are able to ensure that these councils never get too much out of line is to make sure that their members are either party hacks or women that can be kept on a very short leash. Occasionally, members may misunderstand their role and try to really lobby for some serious changes, but the governments take care of this right from the start, one of the major tools being to make sure that they are chronically underfunded.

Interestingly enough, government receives ample help from other feminist groups and activists in undermining the work of the councils. While some of the criticism may be principled, too often it amounts to little more than petty jealousy. The attitude is very much one of, "Why wasn't I chosen for the job? I'm twice as smart as her!" Of course, no one is going to be that honest about their motivations. Instead, the criticisms are couched in the highest sounding terms. Still the hurt pride and the jealousy is there for those who care to look beneath the surface. The best recent case involved Sally Barnes, former President of the Ontario Status of Women Council. Sally had been Press Secretary to the Premier. What galled the feminist leaders in the province was that she had not come through the usual professional feminist ranks. What followed was not pretty. She was literally hounded out of office, not by reactionary males, but by irate feminists. Such infighting drastically undermines the councils' effectiveness. The politicians just laugh. If the feminists are stabbing each other in the back, government doesn't have to look over its shoulder.

The Feminist Lobby and Government: Who Influences Whom?
If we were to believe the media and the many pronouncements of government and the top women's lobbies, we would have to conclude that the feminist lobby in Canada is a great success and though there

are some struggles yet to win, the new age of sexual equality and liberation for women is about to dawn. But ask yourself, apart from some realignments and changes in the economy and in family life, what has changed? By and large most positions of power and authority are occupied by men and when they are occupied by women these women have so abandoned what most of us would recognize as female values as to be almost pseudo-male. They wear three-piece pin-stripe suits, think in terms of the bottom line and exploit, manipulate and order people around just as men have done for centuries. Any changes that have occurred have taken place in that small group of professional and managerial women that are "on their way," breathing new life into the Canadian elite and Canadian capitalism. For the vast majority of Canadian women, life goes on very much as always; they still make much less on average than men. In some cases women are worse off. Marriages end in divorce 40 percent of the time, much more than previously was the case, so the former stability of family life is gone. Now women must not only take care of their families but work in factories and offices as well. The ranks of the poor are coming more and more to be a feminine preserve. The question is, if the women's lobby is so successful at getting government to respond to its demands, why is the situation of ordinary women not improving? The answer is that there may be more to the relationship between the women's lobby and government than meets the eye.

Again, Canada is a country where most important decisions (ones involving money) are made by various elements of the elite before they even find their way onto the political agenda. The conflict then either takes on the mere appearance of conflict or a dispute, played out through the political parties between differing factions within the elite. The politicians and lobby groups have very little room to manoeuvre when it comes to questions of how the elite make their money and maintain control. Of those items that are allowed by the elite to be discussed by the polity, there are some questions that are so controversial as to threaten the continued existence of the government in power. Politicians are not prepared to cut their own throats. Such questions are thus beyond the pale. Lobby in this area and you won't get a hearing.

There are two classes of issues to which government will not listen. They are: issues that threaten to completely change the economic system of the country and who controls it, and those issues which are likely to be so controversial as to result in the party in power losing that power. This means that government is unlikely ever to accede to the following lobby demands in a serious or viable fashion: affirmative action; equal pay for work of equal value; raising the real minimum living standards of women, or men, at the bottom of the social ladder in any meaningful way; democratization or humanization of the workplace and economy; abortion on demand or the elimination of the restrictions on and biases against homosexuals and lesbians.

If any of this seems incredible, consider that the advances women have made in the last decade or so have all been in areas other than these taboo ones. Affirmative action, equal pay for work of equal value, free day care, changes in the economic situation of women and other such programs are still at the stage of being either ignored or rejected on the basis of being impossible to implement or too expensive. There may be some small advances but they are likely to stay at the debate stage for a very long time indeed. Until that time, ordinary women will have to be content with symbolic reforms which aid the climb to the top of their better off sisters, those with professions or who for other reasons are free of the economic worries which plague the majority of Canadian women.

On Whose Behalf Does the Women's Lobby Exert Its Influence?

One of the flaws in the stated ideology of the feminist movement in Canada must surely be the assumption that women represent a monolithic group or a group for whom gender is the most critical feature of their lives. Such an oversimplification of the human condition is not the exclusive preserve of this particular ideology. All ideologies do the same thing. Communism and socialism assume that class standing overrides all else, Nazism assumes that one's race is the be all and end all, nationalism claims to explain life in terms of one's nationality and so on. But people are complex in make-up and rich in their total motivation. We are not one thing but many. So it is with women. The situation of Canadian women differs greatly depending on their circumstances, some of which are determined at birth. So-called "cadillac feminists" such as lawyer Mary Eberts of the prestigious establishment law firm of Tory, Tory, Deslaurier and Binnington, heiress Nancy Jackman, or Doris Anderson share few life experiences with the Canadian women they claim to represent. True, they are all women. But what kind of women? Obviously, if you are a big time lawyer or journalist or a society matron, your concept of what is needed to correct centuries of injustice is going to be very different from that of an automobile worker or welfare mother. For the former group, symbols and an unfettered path to the top are paramount. For the latter group,

stable families, better social assistance, day-care and pro-labour legislation are critical. After all, what are the chances that any industrial or
clerical worker — male or female — will ever make it to be president of
a major corporation or Prime Minister? For working class women this
opening up of positions in the elite to women is like offering a peanut
butter sandwich to a person dying of thirst. It just does not make sense.
This reality is key to evaluating the efforts of the feminist lobby in
Canada. If you use the criterion of opening up of top positions to
women as your measure of success, then this lobby has been extremely
successful, probably more so than any other. If you see success in terms
of improving life for those at the bottom of the social scale, then it has
had very limited success.

It is not surprising that most of the advances and lobby efforts have
been on behalf of well-to-do or professional women. It is their education and high socio-economic standing which makes them legitimate
in the government's eyes in the first place. This should come as no
surprise since every successful revolution has been led by disaffected
middle- and upper-class individuals. These leaders interpret the needs
of their followers in terms of their own needs. What is good for
General Motors is good for America, what is good for Doris Anderson
and Lucie Pépin is good for Canadian women. But the problem is that
the women's lobbies — at least those at the top that have the government's ear — are lobbying as if all women were lawyers or journalists.

How Does Government Manipulate Women's Lobbies?

While on the surface it appears that the various women's lobbies have
been successful at manipulating government, especially during leadership conventions and elections, we have seen that the government is
very successful at manipulating women and women's groups by: determining what issues it will listen to; determining which groups are
legitimate; determining which groups get funded; controlling appointments to most of the lobby groups at the top and setting up reverse
interest groups to pressure it to do what it wants to do anyway.

We have already discussed most of these points, but let's just look at
the questions of funding and reverse interest groups since they illus-
trate rather clever techniques of control.

The women's movement and its lobbying expression is a colossus
but it is a giant with feet of clay. Its weakness is money, that most
sought after political resource in capitalist societies which translates
into political power and influence. Government is happy to fund
feminist organizations; however, there is a price. A very high price.

Officially, the process by which government decides who gets funding and who does not is the ultimate in objectivity and fairness. The good, worthy and needy get funded. The bad do not. According to the Secretary of State, the criteria for deciding on applications is that they fund the operations and project costs of groups and voluntary organizations that: increase understanding of women's issues and promote women's rights (translation: groups with a feminist perspective; non-feminist or anti-feminist groups need not apply); develop women's organizational skills and make women's groups more effective in improving the status of women (Sorry, I cannot translate classical bureaucratese) and encourage institutions to promote the equal representation of women in decision-making positions and to consider women's interests when making decisions (translation: we fund lobby groups who are pressing for affirmative action and job quotas).

REAL Women, an anti-feminist group, had the audacity to apply for funds and was turned down flat. This obvious injustice has not gone unnoticed among the more conservative women's groups. A coalition of REAL Women and anti-abortion groups (like Campaign Life) is presently attempting to pressure politicians to reverse this bureaucratic decision. This coalition is waging a write-in campaign directed at Brian Mulroney and the Minister Responsible for the Status of Women, Walter McLean. The letter which told the group of its rejection betrayed the underlying biases of the bureaucrats. It said, ". . . the promotion of a particular family model is not within the spirit of the objectives of the (Women's) Program. The program concentrates on supporting groups who are working to explore all options for women as they work towards equality in a society that is changing rapidly."[9] All options, except the traditional ones. This is by no means the only bias in the government's funding. There does seem to be a decided bias in favour of big, bureaucratic and establishment-oriented groups at the expense of the smaller, grass-roots organizations.

The Devils: The Anti-Feminist Lobbies
So far we have looked at those groups touted by the media, the government and themselves as being on the side of the angels. Still, what is a morality play without some devils to make it really interesting?

Men's Rights Groups
If you will recall, I suggested that only women and gay men could play the sexual lobbying game and that straight men need not apply. Well, this is a little white lie. There is, in fact, one group that lobbies on

behalf of men's rights. In Search of Justice was founded in 1974 by Ross Virgin. Virgin is an interesting guy who lives just north of Toronto and is an ambulance attendant. My original contact with him was through the feminist media where he regularly gets roasted and branded as some sort of cross between Dracula and a dinosaur. When I interviewed him I was expecting some ham-fisted male chauvinist and woman-hating reactionary. From what I have seen, he is very close to what many feminist women claim they are looking for in a man. He is extremely thoughtful, articulate and at ease with the media. There is a sensitivity and an apparently genuine affection for women as women that is probably not all that common among men. In a funny sort of way he is a "feminist man" or a "new man." I have on occasion wondered if his opposition to feminism does not come from a view that it is a philosophy that is somehow unworthy of women. Whatever the case, it is true that Virgin has become one of the two spearheads (REAL Women being the other) in the counter-attack against the feminist lobbies.

In Search of Justice is not a large organization. According to its founder it has about fifty members and one hundred associate members. The recruitment of this membership is very different from that of most organizations. Up until recently this group has been almost exclusively a support group for men facing charges for such things as sexual assault, sexual harassment or facing custody battles. In this, Virgin's group will help those who no one else will touch. Let's face it, feminist lobbying and media work have left a terrible image of men in most minds, including men's. Common images are "man the rapist," "man the child molestor," "man the wife-beater" and "man the child support evader." When a man is charged with one of these matters, the natural and immediate impulse of most of us is to presume them guilty and treat them like lepers. ISOJ does not do this. Instead it has for the last ten years offered support and legal assistance, which might include helping to research the case in preparation for the trial, attending the trial as a friend of the court or just providing someone to talk to during an extremely difficult period. ISOJ finds that many of these men wish to join the organization following their trials, and that is where many of the members have come from.

Recently the group has come to realize that this old tactic, while useful and important, has been an enormous failure from a lobbying point of view. The result of some soul-searching has been a new direction and stress. It has become involved in a very aggressive media campaign. The remarkable thing about the campaign is that it is virtually *gratis*. The media, after fifteen years of presenting exclusively feminist perspectives, seems ready to give time to the opposing point of view. Virgin has become something of a celebrity on the talk show circuit in Ontario. Indeed, the reception he has received has been surprisingly warm. Not all of it though. Virgin told me of one incident where CBC's *The Journal* was interested in doing a show involving some aspect of men's rights, but the woman researcher who spoke to him before the show became so furious at the idea of men's rights and Virgin's championing of it that she hung up the telephone in his ear. Thus ended his short and unhappy association with the world of "objective" CBC television journalism.

The real weakness of this group is its relationship with government — virtually non-existent. It has been able to break the feminist blockade of the media to lobby the public directly, but has not been able to break the feminist stranglehold of government. At present, ISOJ cannot claim any influence whatsoever with government and, of course, receives no funding.

REAL Women

Those feminists who know of the men's rights movement's existence probably feel little more than distaste. Certainly there is no sense of real threat or anger. The group that provokes feminists' real loathing and hatred is REAL Women.

REAL Women (Realistic, Equal, Active and for Life) began in February 1983 with a core group of four women — Patricia Loughran, Jean Murphy, Gwen Landolt and Grace Petrasek — who met informally to form an organization which would be pro-life and pro-family and would provide an alternate voice for women to that of the National Action Committee. REAL Women incorporated in the fall of 1983. Two events were responsible for getting this group moving. One was the inclusion of several sections in the new constitution and Charter of Rights which could be interpreted as giving precedence to women's rights over human rights. The other was the statement of the then Minister Responsible for the Status of Women to the effect that women who stayed at home were not making a contribution to society and as such should not receive a tax exemption on their husband's tax return.

Probably the major reasons for the hatred this group inspires among feminists lie in its success in presenting an alternative vision of the role of women in Canadian society. Feminism has been successful in making its views those of the government and media because it was the only group with a coherent and vibrant ideology. The old traditional ways of family and sexual life had apparently lost a good deal of their appeal and those who supported them seemed to have lost their nerve. The feminist groups filled this vacuum. What REAL Women has done is to provide an alternate vision. More importantly, they present it unapologetically. In feminist eyes, these women are traitors to their sex.

The vision of REAL Women is very different from that of the feminist groups, although there are some areas of overlap. For instance, this group believes that the government should clamp down on pornography. Still, the areas of overlap are few and far between. REAL Women do not support such causes as abortion on demand, equal pay for work of equal value, affirmative action hiring quotas in favour of women, the legalization of prostitution or no-fault divorce. Instead they stress policies which would help women to stay at home and raise families.

One of the remarkable things about the group is just how fast it has grown and how active it has been in what appears to be a lobbying counter-revolution. In a very short time it has grown to a point where it has a national membership of 10,000. Its major activity has been lobbying the general public through the media, and in this it has been unusually successful. A media which up until a couple of years ago was little more than a mouthpiece for feminist lobbies now seems keen to give this new group a chance on the soapbox. There are a number of reasons for this dramatic about face, one doubtless being the presence of men in the media who were forced to suffer in silence the "man bashing" by their female colleagues for so many years. Another is the media's never ending search for novelty. An anti-feminist women's group? Now there's novelty! Finally, it is probably a reflection of the disenchantment of society as a whole with the liberal and left-wing solutions which have survived with increasingly less relevance from the radical heydays of the sixties. All ideas and movements get tired and lose their appeal. Why should feminism be any different? Whatever the reasons, it is clear that REAL Women has touched a motherlode of sentiment among some elements of the public, and the media sense it.

Politicians are a different matter. They still cling to the feminist lobby groups for fear of electoral defeat the way a drowning man clings to a log. Their attachment to the ten-year-old alliance with feminist lobby groups shows up in a number of ways, especially in the area of funding. This became abundantly clear when REAL Women applied to

the Secretary of State's Women's Program for a sustaining grant of
$93,400 to cover the cost of setting up an office with a full-time
secretary plus a $17,250 grant to assist with the cost of the
organization's first national conference. An acquaintance of mine who
works for the Canadian Advisory Council on the Status of Women
called one of the Secretary of State officials responsible for this decision
on my behalf and was told that the request for funds was denied
because one of the group's policies contravenes a resolution of the
United Nations on contraception. This is without doubt one of the
biggest bits of nonsense I have heard in a long time. There REAL
Women stands condemned by the UN and the Canadian Government,
in the same class with South Africa, the torture states of Central
America and Nazi war criminals. Who says our bureaucrats do not play
fair? Who says they lack a sense of proportion?

The other reflection of this failure to date to get to the government
is the group's singular inability to influence the government in areas
involving women and the family. Not that they have not tried. To date
they have presented briefs to the federal and provincial governments
on prostitution, pornography, pension reform, pregnancy leave, equal
pay for work of equal value, education, birth control and no-fault
divorce.

The Anti-Abortion Lobbies

From groups that are ridiculed by the feminist lobbies and groups that
are hated by feminists let's move on to a group that is feared — the anti-
abortion lobby. For feminist lobby groups abortion on demand is like a
holy grail. This is one matter upon which all of them agree, but it is not
an issue upon which they have achieved their usual victories. In some
sense this issue has shown some indication of being their Vietnam or
Stalingrad. It was during the battle for abortion on demand that it
became clear that they could be beaten in the lobbying war.

The origins of the anti-abortion lobby are a little hazy, especially as
concerns its connection with the Roman Catholic Church. The opponents of this lobby try to assert that it is little more than a political tool
of the Church. The intent of this view is clear. Such critics hope to split
the movement from its non–Catholic supporters or those who favour a
separation of Church and State. The view of the anti-abortion lobby is
quite different. They admit to being extremely grateful for the support
the Church has given but at the same time its leaders claim that the
formation of the lobby was the result of the failure of the Church to
take up the issue in the first place. In this view it is the lobby which has

led the fight and the Church which has only recently caught up on this issue.

Which came first? Whichever it is, it is clear that the Church has been extremely useful as a supporter for the lobby as a source of instant credibility, financing and people. At the same time, it is clear that even if the Church were the major force behind the lobby, its importance is becoming somewhat less as the movement develops a wider base. The demonstrations in Toronto in early 1985 saw support from the more conservative Protestant and Jewish religious groups as well as the traditional Roman Catholic groups. Indeed, there are signs of some differences of opinion between the anti-abortion lobby, Campaign Life and the Church, with the lobby group showing itself to be the more conservative group. An example was the flap over the revelation that some serum for immunizing school children had been developed using tissue cultures from aborted fetuses. The lobby was against the serum; the Church was not.

The significant thing about this lobby is its change of status over a few years from an isolated bunch of apparent yahoos and fanatics to a well-respected, much-feared (by feminists) and mass-based group which is enormously successful in twisting the arms of government and the media. The group's leaders and goals have not changed. The public has. Part of this is the result of the group's lobbying through the media, organizing at the grass-roots level and direct action in the streets. Another part is the change in the public's consciousness. Liberalism and feminism have lost a good deal of their sheen, and old values — like the family — have developed a new patina. The efforts of this lobby have a number of different thrusts:

1. *The development of grass-roots organizations.* This activity, while it has originally taken place within a Church milieu, has begun to reach out to a wider audience.
2. *Coalition building.* Alliances have been developed with various conservative religious groups and more recently with such anti-feminist groups such as REAL Women. Indeed, it was the anti-abortion movement which first permitted the expression of anti-feminist sentiments in polite society.
3. *Lobbying the public directly by use of the media.* This has taken two major forms. One is the standard situation of being interviewed on public affairs shows or in newspapers, letter writing campaigns to the editors of newspapers or magazines or calling in to open-line shows. The other is a little technique they learned

from their feminist opponents, namely, bringing direct pressure on the media to ensure a more even presentation of issues. The best example was the campaign to force the magazine *Homemaker's* to portray the pro-choice side of the abortion question. *Homemaker's*, for those who may not know, is a hard-core feminist magazine which disguises itself with a few recipes and fashion articles as a mainstream women's magazine. Since it is distributed free of charge, readers could not express their feelings by no longer paying for their subscription. Up to this point the magazine had felt no obligation to be objective. By the time the anti-abortion lobby was finished the magazine's editorial staff had a new appreciation for journalistic even-handedness and the strength of their ideological opponents. The approach of the lobby was simple and effective. It organized a letter writing campaign by members and supporters to write the advertisers in the magazine, threatening to boycott their products if they did not withdraw their advertising from the magazine. A few did, most did not. The best part, though, was the protests of "progressive" journalists — feminists and left-wingers — to this tactic which smacked of a threat to freedom. What was amusing was the obvious hypocrisy of this outcry. These same "friends of freedom of expression" had done very much the same thing for years. Direct action, it would seem, is noble only as long as it is you who is employing the technique.

4. *Direct lobbying of government.* This has taken many forms. Lobbyists have dogged the footsteps of parliamentarians with their ghastly pictures of aborted fetuses, always it seems just before lunchtime. They do not represent a good time for politicians, but they represent a lot of votes. So the politicians have to endure this "torture by photo" patiently. Other techniques have involved letter writing and postcard blitzes to the government. After the Morgentaler acquittal in Ontario in 1985, the lobby was responsible for organizing a "jury for life" campaign which saw a postcard mailing to Ottawa by 1 million people. Other techniques have centred around pressuring politicians during election campaigns, aiding "pro-life" candidates and hindering "abortion on demand" candidates.

5. *Direct action.* This is the most spectacular of their many techniques. The less distasteful ploys involve demonstrating in front of abortion clinics, hospitals or public buildings. The really dis-

tasteful ones have a rather bizarre air and involve simulations of garbage cans full of dead babies. They are not pleasant.

The success of this lobby is obvious. Politicians live in terror of it, almost as much as they do the feminist lobbyists who oppose it. It is clear that, were it not for this lobby, the McDonald's style Morgentaler abortion clinics would now be a common feature in all major Canadian cities.

The Rebel Angels

First of all, let me make it clear that I do not see lesbians as being members of this group. They are integral parts of the feminist whole and do not need separate lobbies, although occasionally, they do set them up. An example a few years ago was a lobby of lesbian mothers pressuring government and the courts to recognize their right to the custody of their children upon marital breakup. This lobby, incidentally, was quite successful.

The strange thing about lobbying by gays is that there are very few gay men's lobby groups. The oppression seems real, so why in this age of social activism is there not some huge lobby pressing government to redress the millenia of injustice against them? Virtually everyone else is playing this game. The fact is that such a thing, while it exists in the U.S., does not exist in Canada. Part of the answer may lie in the Trudeau era. One of the first things that he did was essentially legalize homosexuality by saying that the government "has no place in the bedrooms of the nation." In a sense, the gay community got virtually all it could expect in one fell swoop. Another part may stem from the natural conservatism of Canadians. Gays may be a little out of the mainstream, but based on their political behaviour they are still part of that good old Canadian reluctance to assert their rights. Still there have been some lobby actions worthy of notice.

Toronto has to be the homosexual capital of the country. The gay community is huge and important economically and socially, but this has not translated into real political clout. Some of the most noteworthy examples of homosexual lobbying have been responses to police raids on their "recreational centres" like gay bars and bath houses. Such raids have brought sharp reactions from ad hoc gay protest groups plus intensive lobbying pressure, either directly at politicians or indirectly through their media cronies. On a number of occasions these protests have involved besieging police stations and punch-ups with "Toronto's finest." Police and politicians have taken a lesson from these actions. There have been some attempts by gays to take a more consistent and longer range political approach. In one case, homosexual lobbyists got an NDP-controlled Board of Education to study the problem of bias against homosexuals and to include material on homosexuals in some classes. This was not popular with the majority of the straight population of the province. Indeed, Frank Miller, in his brief tenure as Premier, railed against the Board of Education's views on this subject. There was even one mayoralty campaign that included gay rights issues as part of the campaign. The then Mayor John Sewell tried to vie for gay votes by taking their part in the election and promising specific city programs to improve their situation if re-elected. He was not re-elected and his espousal of gay rights contributed to his downfall. He got too far ahead of the electorate and paid the price.

The noisy and flamboyant lobbying days of the late seventies and early eighties have passed. The present thrust of gay lobbies is to campaign for specific issues at the community level. It is not very flashy, but it is a technique that does bear fruit. One of the important issues at present is lobbying for government assistance in fighting AIDS. What they are seeking is more money for research and better facilities and services for the care of AIDS victims. This lobby has a very low profile, perhaps in an attempt to counter the media hype which surrounds this issue. One gay activist told me that in Montreal this low profile is forced upon them by the fear of other community groups that the gay community will use this issue as the thin edge of the wedge for a wider gay rights lobbying push. Apparently, it is not just the hard-hats of this country that have it in for gays. The "cadillac liberals" have their share of homophobia as well.

There are other issues as well. There is the matter of the rights of gay fathers upon marital breakup. Lesbians can get their rights recognized in law, but for gay men it is another matter. They may have opted out of some aspects of the life of men, but they cannot fully escape the oppression that all men experience in trying to be recognized as good and loving parents. The old legal prejudices strike them as well. Other issues involve the treatment of closet gays who are caught engaging in homosexual acts in public washrooms. Pressure has been exerted recently to forbid the media publishing or disseminating the names of men charged with such offences. Finally there have been some attempts to persuade government to include prohibitions against discrimination on the basis of sexual preference in legislation.

The major problem the gay lobbies have in their push for gay rights is the simple fact that Canadian middle-class, liberal society likes to proclaim its enlightenment and tolerance toward homosexuality but the vast majority of these same "bleeding heart liberals" secretly hate, fear and loathe homosexuals and homosexuality. It is not fashionable or nice to express these feelings, but it is true. It is perhaps these real but unspoken attitudes by the majority that may explain the lack of impact and militancy by gay lobbies. They must certainly sense the true extent of this homophobia. And their sense is almost certainly correct. This, then, is the sad fact of life in Canadian sexual politics. Some have more rights than others. Upwardly mobile, feminist women have rights. Well-to-do men do too. Working class men and women, forget it. Homosexuals, never. Thus was it ever so.

Ideological lobbying is depressing, so let's go on to the lobbies of tribal loyalties, those of multiculturalism and language. It may prove better fun.

PART III

TRIBAL LOYALTIES
AND LOBBIES

For all of its technological advances, humanity has not advanced very far in its view of itself, its organization or its place in the scheme of things. Rather than being citizens of the universe, most people still cling to tribal loyalties. In Canada this tribalism — the identification of oneself by reference to some narrow group with very special characteristics of group membership like language, region, race or country of origin — is very strong. In this section we shall look at how "tribal conflicts" are fought out in the Canadian context.

8

The Multicultural Mosaic

The Canadian Government has committed us to a grand and glorious experiment: the creation and preservation of a truly multicultural society. Our politicians have rejected the melting pot model of the U.S. for a variety of reasons, some involving the noblest altruism, many others involving the worst opportunism and self-seeking such as the eternal quest for votes. But whatever the reasons, the State has pledged itself and all its resources to this goal and we are supposed to find some way to make it work.

This is a daring — and dangerous — experiment, for it has not succeeded anywhere else. Truly multicultural nations like Lebanon, India, South Africa, Cyprus, the newly-independent nations of sub-Saharan Africa and now Great Britain are far from being good examples of the peace and joy which result from peoples with very different backgrounds living together. Quite the opposite. Nevertheless our government is determined to elevate Canada to this elect group, and in the process has created an unusually wonderful milieu for ambitious opportunists and would-be influence peddlers.

To some extent Canada has always been multicultural. The first Europeans to arrive here found over fifty Inuit and native Indian cultures. This diversity was, even then, a source of much tension and unhappiness. Some of the more romantic elements of the Canadian intelligentsia have attempted to paint a picture of native peace, plenty and harmony which was shattered by the arrival of the white man, but this image, while charming, lacks reality. True, there was probably a oneness with nature which is lacking in the modern world, but there were other, somewhat darker features of life reminiscent of life today. Wars raged, territorial conflicts erupted; slavery was common, most notably among the Indians of the West Coast. There were massacres. There was torture. Clearly, multiculturalism in the pre-European world had its share of hatred and turmoil. Whatever the faults of the native peoples, however, the arrival of Europeans represented a major step backwards in terms of man's treatment of his fellow man. Europeans brought with them racism and forms of religious, cultural and linguistic intolerance hitherto unknown. Worst yet, they brought new military technology to make their points of view stick. Doubtless the native peoples of the time must have had reservations about the wisdom of an open door immigration policy.

The early European settlers had simple multicultural policies. They warred among themselves and suppressed the customs and religions of others. Those natives who were not killed by the white man's guns and diseases were herded into concentration camps (a.k.a. reserves) and degraded and destroyed as peoples.

Up to the present, multiculturalism has generally involved a great deal of mutual distrust and loathing. Each new wave of immigrants has been greeted with verbal abuse and discrimination by those already here, but in time these immigrants assimilated to some extent and went on to abuse and discriminate against later waves of immigrants.

It may be well to remember that what we now think of as racism and discrimination is paradise compared to what existed up to the end of the Second World War. One need only consider the plight of the East Europeans in the West, the Japanese, Sikhs and Chinese in British Columbia, the blacks in Nova Scotia and native peoples everywhere, to get a true feel for the state of race relations in Canada before 1945. Neither one of the founding groups is exempt from blame for this state of affairs. The history of English Canadian racism — the Ku Klux Klan, some elements of the Orange Lodge, and many other groups — had its shameful counterpart in French Canada. Particularly noteworthy was the vilification of East European immigrants in the early years of this century and anti-Semitism up to and including the present in Quebec. It was and is couched in nationalist rhetoric about the preservation of the French fact on the continent; it was and is racism.

The beginning to our story about lobbying and influence peddling in the multicultural arena involves, oddly enough, the 1963 Royal Commission on Bilingualism and Biculturalism. Originally, this report had been intended to enshrine English and French as the official languages of the country and to expand the role of French Canadians in the running of the country. But there was an interesting twist. Those ethnic minorities in the Prairie provinces, the victims of vilification by French Canadian politicians in the early twentieth century, had come of age. These groups mounted strong opposition to the terms of reference of the Commission since they felt these terms and the recommendations and policies which would flow from them would perpetuate their second-class status as citizens. They were probably right. As a condition of their accepting the idea of two official languages, they demanded the addition of a term of reference of their own — that the Commission would examine the ways in which Canadians of non-British and non-French origins have taken their place "within the two societies that have provided Canada's social structures and institutions." The worm had turned. Those who had been shunned now had the political and economic clout to demand greater recognition by government of their cultural and linguistic rights, and when the Official Languages Act was introduced in October 1968, the Prime Minister's speech attempted to soften the blow for these minorities by saying that these two official languages existed in a pluralistic society.

When the legislation came into force in September 1969, all hell broke loose. The backlash in the West was tremendous. The violent reaction from groups there convinced the government that the "two nations" concept simply would not be acceptable in Canada. The result was a formal multicultural policy introduced in October 1971 as a response to the recommendations contained in Book IV of the Bilingualism and Biculturalism Commission Report. The lobbying had paid off.

Following this policy statement, the Multiculturalism Directorate was established in the Secretary of State's Department and a Minister of State for Multiculturalism was appointed. This part of the history of multiculturalism the government is delighted to mention. The next part usually gets fairly superficial — or even non-existent — coverage because government comes out of it looking so bad. The second phase of the multicultural saga saw a major change in the ethnic and social makeup of the Canadian mosaic. During the 1970s there was a major wave of immigration. Massive waves of immigration are not new, but this one was different. A significant portion of the new immigrants were from the Third World (i.e., not white). All hell broke loose.

Major social change is always painful if the rate of change is rapid and if there isn't adequate planning to ensure that possible problems are anticipated and programs to deal with them are set up in advance. This was the area in which the federal government was negligent, almost criminally so. It should have been obvious that such a major change in the racial makeup of the country would cause problems, but curiously enough, there was no advance planning. There seems to have been an attitude of: "We don't see any problem; therefore, a problem does not exist." Unfortunately, the country was not made up exclusively of cabinet ministers and civil servants with Air Canada passes, subsidized meals and secure jobs. The reaction of the population, especially those in the less well off sections where jobs and even survival are difficult to attain at the best of times, was often xenophobic and racist. In retrospect it is easy to see that a good portion of this reaction had an economic basis. After all, people who are finding life difficult enough do not welcome additional competition, especially if the newcomers appear very different.

While it was bad enough that the federal government had been unable or unwilling to anticipate these problems, the government's reaction, once the problems began, only made the situation worse. It is not usually in the nature of governments to admit to mistakes, but this was particularly true of the Trudeau regime, which was noted for its pride and arrogance. Rather than deal forthrightly with Canadians, admit its errors and try to formulate policies that would both calm the fears of citizens and ensure at the same time a smooth transition and assimilation into the larger society for the newcomers, the government did absolutely the worst thing — it embarked upon a campaign of blaming its own population. The politicians and government, it seemed to be saying, had not erred. Their policies and programs were right. The problem was that the population was "bad." It was racist to the core, and with the guidance and chastisement of government, would be made over in the government's image. A series of new laws, new restrictions, new media guidelines and advertising campaigns were imposed upon the population — all of which had two nasty unintended effects.

First, Third World immigrants, who were already shaken and insecure because of the less than warm welcome they were receiving, grew even more fearful in the face of government actions and statements which seemed to give credence to their worst fears. Clearly, they were indeed immersed in a population of hard-core racists who were just biding their time for an opportunity to get them. Surely, lynchings and cross burnings were likely to follow soon. Demands by them for ever more protection from their neighbours by government — their supposed protector — were entirely understandable. These demands, however, exacerbated a second unintended result of the government's reaction. The existing population was furious at being labelled as somehow less than human and at the new set of government acts that seemed to restrict their freedom and undercut their control over their own lives even more. The "magic" of government policy and intervention had once more ensured that the various segments of the population were well and truly at each other's throats. The stage was now set for yet another act in the influence and lobbying game.

The Players

Because of the complexity and rich rewards that are part of this lobbying activity, there are a large number of players from widely divergent backgrounds and with vastly different goals. The basic players are:

1. ethnic groups.
2. native peoples' groups.
3. politicians and government.
4. other groups (religious, political, feminist, media, etc.).

Canada is a nation of immigrants. All of us have our origins in other parts of the world either directly or through our ancestors. Even native people have their origins in Asia. The groups that embody this diversity are numerous and represent peoples with widely varying interests, goals and resources which vary with the wealth and nature of the memberships. They have widely different focuses too:

1. Organization around the country or region of origin of members, e.g., the National Association of Japanese Canadians, National Congress of Italian Canadians, Federation of Sikh Societies of Canada, National Association of Canadians of Origins in India and many more.
2. Organization around race, e.g., Black Advisory Committee, Canadian Jewish Congress.
3. Organization around religion, e.g., Canadian Council of Christians and Jews, Council of Muslim Communities in Canada.
4. Issue orientation, e.g., Urban Alliance on Race Relations, B'nai B'rith League for Human Rights.
5. Organization around occupation, e.g., General Union of Palestine Students, Canadian Lawyers and Jurists for Soviet Jewry.
6. Parliamentary groups, e.g., Ontario Legislative Committee for Soviet Jewry.
7. Groups within political parties.
8. The ethnic press.

Probably the most important thing to realize about Canadian ethnic groups and their ability to lobby is that all groups are not equal. Some have the government's ear; some do not. Some find easy access to government largesse; some do not. Some are treated in a kindly and sympathetic fashion; others are treated in a savage and almost racist way. Some find government eager and willing to protect them and their members; others are treated in a rather hostile fashion.

The treatment received varies according to political and economic resources. If your community is wealthy and has lots of members, you are likely to receive gentle and considerate treatment from the media and government. If you have strong connections among the rich and powerful, vote more or less as a bloc and act in an aggressive and united lobbying fashion, you are certain to receive favoured treatment. Communities relatively poor in economic and political resources, however, are highly vulnerable to the whims and prejudices of politicians and media people alike. Let's look at two of the "more equal" groups, then at a group with fewer resources.

The Jewish Community

Without doubt, one of the "more equal" ethnic groups is the Canadian Jewish community. It is rich in both political and economic resources. It has not always been in a favoured position though. With the exception of native people, Canadian Jews have probably suffered more in terms of long-term and conscious discrimination than any other ethnic group in society. The present situation of Canadian Jewry contrasts sharply with this shameful past. The reasons for this major improvement lie predominantly in the high socio-economic standing of the members of this community and their influence in the professional, business, cultural and media elites in Canada. Another factor is sponsorship.

A sad but true fact of life in this country is that various elites control most of the really important facets of life, and to be powerful you need to be a member of one of these elites. To be permitted into these magic circles, one needs to be sponsored by those already established. This is as true for ethnic groups as it is for individuals. The sponsorship of Jews into the inner circles has accelerated over the last twenty years. Probably the first major figure to provide this sponsorship was Pierre Elliott Trudeau. The Trudeau years were unusually fruitful for the Jewish community and its struggle for real political clout. This sponsorship by Trudeau of the Canadian Jewish community was best described by Larry Zolf, who said, "Pierre Elliott Trudeau's love affair with Jews is probably the maddest and most passionate fling that Trudeau has ever flung. That Trudeau was their landsman, their Godfather at Ottawa court, their first real access to state power, the Jews of Canada would unblushingly have to agree. The list of talented

Jews given their heads in government, politics and the judiciary by Trudeau is endless."[1] This success in reaching the pinnacles of power and exerting enormous influence is all the more remarkable given the relatively small size of this group, only 300,000. This success in getting sponsorship was based partly on incredible competence. It was not a case of some crude affirmative action program in which individuals are recruited because of their race or sex simply to fill arbitrary quotas. Rather, those who rose to the top represented a vast pool of exceptional talent which had to this point been wasted. Individuals like Bernard Ostry in the bureaucratic elite, Bora Laskin in the judicial elite and Jerry Grafstein in the media elite were clearly the best in their fields.

This process of sponsorship had gone on for some time, and part of the reason that it took as long as it did had to do with the Canadian elite's requirement that prospective entrants be well off and look very much as its members do. That takes time — generations in fact. As well, it was obvious that when the break did come it would be under a Liberal government, because there was some anti-Semitic feeling in the ranks of the Conservative Party of old. This is not to say that such did not exist in the Liberal Party as well — after all it was Mackenzie King who had kept out Jews prior to and during the Second World War — but it was more receptive to Jews and the contribution which they could make. And contribute they did. A good example was the Bronfman family. The Bronfmans have always been enthusiastic supporters of the Liberal Party. This support goes back to their days in Saskatchewan where they started business during the prohibition era. The Conservative Party was somewhat racist and extremely pro-prohibition, which gave the Bronfmans two powerful reasons to support the Liberals. The family became one of the largest and most reliable contributors to party coffers ever. Part of this was motivated by Sam Bronfman's desire to become the first Jewish senator. Apparently he made it clear to Liberal power-broker C.D. Howe, that he would stop his contributions to the Party if he were not appointed to the Senate, but the time for a Jewish senator had not come — at least in the minds of the Liberal Party big-wigs — for they responded not with an appointment but with a threat to raise the excise tax if he was not good. In fairness to the Liberal Party of the time, this refusal to raise Mr. Sam to the purple was also influenced by his bootlegging past and underworld connections, things which do not look nice on the curriculum vitae of a senator. To prove the party's good intentions it later appointed David Croll as the first Jewish senator and later also appointed

Bronfman's lawyer, Lazarus Phillips. It is interesting to note that Phillips was a lawyer-bagman, so the party was just paying back one of its own. The Senate now is a very common happy hunting ground for Jews who have proved their loyalty — there are eight Jewish senators compared to one black, one Greek and two Italians.

This sponsorship of the Jewish community by the elite through the agency of the Liberal Party was not purely the result of nobility or recognition of talent. Another reason was bloc voting by Jews, which has been unusually effective because of their concentration in key constituencies in Montreal and Toronto. The Toronto and Montreal voters are exceptionally dear to the hearts of the parties because they encompass so many ridings and it is virtually impossible to win a federal election without winning support in these two cities. Just ask the Conservatives. Until Mulroney came along, Montreal was a wasteland for them and Toronto was just manageable at the best of times. It usually took a landslide for the Conservatives to see any real support in Hog Town. The advantage Jewish voters hold is that they are concentrated in these very key seats.

There is clear evidence of bloc voting by Jewish voters. The Canada–Israel Committee did an analysis of the Jewish vote in 1984 which showed that of the nine ridings in Canada with more than 10,000 Jewish voters, eight had been represented by Liberals in the last Trudeau government. The same study found that there are fifteen ridings with populations of more than 4,000 Jewish voters, five of which are in the Montreal area. There is a further reason for the importance of the Jewish vote in these and other ridings. Jewish families tend to be smaller than the national average and thus a higher proportion of family members are likely to be of voting age. Perhaps more importantly yet is the fact that Jewish voters turn out more heavily than the national average. It is not just a question of the number of seats that may be affected, it is a matter of the quality of those elected as well. The Toronto ridings are more likely to provide cabinet members — and senior cabinet members at that.

We have already mentioned the love affair Trudeau had with Jews and have discussed some of the very good and obvious reasons. There was one other factor, less obvious, but probably important as well. The 1982 census figures show that Trudeau's riding of Mount Royal had almost 42,000 Jewish voters or 47.4 percent of eligible voters. Clearly, Trudeau could ill afford to offend Jews in Canada unless he wished to change his riding in a hurry. Interestingly enough, his seat was saved for the Liberals during the Tory landslide of 1984 by Sheila Finestone, former head of La Fédération des Femmes, a long time Liberal and Jewish herself.

It is obvious that bloc voting and the prominent role played by many Jews in the Liberal Party have made Liberal governments quite sensitive to the representations of various lobbies claiming to speak for all Canadian Jews or segments of that community. By and large such representations have often been positive in their effect upon the body politic as a whole, with the area of human rights being a good example.

Curiously enough, this support for the Liberals has made the Conservatives exceedingly anxious to listen to and accede to the demands of such lobby groups. In one case the result was disastrous. That was the case with the abortive attempt to move the Canadian embassy in Israel from Tel Aviv to Jerusalem. The original motivation for this move came prior to and during the election campaign of 1979. The Conservatives knew that the election would be determined in Southern Ontario, particularly in the Toronto area, and strategists told Clark that the Conservatives would have to increase their support among Jewish voters in the city.

Clark had been nicely set up for what was to come during his trip to the Middle East, Japan and India. He was accompanied on the trip by two Conservative candidates running for office in Toronto ridings with substantial Jewish votes — Rob Parker, whose riding had a 35 percent Jewish vote and Ron Atkey, who was running in a riding with a 25 percent Jewish vote. There were also two personal friends of Clark's from the Jewish community — Irving Gerstein, president of Peoples' Jewellers, and Jeffrey Lyons, who had supported Clark in his leadership campaign. Not surprisingly, all four urged Clark to commit the Conservatives to moving the embassy. Clark, to his credit, refused. However, the election campaign and the chance of making political gains seems to have gotten the better of him and he made the move Conservative policy after representations and a good deal of pressure from the Canada–Israel Committee. It is still difficult to understand what could have finally persuaded Clark to do this. He had an aide call prominent Conservatives from the Jewish community. Eddie Goodman, one of the most prominent figures in the party, urged him not to agree to this proposal just as Trudeau had done. But Clark went ahead with a commitment to a policy that would soon make Canada a laughingstock in the eyes of the world and lead to threats of lost business and even terrorist attacks.

At present there are many lobby groups representing various causes and points of view among Canadian Jews. Much of the lobbying is concerned with urging government to tighten up hate legislation and to give new powers to bodies such as human rights commissions. These efforts have picked up new momentum, given the perception of the Jewish community that there is a revival of anti-Semitism in Canada. Other activities have included a very aggressive pursuit of those thought to be leaders of this revival. Ernst Zundel of Samisdat Publishers was taken to court for promoting hatred, as was Jim Keegstra, the Alberta teacher who allegedly promoted hatred against Jews by teaching his students that the holocaust never occurred. At another time in Canadian history most people would have dismissed him as some sort of crazy redneck. These, however, are not times that encourage tolerance or calm reflection. The reaction of the Jewish community, the media and all levels of government was, in a word, hysterical. The media tried him and found him guilty, then he was fired from his job. Then — and I emphasize only then — was he charged and tried for inciting hatred toward Jews. It strikes me that all of this is a travesty of justice, no matter what we might think about his nonsensical views.

There is one other major target for Jewish lobbying activity and that is other ethnic groups and their various lobbies and organs. This is usually extremely beneficial to all concerned. Basically the various groups which represent the Jewish community, especially in the area of human rights, attempt to help and encourage other groups in their struggles. There is an almost paternal attitude to the other ethnic groups. Sometimes aid takes the form of funding or providing legal assistance, sometimes it may involve using political clout. This is exactly what has happened in the case of Japanese Canadians seeking compensation from the Canadian government. The Canadian Jewish congress has been heavily involved in using its considerable muscle on their behalf.

Sometimes, however, this paternalistic interest can become a little less than benign. A case in point was the action taken by the B'nai B'rith's League for Human Rights against a Toronto black community newspaper. *Contrast*'s "sin" was that it published an article by Richard Dildy in response to a *Toronto Sun* editorial. Among other things the author had the following observations to make: "Throughout America, but especially in New York City, Jews control a major part of the industry, including real estate, food, manufacturing and retail sales. Most of the absentee landlords, or slumlords, are Jews."[2] The B'nai B'rith came down like a ton of bricks and by the time the whole matter was finished *Contrast* was sorry it ever saw the article. In the end,

Contrast had to agree to write a properly abject apology in editorial form and to publish two letters, one from the B'nai B'rith and one from an "irate reader." The paper had been taught a lesson it would not soon forget. Said Alfred Hamilton, the newspaper's director of publications, "We will guard zealously our relationship with the Jewish community."[3]

The Italian Community

Like the Jewish Community, the Italian community has grown to be an extremely powerful one with enormous political resources with which to lobby and influence government. Also, as with the Jewish community, a good deal of this strength and influence comes from members of the community voting as a bloc. Until recently it has been true to say that the Liberal Party of Canada has virtually owned the "Italian vote," partly because it was a Liberal government which opened the door to the flood of immigration following the end of World War Two which allowed much of this community to come to Canada in the first place.

The incident which really clinched support for the Liberals, however, was the disastrous period from 1957 to 1960 which saw a serious downturn in the economy. This downturn came at the same time as the Diefenbaker regime. The sufferings of the newly arrived Italian community were enormous. The UIC system which existed then was totally inadequate and had a waiting period that was so long that very few could qualify. Understandably, these new immigrants assumed that it was the Conservative Party which was responsible for their situation. After all, hadn't life been good under the Liberals who preceded Diefenbaker? This may not have been fair to the Tories, but it stuck.

What the Jewish community has been able to accomplish through bloc voting, the Italian–Canadian community has been able to do in spades. After all, there are many more Italians than Jews. In Metro Toronto alone there are 400,000 Italian–Canadians, which translates into real political power. At the federal level there is enormous support for the Liberals. In Toronto, there is a strip of Liberal ridings that has remained firm no matter what the political trends. It runs through the west-central part of the city, corresponding exactly with the areas of high concentration of Italian voters. An illustration of just how solid this Italian–Canadian vote is lies in the voting behaviour in many of these ridings during the Tory landslide of 1984. Despite the devastation of the Liberal Party in other parts of the country, these voters bucked the Tory trend by sending two new Italian–Canadian Liberal MPs to Ottawa — John Nunziata and Sergio Marchi.

The Liberal Party tends to be very receptive to the points of view and demands of the leaders of this community, and it has proven to be a major vehicle for the advancement of many Italian–Canadians. Italian–Canadians have found themselves in all of the major positions of power in the Liberal Party hierarchy and in government, including cabinet posts and Senate seats. Once in power these individuals represent powerful voices for the interests of the Italian community.

One of the best cases of the rapid rise of Italian–Canadians is Senator Peter Bosa, famous for his remark that "Canada's like a pizza."[4] Bosa, an immigrant from Italy, was quick to learn the benefit which could be gained from parlaying support among Italian–Canadians for the Liberal Party into patronage appointments and other political goodies. Bosa worked on the election campaigns of Andrew Thompson, Walter Gordon, Charles Caccia and Paul Hellyer — three federal cabinet ministers and one provincial leader. Bosa soon found his political career taking off in a spectacular way. One of his rewards was his appointment in 1963 as special assistant to Guy Favreau, the then Minister of Citizenship and Immigration. He was later appointed to the position of national chairman of the Canadian Consultative Committee on Multiculturalism, a particularly important appointment since the federal government's multiculturalism program relies heavily on this committee for policy recommendations and input on what ethnic committees think about various issues. His final reward was a place in the Senate. (He is one of two Italian–Canadian Senators; the other is Pietro Rizzuto, a construction industry millionaire from Quebec who earned his seat as a result of his past as a Liberal Party bagman. He is Chairman of the Liberal Party Finance Committee.)

Bosa has been, and continues to be, a powerful voice for the interests of the Italian–Canadian community. His more important associations have been COSTI, the Italian immigration education centre, the National Congress of Italian–Canadians and the Friuli Emergency Fund. He represents an important voice as well for the Italian–Canadian business community, as an important member of the Italian Chamber of Commerce and the Canadian–Italian Business and Professional Association.

There has at times been a negative side to shoring up this Italian support, a type of Tamany Hall approach to the "Italian vote" by Liberal Party operatives. An example surfaced in an interview given by

Finance Minister Michael Wilson in late 1984. Wilson, speaking about the difficulty the Tories have in cracking Liberal strongholds in Italian districts of Toronto, had the following things to say about the Liberal tactics: "The election campaigns that we fight in downtown Toronto are: 'Don't vote for the Tories or they're going to send you back to Italy' ... That's the politics of fear that people will play."[5] This did not come as a surprise to political observers and players, but the reaction of some Italian–Canadians active in the Liberal Party indicated that Wilson had touched an exposed nerve. New Liberal MP Sergio Marchi wrapped himself in the flags of both Italy and Canada and accused Wilson of remarks which bordered on racism. Said Marchi, "As an Italian–Canadian, I am shocked that the minister would insult the intelligence and integrity of this proud, hard-working community."[6] Clearly, Marchi was playing to the folks back home (his riding has the largest Italian community in Canada) and avoided answering the accusations by accusing the Tories of something close to being against widows and orphans.

The Liberal Party is not the only conduit of influence used by the Italian community. There are a large number of lobby groups that pressure all levels of government. One of the most powerful is the National Congress of Italian–Canadians. Founded in 1974, this organization claims to speak for 1.2 million Italian–Canadians, 500,000 of whom are located in Metro Toronto. The Congress can really make the politicians dance. At the founding conference of the Congress, External Affairs Minister Mitchell Sharp promised top jobs for Italian–Canadians. He stated that the Italian community in Canada "is not sufficiently represented in senior positions of government ... These changes will come ... Why not a secretary of state for external affairs of Italian origin?"[7] Why not? In fact it might be a good idea to have 150 or so secretaries of state in each one of the ministries to give representation to all the ethnic groups in the country.

This organization has been a major force in the country. Part of its success can be explained by the contribution of Dr. Laureano Leone, twice head of the organization. A thoughtful and far-seeing individual, Leone had a wider vision than most leaders in the multicultural area. He was able to see beyond the parochial interests of any one ethnic group. He founded the National Association of Ethno-Cultural Organizations in 1980 as an umbrella which would represent the common interests of all ethnic organizations in the country and was its president until recently. His vision involved an understanding that the

Italian community had found a proper and prosperous place in the mainstream of Canadian life and could help more recent newcomers. His efforts under the aegis of the National Congress of Italian–Canadians and the National Association of Ethno-Cultural Organizations has resulted in the Italian community finding itself one of the major forces leading the third of the nation made up of ethnic groups. He has, consequently, levered the influence of the Italian–Canadian community into that of a serious national force.

The Congress has been involved in exercising this new-found influence in a number of different ways. It has had major input into decision making by various levels of government in immigration policy, labour law and relations and the operation of government agencies such as the Workers' Compensation Board. In the late 1970s it urged government to funnel savings from the bilingualism program into the area of multiculturalism. It is a reflection of the political clout this organization had acquired that it could get a serious hearing from the Trudeau government as to such a transfer of funds and such a change in priorities. Bilingualism was, after all, a fetish for the Liberals throughout the Trudeau years.

The National Congress is by no means the only organization of importance representing the interests of this community. The Italian–Canadian Benevolent Corporation has taken on itself the task of raising funds for various worthwhile projects benefiting the community. At times this organization has been so powerful that it seemed likely it would successfully challenge the position of the National Congress. Indeed, the Corporation, which is actually part of the Congress, has been highly critical of what it sees as the somewhat "philosophical" and "impractical" nature of the Congress. Frank Fazio, a lawyer and chairman of the Ontario region, criticized the Congress as follows, "They should be practical too. They talk of socialist philosophies but when they need money they want to reach in somebody else's pocket."[8] The weakness of the National Congress in the area of finances was recognized with the election of Ettore Cardarelli in 1983 as president of the Toronto district operation, by far the most important region of the country. He stated that the organization would take a new approach: "We're going to move away from the hip-shot approach to fund-raising. We're doing some serious planning. The congress has done a lot of good for the community but the man on the street often remains unaware of it."[9] In addition, there are a number of social and cultural clubs and societies that represent subsets of the larger Italian community and their special interests. Often these groups represent the interests of Italian Canadians from different regions of Italy.

The influence of the Italian community is enormous and extends to all levels of government. At the provincial and municipal level, this influence is especially important in Ontario and Quebec. The Quebec government was the target of heavy influence by the Quebec wing of the National Congress of Italian–Canadians when it tried to select an advisory council on immigration and ethnic affairs without consulting it. One insider in the Ontario Tories tells me that high level delegations from the Italian–Canadian community closely resemble visits by royalty in terms of the respect shown by top level provincial officials. And municipal government in Toronto is very anxious to ensure that the desires of the Italian–Canadian community are met. A street name was changed to Via Italia in response to a demand by community leaders, which doesn't sound like much of a big deal, except that the Arab community tried to get a similar name change in one of the suburbs and it ran into a brick wall. Then there was the incident in 1979 after the CBC aired a series on organized crime in Canada. In a marvellous display of hot air, Metro Toronto Councillors debated for 2½ hours on the issue of whether or not they should condemn the series' suggestion that some Mafia families might be of Italian background. Alderman Piccinnini delivered a long speech which suggested that the CBC should spend its time telling viewers that explorer John Cabot was Italian or praising the accomplishments of educator Maria Montessori and inventor Marconi rather than on "garbage" that "smears" Italian-Canadians. This fairly typical political rhetoric was made more meaningful by Council's refusal to condemn the Metro Police Association for published attacks on Jews, Pakistanis, blacks and other minorities. One of the councillors called these attacks just a "slight indiscretion."[10]

The Arab Community

Of all the ethnic groups in Canada, excluding native people, the Arab community gets by far the worst treatment at the hands of government, the media and other minority groups. In the media Arabs are depicted in a racist fashion. They are the archetypal villains of the eighties. They are shown as hook-nosed and dirty individuals who are blood-thirsty and lecherous. Islam is often portrayed as a creed which oppresses women and which is little more than a medieval superstition appealing to ignorant and evil fanatics. Often, we are told that it is the

Arabs and their lust for petro dollars which are at the roots of our economic problems. Now, ask yourself, what would happen if Jews, Blacks, French Canadians or women were portrayed in this fashion? The courts and civil rights commissions would be busy for the next ten years dealing with the anti-defamation and anti-hate cases. Strangely, the media — with the tacit approval of government — has a free hand to treat Canadian Arabs in this fashion.

This anomaly has not escaped the notice of the Arab community. At a conference on Arabs in Canada held in Toronto in April 1984, a panel of academics dealt with this question, and concluded that the stereotyping of Arabs in the North American media created an impression that it was socially acceptable to discriminate against Arabs. University of Illinois professor Jack Sheehan stated that "Today's Arab is very much like yesterday's Jew, back in the '20s . . . They've taken the Jewish nose and put it on the Arabs."[11] Professor Tom Naylor of McGill University, accused the CBC of extreme bias, claiming that, "The CBC is a particularly scandalous example in portraying Arabs . . . *The Journal* is historically the most manifestly biased. *The Journal* in my view is a highly fictionalized source of information about the Arab world [but] in the last year, there's been a little improvement."[12]

The unavoidable conclusion is that the vulnerability of an ethnic group depends on whether your people are members of the media and if you have the political and economic resources to hurt the government and media if you do not like the portrayal of yourself. Forget about human rights. Not possessing power means that you are everyone's potential scapegoat.

Government is not blameless either, often bending over backwards to please the Jewish community. The sad result is that government representatives often make statements which verge on anti-Semitism, this time directed against that other group of Semites. One ironic example of this involved Canon Borden Purcell, head of the Ontario Human Rights Commission. At a speech given at a Toronto Synagogue he declared that anti-Zionism is really just a form of racial and religious prejudice. He said, "We should all recognize that for the most part anti-Zionism is anti-Semitism."[13] Arab-Canadians, being Semites themselves, were surprised that their support for the Palestinian cause was actually considered racism against their own group. In a few short sentences the good Canon had dismissed the yearnings of an entire people and defamed Arab-Canadians. I suspect his words were guided somewhat by the location and his appraisal of the relative strengths of the two communities in question. The Arabs were clearly dispensable.

Arabs should not have been surprised at this outburst by a government official. It was not the first. Another example was the furor over whether the PLO should be allowed to testify before a Senate committee studying Middle Eastern affairs. The testimony of the PLO representative was very nearly cancelled at the last minute due to pressure from the Jewish community and sympathetic MPs. How can one consider peace in the Middle East without a *thorough* consideration of the Palestinian question. "Thorough" must certainly mean consideration of the Palestinian — and thus PLO — perspective. This point of view was presented by the then Prime Minister Trudeau at a Liberal caucus meeting held to discuss the matter. Trudeau's even-handed approach was very much a case of crying out in the wilderness. The media and many officials loudly proclaimed the PLO to be simply a bunch of terrorists and thugs and that support for the PLO was tantamount to racism. The then Solicitor General, Robert Kaplan, described the PLO as a "major terrorist group," and Rolande de Corneille, Liberal MP, called the decision to let the PLO representative speak "distressing, disappointing and really disgusting." This should not have been too surprising since his riding has a very high proportion of Jewish voters. Liberal MP James Peterson, also from a heavily Jewish riding in Toronto, described the move as "naive and unsophisticated."[14]

This was not all though. The Liberal caucus was really up in arms. One MP went so far as to suggest that Trudeau was giving comfort to the PLO. The Tories were no better. Ontario Premier Davis sent a telegram to Trudeau protesting the invitation to the PLO and both Mulroney (then opposition leader) and his external affairs critic damned the visit. Was their opposition real or a cynical appeal to the Jewish community? Certainly, Mulroney is no stranger to cynicism.

All of this was just the same old thing for the Arab community, just at a higher level than usual. The lesson in all of this is that treatment by the media and government of your ethnic group has nothing to do with justice or fair play. It is simply a matter of politics at its worst. If you are powerful like the Jewish, Italian and other such communities, the politicians and media will love you and plead your case. If you are weak the politicians and media will treat you like dirt. If the Arab community becomes rich, powerful and well-organized, the media and government will suddenly change to being pro-PLO. It is as simple as that.

Issues
As noted earlier, the issues and demands which preoccupy the various ethnic lobby groups vary enormously with the nature of the ethnic

group, its membership and political and economic resources. Still there are some issues which seem to stand head and shoulders above the rest: immigration; employment; racism and human rights; politics in home countries and language and culture.

Immigration

Canada's immigration policies have been and remain a curious mixture of the finest idealism and the crassest political and economic opportunism. On the one hand, Canada's traditional view toward refugees and displaced persons (with the notable exception of the Jews in the Hitler period) has been generous and humanitarian. Recent examples of this high-minded behaviour were the Indo-Chinese "boat people" and the political refugees from Central America. The admission of these individuals was especially remarkable since it occurred during periods of high unemployment, which definitely qualifies as "giving until it hurts." That takes care of the idealism.

The opportunism is more important. Part of this opportunism is of an economic nature. Instead of instituting serious apprenticeship and on the job training programs for existing Canadians, Canadian employers have through their lobbying of government ensured that there will be a constant supply of well-trained and skilled workers as a result of immigration. There is a correspondence between the manpower needs of Canadian industry and the nature of immigration. During the building and developing boom following the Second World War we saw a massive influx of trades people from Italy. The demand for labour of all kinds in the late sixties and early seventies saw a massive influx from Third World countries. That wasn't all that has come from Third World countries. The sudden conversion of immigration policy to a non–racist orientation resulted in enormous amounts of capital flowing from such Third World countries as Hong Kong, Uganda and India. In addition, Third World immigration has been very helpful in compensating for the inadequacy or unwillingness of Canadian medical schools to produce a sufficient number of doctors and other medical personnel.

This economic opportunism has definitely been good for the Canadian economy, but it has been a disaster for the countries of origin of the new immigrants. It seems strange that Canada should trumpet its desire to see economic development and well-being in the Third World and then rape these same countries for their capital and most skilled and most critically required citizens. This is most evident when one considers that the present policy is directed toward attracting those who are likely to bring lots of money with them when they come. If you don't have relatives in Canada or qualify as a political refugee in danger of death, the only other option is to be rich. If you are poor, forget it.

Immigration policy has been an unusually active arena for lobbying activity. Because it touches so many exposed nerves, it is a hotly contested matter. Indeed, it is really the only area where influence is brought to bear by representatives of the two majority groups. In French Canada, the Quebec government has fought hard to retain the sole right to determine the guidelines for who may immigrate to Quebec (French-speaking only), and in English Canada, business and labour groups have lobbied for and against immigration based on prevailing economic conditions. Sometimes the grass roots gets into the fun as well, as with the National Citizens' Coalition's mobilization of public support against letting in more "boat people."

Ethnic lobbies get very involved in immigration issues. The West Indian communities have lobbied hard to get the government to recognize common-law marriages and illegitimate children when deciding whether or not to allow a potential immigrant in on the grounds of reuniting family members. Almost all groups have lobbied government never to return to a North European immigration policy. The Jewish community has successfully lobbied for the elimination of visas for Israeli citizens wishing to visit Canada. Then there are the innumerable pleas concerning immigration or deportation hearings. While the occasional case gets fought in the media or at the highest levels of government, the vast majority of lobbying takes place in the constituency offices of MPs across the country. Sadly many of these cases are not decided on their merits but on the political value of those lobbying the MP. One Toronto MP told me that electoral success for MPs is often determined by how successful he or she was in getting landed immigrant status for the brother-in-law or aunt of an influential leader of some important ethnic group. The poor, as always, get the "bum's rush" and empty promises.

Employment
Jobs represent life to immigrants. Excellent jobs represent status and comfort and acceptance by the larger community. They represent exactly the same things to those whose families have been in Canada for a long time. Regrettably, jobs are in short supply and the result is a very fierce competition between immigrants and citizens. Those born here, of course, have enormous advantages — they speak the language of business, they know how things work, they have contacts, they are

part of the culture and so experience no culture shock and do not unwittingly offend the cultural sensibilities of others. Traditionally, immigrants have just gritted their teeth, worked hard and tried to give their children the education and advantages that would ensure that they would achieve full and equal status in the wider society. But these are different times. Newcomers no longer are prepared to be patient. Lobbying and bringing influence to bear on government evens up the score and speeds up the process.

One side to this lobbying is the traditional use of influence exercised at the level of individual jobs. Often this involves approaching a politician or political boss. Usually it is just a case of the official making a few calls and "presto" there is a job. It might be at the municipal level in, say, a road maintenance crew or in an office, it might involve low-level patronage units like the Ministry of Supply and Services or a job in a liquor store, in the case of provincial patronage. Then again, it could be some of the lovely and high-paying morsels in the federal pork barrel. The bad news is, there is no free lunch. If you get something from a politician, he or she will want something in return. Largesse from politicians to members of ethnic groups is given with the expectation that this will translate into votes, contributions and campaign workers. The practice need not involve just low level goodies. Some leaders of ethnic communities are extremely sophisticated and wordly-wise. One "backroom boy" told me with just a little sadness that ethnic community bosses have become a little greedy. They are no longer content with slaps on the back and warm thanks. They want to be able to loot the system, just as their native born Canadian brothers and sisters have done for centuries. And they are starting to get their chance, with real "goodies" like directorships on the boards of Air Canada, the CBC and other top-flight crown corporations. Then there are always the glory jobs in Human Rights Commissions, advisory councils and other cogs in the government multiculturalism machine.

This lobbying for individual jobs has been augmented recently by the use of lobbying for a bigger piece of the pie for the group as a whole, always, I might add, couched in the highest moral terms (human rights, the fight against racism, equality and that sort of thing) rather than the more appropriate "gimme!" One of the newer techniques in the quest for jobs involves demands for affirmative action and quotas based on race and origin.

Normally, this would not have gone anywhere. It is clearly a form of reverse racism and will be extremely costly for companies in terms of administrative costs and lower staff morale. However, leaders have shown a touch of genius. They have formed an alliance with one group that does count for a great deal in government eyes — the feminist lobby — and together they are carrying the day. The best example of the working of this alliance was the Royal Commission on equity in the workplace (translation: sexual and racial preferential hiring) under Rosalie Abella. It is hard not to be cynical about this one. The results of the commission's findings probably could have been released even before the Commission was struck. The government was facing an election and wanted to shore up its support among women and ethnic voters. Therefore, the call went out for a report that would call for reverse discrimination in favour of those voters the Liberal government was seeking. Certainly Abella held up her end of the bargain. She recommended just what the doctor (or Prime Minister) ordered. Unfortunately for her the timing was bad. Her report came out after the defeat of her political masters. Pity.

Government commissions have proved extremely useful to the efforts of groups lobbying for affirmative action. The major benefit is that these commissions enshrine the lobbyists' points of view as virtual dogma. The research findings and recommendations are quoted uncritically and so frequently by both government and media that they soon become accepted as fact rather than mere opinion. The political motivations and patronage which underlay them are soon forgotten, and all that is left is a document that soon comes to challenge the ten commandments for credibility.

The question of affirmative action and quotas is a nasty one since there will almost certainly be unintended effects that may make the lives of members of various ethnic groups more difficult in the future. One of the effects will be to create racist feelings in many of those who will be hurt by these policies. There is a simple fact about Canada at present and that is that we have a "zero-sum" game in the economy. (A "zero-sum" game is a game where, if I win, you lose.) If members of visible minorities are hired in a preferential fashion, that means members of the majority group will not get the jobs. That is asking a lot of any population. If people get jobs or promotions on the basis of their race or sociological characteristics, the generation of racist and sexist feelings among those who are being discriminated against is virtually inevitable. It is already happening. The government won't admit it and the media won't discuss it, but it is a fact.

Racism and Human Rights

Concern with this issue cuts across all those groups that might possibly be affected by racism. There are groups in Canadian society for which the question of racism has an immediate and acute relevance — the Third World immigrants who came here in such large numbers starting in the late 1960s. These groups have had considerable success in influencing government to accept their position that the protection of visible minorities from racism is a major priority. Part of their success has come from the powerful allies who have joined them in this battle. The media has used its full weight to popularize their positions and government has responded enthusiastically to their demands, setting up new laws, guidelines for the media and the educational system, affirmative action programs and Royal Commissions to promote these policies. Other ethnic groups with powerful political resources — like the Jewish and Italian communities — have used their contacts to promote these demands and the more liberal churches have latched onto race and human rights issues as part of their constant search for relevance. Feminist and other social change movements have made common cause with visible minorities especially in conjunction with lobbying for heftier censorship, affirmative action and employment quotas and the redistribution of power and income.

Just as with affirmative action, the lobbyists for more punitive human rights measures have found Royal Commissions the royal road to instant credibility, media attention and government funding. This is not to suggest that this is the only technique that these groups employ or that the federal government is the only target of their attention. Far from it. One of the major targets of their lobbying is made up of organs of information. The reasoning is that if you control the sources of information, the means of communication and education, you have it all. In this they are probably correct. Targets of their influence are the media, the educational system and advertising.

The media have proved to be easy targets. First of all, the government has been good enough to do much of these lobbies' work for them through the use of the Broadcast Act and CRTC guidelines which forbid the portrayal of minorities in such a way as to incite hatred toward them. That seems pretty innocuous and noble, but unfortunately, it often goes far beyond what was originally intended. Guidelines are sufficiently vague that no one really knows what the government means and, given this vagueness and the onerous penalties for transgressing the guidelines, there is an enormous amount of self-censorship which goes far beyond what is reasonable or was intended. The old stereotypes where blacks, orientals and Jews were always either evil or stupid have been replaced by new stereotypes where *all* members of these groups are *always* exceptionally good, intelligent and capable. The media just don't seem to be able to get it right.

Other lobbying techniques that work can involve direct lobbying of the media and the government as issues come up. One of the more celebrated incidents involved a CTV television show which seemed to claim that so many Chinese students were in the professional faculties in Toronto universities that Caucasian students did not have a chance of getting positions and, thus, access to those professions. This show was not one of the year's more popular ones in Chinese–Canadian homes and politicians' and media executives' telephones rang off the hooks as leaders in the Chinese–Canadian community exercised their considerable influence. CTV executives were only too happy to apologize abjectly. Then there was the CTV reporter visiting a Persian Gulf state who agreed to read a portion of the news on the state television station. The item that got him in trouble was one which labelled an Israeli leader a criminal and terrorist. He was fired. Then again, any show which portrays the Mafia, that organization which we are told does not exist — as having members who are Italian–Canadian and Italian–American, always provokes an endless stream of complaints about racism. Mafiosi of Italian origin? Ridiculous! Everyone knows they are Swiss.

The educational system is an ever popular target. Textbooks are examined in great detail by provincial bureaucrats who ensure that the racial backgrounds of the characters in the books reflect the composition of the community. There is some sense in this; however, the bureaucrats and ideologues manage with unerring skill to perform this task with the ultimate in ridiculous results. In Alberta, for instance, some of the fallout from the Keegstra affair was the removal of some Ukrainian-language textbooks which seemed in the opinion of the Alberta "thought police" to be of an excessively nationalistic character. Not racist, mind you, but too nationalistic. Then Alberta bureaucrats felt that a book called *The City is for People* portrayed visible minorities in insufficient numbers and when it did portray them, did not portray them often enough in high status situations. This same text had been used without complaint in Ontario schools for some time, but when they found that Alberta had tried the book and found it guilty, Ontario officials decided to give it the fifth degree as well.

Those groups which have set themselves the task of combatting racism claim that advertising has a role to play in the problem. One of the most radical lobbies in this area must surely be the Toronto-based Urban Alliance on Racial Equality, whose president, Carol Tator, seems to be unusually successful at capturing media attention. The extent of media coverage is all the more remarkable because Tator's lobby has a membership that could fill a telephone booth — just. Still, her success at getting attention has politicians running scared. She recently charged that racism was rampant in advertising. This charge was trumpeted by the media, and both government and the advertising industry caved in immediately. With many *mea culpas* they promised to mend their ways. The advertisers promised to right the wrong, and the government assigned people to monitor the situation and enforce compliance.

Politics in Home Countries

One of the problems of personal change is that all of us see ourselves as we were two, three, four or more years ago. We carry emotional baggage with us wherever we go. This is true at the individual level. It is also true at the group level. Various ethnic groups are continually lobbying federal, provincial and even municipal governments to exercise their power and influence so as to either bring down or influence governments in their home countries. Most of the time this takes on an understandable, but pathetic, quality. It is difficult to shed a lifetime of conditioning and nationalistic or parochial feeling simply because one now lives in another country.

Sometimes this struggle has the quality of a just, but hopeless battle. A good example would be the efforts of Canadians of Jewish and East European descent to force the Canadian government to meddle in the internal affairs of the Soviet Union. This is a hopeless task if there ever was one. Occasionally it results in the release of the odd political prisoner, but usually these lobby efforts come to naught. About the only result of demonstrations, mail-in campaigns and meetings with MPs and cabinet ministers is to enhance the nationalistic and parochial sentiments of the group members and give everyone concerned a nice warm feeling that something is being done. Other examples might involve South Africa and South and Central America. Nothing significant comes of it. The governments of these countries do not change their policies and the Canadian government does nothing. How could it be otherwise? After all, we may not like other governments and their policies, but we have to co-exist on the same planet.

Often these lobby demands are made to cabinet ministers who are invited to speak at celebrations marking national days of the home countries. The advantage of such an approach is that the minister is almost always softened up in advance by folkdancing and singing, good food and drink and pretty girls in native costumes. In addition, the minister is vastly outnumbered. It is the most polite and delightful form of ambush known to man. A typical case of this was the get together of the Macedonian Patriotic Organization in 1979. Norm Cafik, the minister then responsible for multiculturalism, was the guest of honour. The request was simple. The Macedonians wanted him to get the Canadian government to press the Yugoslavian, Greek and Bulgarian governments to give up parts of their countries for the creation of a new and independent Macedonian state. Norm turned them down flat. The Macedonians must not have many votes. Usually the government obfuscates a bit before it lets such matters die a quiet death. Such directness is uncommon.

Things are not always as civilized as this. Sometimes representatives of ethnic groups get nasty. There have been bombings by fringe elements in the Croatian–Canadian community, some small support for fanatical attacks by Armenians on Turkish diplomats, abortive attempts by some Guyanese–Canadians to purchase arms in the United States for an overthrow of the government in Guyana and contributions by Irish–Canadians to groups which front for the IRA. The worst of all has to have been support — financial and political — for the Sikh secessionist movement in India. The Indian government claimed that some of the weapons held by Sikh rebels had been purchased with money from Canada. Some members of the Sikh community claimed to be part of the underground and called for "hit teams" to assassinate prime Minister Indira Gandhi. As we know, such a hit team was ultimately successful and horrid internecine massacres followed the assassination. Some Sikhs celebrated the assassination in Canada with dancing and rejoicing in the streets and by offering sweets to passersby. This did not represent one of the high points of multiculturalism in Canada.

One of the more fascinating examples of this "fists across the sea" approach is that of the Latvian community in its attempt to resist the Russification of the Latvian portion of the Soviet Empire. The birth rate of the Latvians is so low and the rate of immigration by Russians so high that soon Latvia will lose its distinctive character. (It's similar to the problem of francophones in Quebec.) Part of the problem has been one of obtaining adequate housing in Latvia to allow larger families. At present, many Latvian–Canadians are sending money secretly to bribe Soviet officials and provide money to Latvians for the acquisition of the housing and other necessities which would make larger families possible.

Language and Culture
It is hard to break with the past. There are so many associations and memories involving the country of our birth that if we have to leave that country, we carry with us to our new home a nostalgia and longing for our culture and language. And it is frightening to find that one's children no longer know or value the old language and customs. The desire to try and retain and reinforce the old often leads to demands that government provide funds and facilities to promote and teach the languages and customs of the various countries of origin. Usually, this is reasonable and involves small (by government terms of reference) grants to the ethnic press, the foreign language book publishing industry, cultural societies and after-hours language instruction for immigrant children. The problems begin when ethnic lobbies and their political allies begin to lose their sense of proportion and draft truly grandiose schemes for the use of public money and institutions. The results are often wasteful, occasionally disastrous.

A good example of what can happen is seen in the heritage language programs now beginning to surface in boards of education across the country. Toronto, for example, is a fabulous mixture of virtually all of the races and nations in the world, and it is not surprising that there would be an enormous demand for the teaching of "heritage languages." Indeed, various ethnic communities have long been involved in teaching these languages to their children as a way of ensuring the survival of their cultures. The classes often took place in church basements and community centres after school or on the weekend and the quality of instruction was often quite high. There was never a problem. Then during the seventies the development of economic and political power by many groups encouraged a new and enhanced sense of pride in their heritage. The reasoning of many was that this rise in the importance and the idea of multiculturalism as a whole should be recognized by educational authorities. After all, their languages are in no way inferior to French and English. Having to teach their children these languages after hours seemed to imply a second class status. Rather, these heritage languages should be taught during regular school hours by Board of Education staff. The problem was that not every child was likely to want to learn Modern Greek, Serbian or

Macedonian. What to do with these other children and their teachers in the meantime?

Daytime heritage language programs began about seven years ago in a controlled and experimental fashion in two Toronto schools, now expanded to 12 schools with 113 classes in 8 languages. In theory, teachers are supposed to run remedial or enrichment classes for other students during these periods and everything is supposed to work out just fine. The immigrant students will have increased self-esteem as a result of the teaching of their parents' native language. Official recognition will raise their standing in their own eyes and in the eyes of their fellow students with a lessening of any racial and ethnic tensions which might otherwise occur. The theory was great. The practice has been terrible.

Most unhappy with this program are the teachers. No one bothered to consider that teachers were being asked to work an extra half hour without any advance consultation as to their feelings and without extra pay. Imagine how you would feel if your boss called you into his or her office one day and informed you that from now on you would be working an extra half hour a day for nothing. Toronto teachers were furious. They reacted by refusing, as a group, to supervise any after class activities like sports or clubs and made it clear that the "extended day" was going to be the one non-monetary issue in upcoming negotiations. Separate school teachers indicated that they would probably follow the same path as their public colleagues if the situation did not change.

The real losers were the students. For a time many found themselves engaging in busy work or idle time during the time set aside for the teaching of the heritage languages. In response, the Board of Education got the bright idea of employing artists, writers, poets and so on to speak to classes during this time. The bill for this was to be $150,000. Some parents branded this as "babysitting." Furthermore, the 90 percent of the students not in these classes found that as a result of language programs they now had to be in school for an extra thirty minutes and could no longer take part in extra-curricular activities as before. They were not pleased.

As noted before, part of the rationale for these classes was a belief that they would result in more inter-racial and inter-ethnic group harmony and an enhanced sense of self-worth by the students taking the classes. To some extent, they have resulted in quite the opposite. Some ethnic leaders claim that the furor over the question has resulted in more racist feeling in the schools. Alberto DiGiovanni, the leader of the Italian parents, said that the debate has resulted in racial incidents at several playgrounds: "Some students are being told that because of the foreigners, we have to stay an extra half hour and we cannot take part in sport activity."[15] Keren Braithwaite, a spokesperson for a group of black parents, said that the Black Culture Program was called "the nigger program"[16] during a conversation in one Toronto school playground.

There was a nasty reverse racism and self-righteousness on the part of those supporting the program as well. Teachers were the objects at whom charges of racism were levelled as well as parents who spoke out against the programs. One woman who fought against her son's school being declared a heritage language school found herself branded a bigot: "They made me feel like I was a bigot because I wanted my son to get a sound education in the basics."[17] Indeed there seemed some reason to believe that many ethnic leaders were a bit too free with the charges of racism. The *Globe and Mail* reported: "Spokesmen for several ethnic groups say that many critics of the program are racists and that teachers encourage racism by dragging the heritage language program into a labor dispute."[18] That pretty much takes care of everyone who disagrees with their viewpoint.

Obviously a situation does not get as big and as nasty as this without a lot of help from lobbyists, politicians and special interest groups who had good intentions yet paved this particular road to hell.

The real origins of this crisis lie in the NDP's domination of the Toronto Board of Education; no small victory for the party. The board's annual budget is larger than the entire budgets of most municipalities in the country — in the $300 million range in 1984. The control exercised by the NDP is very tight. The caucus meets with party officials and members of the Labour Council on a monthly basis to decide on the policies the board will pursue. Once this meeting is held, the matter is virtually settled. The automatic majority clicks into position and that is that. One thing the NDP members have done is to ensure that they have left-wing militants in as many sensitive positions as possible, so that if the party should lose its majority on the Board it would still wield some measure of control through these unelected officials. There is another and more pressing reason, and that is that they prove extremely useful in furthering policy in the here and now. Such was the case with the "heritage language" affair.

One of the key bodies in the "heritage language" matter was the School Community Relations Department, employees whose stated goal is to smooth out relations between the community and the school system but who in fact tend to be hand-picked plants whose purpose is to facilitate and lobby for a shift to the left in board policies. The language issue illustrates how this works. This department consists of what one trustee referred to as "sixties radicals." Having left-wing politics is very important in getting a job in this department. The other major asset is that you be a member of one of the major ethnic groups in the city. These people are extremely powerful in influencing parents. They speak the languages of the parents and are a part of their culture. This means that the parents who are unable to understand English well — and that is very many — are totally dependent on these people for any information they might get about the issues facing the school system. Their other asset is that they are in a position of authority in the parents' eyes. This lends credibility and commands respect and obedience from parents.

Prior to the meetings which finally resulted in acceptance of the heritage language program, members of this department spent a great deal of time lobbying their respective communities on the necessity and desirability of active support. Often the program was sold on the basis of opposition to racists who were opposed to the program, so opposition to racism and nationalistic pride got mixed in. Not to support the program became tantamount to caving in to racism. Once the time for meetings came, this alliance of NDP trustees and employees really swung into action. At one meeting people were bused in at five o'clock to fill the board chambers. Those who spoke to oppose the program were summarily dismissed with charges of racism. Once the program was approved, there was the little matter of the Provincial Government to attend to. Officially, this program was against the law; the Education Act says that the languages of instruction are English and French. Pressure was put on the provincial government and a ministerial order exempted the Toronto board from the law. The matter was over, except for the increased conflict and racism which was to result.

Native People

So far we have looked at groups that have come to Canada in the last hundred or so years. Indeed, when most of us think of racism or the problems of multiculturalism, we almost always think of immigrant populations and second or third generation Canadians with their roots abroad. This betrays a very common blindspot in the Canadian psyche.

There is one group that has suffered more than others and continues to do so — the native people.

Consider the situation of native people in Canada. They and their ancestors have been residents for tens of thousands of years. When the settlers came, native people were killed by white soldiers, ravaged by diseases imported from Europe and finally herded into concentration camps called reserves. The vast majority of their lands were stolen from them and when the soldiers, merchants and settlers had done their worst, the missionaries and representatives of various Christian churches finished the job. They destroyed the old cultures and religions and left people with values and beliefs that made no sense to their lives.

When you are in such a situation, it is difficult to know where to start and how. You have no resources, no confidence and almost no knowledge of how the "white man's government" works. But the native peoples' lobbies have done remarkably well over the last fifteen years from such a cold start.

Probably the major event which sparked a revival of the native peoples' movement was the caravan which started in British Columbia and ended in Ottawa at Parliament Hill. One of the demands of the members of the caravan was constitutional recognition of treaty and aboriginal rights in Canada. (This has since appeared in a somewhat watered down version in the new Canadian constitution.) The caravan ended September 30, 1974, the same day the thirtieth Parliament was opening, in a riot involving the RCMP's tactical squad and 200 native demonstrators. In a sense this was not surprising given the general tenor of native agitation at the time. During the early seventies there was a serious split in many native groups between the leadership of bands and extremely militant young people who often formed warriors' groups or societies which engaged in direct action. Examples of such action were the armed occupation of Anicinabe Park near Kenora, Ontario, and the seizing of an abandoned river mill that was dubbed the Native Peoples' Embassy. Usually these actions were peaceful, but not always. Probably one of the worst examples took place in the Caughnaiwaga reserve near Montreal. On October 15, 1973 the Warrior Society, a militant group of Caughnaiwaga Mohawks, conducted a systematic house to house search for eighty white families to whom it had sent eviction notices three months earlier. In the early afternoon the Quebec Police Force riot squad marched onto the reserve to prevent an outbreak of violence. This violence was not long in coming. By the end of the day three officers had been injured (one had been struck in the face with an axe), three police cars had been overturned and 500 Mohawks had stormed the local jail and released several of the men who had been arrested.

Incidents like these had a profound impact on the native organizations' leaders. These leaders moved to shore up their support among their members by moving to radical stances themselves. This had two effects. First of all it eliminated the challenge to their own leadership by radicals. Second, it resulted in greater success in lobbying governments at all levels. It had an effect on governments too, especially the federal government, which has major responsibility for native people under the Indian Act. Government began to realize that if further violence involving almost 400,000 people was to be avoided, the demands of native people must be addressed. One of the first acts following the riot on Parliament Hill was the formation of a joint working group of representatives from the federal Cabinet and the National Indian Brotherhood to try and solve some native grievances. This group was not especially effective and later died out. It did, however, establish a precedent leading to the involvement of all aboriginal people in the constitutional process.

An even more important result of aboriginal militancy was a new and serious government approach to funding native peoples' lobby groups. The federal government in particular began to fund native lobbies in such a way that they could better articulate and express their concerns and demands to government. The result has been the development of a number of effective, highly professional and successful native peoples' lobbies.

There are about 400,000 people who might be classed as "native people." These are then subdivided into a number of groups — Inuit, Status Indians, Non-Status Indians, Dene, Métis, etc. These are then subdivided into regions, bands and sexes, each with their own needs and demands. Often the needs of some groups conflict with or are diametrically opposed to those of others. Obviously, such a situation creates problems not only for government in trying to understand what is what but also for native leaders trying to hammer out common positions.

At present some of the major players in the native peoples' lobby are:

1. *Assembly of First Nations.* This is perhaps the most powerful native group in the nation. It has a number of leaders with national profiles, David Ahenakew, the National Chief, and

Georges Erasmus, vice president and former president of the Dene Nation. It represents most of Canada's 320,000 Treaty Indians and a great majority (570) of the Indian bands.

2. *The Native Council of Canada.* Under President Smokey Bruyère, this group represents Métis and Non-Status Indians. Until 1983, it represented all of these people. Now it no longer represents Western Métis.

3. *Métis National Council.* Its president is Clem Chartier. This group represents Western Métis. These people broke away from the Native Council of Canada and formed their own group just before the Constitutional Conference in 1983.

4. *The Inuit Committee on National Issues.* This group, headed by John Amagoalik, represents the Inuit of the far North.

5. *The Dene Nation.* This group brings together all the native people, with the exception of Inuit, who live in the Mackenzie Basin (from Northern Alberta to the Arctic). Included are Métis, and both status and non-status Indians.

This in no way properly captures the complexity of the groups representing native people. There are provincial and territorial associations representing Indians and/or Métis and/or Inuit, groups representing tribes, bands or nations, womens' groups, single-issue groups. The list is endless. Worse yet, they often disagree on major issues. The manner in which different positions are formulated and presented often complicates the resolution of problems.

Self-Government
One issue upon which virtually all native groups agree is the need for self-government. This issue involves a concept very close to that of the Parti Québécois' "sovereignty association." There is no clear understanding of exactly what "self-government" would mean in practical terms. A full page advertisement placed in some major Canadian newspapers in May 1984, said that it would involve native people having control over: the use and development of their lands and resources; the money received from the sale of minerals, oil and gas on their lands; courts and law enforcement on their lands; their education; social and child welfare services and health care services.

This concept has a fascinating history, especially in as much as it shows how easily politicians can change their minds under pressure. Former Prime Minister Trudeau opened a constitutional conference in 1984 with a plea for native self-government as a way to end centuries of injustice. This was the same Trudeau who had originally seen assimilation as the only path to improving the lot of native people. After Trudeau made this sterling appeal, federal, provincial and native officials worked through the night in vain to try and come up with a compromise that would at least make a symbolic gesture of support for native rights, but no one had a clear idea of what these rights might be. While it is true that the constitution states that aboriginal rights have always existed, it does not define what they are. Trudeau need not have worried too much though, because this conference was just the second of four meetings which are to be held by 1987 aimed at defining what unique rights native people have in law. The ultimate sticking point in getting a constitutional amendment lies with the provinces anyway. Under the constitution seven out of ten provinces with 50 percent of the population must approve any amendment before it becomes law. Trudeau's draft amendment presented at this conference received the approval of only three premiers.

In spite of provincial opposition, self-government remains a key demand of all groups. The Assembly of First Nations has been particularly active in lobbying for this and has shown great sophistication in its lobbying techniques. Besides the advocacy advertising already mentioned to help mould public opinion, it has also lobbied heavily using Gallup polls to prove that Canadians support this concept.

Women's Rights
Probably the hottest potato that native organizations have had to deal with in recent years is the matter of clause 12(1)b of the Indian Act, which specifies that native women who marry non-natives lose all property and status. However, it appears that this restriction does not apply to native men who marry "out of the faith," as it were. In an age of women's rights such is a "no-no." This one caught male native leaders off balance. They were used to making charges of discrimination against all and sundry, but when it happened to them, they were considerably less than pleased.

The start of this whole matter was the challenge to the act by Janette Lavelle in 1973 in the Supreme Court. She lost. Next was Sandra Lovelace, a New Brunswick Indian, who took her appeal of the law to the UN. The UN Human Rights Committee ruled in her favour. Apparently Canada had signed an international covenant in 1976 and this clause put Canada in violation of that agreement. Next in the line of petitioners headed for the UN were Paula Sissom and Laura Nadeau, also from New Brunswick. The New Brunswick Human Rights Commission backed up their efforts to petition the UN Human Rights Committee where Canada stood condemned as a human rights violator right up there with Chile and South Africa. At this point the feminist lobby got into the act. The Native Women's Association of Canada sought support from the Canadian Advisory Council on the Status of Women and other women's groups. This is where the native rights lobbyists found out what real lobbying was. Unfortunately, they were the victims of it.

What followed was a merciless barrage of media propaganda against this clause and against the "evil" and male native leaders who for no reason, other than pure nastiness (or so the media and feminists seemed to be suggesting), wanted to perpetuate this horror. Everything was cast in the starkest black and white terms. At virtually no time did native leaders have a chance for a fair presentation of their side of the story. Despite the propaganda onslaught, they too had a point of view. Their objection was two-fold. They feared that repeal would prejudice their bands' ability to decide who was and was not going to be a member, and were terrified that the potential addition of 23,000 women and 40,000 children to band rolls asking for money and services would bankrupt them. Never mind their arguments. The media and feminists had made up their minds and nothing else mattered. The politicians caved in (as always) and twisted the arms of native leaders. A bill designed to amend the act was rushed through. Unfortunately for the intrepid feminist lobbyists, an Inuit Senator, Charlie Watt, felt that the whole thing had an air of indecent haste and since the bill required unanimous support, it failed.

Politicians and Government

Thus far, the impression is one of a poor harassed collection of politicians and governments hard pressed by a group of highly independent and tough ethnic lobbyists who are able to bring to bear irresistible pressure to which the only response is acquiescence. There is some truth to this, but there is some question as to who is the puppet-master and who the puppet.

Again, the federal government originally had no intention of promoting or supporting the idea of multiculturalism; this was strictly a side-show to the real action — bilingualism and the enshrinement of the compact between French and English Canada. The Feds realized they would have to throw a sop to the ethnic communities if they were ever going to sell bilingualism west of the Ontario–Manitoba border and so espoused the idea of multiculturalism. At first this was a forced and highly reluctant conversion. The federal government was dragged kicking and screaming to this new ideological marriage bed but what followed these initially forced trysts was a great love affair based on self-interest.

The politicians grew to love multiculturalism; it provided them with a new technique for social control and electoral success. The bureaucrats loved it; civil servants found in it new career paths and new ways of increasing the size and budgets of their departments and thus their power. The leaders of various ethnic groups loved it; it gave them real importance for the first time, and with it, fabulous job and funding possibilities. It opened up the doors to them for real power. In a masochistic way the English and French Canadian groups loved it too; a simmering and deep-seated guilt that had grown out of the civil rights movement in the United States and national liberation struggles in the Third World cried out for sackcloth, breastbeating and penance. Multiculturalism and the human rights industry, with their accompanying finger pointing and accusatory laws, regulations, royal commissions and media guidelines, offered that penance and punishment for which remorseful Roman Catholic and Orange souls cried out. The Gordon Fairweathers of this country made certain that they got that which they desired. With the flood of Third World immigration during the late sixties and throughout the seventies the doctrine of multiculturalism went from theory to dogma.

Funding
One of the major tools government uses to control and manipulate multicultural groups is funding, which is enormous and takes place at all levels. The federal government is of particular interest in this area, both because of the amounts involved and the rather shameless way it uses funding to manipulate opinion and behaviour of ethnic groups. It is probably impossible to develop a total figure for the amount of funding for multicultural groups because of the way in which it is handed out — every ministry gives support through various programs. The major conduits for government funding are Employment and Immigration, the Secretary of State, Indian and Northern Affairs and the Ministry of Justice.

What this funding does is give the government enormous control over the groups that are supposed to be lobbying it. All the government has to do is cease funding the organizations and many would go under within the year. Take the ethnic press, for example. These companies and individuals learned prior to the last federal election just how vulnerable they are to government pressure. Government advertising represents a major part of their revenues; for many it is the difference between success or failure. One recent example of how government uses this spending power involved a $200,000 ad campaign placed by the federal government in early 1984 in many ethnic papers. Very quickly the placement came to suggest arm-twisting. Some papers received three to five times as much advertising as similarly sized competitors, some received none at all. Czaba Gaal, editor of Canada's largest Hungarian-language newspaper and manager of a company which prints almost all of the ethnic papers in Metro Toronto, accused the government of "trying to blackmail the ethnic media. An election is coming."[19] Furthermore he expressed the view that his paper was seen as against the Liberals and for Mulroney and as a result was getting fewer of the multiculturalism ads than his smaller Hungarian-language competitors. It was, he felt, the government's way of reminding him "who controls the money." Another publisher said that "this kind of thing always happens when an election comes around." Albert Vanderheide, publisher of the Dutch-language *Windmill Herald* in New Westminster B.C., said that the "unexplainable and contradictory campaign suggests we're back to politics in determining the use of government advertising."[20]

Control of groups by funding is endemic in this area. In Ontario, NDP leader Bob Rae charged that the Ontario government was cutting aid to agencies that help immigrants, so that it can do more of the work itself and get more of the credit. The fact that this would hurt the valuable work already being done by community groups was of little interest. As Rae put it, "You've got to show some respect for the expertise of the people in the field every day . . . I think the government of Ontario and the Tory party of Ontario is determined to maintain itself in power."[21]

In some cases the government acts as a catalyst for the creation of ethnic lobby groups that previously had not existed. An example is the National Congress of Italian–Canadians founded in 1974. The two day conference which set up the organization was funded by a $9,500 multiculturalism grant which paid for such expenses as travel and accommodation costs for conference delegates.[22] Fascinating. The government paid for and helped to organize the creation of a pressure group whose purpose was to lobby the very same government. These set up costs were just the beginning. The National Congress, like so many other ethnic lobbies, went back to take nourishment at the breast of Mother Government on a continuing basis.

This dependence on government for funding casts some doubt on the independence of these lobby groups and ethnic organizations. Nevertheless, this is nothing compared to those organizations which are apparent reverse interest groups, that is, organizations which are the creation of government and which are virtual fronts for the government. One such example involved an Italian–Canadian social service organization, the Alliance Community Services.

Originally, this group billed itself as a counselling agency for the Italian–Canadians. If their intention was to raise the party's profile, mildly famous (or infamous) when it was discovered in January of 1984 that the group received a $580,000 grant. This was outrageous for a number of reasons. First of all, it was unheard of that an agency which had not previously existed should receive such an enormous grant. Second, the long established service groups for the Italian community had never received such a large grant. It began to look as if the agency might in fact be a Liberal Party front. The board of managers and senior officers were predominantly Liberal Party activists. Several had previously written a paper on how to raise the party's profile among Italian-Canadians. If their intention was to raise the party's profile, they succeeded. The furor over the agency led to the discovery of the $300 million national program called Special Employment Initiatives Grants. (This was indeed special since a disporportionate portion of the grants went to Liberal ridings; this was not too surprising since the grants were being initiated by Liberal MPs rather than federal employment and labour departments.)

Patronage

In the multicultural mosaic there is no lack of patronage jobs that pay too much, demand too little and are too much fun for anyone in their right mind to want to jeopardize them by stepping out of line. Certainly, if I had had better luck at birth and my "demographics" had been right, I would be looking for a nice cushy job with one of the many multicultural advisory commissions. They are wonderful. The problem is that the government uses them to control ethnic groups and to manipulate debate on vital issues and the media's expression of them. Take, for example, the fifteen person council set up by the Quebec government to advise it on policies involving immigration and "ethnic affairs." The appointments had the strong scent of patronage and political control, since the government never bothered consulting the ethnic groups involved as to whom they would like to see appointed. Still, for real corruption and manipulation you could never go wrong with the Trudeau regime. Speaking of the federal government's advisory committee on multiculturalism, the then head of the National Congress of Italian-Canadians, Dr. Laureano Leone, said, "The Multiculturalism Program relies on a National Consultative Committee whose membership, we think, is too partisan in favour of government. As a reflexive voice of the groups themselves, the present structure of the Committee is unsatisfactory."[23] The effect of these patronage or "sweetheart" appointments is that the government is able to ensure that the government gets what it wants and is able to control what is thought, recommended and done in the multicultural area. This does not apply just to advisory councils, but to policy making, implementation and enforcement — human rights commissions, multicultural directorates, royal commissions, studies, etc.

Legitimacy

Funding and jobs are not the only tools available to government when attempting to manipulate multicultural lobbies or ethnic groups. Another technique that is frequently and successfully used is the dispensing of legitimacy by government to selected individuals and groups in the multicultural community. Government is able to determine what leaders and groups will be successful by means of its power to decide to whom it will listen and whom it will appoint to various commissions, study groups and advisory bodies. Being chosen means instant credibility with the media, other multicultural groups and one's own ethnic group. Conversely, if the government will not listen to you, your influence and power is zero. Your base of support is almost certain to melt away if this should happen.

In fairness to the government this decision as to who is *the* representative group of a given ethnic group is not an easy one. The former Minister of Multiculturalism, David Collinette, told me that one of the problems is that some of the ethnic groups are in fact fronts for the governments of the home countries. He cited the problem which he had as Minister in deciding which of the two major Filipino groups to pick as the representative group for that community. The matter was finally decided when his officials advised him that one was actually a front for the Marcos government. Of course, not all of the decisions are as clean as this one. There was a problem for one of the Chinese community organizations when a rumour circulated that it was an NDP front. It found that its channels of funds and access had mysteriously dried up until it could explain its side of the story and convince the Liberal government that it would never dream of supporting the NDP. Once explained, all was well again.

Direct Government Action

We have looked at many indirect techniques used by government to influence and manipulate multicultural and ethnic lobby groups. Indirect means are not the only ones available. Sometimes, the government takes no chances and gets into the ring itself. The most prominent examples are the federal and provincial human rights commissions, which are often a means of controlling ethnic communities and their leaders. Apart from the much touted noble purpose of improving the human condition, there are a couple of reasons for their existence even more important than the stated ones — to dispense patronage to members of the ethnic communities and to shore up ethnic support for the government in power.

The patronage quality of these commissions is obvious and exists in all of them. In Ontario, for instance, the commission there was until recently the personal pork barrel of Roy McMurtry, the former Attorney General. The appointees were not all good Tories (although some were); McMurtry was more subtle than that. He wanted people who would be relatively easy to control and who would not cause too much trouble for the party with the white majority. He also wanted people who would be personally loyal to himself. The Saskatchewan Commission was used by the former NDP government as a patronage funnel as well. Indeed, a little orgy of house cleaning took place in 1984 when a number of these NDP patronage appointments were dumped. Two had obvious partisan connections: Louise Simard, who took a leave of absence from the commission to run (unsuccessfully) for the NDP, and Bill Rafoss, who had been an executive assistant in the previous NDP government. These two provinces are not unique.

From a government's point of view, this tight control over appointments is key. Once in place, these people have the ability to do a great deal of harm to the government's main base of support — business (or organized labour in the case of the NDP) — if they take themselves and their function a bit too seriously. This does happen. It happened in Ontario. One appointee, a black activist, mistakenly supposed that the government was really serious in attacking racism as he understood it, and treated the good citizens of Ontario to a steady diet of black power. His appointment was not renewed. In Saskatchewan the Director of that province's human rights commission, Shelagh Day, was fired after she had been a bit too aggressive in her approach and would not accede to government suggestions that she take it easy. In Quebec a member of that province's human rights commission was informed that her appointment would not be renewed, apparently for the same reason.

Control of the budget coupled with threats of lower funds next year, seems to have a calming effect on many commissions. If worse comes to worse and the whole business gets entirely out of hand, you can always disband a particularly difficult commission and later replace it with a captive one. This happened in British Columbia.

To say that these groups are made up of political appointees and tightly controlled is not to say that they do nothing. Far from it. The commissions have set aside for themselves a two-fold role — to hear complaints and to lobby for new legislation. There is something a little scary about this. It is almost as if this mandate makes them police, judge and jury. They lack the apparent objectivity and independence from politics of the court system. The word "kangaroo court" comes to mind.

While all of the commissions are involved in lobbying, the most notable must surely be the Canadian Human Rights Commission and that lobbyist *par excellence*, Gordon Fairweather. He is a busy boy. To judge from his lobbying activity *everything* is a human rights issue and the proper object of his group's attentions. In 1983, for instance, the commission was involved in lobbying government on legislation connected with the Unemployment Insurance Act, the Income Tax Act, the Veterans Land Act, the Farm Credit Act, the Indian Act, the Prairie Grain Advance Payments Act, the Veterans Allowance Act, the Civilian War Pensions and Allowances Act, duty-free religious articles, immigration regulations, perceived discrimination on radio and TV and various RCMP regulations. The commission seems to be trying to ensure that it will have problems to deal with for a very long time. Just when it seemed that overt discrimination was on the wane, the commission discovered the concept of systemic discrimination — discrimination that is not intended but just somehow happens because of the way an organization works. It's mysterious and so subtle that only a few adepts can actually understand it or detect it. Among these favoured few are members of the Human Rights Commission. Coupled with this is Fairweather's lobbying foray into the area of affirmative action and job quotas. This should be excellent for the future of the Commission.

The resulting injustices and abuses of such programs should ensure that we begin to see a revival of real racist feeling and resentment once again. This will of course lead to demands by Gord and his merry band for more funds to combat the new racism caused by backlash to these programs. The Commission will win no matter what happens. It is certain to exist forever, as will the social problems it seems to have a vested interest in perpetuating.

9

The Forked Tongues: Bilingualism

Canada has been characterized as the world's richest Third World country. Indeed, Canada's colonial past has resulted in problems which resemble those of many of the Third World countries. One of the nastiest tricks used by the colonial masters of most countries was the "divide and conquer" ploy in which they created unholy unions of peoples who were traditional enemies. The reasoning was that if you set the inhabitants at each others' throats they would be so preoccupied with attacking each other that they would have neither the time, energy, inclination nor the resources to oust the colonial masters. It worked for centuries. Unfortunately, when the colonial rulers left, they left behind nations that were virtually ungovernable — nations divided by racial, linguistic and tribal hatreds and suspicions that are enormously difficult to resolve. This is the heritage of countries like Nigeria, Uganda, South Africa and India. It is Canada's heritage as well.

Relations between our two major linguistic groups have never been particularly good. Virtually every approach has been used to try and resolve the problem — war, insurrection, assimilation, provincial isolation and deportation. These techniques have not worked well at all. The present orthodoxy is official bilingualism — a policy perhaps best described by Dalton Camp as "a noble experiment, wretchedly conducted."[1]

This, then, is the fertile ground which has spawned a whole new breed of lobbies and lobbyists. They represent many different interests and demands, political, economic, cultural, educational, linguistic and so on. There are four major categories: French language groups, English language groups, media and government.

French Language Lobbies
Contrary to what many English Canadians may think, this group of lobbies is far from monolithic in their view of what "the French fact"

is, or should be, in Canada. Part of this diversity results from the membership and financing of these groups, part from geography. Clearly, the geographical focus of a lobby determines its view of the world. Quebec-based groups tend to be preoccupied with the health of the francophone community in Quebec, and at times it seems as if the rest of Canada does not exist. Groups outside of Quebec tend to see things more in national terms. The solutions sought and the demands made thus tend to be quite different.

Consider the situation of francophones in Quebec. At the time of the fall of Quebec in 1759, the non-Indian population of Canada was totally French-speaking and was clustered almost exclusively in what we now call Quebec. Thus, Quebec was Canada, and Quebec was French-speaking. Demographically speaking, the situation has deteriorated progressively since. At present the francophone population of Quebec represents about 5¼ million or only about 22 percent of the total population of Canada. The situation is even worse if you look at the French population of Quebec compared to that of the continent. At present the English-speaking population of Canada and the United States is about 249 million, compared to the 5¼ million francophones in Quebec, which means that French-speaking Quebec represents only about 2 percent of the total population of the continent. Worse yet, the vast majority of these anglophones are made up of the people of the United States, the most powerful military, economic, cultural and linguistic force in the world. Now, I ask you, if you were a French-speaking Quebecer, how would you feel? Threatened.

This sense of isolation and threat has produced a series of French language lobbies in Quebec with what can be best described as having a siege mentality. Chief among these lobbies is the Parti Québécois, the party which was, at the time of writing, the government of the province. Its raison d'être is the representation of francophone interests in the province. Traditionally, this group has felt that francophone language minorities outside Quebec are lost and that the French language only has a chance for long term survival within the boundaries of the province. As a result, the Quebec government under the PQ has been largely inactive in lobbying for French language rights outside the province, while within the province it has pursued policies clearly aimed at the creation of a unilingual French-speaking province. In fact, the PQ is very much an umbrella organization for a number of other French language groups, spanning almost the entire political spectrum, ranging from the trade unions and some far-left political groups, to the Saint-Jean-Baptiste Society which has a decidedly conservative nationalist perspective. One of the major problems of the PQ has been that of bringing together these differing interests into one more or less coherent program. This has not been an easy task. The problems of Premier Lévesque in late 1984 and early 1985 show just how difficult that task is at times.

One of the great dreams of the separatists in Quebec has been the formation of a federal force which would take the struggle to Ottawa. The success of the Parti Québécois at the provincial level contrasts dramatically with the notable failure of these forces at the national level. There have been many ill-starred attempts at creating such a force. One of the earliest attempts was the Union Populaire, formed in 1978 under interim president Henri Laberge. It clung to the hope of electoral success on the basis of a poll which said that 25 percent of Quebec voters would support a separatist party at the federal level. So much for polls. This group never got a seat. Then there was the Parti Nationaliste formed in 1984 to fight the federal election under interim leader Marcel Léger, a former PQ MNA. It was aiming at the 40 percent of the population who voted yes to sovereignty association in the Quebec referendum. They did not get a seat either.

No matter what happened at the federal level, the PQ retained its role as the sole voice of Quebec nationalists at the provincial level. Even this role was challenged in late 1984 with the creation of a coalition which sought to pick up the mantle of separatism from the PQ. This coalition was composed of some PQ politicians, Denis Monière of the Parti Nationaliste, Gerald Larose, president of the 200,000 member Confederation of National Trade Unions, Gilles Rheaume of the Saint-Jean-Baptiste Society, writer Michelle Lalonde and Marcel Pépin, president of the Mouvement Socialiste. It should be noted that Pépin and his Mouvement Socialiste were aiming for the launching of a pro-independence socialist party in the spring of 1985. Clearly, the PQ was starting to fail in its role of accommodating the varying interest groups in Quebec society.

Basically, francophone groups at the federal and provincial levels are after virtually the same things — the extension of the use of French outside of Quebec and the opening up of new job opportunities for francophones. Whether it be the Association des Francophones Hors du Québec (the national group) or the various provincial French rights groups, the thin, cutting edge of lobbying activity has always been the same — "official bilingualism."

Bilingualism

Let's face it. Except for francophones outside of Quebec and anglophones in Montreal, bilingualism is one of the most universally loathed policies ever foisted onto Canadians. Francophone Quebecers hate and fear it because they feel — rightly — that it is a threat to their national sovereignty and existence. English Canadians see it as a stupid and expensive failure which seeks only to perpetuate a historic bad joke and which gives unfair job advantages to a tiny French-speaking minority. In areas like Toronto or the West where Italian, Ukrainian and German groups far outnumber francophones, this cultural and employment favouritism seems grossly unjust. And it is. Still, the secular dogma of bilingualism as enshrined in the Charter of Rights and by twenty years of government policy gives francophone lobbies a lever which they find impossible to resist.

The declaration of official bilingualism tends to be extremely expensive for any province or territory. It involves some duplication of services, new services and almost always an expansion of government. It also tends to be enormously unpopular with the majority of anglophones in a province or territory. Usually this is explained by the media and spokespeople for government and French language groups in terms of racism and bigotry. It is probably closer to the truth to see this opposition in economic terms. What government and French language groups are really asking the anglophone majority to do in most cases is to pay a new cost in terms of higher taxes and lost job opportunities for measures which cannot possibly benefit it. In such a situation resentment is inevitable.

Lobbying by provincial groups for official bilingualism has been extremely successful despite this opposition by the anglophone majority for a number of reasons. Where there is a substantial francophone minority, the declaration of official bilingual status is a powerful temptation for a party in power. One province in which such a situation has occurred is New Brunswick which has a French-speaking minority which represents about 35 percent of the population. Before the declaration of official bilingualism, the Tories could not get a dogcatcher elected in a riding with a high proportion of French-speaking voters. Now, after years of official bilingual status, aggressive administration of the program and serious attempts to increase the number of francophones in the provincial civil service, the ruling Conservative Party virtually owns the Acadian vote. For Premier Richard Hatfield, official bilingualism has been a political godsend. If the Acadians did not exist, he would probably try to create them.

In provinces where the proportion of francophones has not been as large, the lobbying for official language status has been more difficult. The reason is that politicians are primarily driven by strictly political considerations and are not anxious to provoke the ire of English-speaking voters if there are few French-speaking votes to garner. Fortunately for francophones, they receive massive help from "Big Brother" in Ottawa. The federal government makes life a great deal easier for these groups. First of all, it has included official language guarantees for linguistic minorities (French and English) in the constitution. This allows these groups a constitutional hook to hang their hats on if they choose to go the legal route. In addition the federal government has been quite enthusiastic about providing legal assistance for challenges to provincial laws and in picking up the court costs and legal fees of French language groups seeking to challenge the constitutionality of provincial laws.

In conjunction with the federal government, provincial French language lobbies have challenged the constitutionality of laws in Ontario, Manitoba and the Yukon. One of the favourite causes célèbres of these lobbies seems to be traffic tickets. In the Yukon and Manitoba, French language groups initiated major political and legal crises by arguing successfully before the courts that English language traffic tickets were unconstitutional. The challenge in the Yukon led to the declaration of official bilingualism in the Yukon and Northwest Territories. The successful challenge by Roger Bilodeau in Manitoba resulted in an agreement involving the Manitoba government, the federal government, Bilodeau and la Société Franco-Manitobaine. The agreement had the following elements: in exchange for a halt to court proceedings which would probably result in the invalidation of the province's laws, the provincial government agreed to gradually translate the province's laws into French and accept entrenchment of extended French language services for the French language minority in the Constitution of Canada. It was a good day's work for la Société Franco-Manitobaine. Unfortunately for this lobby and the other principals of the agreement, a large part of the English-speaking majority had a different concept of justice and opposed the agreement strongly and effectively. The whole mess was decided before the Supreme Court of Canada.

Ontario has been the "happy" object of this alliance of the federal government and provincial French language lobbies seeking to make the province officially bilingual. Part of this lobbying has taken a similar form to that used in the provinces and territories mentioned above. Certainly, Ontario has been very receptive to demands for informal bilingualism in the province. Indeed, the Ontario government now provides services to the French-speaking community in virtually all the areas that would be demanded of it if it were officially bilingual — bilingual laws and government documents, the ability to be tried in French, French language education and significant programing in French on the government owned television network, TV Ontario. Even the French-speaking community and the federal government concede that Ontario provides meaningful and significant services and rights to the French-speaking minority (about 5 percent of the population). Still, only total victory seems to be satisfactory to these two sets of lobbyists — they insist that bilingualism must be entrenched in the constitution. Part of this lobbying takes the form of direct pressure from various high level federal government officials. Just before the retirement of Pierre Trudeau both the Prime Minister and Commissioner of Official Languages made direct appeals to Bill Davis to do the "honourable" thing and make Ontario officially bilingual. The Ontario Premier sensing the deep resentment which this would create in the province and cognizant of the deep divisions caused in Manitoba and New Brunswick by the entrenchment issue, decided to play it safe.

Of course, not all lobbying efforts are directed at official bilingualism at the provincial level. One of the most contentious issues in Ontario has been the question of funding and control of French language education in the province. In June 1984, the Supreme Court of Ontario appeals branch ruled that parts of the Ontario Education Act violate the rights of French-speaking citizens because the Charter of Rights and Freedoms supersedes any restrictions placed on minority language education by the Education Act. This appeal had been launched by two French language groups, l'Association Canadienne d'Education and l'Association des Enseignants Franco-Ontariens in conjunction with four individuals.

Prior to the action, the Education Act had promised French language instruction where numbers warranted. In practice that meant about twenty to twenty-five children. The ruling now meant that the government would have to provide education in French no matter how few students were involved. The province immediately announced its intention to table legislation that would do just that. This was a great victory since a similar group composed of l'Association Canadiennes-Française de l'Ontario, l'Association des Enseignants Franco-Ontariens and four families had its constitutional challenge thrown out in January of the same year. Clearly persistence pays. These same lobbyists learned though that no victory is necessarily either complete or forever. Late in December 1984 Serge Plouffe, the president of l'Association Canadienne-Française de l'Ontario, expressed fears that the Ontario government's plan to provide full funding to Catholic schools might hurt French high schools.[2] Since most French Canadians were Catholic, this funding of Catholic schools might draw students away from French high schools. And besides, these funds were going to anglophone Catholics and not francophone Catholics. This had a petty quality to it and seemed to suggest that social justice was fine only as long as the members of Plouffe's group were the beneficiaries. If it cost them, it was no good.

English Language Lobbies

French language lobbies have made enormous progress in advancing the interests of their members. With the enormous resources of the federal government behind them — money, lawyers and moral support — and with government pushing through constitutional changes with minority language guarantees, the results were inevitable. Centuries of injustice have been redressed. Unfortunately, there have been some unintended results as well. Where one side wins, there is always the possibility that the other side will lose. This is almost certain when emotion plays a large part in the process and the administration of the programs aimed at promoting change are badly or insensitively handled. When this happens — and there seems ample evidence that this happened in implementing bilingualism — new injustices occur. The fundamental law of physics which states that for every action there is an equal and opposite reaction is as true for politics as it is for physics.

From an English Canadian point of view, the fundamental fact of Parti Québécois rule is that the Party attempted to reverse 200 years of oppression in a decade. The measures the PQ used to do this have succeeded in some measure, but the human cost has been enormous. One of the most important things to realize about the plight of English Canadians in Quebec is that whatever they faced they faced alone. English Canadians outside of Quebec made no attempt to support them. Rather, Anglo-Quebecers were portrayed as hopeless bigots who had lived in a French-speaking environment and yet had made virtually no effort to accommodate themselves to the demands and sensibilities of the majority French-speaking population. They were left to their fate. The federal government, that supposed champion of minority language rights, has until recently turned a blind eye to the oppressive government measures which found their culmination in Quebec's Bill 101. Without doubt, some of this was based on the very practical decision that any support for the English Canadian minority would feed the separatist tide. Perhaps the feds were correct. The end result, though, was that Quebecers were pushed up against the wall without any outside champion or allies. Many left the province. Many of those who did not, formed their own interest groups and began lobbying.

The roots of the anglophone lobbying activity go back to 1974 when the Liberals under Robert Bourassa passed Bill 22 which declared French the official language of the province. One response by anglophones was a petition with 600,000 signatures. The government's response was a refusal to compromise. This was unwise since the anglophone community has always represented a major and solid source of support for the Liberal Party in Quebec. As a result of the government's refusal to negotiate, a significant number of anglophones voted for the Union Nationale. This was disastrous for both the Liberal Party and the anglophone community. The Liberals lost the election and the anglophone community discovered that it had helped to elect a far worse (from its point of view) government, the Parti Québécois. Bill 101, passed in 1976, made Bill 22 look like a love letter to anglophones. Among other things Bill 101 restricted access to English schooling; banned commercial signs in any language other than French; declared that any internal or external communications by English businesses or institutions must be in French; forced anglophone professionals with fewer than three years of full-time study of French at the secondary level to pass French proficiency tests in order to be able to practice in Quebec and set up the Office de la Langue Française, otherwise known by anglophones as the "language police" and "tongue troopers."

The initial reaction to these measures on the part of the English-speaking community was one of shock. This extreme pressure by government was met by a disorganized and unco-ordinated series of briefs by virtually every non-francophone organization in the province from churches to service organizations to theatre groups. As time went by the opposition to this law began to coalesce into groups whose sole goal was to oppose the PQ measures against the English-speaking community.

One group which claimed to speak for the anglophone community was the Positive Action Committee (PAC) founded by a group of 115 professionals and business people in 1977. This group recognized the special place of the French language in Quebec society but sought incentives for its use rather than Draconian measures against the anglophone community. Its lobbying of the Quebec government did not really achieve very much by way of results. One measure it took that did win support from the government, however, was its campaign to try and stanch the flow of businesses out of Quebec. This group was criticized for being just a remnant of the old English Canadian elite.

Another group which was formed a little bit earlier was Participation Quebec. It was founded by about one hundred students and professionals, one of whom was Eric Maldoff, who would go on to become leader of Alliance Quebec. Whereas the PAC had a predominantly WASP character, this group was perhaps more representative of the Jewish community. This group had very little to show for its efforts but was viewed in a more positive light than the PAC because it was perceived to be more enlightened — it was more willing to accept the new linguistic and political reality.

Both the PAC and Participation Quebec received their major funding from the federal Secretary of State. Very quickly this federal department began to pressure both to form an umbrella organization which would speak with one voice for the anglophone community in Quebec. The pressure was successful. In 1977 the Council of Quebec Minorities was formed to bring together twenty-two interest groups, among which were the PAC and Participation Quebec. The re-election of the Parti Québécois in 1981 led to an understanding of the need for a broadly-based group which would represent the needs of the entire English-speaking community. The result was the ad hoc Coalition of English-Speaking Quebecers representing more than fifty organizations. This lasted only a month and was replaced by Alliance Quebec, the lobby which now purports to speak for all anglophone Quebecers.

Once created, Alliance Quebec was quickly blessed by all the appropriate governments. Soon after its formation, it was granted an "audience" with Premier René Lévesque, an unprecedented move by the Quebec government and a public expression of the government's recognition of the group as the legitimate voice of anglophones in the province.

Alliance Quebec has come a long way in terms of a lobbying force. It is large. Its membership is about 40,000 and as such is five times the size of its two rival organizations combined. It is well financed and has enormous political clout, as much as anything the result of its powerful connections with the Liberal Party. It is extremely well organized too.

All of the organization's activities are co-ordinated by a nine member executive committee. To deal with specific issues there are special committees and task forces to study problems and suggest policy. Such issues often include education, health, social services, the business climate in the province, employment and community development. This structure is replicated in the sixteen Alliance Quebec chapters and the five regional anglo rights associations. The Alliance has a full-time staff of thirty in its Montreal office who do research, prepare briefs for hearings and assemble documentation for court cases.

The activities of the Alliance are many and varied. At one level it acts almost as a social agency. It provides services in the area of language training and career counselling for those who would like to stay in the province. But where it really flexes its muscles is in lobbying government and supporting court challenges to provincial laws.

The most important successes of the Alliance have been the result of its support for challenges in the courts between 1982 and 1984 which have virtually gutted Bill 101. The courts have ruled against clauses dealing with the provincial language tests for professionals, unilingual signs and restrictions to English language education. In virtually all cases the Alliance provided significant support in terms of money, legal staff and publicity campaigns in the media.

The Alliance's lobbying effort has been significant but with somewhat mixed results. Certainly, its relations with the PQ government have been better than virtually any anglophone organization. Of course, when one considers how bad these relations have been, that is not so very hard to do. The Alliance has had some important successes, the first being its recognition as the sole anglophone voice by the Quebec government which has resulted in access to decision makers at the top and funding for the organization from the PQ government. This recognition cost, however; the Alliance has had to agree to the English-speaking minority being viewed simply as another minority group. That represents a major victory for the PQ. Nevertheless, the Alliance's conciliatory approach has borne fruit on occasion. For instance, it collaborated with the government on the drafting of Bill 57 which entrenches recognition of the English-speaking community's institutions in the preamble of Bill 101.

One of the major problems with Alliance Quebec is its incredibly complex structure which has given rise to an enormously bureaucratic nature. Part of this is positive, since all governments like to do business with highly bureaucratic interest groups. The bad news is that such groups become more alienated from the wishes and needs of their memberships. The result is that the organizations come more and more to serve the needs of their leaders and less those of their membership. This process of bureaucratization is at work in Alliance Quebec and the leaders have become remote from the general membership. This situation was alluded to by Graeme Decarie, head of Concordia University's Institute for Anglophone Studies and advisor on the Alliance's education committee: "I haven't seen Eric (Maldoff) in over a year, and I *know* the guy. I see very few members of the board of directors. The criticism has been made that the power was moved from old Westmount farts to the young Westmount farts. And there's a lot of truth in that."[3] Another problem is that a vast majority of members live in Montreal and district. What this means is that many anglophones who live in other parts of the province often feel that the Alliance is neglecting their interests. And with policies that are so conciliatory toward the Quebec government and so in step with the federal policy of official bilingualism, some critics have charged that its name should be "Appliance Quebec." Is this label and charge justified?

One of the most important features of the Alliance is its powerful financial support from government at all levels. An examination of the federal government Public Accounts for the fiscal period 1983 to 1984 reveals that the federal government doubled its support to the group in this year from the previous year — the Alliance received a million dollars from the Feds and funding for the regional affiliates contributed another $531,500. What is interesting is that the other major anglophone organizations, the Freedom of Choice movement and Quebec for All, did not receive a penny. Of course, the Secretary of State, the funding department for Alliance Quebec, was the catalyst for the formation of this group in the first place. The curious funding, however, came from the PQ government which in the same period gave the Alliance $33,000 through the Quebec Ministry of Cultural Communities and Immigration. The Alliance also has powerful Liberal Party connections. Executive member Sheila Finestone, was a permanent staff member of the Quebec Liberal Party and has since gone on to be a Liberal MP for Mount Royal, Trudeau's former riding. Directors Caspar Bloom and Sam Berliner are Quebec Liberal activists, former director John Parisella works for the Liberals and was one of their senior regional campaign organizers, Michael Goldbloom is a long

time political fundraiser and is the son of former Liberal MNA Victor
Goldbloom. There is little doubt that a close and special relationship
exists between the Quebec Liberal Party and the Alliance.

Certainly support for the Alliance has been quite profitable for the
Liberal Party both at the federal and provincial levels. At the federal
level, support for this group has had two major benefits. One has been
to shore up support for the Liberals among anglophones in the Montreal area. The doubling of funding immediately before the 1984 federal
election led to suggestions that the increase might be an attempt to
prevent any swing among Montreal anglophones to the Conservatives.
These accusations were sufficiently annoying to draw an angry denial
from then Secretary of State, Serge Joyal.

Another major benefit has been to use the Alliance as a mouthpiece
for drumming up support in English Canada for the unpopular official
languages program. When it became clear that the deal between the
Manitoba provincial government, the federal government and the
Société Franco-Manitobaine was in trouble, Eric Maldoff, President of
the Alliance, was trotted out to Manitoba to try and sweet talk the
anglophone majority into buying the deal. He got a cool reception.

The provincial Grits also have a powerful vested interest in the
continued survival of the Alliance. Up until the creation of the Alliance, the Liberal Party was dogged by accusations by the PQ that it was
taking the side of anglophones, which hurt them with francophone
voters. The Alliance was a godsend. English language rights could be
supported through the Alliance and the Alliance would take the criticism. Even better, having Liberal Party activists in leading roles in the
Alliance ensured that the Party could control what was being said and
done. In any case, the anglophone community in Quebec is a virtual
hostage to the Liberal Party. The only alternative is the PQ and it is
almost totally hostile to the anglophones. There is another major
shared benefit for the federal and provincial Liberals. Both Serge Joyal
and Michel Gratton, provincial Liberal language critic, have openly
expressed hopes that Alliance Quebec will double as a springboard for
Liberal politicians. When asked about this possibility, Eric Maldoff
replied coyly that if some of the leaders happened to take that path that
is the way the chips fall.[4]

There are other anglophone lobby groups that are smaller, grass
roots expressions of anglophone fear and rage. They are anything but
stodgy. One of the two major ones which have chosen to stay outside
of Alliance Quebec is the Freedom of Choice Movement founded in
1978. It has about 3,000 members and lists William Shaw, former MNA,

as its most prominent member. Shaw is a study in himself. He is a prosperous dental surgeon who ran successfully for the Union Nationale and after breaking with the Party sat as an independent. Part of the Union Nationale's problem with Shaw was his views on national unity, which seemed somewhat redneck. The other problem was his link with the Eleventh Province Movement, which wanted large pieces of Quebec taken away from Quebec and used to form another province if Quebec separated. Shaw is feisty too. When asked if he was afraid there would be violence in the struggle for English language rights, he replied, "Anyone who is afraid of violence is a coward and I'm not a coward."[5]

The tactics of the Freedom of Choice Movement have differed enormously from those of the Alliance Quebec. Unlike the Alliance which favours behind-the-scenes lobbying and court challenges, this movement favours direct action. Sometimes this has taken the form of running candidates in elections. The Movement ran Dr. David DeJong in a provincial by-election in 1978; he ran second with an impressive 25 percent of the vote. On other occasions the direct action has taken the form of demonstrations and picketing. On one occasion the Movement picketed the Steinberg supermarket chain because it was quick to comply with the unilingual sign law. Perhaps the most famous occasion was when they picketed the National Press Club in Washington when Lévesque spoke there in 1979. Lévesque was furious and referred to them as "racist" and "fascist." The joke here was that just a few years before Quebec nationalists had done very similar things to promote their cause, but when they did, it was called a fight for freedom.

The other group is Quebec For All, founded in late 1981 by Carol Zimmerman, a social worker. This group, which claims 5,000 members, uses attention grabbing tactics similar to the Freedom of Choice Movement. Some of these stunts have included protesting while in chains or with gags labelled "Bill 101" in their mouths and holding a mock funeral procession through east end Montreal to mark the death of anglophone rights (east end Montreal is a traditional centre of Quebec nationalism). Zimmerman has considerable charisma and is able to fill halls wherever she speaks. The position of her group is that it is impossible to work in a conciliatory way with the PQ because it is an extremist government.

English Language Groups Outside of Quebec
There are very few organized groups in English Canada involved in the promotion of the interests of the English-speaking community. A

large portion of this is undoubtedly because they represent the large majority of the population and have very little reason to feel that their existence as a group is threatened. Still, there have been many difficult changes which have been forced on this group as a result of the worst abuses and poor administration of the bilingual program at the federal level. To a very great extent this program has been an affirmative action hiring program at English Canadians' expense. Many have been hurt in terms of employment or promotion. The program has involved a great deal of badgering, hectoring and blaming — all extremely noxious to the English Canadian psyche, yet there has not been much by way of organized opposition at the federal level.

This cannot be said about the provincial level. Two of the most notable examples involve the implementation of official bilingualism in Manitoba and New Brunswick. In both cases, the English-speaking majority decided that enough is enough and organized effectively.

Without doubt the Manitoba incident must qualify as one of the great moments in hypocrisy and self-righteousness by the Central Canadian media and political elite. Between the two they managed to trash the entire province and virtually all of its people in the role of bigots. This issue had its origins in 1870 with the Manitoba Act, the act by which the province joined Confederation. According to this act, both English and French were to be official languages of the courts and legislature. This made perfect sense since the population was about evenly split. As time passed the province was flooded with English-speaking Ontarians or immigrants who would eventually become English-speaking, and in 1890 the Manitoba legislature abolished the use of French in the courts and legislature. It was an obvious breach of the Manitoba Act, but politicians argued that the numbers warranted it. That is where the matter stayed until 1979 when the Supreme Court ruled that the 1890 law was unconstitutional. The real crunch came in 1980 when Roger Bilodeau, supported by the federally financed Société Franco-Manitobaine, challenged two of the province's traffic laws because they were in English only. The possibility of his winning this case terrified the provincial government. If successful, it could well result in the rest of the province's laws being declared illegal. The province started translating its most important laws into French and began serious negotiations with the Société Franco-Manitobaine in search of a negotiated settlement.

The only problem with all of this was that times had changed since the late nineteenth century. By the beginning of the 1980s the French-speaking population was only about 50,000 or about 5 percent of the population. In addition the majority of citizens in Manitoba did not view their province as bilingual, official or otherwise. Instead they viewed the attempt to force official bilingualism as yet one more move by the Central Canadian elite to force its will upon western Canada. This view was confirmed by polls at the time that indicated that 76 percent of Manitobans opposed the Pawley government's plan.

Once it became clear that the Manitoba government was intent upon negotiating a deal with the Société Franco-Manitobaine that would result in official bilingualism, a number of groups were formed, almost all of which died quickly. The one group that did survive was Manitoba Grassroots, a loose coalition led by Grant Russell, a former RCMP officer and intelligence agent with the federal immigration department. Grassroots was well financed and well organized. One tactic it used was to send members to meetings where NDP ministers were likely to be present. They would then attempt to heckle or ask the ministers embarrassing questions. They also used the usual techniques that have proven so successful for grass roots organizations in other areas. They swamped open-line shows and the letters to the editor section of newspapers. They collected names on petitions and organized meetings. These meetings were notable successes. One Grassroots rally at the Winnipeg Convention Centre drew more than 3,000 supporters in early 1984. Once it was clear that there was major support for the movement the politicians began to flock to it as supporters. At one rally the speakers included the former Manitoba Premier Sterling Lyon and Sidney Green, leader of the now deceased Progressive Party, a right-wing NDP splinter group that had included non-entrenchment in its party platform. Another supporter of the movement was Russell Doern, a member of the NDP government who had broken ranks with his own party because of the opposition he sensed among his constituents. This group was enormously successful. Its opposition led to the government watering down its plans on a number of occasions. Perhaps its greatest success was to instigate a number of municipal plebiscites which showed massive disapproval among voters for the government's proposed deal.

Probably one of the most important allies of the Grassroots movement was the Manitoba Conservative Party. It was the concerted and uncompromising support of the Tories for the groups opposing entrenchment which led to the ultimate demise of the legislation intended to solve the constitutional problem. Every time the government rang the division bells to call members to vote on a closure measure which would close off debate on the issue, the Conservatives would walk out of the House. The result was a complete paralysis of the Legislature. The government finally recognized defeat and let the bill die.

As an interesting sidelight, even the Premier's own party was affected by the crisis. Besides MLA Doern, there was another NDP member, Winnipeg businessman Herb Schulz, who created a sensation by his opposition to the government's policies. Schulz used the formal appeal of his expulsion from the NDP to protest the government's language policies and to say that the NDP had "embarked on a course that can only lead to its destruction."[6] They must not have liked his speech. He discovered that he only had the support of five delegates and dropped his appeal before a formal vote was taken. He was especially noteworthy because he was the brother-in-law of the then Governor General Ed Schreyer, the former NDP Premier.

A fascinating postscript occurred in November 1984 following the defeat of the bilingualism deal. Grant Russell was fired from his job with the federal government. The government claims it was on account of his health. He claims to have obtained a confidential government document which indicates it was because of his political activities.[7]

One of the fascinating ironies of the Manitoba crisis was the speech given by New Brunswick Premier Richard Hatfield which urged Manitoba's anglophones to mend their ways and embrace official bilingualism as he had done in New Brunswick. In a speech in March 1984, Hatfield criticized Manitobans for opposing their government's moves to entrench bilingualism in the constitution and predicted that their refusal to go along with the agreement would lead to instability and that Manitobans were going to pay a heavy price for their intransigence.[8] This was the height of irony, for little did he know it, but his already official bilingual province would begin in a few months to pay this very price as he tried to extend the scope of bilingualism.

In terms of practicalities and demographics there is a much stronger case for official bilingualism in New Brunswick than in Manitoba since about a third of the population in New Brunswick is francophone. It was with this background and the increasing pressure by francophone groups that the New Brunswick government passed its Official Languages Act in 1969 which declared the province officially bilingual. The relationship between the English and French-speaking residents has never been perfect and the implementation of the Act caused some tensions. Still, there were many positive results, one of which was increased representation by francophones in the New Brunswick civil service. As the process of implementation proceeded and anglophones found themselves losing jobs and promotions to Acadian candidates, the ground became more fertile for some sort of protest movement. All that was needed was some form of provocation for the English-speaking majority. Unfortunately, the Hatfield government provided more than one. Once the government had lit the fuse, an explosion was inevitable.

The English language rights movement took almost the same form and route as that in Manitoba. In New Brunswick the impetus for the development of the movement came from two events. One was symbolic — the decision by the government to fly the Acadian flag next to other official flags for a year as a sort of symbolic gesture of goodwill to francophones. The other involved the setting up of the Poirier-Bastarache committee to investigate the possibility of extending the rights of francophones. Like events in Manitoba, these two events seemed to persuade many anglophones that enough was enough. Also as in Manitoba, the movement developed an alliance between grass roots groups and members of the legislature.

The Association of English-Speaking Canadians formed in 1984, has a membership of about 12,000 people and is led by Leonard Poole, a former Fredericton city councillor. According to Poole, the catalyst for forming the group was the government decision to fly the Acadian flag. Apparently, he was furious at this move since it would cost $50,000 to build the necessary flag poles when the Fredericton campus of a community college was going to close because the provincial government supposedly could not find $10,000 as its share of the funding. Hatfield with a nice touch of delicacy pushed an amendment through the legislature extending the original period of one year for flying the Acadian flag to make it a permanent feature. This matter of the flag was just the start.

The real crux of the matter revolved around the 1982 report entitled *Towards Equality of Official Languages in New Brunswick*. Now, one of the interesting things about the Conservative government's moves in the area of official languages is that they always seem to coincide (quite accidentally, of course) with coming provincial elections. The 1982 report came just before the last provincial election. As to the most recent committee's hearings, Bernard Richard executive director of the National Society of Acadians had the following comment, "We didn't hear anything about it for two years, and now that we are getting to another election, it's being pulled out again."[9] The report itself was nothing if not controversial. Its recommendations, if implemented, would result in increased levels of francophone employment in the civil service. Among other things it recommended the establishment of anglophone and francophone units in the civil service and higher levels of service by government for francophones. This was too much for Poole and his organization.

The major thrust of Poole's group is that it is becoming increasingly difficult for anglophones to find employment and advancement in the civil service. As Poole puts it, "For two years now, ordinary people have been telling me they're getting pushed aside in their jobs. French people are taking over as bosses who have little experience, while they themselves have been working for 15 years."[10] Interestingly enough, this group seems not to be against the idea of more jobs in the public service for francophones, only the way in which it is being done. Says Poole, "I'll be honest with you, back a few years ago there weren't enough francophones in the civil service compared to the number of anglophones. I think that should change. Since the francophone population is roughly a third of our population, a third of government jobs should be occupied by francophones. And in areas where francophones predominate, of course French should be the language government uses. But duality (the practice of separate English and French work units) is just crazy."[11] In addition the group claims that anglophones are no longer being treated equally in hiring. Where bilingualism was once considered just an asset in some jobs, it is now considered a necessity.

One of the problems which this group has experienced has been a virtual refusal by government to talk to it. Faced with this, the group has made a direct appeal to the people. Members have become increasingly aggressive in their appearances at hearing meetings. Toward the end of 1984, these meetings had on two occasions become extremely nasty. Proceedings degenerated into cat calls and invective of a particularly distasteful form. In one case a francophone woman and an anglophone man almost came to blows after the man had knocked over a Radio-Canada television light.

The Association's direct approach has proved to be highly effective. By the end of the year Hatfield was faced with a virtual uprising by his own caucus which he handled with great difficulty. According to one government source, twenty-one out of thirty-nine Tory caucus members were critical of the way in which the report was being handled. In addition, Social Services Minister Nancy Leark Teed complained of the high cost of implementing the bilingualism proposals. Worst of all, the committee co-chairman, Horace Hanson, resigned. In his letter of resignation he stated, "There have been attempts to manipulate the committee by the Official Languages Branch, which is composed entirely of bilingual francophone civil servants."[12] To complete this linguistic and political storm the Opposition leader expressed the feeling that the committee hearings were divisive and that further hearings should be cancelled.

Hatfield, who had just a few months before castigated English language groups in Manitoba, found himself under heavy attack by a similar group. His self-righteousness had come back to haunt him.

Looking outside of Quebec, it sometimes seems that English language groups that support bilingualism are about as common as white crows. But there is an Anglo group that supports the extension of bilingualism. Canadian Parents for French sprang up in 1977 with the objective of "ensuring that each Canadian child have the opportunity to acquire as great a knowledge of the French language and culture as he or she is willing and able to attain." This group, promoting the effective teaching of French, lobbies provincial governments and local school boards. Among its most notable successes has been its campaign for more immersion classes and schools. It also has uncomfortably close ties with the federal government, receiving a $190,000 grant in FY 1983–84.

There is one terrible irony which surrounds this group. It is lobbying for what federalist French Canadians have been calling for over the years — a large group of bilingual anglophones. That is good, right? After all, the theory behind bilingualism is that once there is a large group of bilingual Canadians of both French and English Canadian origins there will be understanding between the two groups and a decline in tension. Unfortunately, there are signs that such is not happening. A recent study done by the Ontario Institute for Studies in Education, found that bilingualism is in fact producing a new anglophone elite that is resented by francophones since it threatens their advantage in competition for jobs based on their almost exclusive possession of a bilingual competence.[13] This competitive advantage in access to managerial jobs, especially in government, will disappear as more anglophone children pass through French immersion classes and schools and hence into the job market. This report must make the idealists in Canadian Parents for French want to cry. It may, however, come to the nub of the whole bilingual issue.

Government

Probably the most powerful lobbyist on the language issue is government itself. We have already seen a lot of evidence for this in the way in which the federal government used its funds and influence over the media to encourage the francophone groups in Manitoba and New Brunswick. We have also seen how the Quebec and federal governments encouraged the growth of Alliance Quebec and discouraged other movements in Quebec by judicious use of its powers of funding, access to contacts and the bestowing of legitimacy. It is now apparent how the federal government has funded challenges to provincial laws and in some cases lobbied provincial governments (like Ontario) directly for changes in their linguistic policies and approaches. Let's deal with this whole question in a little bit more detail and try to get a more comprehensive picture of how governments cast themselves in the role of lobbyist.

The federal government has been especially active in encouraging provincial language lobbies. Below are some of the provincial and territorial groups which receive funds from the federal government.

Selected Grants for Language Lobbies
From Federal Secretary of State's Office
(FY 1983–1984)

Province	Group	Amount
Quebec	Alliance Quebec	$109,977
	Alliance Quebec	$1,000,000
		$1,109,977
Alberta	Assoc. Canadienne Française de l'Alberta	$64,000
	Assoc. Canadienne Française de l'Alberta	$648,000
		$712,000
Ontario	Assoc. Canadienne Française de l'Ontario	$51,093
	Assoc. Canadienne Française de l'Ontario (Régionale Sudbury)	$885,000

	Assoc. Canadienne Française de l'Ontario (Rég. Rive Nord Elliott Lake)	$50,400
	Assoc. Canadienne Française de l'Ontario (Régionale Timmins)	$51,500
	Assoc. Canadienne Française de l'Ontario (Régionale du Grand Nord)	$53,000
	Assoc. Canadienne Française de l'Ontario (Conseil du Niagara)	$50,400
	Assoc. Canadienne Française de l'Ontario (Région de Prescott Russell)	$50,300
	Total	$1,141,393
Saskatchewan	Assoc. Culturelle Franco Canadienne de la Saskatchewan	$649,000
Newfoundland	Assoc. Francophone du Labrador	$70,781
	Fédération des Francophones de Terre-Neuve et du Labrador	$130,330
	Total	$201,111
Nova Scotia	Fédération Acadienne de la Nouvelle Ecosse	$808,128
B.C.	Fédération des Franco Columbiens	$60,319
	Fédération des Franco Columbiens	$567,661
	Total	$627,980
Manitoba	Société Franco-Manitobaine	$108,421
	Société Franco-Manitobaine	$882,000
	Total	$990,421

The important thing to realize about this is that it is only a partial list. The federal government is involved in funding groups in all provinces and territories. Some of this is for ordinary community and cultural activities; very often it is for the support of lobbying activities. What is interesting is who does not get funded. In the above list there are no separatist or English rights groups outside of Quebec. I should point out that it is not just groups which get funded. Individuals get money too. Usually this happens in connection with challenges to provincial legislation. Below are some individuals who have received funding from the federal government.

The Funding of Language Lobbies
Grants to Individuals

Name	Province	Amount	Year
Daniel St. Jean	Yukon	$25,000 for appeal of traffic conviction (English only ticket)	1983
Duncan MacDonald	Quebec	agreed to pay up to $47,350 of Supreme Court costs (Gov. has already paid $20,000 for costs in lower courts)	1984

Source: *Public Accounts* FY 1982-83 and 1983-84. Reproduced by permission of the Minister of Supplies and Services Canada.

In fact in FY 1983–1984 the federal government set aside $150,000 for challenges by individuals to provincial language legislation. Still, all of this understates the federal government's commitment to official bilingualism. This becomes even clearer when you realize that grants and contributions under the Secretary of State's official languages program totalled almost $200 million in FY 1983–84, while grants and contributions available for groups promoting official bilingualism and for challenges to provincial language legislation under the Secretary of State's Citizenship and Culture Program totalled about $21.5 million for FY 1983–84. In brief, then, the Secretary of State provided just under a quarter of a *billion* dollars for the promotion of the dogma of bilingualism.

Other tools used by government to influence which groups survive long enough to become the interest group that finally pressures government, is the bestowing of legitimacy and permitting access to the upper levels of power. Both the Manitoba and New Brunswick governments attempted to destroy the English rights groups that were trying to lobby on behalf of anglophones by smears in the media and by refusing to talk to the groups. The Quebec government tried the same tactic in choosing to speak only with Alliance Quebec. As we saw, the Quebec government had better success with this tactic.

Not all of government lobbying activities are of an indirect form. All governments exert enormous influence over the form and nature of the struggle by interest groups in this area through their ability to pass legislation. At the provincial level we have seen how government legislation in Ontario, Quebec, Manitoba and New Brunswick have set the ground rules and determined the field of battle for lobbies. Once again the federal government holds the aces. The Canadian Constitution has been used by the federal government to raise the policy of official bilingualism to the status of dogma and to prevent any turning away from the policy. Considering how difficult it is to change the constitution, it is certain that the linguistic policies in Canada are unlikely to change for a very long time.

The Trudeau government was extremely keen on the use of direct influence. It attempted to influence both public opinion in general and the Quebec referendum in particular by means of advertising (some called it propaganda) emanating from the Canadian Unity Information Office. Strictly speaking, the Office should have disappeared after the Quebec Referendum had been settled. However, top-level Liberal government insiders discovered that the Office served the Party too well to let it die. It was extremely valuable because it provided an easy organ for direct influencing of Canadian public opinion; provided a vast storehouse of patronage jobs for faithful Party workers and provided valuable patronage contracts to Liberal Party-dominated advertising and polling companies. In its last year of fiscal 1983–84, it had a budget of $21,878,000.

Another agency used to lobby both the public and government on behalf of official bilingualism has been the Office of the Commissioner of Official Languages. This office has lobbied for official bilingualism in Ontario, Manitoba, the Yukon and Northwest Territories; the extension of government services in federal government offices across the country; improved instruction in the two official languages and increased powers for both the Official Languages Act and the Office. In many cases it has lobbied for increased hiring of francophones in the federal civil service. Indeed, there are persistent rumours that Trudeau made Max Yalden, an English-speaker, the first Chief Commissioner of Official Languages because he believed that English Canadians would take the bashing to come better if it came from an English Canadian.

My favourite example of the feds' direct approach to lobbying on behalf of official bilingualism was its "bilingualism by fiat" approach in the Yukon and the Northwest Territories — an excellent example of the arbitrary use of power. Bilingualism in the North began, as it seems to begin everywhere else, with a challenge to a traffic ticket. Daniel St. Jean argued in Yukon Territorial Court that his two speeding tickets contravened the Charter of Rights and Freedoms because they were printed in English only. The court ruled against him, but Mr. St. Jean appealed, backed by a $25,000 grant from the Secretary of State. The case was never decided upon.

In a hastily prepared press conference, Northern Affairs Minister John Munro announced that the government would introduce legislation making official bilingualism the law in both territories. The reaction of northerners was far from positive. The Yukon Legislature unanimously condemned the legislation. Richard Nerysoo, the Northwest Territories government leader, said that the proposal was a "serious infringement" on the constitutional authority of his government. Larry Tourangueau, president of the Métis Association of the Northwest Territories, was puzzled by the pending legislation. He said, "There are a lot of languages here and if most people had a choice of having (a second) official language it probably would be one native language as opposed to French."[14] This made some sense since about 50 percent of the population of the North speak a native language. Still they did not have a choice.

Thus our two northern territories have now been made bilingual to suit 1.3 percent of the population, or 860 people. Sure, it is a terrible waste of money considering the better uses that could have been made of it for development and the alleviation of poverty. But look at the bright side. Think of the jobs it has created for translators, although cynics might conclude that most of the jobs will go to carpetbaggers from the south.

Sometimes federal ministries pressure bodies dependent on government to toe the "party line." A good example was the Ministry of Fitness and Amateur Sports. In early 1984, MP Jacques Olivier was made the minister and one of his first acts was to order his officials to review the Ministry's contracts to ensure that the principle of bilingualism was being upheld. The Minister was clear about what would happen to those who were unwilling to knuckle under: "If they [sport officials] say they need more money to provide bilingual services, they should tell me and I'm ready to take a look at it. But if they say no, maybe they'll lose the contribution I give them."[15] No one can accuse Ottawa of being subtle about the matter. It can make the private lobbyists seem shy in the exercise of influence.

PART IV

THE LOBBIES OF GREED

With lobbies and influence peddlers whose objective is to advance either a set of ideas about the world or one's group as defined by language, race, region or country of origin, demands are couched in lofty terms involving the good of mankind or human rights, although this is sometimes just a cover for fairly selfish personal needs and wants. In this section we shall look at those groups and individuals who are totally honest about what they want and why. Their demands may be summed up in one word — "gimme!" They are the lobbies of self-interest, or to put it another way, the lobbies of greed.

10

Dialling for Dollars: Business and Government

One of the basic axioms of influence peddling and lobbying is that you must start from where you are. You have to recognize your strengths and weaknesses and use whatever resources are at your disposal to get what you want. So far we have looked at groups whose major resources are ideas and people. Now for a change of pace. In this chapter we will look at a group that really only has one idea — institutionalized greed. We call this group the business community. This group has only one resource at its disposal, but it is a dilly. It is money.

Suppose for the moment that you are a business person who wants to get help from the government for your own noble purpose, i.e., to become rich or richer! You don't have some noble moral or ethical argument with which to make your appeal. You don't have a large number of supporters whose potential votes can be used to blackmail the politicians. The media are antagonistic to business anyway, so you cannot make use of them to propagandize your point of view. Obviously you are in a spot since you cannot use any of the levers that other influencers use. What would you do? How about using your money to buy the decisions you want? And that is exactly what the business community does.

Let me say it right from the start. You cannot usually buy politicians and highly placed friends in politics. You can, however, rent them.

Political Contributions

Political contributions are the life blood of all political parties. For corporations, political contributions are as close as they can come to bribing without actually committing a crime. What they do is buy access to power and a hearing from powerful officials. Large gifts to the party in power will almost certainly ensure that you will be able to discuss your problem with a Cabinet Minister or Deputy Minister. With heavy giving at election time, you will be able to get exemptions to upcoming or existing legislation, you will be given lucrative government contracts that somehow never seem to go to tendering, your firm will be given grants that it was previously ineligible for on the pure merits of the case, or you will find that bureaucratic red tape just seems to melt away. It happens every day.

This is not a problem that involves just a few people at the constituency level. The fact is that this system of influence operates at the very highest levels and has nation-wide significance. The amount of money involved is enormous and the would-be persuaders represent the wealthiest and most powerful in society. Below is a table listing some of the largest contributors to the three major parties in 1983:

LARGEST CONTRIBUTORS TO
POLITICAL PARTIES IN 1983

CONTRIBUTOR	*LIBERALS*	*CONSERVATIVES*	*NDP*
Canadian Pacific	$51,958	$50,000	Nil
Brascan	$44,344	$18,056	Nil
Power Corp.	$39,154	$37,814	Nil
Dofasco	$37,249	$36,671	Nil
Imasco	$31,113	$35,556	Nil
Bank of Commerce	$31,500	$30,000	Nil
T-D Bank	$30,101	$19,147	Nil
Bank of Nova Scotia	$30,000	$30,000	Nil
Bank of Montreal	$30,000	$30,000	Nil
Northern Telecom	$30,000	$30,000	Nil
Montreal Engineering	$22,070	$20,550	Nil
Noranda Mines	$21,872	$21,375	Nil
United Steelworkers	Nil	Nil	$20,687
B.C. Fed. of Labour	Nil	Nil	$20,450
B.C. Bldg. Trades	Nil	Nil	$20,000

Source: David Vienneau, "CP gave $102,000 to Liberals, Tories," *Toronto Star*, July 12, 1984, p. A1. Reprinted with permission — The Toronto Star Syndicate.

It was a big year for the parties, with contributions to the three major ones totalling almost $30 million. A breakdown is shown in the table below:

TOTAL CONTRIBUTIONS TO MAJOR PARTIES IN 1983

Progressive Conservative	$14,108,012
NDP	8,590,942
Liberal	7,285,115

Source: Elections Canada. Reproduced by permission of the Minister of Supply and Services Canada.

It is interesting to note that the Liberal Party collected less than the NDP. Usually the Liberals and Conservatives collect about the same amount, certainly more than the NDP. The answer lies in the unpopularity of Trudeau with the business community and its perception of his government as being anti-business or "socialist." The lesson is that you should not mess with those that pay the bills. The PCs almost made the same mistake during the election of 1984. In a July 23, 1984 interview with the *Globe and Mail*, Sinclair Stevens stated that a Conservative government would exclude four areas of the economy from foreign investment. This article enraged Alberta oil-drilling operator and rancher Peter Bawden, who is no ordinary taxpayer and voter. He is a former Conservative MP and most important of all, he was the largest individual contributor to the Conservative election campaign in 1980 with a donation of $26,000. Bawden threatened to halt his contributions to the party if this stance remained. Within days both Mulroney and Stevens publicly reversed this stand. Justice — and money — had triumphed.

It looks like a perfect strategy, doesn't it? It is simple and it works. You end up with friends in high places who are only too happy to help you at some point in the future. What can go wrong? You can. One possible problem might be that you will get yourself in such a mess that even the politicians will not be able to get you out of it. As we saw in the chapter on the real world of politics, there is a concept of "bad" corruption among the movers and shakers of the political system. If you find yourself in this position and attempts at a coverup fail, you will be thrown to the wolves, no matter how much you have donated up to this point.

Below is a portion of a transcript of a wiretap made by the RCMP during its investigation into the Hamilton dredging scandal. The two men involved are Kenneth R. Elliott and Horace Grant Rindress. Elliott was charged and convicted in connection with the scandal, Rindress was the Vice President of one of the dredging companies accused of rigging bids. As you will see, Elliott seems to feel that he is the victim of politicians' short memories and ingratitude.

E: ". . . the way I busted my ass for all them politicians, the money I've got them over the years.

"Now they all go run and hide, including Munro.

"That's one that irks my ass more than anybody, Munro."

R: "Well, he started this whole thing, didn't he?"

E: "You bet your ass he did."

R: "Nice guy."

E: "Bitch. Joe, they're all . . . look at your bosses . . ."[1]

Clearly if you step over that fine dividing line between "good" corruption and "bad" corruption and get caught, they will crucify you. Elliott was really treated roughly, according to his account. In another wiretap he is quoted as saying that his mother was served a warrant on her deathbed just before she closed her eyes and slipped into a final coma. Now, that's playing hardball.

So far, all of this has been pretty crude stuff. I give you some money, people or advertising for your campaign and you give me patronage or do me some legislative favours later on. The advantage of such a system is its simplicity. Still, as you can see above, there are dangers — big dangers. One is obviously that of detection. Any Tom, Dick or Harry can examine the lists of election contributors that are required by federal and provincial law. Another problem is that this system is inefficient at the national or provincial level, especially where big contributions are involved. From the parties' point of view the biggest danger in the more personalized and informal system is that they will not harvest enough from their corporate friends (or patsies). Fortunately, there is an answer to everything.

Political parties are faced with three major problems in squeezing their corporate "friends." These are:

1. Knowing how much to ask for. If you ask for too much, you risk alienating them forever. After all, business has only so much to spend. The other danger is asking for too little. It would be hard

on the pride of any party to think that it got less than the competition.

2. How to canvass the corporations in as efficient a manner as possible so as to maximize the amount collected and to minimize the cost of collecting it.

3. How to collect the money in as secret a way as possible. Many of these corporations may be asking favours later on and so would like to avoid publicity if at all possible. The only groups that ideally should know about the donations are the parties themselves and only at the highest level possible.

The answer to all of these problems lies in the bagmen; those people entrusted by the parties with the task of canvassing the various corporations and the wealthy for donations to the campaign warchests. Their role is key to the waging of election campaigns, for without bagmen and the money they bring in, the parties would be unable to finance their activities.

Political bagmen and women are well-placed for their roles. They are usually lawyers, business people or long time political activists (unkind people call them "hacks") and know who the parties' supporters are, which officials have money to spend and how much each company can be expected to give.

Because of their position in the process, political bagmen become enormously influential after an election. First of all, they know who was generous and how generous they were. Business people wishing favours from the party in power may well seek out the help of these bagmen in getting access to those in government who can help them with their "problem." Because of their importance to the parties, bagmen's calls are always returned, no matter how busy and how important the official. Obviously, not every businessman wants a receipt or a written record of his gift. Receipts mean public disclosure and this can lead to embarrassing questions later on when favours are bestowed or contracts given out. Still, it is important that the party be aware of where the money has come from so that proper gratitude can be shown later on. This is where the bagman comes in. Only he knows and he will not tell except to those that need to know when the time is right. This is particularly important in those delicate situations where the money may come from such tainted sources as organized crime. If there is a scandal, the politicians will be able to honestly say that they never knew a thing about the origins of the money.

The payoff is that these individuals can expect and get the choicest plums from the patronage trees. What would you like? A senatorship? An ambassadorship? A directorship of a Crown Corporation or a place on a regulatory body like the CRTC? How about lieutenant governor? They are all possibilities. In fact some of our leading "elder statesmen" are former (or current for that matter) bagmen. The present Ontario Lieutenant-Governor John Black Aird is a former Liberal bagman. Trudeau appointed him to his lofty position as a reward for his efforts. Look at the following names and tell me what these people have in common: Sen. John Godfrey (L), Sen. Bill Kelly (PC), Sen. John Nichol (L). They were all big time bagmen. The story of Kelly is especially funny. Trudeau intended to appoint a Tory senator to try to prove that appointments were not political. After looking at Joe Clark's list of possibilities, he treated Joe with the usual respect and promptly called Ontario Premier Bill Davis and asked him who he wanted. Davis gave the nod to his provincial bagman. Kelly was in.

In addition to the bagmen there is another group that is key to this aspect of the business/government influence peddling system — lawyers. As noted before, one of the major requirements for many businesses wishing to influence government as result of donations is secrecy. The fewer people who know of the origins of the money the better, especially if the money comes from a tainted source. This is where lawyers come in handy.

Lawyers act as frontmen for many people and corporations wishing to make secret donations to political parties and to particular political campaigns. The lawyer will make a donation to the political party and then bill the cost of the donation back to the client. The advantage of this arrangement is that only the lawyer's name will appear on the forms demanded by the Elections Act. The privacy of the client is assured. No pesky reporter will be able to know that the company gave money and put two and two together. If the client's favourite candidate loses, the client need not fear retribution by the winning candidate. There is another benefit as well. Suppose that the lawyer has a hundred clients that individually wish to give $5,000 each to Party X. If they had given that $5,000 individually, that $5,000 would not have bought them very much influence. However, suppose that the lawyer gave in their place. That represents a donation of $500,000. This buys the lawyer *enormous* influence. Anytime he or she picks up the telephone on behalf of his or her client, the lawyer can be certain of getting a meeting with the highest officials, and a very sympathetic hearing at that. By giving through the lawyer, the client has achieved a quantum leap in the influence which he or she is able to bring to bear.

Another advantage may not be immediately obvious. By giving to one party through a lawyer the client may in fact be ensuring himself influence with the other party as well. Most legal firms cover their bets. They try, wherever possible, to ensure that there are partners in the firm with connections to both political parties. That way, whoever wins the election, they and their clients win. This was particularly true in the West during the Trudeau era. There was a joke that 80 percent of the members in the Liberal Party in Alberta were lawyers seeking legal work from the federal government. As the saying goes, "it's a dirty job, but someone has to do it." Once the cheque is cashed, the money seems to lose its smell.

What's in it for lawyers? Lots. For starters they can look forward to getting the designation Q.C. after their names if they do this long enough, which doesn't mean much in strictly legal terms, but it is good for business. Then there is the possibility of doing work for the party in power. There is lots of money in this. Times are tough for lawyers and every little bit helps. Also, there is the matter of influence over government. This can take a number of different forms — influencing future legislation, getting changes and exceptions to existing legislation, getting favourable rulings from quasi-judicial bodies, etc. The sky is the limit. Finally, if you are very good at this, you can look forward to the same goodies as the bagmen. In fact, if you are this good at getting donations for the party of your choice, you are probably already a bagman yourself.

In fairness to lawyers, I should add that this type of activity is almost forced on them since almost all of their clients expect them to have political influence. If they do not have it, their clients will probably take their business to a lawyer that does. What choice do they have? It's very seldom that human beings pick morality over money.

Direct Political Strategy

Of course, using money to buy influence with political parties is not the only way that business can influence their behaviour. Another way is for members of the business community to actually get involved in politics themselves. The success of this tactic seems to vary considerably with the level. As we have seen already, the municipal government is the virtual playground of the development, construction and property industries. The Senate — as we shall see later — is little more than a permanent business lobby maintained at the expense of the Canadian taxpayer. Elective office at the provincial and federal levels seems to result in mixed reviews. Actually, day-to-day lobbying by MPs and MPPs is probably uncommon. Instead, the existence of business-oriented Members probably has the effect of reinforcing Parliament's or the provincial legislatures' bias toward a capitalist organization of the economy and society.

Whatever the purpose or effect, the presence of business is there. One study by the Library of Parliament in 1984 showed that fifty-nine MPs had business backgrounds. When you add in the sixty-eight lawyers — a group usually identified with business, except for a handful of NDP types — you end up with a Parliament that probably has somewhere between 35 and 40 percent of MPs with an *automatic* pro-business bias. One interesting fact concerning these business MPs is that they are almost exclusively big business representatives. Small business, that most vibrant sector of the Canadian economy, is virtually unrepresented. A good part of this absence is the result of the clash of values between small business and government. John Bullock, head of the Canadian Federation of Independent Business, stated that, "combining business and politics is 'absolutely unnatural' for the entrepreneur. Their whole drive is centred around independence. . . . Politics is the absolute opposite. You're totally at the mercy of events. If your leader pats somebody on the bum, you may be wiped out before you even start. You can't control your own life."[2]

This monopoly of business expression by big business has its effects, almost all of them negative. Big business in Canada is fat, lazy, inefficient, bureaucratic and highly innovative in developing new techniques for restraining competition. When its representatives enter government, which is also fat, lazy, inefficient, bureaucratic and restrictive, it acts as an accelerator rather than a brake on already present tendencies toward stupidity and waste in the political system.

Lobbying

Business has always had a tremendous influence over policy making and administration by government. Even though it has a long history, the way in which this influence has been exercised has undergone a tremendous transformation. Formal lobbying activity by business is a very recent phenomenon. Up until about twenty years ago, "lobbying" as such was conducted in a very informal sort of fashion. This process might be best described as "friendly persuasion." The structure of business and government was simpler in those days and the amount of government intervention in and regulation of the economy was minimal. Business ruled its sphere, government ruled its sphere, and there was very little overlap between the two. When there was interdependence or interaction, all that was required was a telephone call by a business leader to a cabinet minister, a top civil servant or the Prime Minister to explain the problem and work out a mutually agreeable solution. The number of players in the game was smaller, with a relatively small and well developed network of top government and business leaders who knew each other, belonged to the same clubs and went to the same parties. They were friends. Most importantly, they shared very much the same point of view. Perhaps the epitome of this business and governmental consensus was C.D. Howe. Howe was, of course, the key figure in the development of economic policy and the architect of the growth in the Canadian economy for decades. He was also one of the greatest figures in the Canadian business establishment. His biographers, Robert Bothwell and William Kilbourne, state that "Howe was . . . the leader of a national business community as well as a party leader and a minister of the crown . . . who saw no contradiction in his role; it was his job to enforce the public interest and the public interest was, ultimately, business' interest."[3]

This idyllic world of government and business co-operation (idyllic from a business perspective) began to slip in the early sixties, and the process accelerated to the present. Part of this slippage in the quality of the relationship is the result of profound changes that have occurred in the structure and function of the state in Canadian society and the Canadian economy. The last two and a half decades have seen a dramatic increase in government intervention in the operation of business activity and the economy, which has not pleased the business community to say the least. Indeed it has lead to a major and growing divergence in the outlooks of business and government. While the outlook of business has remained very much the same, the ideology of government has altered dramatically. To paraphrase the words of former U.S. President Franklin Delano Roosevelt, politicians discovered that there were more votes on Main Street than on Bay Street. Government intervention won elections; fiscal restraint and laissez-faire economics did not.

As the role of government changed, its structures and methods of making decisions changed dramatically in an attempt to manage the work of the vast bureaucracy which had been created. And as government changed, the type of person doing the lobbying, and the techniques that he or she uses have changed as well. With the growth of government, the creation of new central bodies of government and frequent changes in responsibilities and personnel in various ministries and departments, it was no longer possible for business leaders to pick up a telephone and lobby government as they had in the past.

The early sixties saw the rise of the professional Ottawa lobbyist. This happened in response to the need for an intermediary who was familiar with how government worked, knew how to identify the various power centres in the policy process and could explain this process and interpret developments for senior executives. At this point the type of person sought after by business for lobbying was someone who had graduated from the upper ranks of the public service, such as David Mundy, former Assistant Deputy Minister of Industry, Trade and Commerce, who went to work for the Air Industries Association. The Canadian Export Association recruited Tom Burns, formerly an Assistant Deputy Minister at Trade and Commerce. Henry de Puyjalon joined the Canadian Construction Association; he had been at the Treasury Board. Ernie Steele, former Under-Secretary of State responsible for broadcast policy and with a career in government that spanned eighteen years, joined the Grocery Products Manufacturers of Canada in 1968, which might seem a tenuous link, but in 1978 he was able to use his background to better purpose when he became head of the Canadian Association of Broadcasters.

In the 1970s there was a rapid circulation of cabinet ministers and deputy ministers from one department and ministry to another. One result was a belief among many that they had become out of touch. There was a feeling that only people below ministerial and deputy ministerial rank — ADMs, Director Generals and Directors — possessed a firm grasp of the issues at stake in their ministries. These became the new foci for lobbying activity. They developed policy. They held power.

For a time this lobbying strategy worked, but only after a fashion. The lobbying activities of business were good when used as special efforts aimed at influencing, changing and defeating specific legislation, but when it came to the larger issue of public policy, this strategy was a failure. Partly this was the result of the decline in the role and influence of the public service in the area of public policy, a process which began in the early and mid-seventies but really began to gather steam with the return of Michael Pitfield in 1980, to the position of Clerk of the Privy Council. Pitfield instituted a system whereby cabinet ministers would determine priorities and public servants would be preoccupied with their implementation. Briefly, the system involved a process whereby two or more ministers with responsibilities in the same area were given a lump sum and told to fight over it. The result was a dramatic shift in the policy area back to the politicians, at least those at the highest levels. This resulted in a major shift in the way to lobby government and the type of person recruited to do the lobbying.

Up to the early 1980s, the majority of Ottawa lobbyists had been people who had worked in the upper ranks of the civil service, but now there was a need for lobbyists who had worked in ministers' offices. This shift was accelerated by the November 1981 budget fiasco. The budget was so bad that it resulted in a shaking of faith of many ministers in the public service. Ministers were now anxious to speak with lobbyists who could give another perspective and who shared the politicians' approach. The Canadian Petroleum Association provides some good examples of this new type of lobbyist. One CPA acquisition was Janice Deacy who had been Executive Assistant to Energy Minister Alastair Gillespie. Jodie White, former Communications Director for the Progressive Conservative Party, started to work for the CPA under contract. Jim Bennett, who had worked for Jean Chrétien and Jack Horner, two cabinet ministers under the then Prime Minister Trudeau, went on to become Director of National Affairs for the Canadian Federation of Independent Business and later worked for the Canadian Wine Institute.

There are four major groups of lobbies in the business area: trade associations, public affairs consulting companies, lawyers and company staff.

Trade Associations

At last count there were about 700 Canadian national trade associations. Their composition and areas of interest were as many and as varied as Canadian business itself. Basically trade associations can be broken down into two major categories: broad-based organizations which seek to influence the general direction of national policy, and those associations with a narrower focus and more specific and short-range goals. These groups may be organized by sector, industry, product, activity and size.

There has been a trend in Canada toward a proliferation in the number and type of interest groups, part of a tendency toward specialization. This sort of specialization can be explained by the emergence of new industries, products and trade associations, to protect and promote the interests of the new industries and make government sensitive to the nature and implications of the new products and technologies. There have, of course, been other factors that have led to this proliferation. Differences between protected and export industries, labour intensive and capital intensive industries and domestically owned and foreign owned industries have led to a large number of different needs and therefore different trade organizations. The growth of government itself has led to new associations as businesses have attempted to cope with and respond to new forms of government regulation and organization. Finally, the fact that so many of Canada's industries are subsidiaries of or in competition with foreign companies has meant the establishment of organizations parallel to those existing in other countries, most often the United States.

Up until recently, the tendency toward the proliferation and specialization of trade associations has led to a bias in favour of the narrow-based and specific issue type of lobby at the expense of the association interested in the general direction of long-term government policy. Until recently most of the activity of trade associations in Canada was restricted to setting standards, writing model contracts, micro-economic analysis and making government aware of their members' views on upcoming legislation. Recent trends in government activity and a general perception of a growing hostility on the part of the government to the business point of view have led to an understanding that it is no longer any good to respond on a case by case basis because you are almost always too late to effect any change. The answer was to begin lobbying earlier and lower down, in the hierarchy of the civil service. The real shocker for business was the realization that even this change was not enough. What business discovered was that it was always responding to someone else's agenda. Business was winning many of the battles, but it was losing the war. In fact, it was facing annihilation. The appreciation of the value of influencing public policy before it was formulated — years, even decades before it might see the light of day — lead to a dramatic increase in the importance of associations aimed at influencing general policy.

Probably most of us (myself included) are used to thinking of groups such as the C.D. Howe Research Institute and the Conference Board of Canada as just public-spirited and non-partisan bodies whose sole purpose is to do research and advise government of economic problems and prospects. What is less obvious is that these two groups are in fact trade associations devoted to influencing the formulation of government policy in the general interest of the Canadian business community. They are just small time compared to the Business Council on National Issues.

Make no mistake, the Business Council on National Issues is the voice of the "big boys." You won't find a neighbourhood grocer or gas station owner in the bunch. There's nobody from your bowling league here. This organization represents the opinions of the chief executive officers of the largest companies in the country. If you aren't the CEO of some company like Imperial Oil or Bell, don't bother applying for membership. The organization was formed by Letters Patent in March 1977 by the chief executive officers of 125 of the major corporations in Canada. Apparently one of the leading forces in its inception was Bill Twaits, then chairman of Imperial Oil. At last count the organization has about 150 CEOs of the largest corporations in Canada, including Paul Demarais of Power Corporation, Jean de Grandpre of Bell, Charles Bronfman of Seagram's and Kenneth Harrigan of Ford. Just to put icing on the cake it also has the CEOs of the five largest banks. These members administer $450 billion in assets and employ two million Canadians. That is definitely clout to which the government is likely to respond if asked nicely.

The BCNI differs dramatically in philosophy and practice from virtually all other trade associations. Unlike groups representing grocers, haberdashers and coffin makers, the BCNI does not dirty its hands with the more sordid day-to-day aspects of business lobbying. Its world is the lofty and noble stratum of heaven populated by Prime Ministers and Cabinet Ministers and its nourishment and raison d'être are made up of long-range studies. No vulgar ADMs for these gents. No nasty haggling over mere billions and who will get a grant for what company. Nothing so common! Thomas D'Aquino, its President, captures the somewhat patrician essence of this organization when he says, "The BCNI is a new kind of organization . . . We are different in style, composition, philosophy and methodology. We don't shoot from the hip; our members are eminent CEOs who detest confrontation. We bring the senior voice of business to government in a more sophisticated, better prepared way."[4] The really long-range and far-reaching goals of this organization were best articulated in an interview D'Aquino gave to *Canadian Business* in March 1983 where he said, "The council's main aim is to be the most influential voice of business in the national public arena, to try to change some of the values, as well as the policies, of our society while respecting the fundamental aspects of the market economy."[5]

Sounds ambitious. Still, if anyone can do it, D'Aquino can. His background is the epitome of that new breed of lobbyist. Professionally and politically, his credentials are unimpeachable from the perspective of upper crust Ottawa society. A native of Nelson, B.C., he roomed with Joe Clark at the University of British Columbia. Following graduation with a degree in law, he worked on Trudeau's successful attempt for the leadership of the Liberal Party. From 1969 to 1972 he worked in the Prime Minister's office as a special assistant and speech writer. The next three years were spent in international law and financial consulting in London and Paris. In 1975 he returned to Canada to set up a consultancy practice in Ottawa to help businesses with their relations with government in the areas of policy and regulatory problems. During this time one of his major clients was BCNI. One thing led to another and in 1981 he was made president of BCNI.

D'Aquino is well connected to the holders of power in Ottawa of both the major parties. The link with Trudeau during his time in office was useful. There was his stint in the PMO and work with cabinet minister James Richardson. He has lived a charmed life on the Conservative side of the House as well, especially through the agency of Joe Clark, Esq. Rooming with him at college was a nice start. Apparently they stayed quite good friends. He just happened to be sitting with Maureen McTeer when her husband was chosen leader of the PCs. Clearly he and his organization are positioned nicely whoever wins any given election.

As I said before, the BCNI and its members are spared any of the more unsavoury aspects of lobbying which we mere mortals might have to engage in. If you are looking for greasy and slimy backroom boys making dirty deals in smoky rooms for a few measly dollars, look elsewhere. Our friends at BCNI would never dream of it. They don't have to. Actually the Council operates through a twenty-three member policy committee. This committee meets four times a year and decides which issues should be studied. The work is farmed out to task force members and the research is done by top-flight consultants. A typical example was their report on defence policy which was done by Peter C. Newman! The organization has the resources to do first class work, too. The budget in 1983 was a little more than $1 million. In addition to this money, the BCNI is able to draw heavily on the resources of the member companies. BCNI people are used to dealing with la crème de la crème of Ottawa people in government. Says D'Aquino, "Chief CEOs like talking to their counterparts — the people who make the decisions."[6] Apparently BCNI has excellent relations with senior economic ministers, and select BCNI members have informal meetings with the Prime Minister.

While increasingly important, lobby groups concerned with the long-term influencing of public values and perceptions are still the exception rather than the rule. The more common variety of business lobby is the trade association that operates on behalf of members made up of companies with a rather narrowly defined set of problems and lobbying objectives. These people are not out to change the world. They only want to make their little piece of it a little sweeter and a little easier to operate in. As we noted before, these lobbies may be organized according to: sector (e.g., Canadian Manufacturers' Association), industry (e.g., Grocery Products Manufacturers of Canada), product (e.g., Canadian Carpet Institute), activity (e.g., Canadian Exporters Association) or size (e.g., Canadian Federation of Independent Business).

These organizations tend to restrict their lobbying to matters of intimate and immediate concern, such things as taxation, accounting practices, business procedures and practices, applied research, marketing and promotion of trade, statistics and attempting to modify government regulations and legislation to the benefit of members. Their target audience can be either the government or the general public. Obviously, they do not do all of these activities all the time nor do they do all of them equally well. The table below is the result of research conducted with the co-operation of the top 143 trade associations in Canada. It shows some of the activities undertaken by these lobbies and just how important each one is.

ASSOCIATION ACTIVITIES
RANKED ACCORDING TO OVERALL IMPORTANCE

	Frequency
Government Relations	90
Industry/Market Information	60
Public Relations	54
Product/Service Standards	38
Inter-Industry Relations	36
Industry Promotion	36
Interest Group Relations	29
Other	22
Education	14
Employment Standards	11

Source: Isaiah A. Litvak, "National Trade Associations: Business–Government Intermediaries," *Business Quarterly*, Autumn 1982, p. 36. Reproduced by permission.

As you can see, "government relations" is the hands down winner in terms of importance. Simply put, this means lobbying the government. As much as these groups may tout their efforts in the areas of education, product standards and what not, when all is said and done, they are there to promote the interests of their members. If the public's and their interests coincide, so much the better. If not, too bad.

Public Affairs Consulting Companies
Not all businesses are fortunate enough to be able to rely on the services of a knowledgeable, skilled and hard-working trade association. Or perhaps they have a special need for a sensitive matter that involves government and which also involves their competition. In such cases, the use of a trade association would either be inappropriate or disastrous. That's where the services of a public services consulting company come in handy.

This type of company can provide a number of critical services to a company dependent on government. Some of the more important are providing an early-warning system for changes in existing legislation and new policies that will appear in the future. The idea is, as noted earlier, to start work on influencing policies before they become fully articulated or are announced. The sooner the better is the watchword of lobbyists. In addition, these companies will identify the people to see and outline how to approach them and what to say when you get there. It should be added at this point that this grooming of executives and rubbing off the rough edges is critical and usually badly needed.

Contrary to popular opinion, most executives lack any sort of personality or political sensitivity when it comes to dealing with bureaucrats or the government. Oddly enough, many of the trade associations are no better. A premium seems to be put on speaking bluntly and lecturing bureaucrats on their failings and their proper place in the scheme of things. John Godfrey, a man of great influence in the federal Liberal Party and the Trudeau government made the following remarks about this tendency toward less than delicate or sensitive behaviour on the part of business lobbyists and executives: "If the Chamber (the Canadian Chamber of Commerce) has ever had a president whose political philosophy was not well right of Louis XVI, then he has been remarkably successful in concealing it . . . such organizations who reiterate such completely predictable views *ad nauseum* simply lose their credibility with the upper echelons of the government. . . ."[7] That's where the consulting firms come in. It is often their unenviable task to civilize these would-be lobbyists and somehow help these business types to make the long and painful leap from the eighteenth to the late twentieth century. They earn every dollar they make.

These companies are usually well equipped for the task. In most cases they are staffed by people who were either cabinet ministers themselves or were aides or assistants to ministers. Extra influence goes to those firms with alumni from both sides of the House. Take, for instance, Public Affairs International Ltd. It has managed to recruit ex-aides and assistants of Liberal and Conservative cabinet ministers such as Don Jamieson, Judd Buchanan, Herb Gray and Marc Lalonde on the Liberal side and Ray Hnatyshyn and John Crosbie on the Conservative side. No matter who wins an election you can be sure that firms like this will have the inside track in cabinet and get their telephone calls returned.

Lawyers

Whenever and wherever there is money or power around, there seem to be lawyers in place doling out or managing both. Beyond handling donations of tens or hundreds of thousands of dollars of his and others' money to the party's coffers, another source of a lawyer's political clout comes from the fact that lawyers dominate the House of Commons and Cabinet. When they retire from politics or are retired by the voters, it is totally understandable that many of them would find themselves lobbying on behalf of clients once they return to their practices. Whatever the source of their influence, lawyers play an important role in the lobbying programs of very many businesses and business groups. Robert Presthus, in his seminal work on the role of the elite in Canadian politics, notes the role of lawyers explicitly when he states that 40 percent of all groups, led by business, social-recreational, and professional groups, have at one time or another employed a lobbyist or a lawyer to represent them.[8]

Staff

The final technique used by business to lobby government is to have individuals on staff whose sole purpose is to keep abreast of events, personalities, policies and trends in ideology in Ottawa or the provincial capitals. These employees are not exactly what one would describe as political virgins. As with other professional influencers, they too have pasts involving work with the parties or in the highest echelons of government. There are two divergent philosophies as to where these people should be located. One school of thought sees their natural place as being in Ottawa or the capitals. The advantage of this is that they can know the game and the players at first hand; the disadvantage is that they will be corrupted by the system. All too often lobbyists who work on a day-to-day basis with the bureaucracy come to hold the same opinion as the bureaucrats, which is often at variance with the opinions of those who pay their salary. They become co-opted. The other philosophy is to have these people in the home office, even if that office is in a different city from the capital. No fear of co-option here. The problem is that they are far from where it is happening and must rely on trade associations in the capital to act as a listening post.

Lobbying Stategies

The best business lobbying efforts have seen campaigns that involved targetting and styles that corresponded to the political realities of the time and the personalities involved. Needless to say, the number of stupid, clumsy and ill-timed campaigns usually seems to outnumber the excellent ones. Let's have a look at those factors that make for a winning or losing lobbying effort by business.

Lobby Targets: Legislators

Relying on the influence of legislators means defeat, as the table below indicates.

IMPORTANCE AS INFLUENCE ON GOVERNMENT*

	Frequency
Interaction with Senior-Level Civil Servants	75
Interaction with Cabinet Ministers	50
Favourable Media Coverage	36
Public Opinion	35
Participation on Joint Bus./Gov't. Committees	32
Support of other Trade Associations	28
Interaction with Jun./Mid-Level Civil Servants	22
Contact with Prime Minister's Office	22
Appearances before Parliamentary Committees	21
The Support of Special Interest Groups	18
Union Support	12
Interaction with Government MPs	6
Interaction with Opposition MPs	4

*Defined according to number of associations who ranked category as 'very important'.

Source: Isaiah A. Litvak, "National Trade Associations: Business-Government Intermediaries," *Business Quarterly*, Autumn 1982, p. 39. Reproduced by permission.

Lobby the Prime Minister. Lobby the Cabinet. Lobby the media, parliamentary committees or unions. Lobby the janitors and security guards. You may even lobby senators. But never, ever, lobby MPs because they count for nothing as far as power and influence are concerned. Not only are they nobodies twenty minutes from Parliament Hill, as former Prime Minister Trudeau announced, but they also seem to be nobodies within twenty minutes of the Parliament Buildings. Their wives or husbands love them, their dog loves them, their parents love them, sometimes even their secretaries love them, if we are to believe the gossip. But that's it. As one experienced lobbyist put it, "When I see members of Parliament being lobbied, it's a sure sign to me that the lobby lost its fight in the civil service and the cabinet."[9] Only if the MP lobbied happens to be a cabinet minister, can it be worthwhile. There has been the occasional success in lobbying Commons committees, but it's just that, occasional. About the only lobbying of MPs that seems to show any promise is a long-term strategy based on wooing young MPs who seem to be future cabinet material. Still, that's a ten or fifteen year gamble and a slim one at that.

Cabinet and the Prime Minister

Business has had quite a bit of success with approaches at this level. Two factors seem to maximize business lobbying success here. If you have been a generous contributor to the election coffers of the party in power, ministers may listen to you and meet your requests if they are reasonable and if they are within their power. Otherwise, they may not return your calls. The other factor involves the nature of the evolution of legislation. Business has had good success in influencing top-down legislation, legislation emanating from Cabinet. Implementation is then passed to the civil service. Joe Clark was particularly fond of this approach, probably because he knew he could not trust his bureaucrats. This was especially true of his energy legislation.

When businesses are seeking some favour involving a regulatory agency or quasi-judicial body, they've got it, once again as long as they have been generous beforehand. It is as easy as it is because the members of these bodies are almost all political appointees. The media tend to be a great example of this sort of thing. Take the CRTC. Getting it to pass favourable regulations or grant a licence is either easy or impossible. It all depends on your politics. All it takes is a telephone call from the Prime Minister or a cabinet minister.

Still, Cabinet and the Prime Minister are not always the places that business should go to for help. If the legislation is of a bottom-up nature or if cabinet is relying on the bureaucracy for guidance, then business finds itself having to mingle with the masses in the civil service.

One last thing. Once a year Cabinet will call in big shots from the highest levels of business for direct briefings. Have no fear. Nothing of significance happens behind your back at this time. It is rather like watching trained seals at the zoo. The Prime Minister and his cabinet nod at the right places and smile, but that's about as far as it goes. All that is really happening is that a few delicate corporate egos are being massaged. The really dirty trench warfare is being conducted by their underlings on a day-to-day basis in mortal combat with the bureaucracy.

The Bureaucracy

It is amazing that such a powerful group has received so little attention until recently. However, even business, that great lumbering giant, so slow to learn, has finally realized that much of the real power lies here. A good deal of business lobbying attention is now — finally — being directed at the civil service. Says one lobbyist, "Really, most new ideas begin deep in the civil service machine. The man in charge of some special office . . . writes a memo suggesting a new policy on this or that. It works its way slowly up and up. At that stage civil servants are delighted, just delighted, to talk quietly to people like us, people representing this or that corporation or industry directly involved. That is the time to slip in good ideas. Later it oozes up to the politicians and becomes policy."[10] Style seems to count for a lot at this stage. Civil servants are a timid lot and easily frightened. One must look and act like them if at all possible. Above all, industry lobbyists must be gentle with them. None of this aggressive business stuff. As one observer notes, "While constantly defending their line of work as honourable, lobbyists do admit that the kind of relationships they have with people in government can make a difference in how their message is received. And the best way to get to know civil servants is casually, over a drink or a meal at Ottawa's elite Rideau Club, or even better, the fairway of the Royal Ottawa Golf Club."[11] Business lobbyists have the budgets to cultivate these connections and use them to their fullest extent. It's good for business, even though it may be bad for the public at large.

The Senate

The Senate is often ridiculed as being useless and ineffective, but it is useful and effective in one important area. Many senators act as lobbyists for various business and industry interests. One observer has called it the "lobby from within."[12] This role is reprehensible since the cost of this business lobby is being borne by taxpayers, the very group which is probably being fleeced by these interests. The worst part of it is that many of the activities are unethical even by the senators' meagre rules of conduct.

One of the most upsetting aspects of the senate as business lobbyist has been its role in the process of the review of business legislation. This review has proved time and time again to be almost completely biased in favour of big business interests. The worst offender in this respect is the Banking, Trade, and Commerce Committee. One of the darkest moments of this committee occurred in the area of banking legislation. It has consistently shown itself on the side of the established banks and against any sort of decentralization of the banking system. In 1964 it pigeon-holed three bills which would have granted charters for the Bank of British Columbia, the Bank of Western Canada and the Laurentide Bank. Several senators argued that there were already enough banks. That must have been music to the ears of the established banks. Some senators argued that the Bank of British Columbia was a threat to free enterprise since the province of British Columbia would control it. The true nature of this affair became apparent when the press revealed that four members of the banking committee held directorships in chartered banks.[13] There was clearly a conflict of interest.

Another black moment for this committee occurred in 1968 when it proposed so many amendments to the Hazardous Products Bill that the bill died when referred to the House of Commons. The bill was revived in 1969 and was once again emasculated. The Investment Companies Bill of 1969 saw this committee go into action again. The bill was designed to give the government licence to monitor the activities of investment companies so as to provide protection for consumers. Accusing the bill of dramatically aiding the government in interfering in private affairs, the committee went to work with changes and deletions that diluted the bill considerably. Two amendments are of special interest because they shed light on the apparent lobbying of the committee on behalf of business interests. One amendment ruled that manufacturing companies did not have to comply with the "surveillance" legislation if they owned subsidiaries which in turn owned subsidiaries themselves. The second said that car manufacturing companies with sales finance and acceptance companies "downstream" would likewise not have to comply with the surveillance.

Senator Hayden, head of the committee and a top corporate lawyer and businessman, revealed how these two amendments came into being. The first amendment occurred because Labatt's, Molson and Weston pressured the Senate committee after their representations in the House of Commons failed. The second amendment was the result of automobile companies having persuaded the committee that car dealers who have trouble raising capital benefit when manufacturers lend them money. The committee ruled that such loans were temporary and incidental to the principal business of the shareholder.[14]

Influence directed by the business community through the Senate is often subtler than this. In many cases, individual senators or committees may court favour with civil servants who are responsible for the legislation in question. Without declaring the original origin of the query, the senators may convince the civil servant of the virtues of making this "minor" change. No fuss, no muss. No one is the wiser.

There is more fun that this, though. In 1976 and 1977 the Senate Finance Committee was studying federal government rentals of office space from private corporations. This investigation was the result of charges that the Liberal government had shown favouritism to the Campeau Corporation in financial arrangements for a multimillion dollar federal office complex in Hull. There was some doubt as to the impartiality of the committee. During fiscal 1974-75, eight senators were directors on the boards of twelve companies which rented space to the federal government. Three of these were listed as members of the Finance Committee when the inquiry began. One of the three was Senator Louis de G. Giguère, famous for his involvement in the Skyshops scandal. Giguère had served as a director of Campeau Corporation up until the scandal broke in 1975. Campeau had been unusually well blessed among the firms renting space to the federal government which had senators as directors. During fiscal 1974-75 Campeau had received 10.1 million of the 15.3 million.[15]

The Public

As a last resort business will sometimes make a direct appeal to the public. In this area business is at something of a disadvantage. After a few centuries of buying the ideological explanations of its "betters," the Canadian people does not seem in the mood to buy the point of view of the business establishment any more. The public is fed up with calls to a higher national interest and seems intent upon satisfying its own individual self-interests, while the media are antagonistic to business and its outlook. Nobody seems to want to hear what business has to say. Still business realizes that it is light-years behind its enemies in communicating its point of view. The question is "how?" The answer has in many cases been advocacy advertising.

Advocacy advertising, in the business setting, takes the form of two different types of campaigns. One is a long range campaign to develop a consensus over time of an industry's perspective. It may take the form of messages in support of the free enterprise system, as was done by the Insurance Council of Canada, or involve whipping up support for a particular problem or industry. This seems to be a favourite with the energy industry. The funniest though must surely be the campaign by the Canadian Bankers Association to convince us that banks love small business. They do love small business, but in the same way that butchers love cattle.

Lobbying Style

So far we have discussed style very much in terms of whether business tries the one-shot effort in response to a perceived danger (which definitely does not work), or the ongoing "be my pal" approach, which does work sometimes. The question of style cuts another way too. Two major stylistic options open to business lobbies are the quiet diplomacy style employed by the wise and the confrontational style public campaign employed by corporate kamikazes.

Quiet Diplomacy

Let's face it, there is a natural tendency for most political decision making and policy formulation to be done informally, behind the backs of Canadians. Again, this sort of thing has a long tradition in Canada and is certainly not unusual or an aberration. There is a profoundly elitist tendency which runs through Canadian history and politics. The political system has favoured, and still does favour, elite accommodations as the principal form of decision making. It's hard to accept, but it is a fact. There is one more reason for this tendency toward the backroom deal — the political culture of the country. Canadians — at least English Canadians — are a somewhat timid and reticent people. They shun conflict, especially public conflict. Not for them the feisty self-assertion of rights so typical of the United States, so crude and unpleasant. Instead Canadians prefer accommodation, compromise and consensus seeking. If it never hits the papers, so much the better. All of this makes "quiet diplomacy" the preferred strategy. This is a game like any other and as such has certain rules:

1. Recognize that the federal bureaucracy is a collection of people. With this in mind it becomes clear that lobbying bureaucrats and politicians is an exercise in human relations rather than hand-to-hand combat. Too many business lobbyists make the mistake of assuming that superior analysis and reams of figures will win the day. People come first.

2. Develop a long-range plan of what you wish to achieve and how you will go about it. Do not use the short run blitz techniques that business had relied on in the past. The show of all that power and passion, especially coming out of the blue, seems threatening to bureaucrats and politicians. They may cave in as you wish, or they may react in exactly the opposite way. It is so unpredictable. Part of this long-range strategy might involve releasing some of your top executives to work in federal government programs. It may seem like an enormous investment, but it will pay big dividends in the end. You will develop powerful contacts in government and more importantly, you will understand for the first time how the government works. The result will be that you will be more successful at lobbying and it will cost you less.

3. Understand that the bureaucracy is unable to respond quickly. It is, after all, like a great elephant, heavy, ponderous and slow. There is good news though. Once it begins to move, its enormous inertia carries all before it.

4. Understand that most civil servants are competent and conscientious people just like you. They have dreams and they want to do a good job. Indeed, most do a remarkably good job considering how the cards are stacked against this happening. Treat them with consideration and respect and they will rise to your high expectations.

5. Realize that you are not the only interest in the country. Politicians and civil servants have other problems besides yours. They have their careers and re-election to worry about, other groups' demands to consider, and the defence of the national interest (as they understand it) to think about. All of this has an impact on the type of lobbying pitch and campaign you will mount. One of the important things to realize is that your pitch must show how giving in to your demands will help the politicians and bureaucrats with their own selfish goals. Furthermore you must show how your demands are in the national interest. Too many business people act like primitive

social-Darwinists and Ayn Rand fanatics. Reference to naked self-interest and survival of the fittest may buy you something with the boys in the locker room at the squash club, but it is like cancer with the government. The only self-interest of any value to them is their own, not yours. So tell them how you can help them, not the other way around.

6. Skip ideology. Many business lobbyists cannot seem to stay away from ideological stereotypes. Groups like the Canadian Chamber of Commerce had a tendency to treat the Trudeau Liberals like a reincarnation of the Bolsheviks. This prejudice was quickly communicated to those they wished to lobby. Government was not amused. The same lobbies made a similar mistake with the Mulroney PCs. Somehow they got the crazy idea that the PCs in power would be born-again right-wingers and so only too happy to give away the shop to business. Wrong again. The fact is that no party in power is ideological. All governments play the game of brokerage politics. They hug the centre like a child his teddy bear. They hold no ideas as dear as that of staying in power. They would sell their grandmothers if they thought it would help. They will sell you too unless you can persuade them that you are useful to *their* success.

7. Stress consensual solutions. Government hates conflict and confrontation and ignores or crushes those who use it. It loves bureaucratic — and quiet — groups made up of pleasant and agreeable people who never rock the boat.

Public Campaigns

While the natural preference for business is to take the path of quiet diplomacy, there are times when even business is prepared to use the public and the confrontational strategy, especially when the path of quiet diplomacy does not work. You may recall the so-called energy crisis at the end of the seventies and early eighties. The shock of rapidly rising gasoline prices and line-ups at gas pumps produced an outcry from the general public that led to a government inquiry into profits in the petroleum industry. The Bertrand report which followed was released in March 1981. The report did not actually accuse the petroleum industry of illegal activities, but it did have some rather revealing things to say about the possibility of a rip-off of the consumer and the sad state of the Canadian oil marketplace. Among other things, it alleged that Imperial Oil and other oil companies had overcharged the public by about $12 billion. This had apparently occurred, said the report, because of the lack of much real competition in the oil industry. Headlines appeared in newspapers across the country which went something like: "Oil industry rips off Canada." Clearly the oil industry in general and Imperial Oil in particular had failed to control events and the commission's findings by means of quiet diplomacy.

The industry's assumption at this point was that it was being made a scapegoat by government and the press. It was the industry's view that more quiet diplomacy was unlikely to encourage government to help it limit the damage that had already occurred since it appeared that the federal government had many compelling reasons to let this affair continue. For one thing, the government could garner considerable public support by portraying itself as the protector of the public from these awful speculators and exploiters. For another, the scandal which followed helped to soften up public opinion for later government moves to intervene dramatically in the workings of the oil industry. Third, there was a suspicion among some that the federal government identified the oil industry as a supporter of its political enemies. With this in mind the industry felt it had nothing to gain by continuing quiet diplomacy and everything to gain by going public.

This was serious business. The public obviously had pronounced the industry guilty. Polls showed that negative attitudes toward the oil industry had increased to 70 percent of respondents. Imperial was besieged by angry letters and telephone calls. Employee morale plummeted as employees were assailed by friends and acquaintances as to why they continued to work for a company that was profiteering. All of this was beginning to hurt in ways that business people understand — on the profit and loss statement.

Imperial did something that is rather uncharacteristic of Canadian business. Most Canadian companies are used to being abused by the media and supporters of social change. Instead of fighting back, they take it on the chin like good soldiers and hope it will go away. Imperial decided it had to fight back. Two days after the original statement by the Combines Director, Imperial Oil executives held a press conference where the press had the opportunity to grill the company's Chairman, President and Director of Marketing. Following this it held a number of press briefings across the country and Imperial executives and public relations representatives appeared on various TV and radio interview shows. The company also tried direct communication with its customers. It enclosed a pamphlet with monthly credit card billings that told the company's side of the story. Actually, I wonder at the wisdom of this ploy. I know how happy I am to receive bills and I suspect most people are like myself in viewing anything accompanying a bill with a pretty negative attitude. Finally, and perhaps most importantly, the company launched an advertising campaign to tell its side of the story and to convince the public that the charges were false. Two ads ran in thirty-seven newspapers across Canada. To supplement the newspaper campaign there was a television commercial starring the company president, Jack Armstrong.

This court of last resort approach is only a part of the trend toward more public campaigns. Another part stems from a belief among many business people that the whole world is against them. They are probably right. The old and easy days of agreement between business and government (collusion might be a better word) seem to be a thing of the past. The increasing number of regulations imposed upon business by government indicates that government no longer loves business. The media seem to be biased against business, and permanently so. Business is constantly under attack by various church, women's, environmental and union groups, and these attacks are reported in an uncritical fashion. Many business people believe that if they keep their heads down it will all blow over, but others are now becoming aware that a long term shift in public sympathy away from business, ultimately translates into more government regulation and an increasingly difficult business climate.

This danger has spurred some companies and industry groups to try to make public appeals for support for their own business operations and to buttress flagging public support for the free enterprise system as a whole. This is a bit of a joke since Canadian business is the group most terrified by a return to free enterprise. It has obtained nourishment at the public teat and sought shelter in monopolies and oligopolies for so long that it is somewhat doubtful whether it could cope with a return to pure capitalism. Still, it is part of the business mythology and business feels compelled to mouth the words. This has led to two rather noteworthy thrusts. One is to try and mobilize employees to support their companies and to lobby on their behalf to their MPs and MLAs, the effect of which is small given the extreme limits of freedom available to the typical MP. The other technique, one which offers more promise, is that of advocacy advertising.

Advocacy Advertising

Crudely put, advocacy advertising attempts to sell ideas and points of view in the same way advertisers market soap, corn flakes and toilet paper. Full page ads, thirty second spots on the radio and slick television commercials attempt to persuade us that the oil industry is our best friend, the forest industry is leaving the North with even more trees than were there before and that a return to the bracing days of unfettered free enterprise will cure unsightly acne in teenagers.

So far advocacy advertising has been something of a failure. Even the federal government under Trudeau used this technique to try and buttress what had become an increasingly unpopular regime. Yet it went down to the worst electoral defeat in history. The oil industry's use of advocacy advertising to try and persuade the public that they are not being gouged has also not met with success. People still think the oil crisis was a fraud used by the industry to garner obscene profits. The funniest ad campaign of all has to have been that of the Insurance Bureau of Canada which touted the merits of the free enterprise system. No brash and obvious campaign, this. It was tasteful and subtle. The problem was that it was so subtle that very few viewers who watched it could figure out the message. A viewing public that had for decades been hit over the head and whose intelligence had been insulted so many times by advertisers was shown to have been unable to understand one of the first intelligent and subtle commercials in decades.

Apart from the danger of being too subtle, companies attempting to influence public opinion in this manner have found that there are other dangers as well. Terence Hill, the director of the "Let's Free Enterprise" campaign, put it this way, "Don't do it . . . unless you absolutely have to. Advocacy advertising is so loaded with potential problems . . . that to take on a campaign of this nature should be looked at only as a last resort."[16] Not too encouraging coming from the director of one of the biggest of these campaigns, is it? One of the potential dangers is that it may inadvertently help your enemies. INCO learned this painful lesson the hard way. For many years environmentalists had been nagging the Ontario government to force INCO to clean up its emissions from its Copper Cliff, Ontario smelter. INCO counter-attacked with an advocacy campaign giving a detailed breakdown of the emissions. Everyone's eyes popped out when they saw the figure of 2,000 to 3,000 tons of emissions per day. Virtually no one had realized that the problem was that bad. INCO, having given an enormous boost to the efforts of the environmentalists, slunk away and hid, never again to return to the fight in public.

Another example of the sort of trouble business lobbyists can get themselves into involves the Toronto Home Builders Association. On September 15, 1981 this group placed an ad addressed to the Prime

Minister which accused him of destroying the industry with his policies. On the same day a spokesman for the industry stated in the
Toronto Star that new home starts had ground to a near standstill.
Unfortunately, just a few pages later there was a story which stated,
"Despite escalating mortgage interest rates, housing construction
starts in Peel (a region adjacent to Toronto) increased 59 percent in the
first half of this year compared with the same period in 1980."[17] This
effectively destroyed the ad and made the builders look considerably
worse than just being ill-informed.

How Effective Is the Business Lobby?

The effectiveness of business lobbies is quite variable, depending on
the issue, the skill and access of the lobbyist, the resources at the lobby's
disposal, the legitimacy of the lobby and the strategy used. What is
clear is that the single issue lobby has, at least until recently, been
relatively more successful than those that have been involved in trying
to change long term attitudes toward business and the economy.
Government has been particularly receptive to business lobbyists
where technical issues were involved and where there was a need for
expert input and information was difficult to obtain from business on
legislation, either about to be introduced, or under review by Commons
or Senate Committees. Such areas as tax rulings and reactions to
technical features of draft legislation and regulations have seen government welcome with open arms the input of business representatives. Lobbyists are seen as experts in their field who are merely
helping former colleagues in complex areas and sharing the goal of
making the system more workable. A good example of this process was
the Grocers' Association's influence on the 1976 Consumer Packaging
and Labelling Act. The association was successful in producing recommendations that satisfied both industry and the government. Recommendations that can do this find their way into law.

One area that business has had great success in, is in the area of
either altering regulations or appealing their application. Interestingly
enough, business has had the most success in exerting influence over
taxation. Most people feel that when it comes to taxation, you just
cannot fight city hall. This is definitely a point of view that Revenue
Canada types would like to foster. It makes life so much easier for them
and it means that they have no trouble in meeting their revenue
targets. But the fact is that taxation is one of the easiest areas in which
to lobby for changes or relief. You just have to be aware of the hidden
agenda of tax officials and phrase your lobby's pitch so that it seems to

support their plans. Basically, tax officials are concerned with protecting the government's revenue base. They have to feel sure that they are not opening the floodgates for a mass of other businesses if they grant an exemption in your case. The trick then is for business lobbyists to phrase their appeals in terms of the injustice of the specific ruling rather than in terms of saving businesses part of their tax bill. Of course, it depends on the environment and timing as well.

The soft drink industry tried for ten years to get $73 million in tax relief by having their product classified as food. It was turned down decisively by then Finance Minister John Turner as simply costing the government too much money in lost tax revenue, but the same appeal was accepted the next year. What was different? The timing and the political and economic environment. In that year the government had introduced an expansionary budget, so such an exemption now fit into its plans.

Very frequently both Revenue Canada and the courts turn out to be very amenable to requests for relief. Nevertheless, businesses often find the path not as smooth as they had thought. Having successfully gotten the revenuers or the courts to see things their way, they are often stymied by the Ministry of Finance when, in its role as watchdog of public revenues, it decides to change the rules of the game. Johnson and Johnson Inc. of Montreal and Playtex Ltd. of Toronto, for example, won decisions to exempt sanitary napkins and tampons from tax on the grounds that they were clothing, but the Finance Department immediately had the clothing regulations which were part of the Excise Tax Act amended while it appealed the Playtex ruling. Fortunately for these two companies they seemed to have some pretty clever people leading their lobby effort. Both companies began to lobby in earnest and managed to persuade three important cabinet ministers to support their case. Obviously two can play at Finance's game.

Another area of successful lobbying activity involves trying to influence the government's buying plans. The federal government has enormous buying power. Sell one big contract to the feds and you can go golfing for the rest of the year. As a result competition for government business tends to be extremely severe. One of the industries where this is particularly true is the computer and computer services industry. For these companies lobbying is one of the key success variables in getting government business. Some years back I used to work for a subsidiary of a giant U.S. computer services company. For many years the company had been unable to get any sizable business placed with the federal government because it was not a truly Canadian company. At some point, I noticed that we were suddenly getting federal government business we would not have dreamt of getting before. Being young and foolish, I asked my boss, the National Marketing Manager, why this was. The reason, he told me, was that the company had retained the services of an Ottawa lobbyist and after a few telephone calls and an occasional dinner in a fine restaurant, a U.S. subsidiary was now a native-born son. Had there been a bribe? Was it a case of just an intimate chat with former colleagues? I'll never know. All I do know is that the previously impossible had become the actual.

A more recent case involved a Canadian computer company, Comterm Inc., lobbying the federal government to reverse what it saw as bias in the awarding of contracts for microcomputers. According to Comterm, the government was arbitrarily deciding to award contracts to IBM Canada without giving other companies a chance. I might add, that at this point Comterm made a microcomputer called the Hyperion which was very highly thought of in the industry. It was what is known in the industry as an IBM clone. This means it looked and acted almost exactly like an IBM/PC, the IBM microcomputer, performed very much like the IBM machine and compared favourably with IBM in terms of price and quality. Comterm assumed that it should be getting its share of the federal government's business, but this seems not to have been the case if we are to believe the president of the company. He claimed in September 1984 that the federal government had a policy of giving IBM the business without giving other companies a chance to compete, and in stepped the lobby group which represents businesses like Comterm, the Canadian Advanced Technology Association. Its executive director went to bat for the company and in an interview with the *Toronto Star* he presented the position his group would be taking. He was quoted as saying that the practice of buying only from IBM was hypocritical, since on the one hand, politicians extolled the virtues of the Canadian high-technology industry and on the other "there's an overt discrimination by government against those companies in this country."[18]

These remarks are an excellent example of how the lobbyist works. He was not telling the government to give his people more business because they want to make big profits and so enable the executives, owners and salesmen to retire to the Bahamas. This would have meant instant rejection by a government publicly committed to a view that businesses were making too much money off the backs of ordinary citizens (even though the ease with which they accept political contributions from business and the fact that the majority of them are either lawyers or business people puts the lie to the rhetoric). Instead, he phrased his appeal on the basis of support for a stated government goal, namely, the development of an indigenous Canadian high-technology industry. What he was proposing — fine tuning the administration of government policy — was an acceptable message. In theory at least this should lead to more jobs, a larger tax base and more tax revenues for the government and more government control over the country's economy. Moreoever, it would allow politicians who supported his ideas to tout themselves as patriots and nationalists. Appeals like this are difficult for government to refuse.

Of course, business lobbying is not always individual companies or lobbies fighting for small victories. Sometimes the goals are of national significance and historic proportions. When the stakes are this high, individual lobbies band together into coalitions, some of which have been exceedingly successful.

One of the more successful coalitions was the one formed to fight the MacEachen budget in November 1981. I have already mentioned this ill-fated budget and I suppose it would be unkind to dwell too much on its many horrible features, so suffice it to say that it was a grade A turkey and many a career ended as a result of it. For business lobbying, however, it was one of the great moments, the start of new directions in dialling for dollars. For business this budget and the economic tailspin which it engendered was a disaster. There was virtually no segment of the business community that did not loathe it. Virtually every business-oriented group in the country revolted. Angry telephone calls were made to cabinet ministers. Letters from the usually staid and the almost moribund sparkled with vitality and passion and threatened the physical well-being of the Finance Minister and anyone else connected with the Liberal government if they ventured out of Fortress Ottawa. It was the opposite of a love-in and the government was the guest of honour. The results amounted to one of the greatest victories in business lobbying in Canada.

The old budget was torn up and replaced seven months later by a new budget. It was not actually called a budget. To save face, it was called an economic statement but the only group fooled by this euphemism was the government itself. A whole world of pain seemed to fall upon MacEachen as a result of business lobbying against his budget. The final result was his removal as Finance Minister and his being put out to pasture in his home away from home in External Affairs. He finally made his home in the Senate.

Not all big business coalition campaigns are protests against gov-

ernment policies. Some reflect conflicting interests of various segments of the business community. In some cases the lobbyists are
egged on by the government. Such was the case with the Crow lobby.
The whole issue of the Crow freight rate was a fascinating one since it
shed so much light on the contradictions and centrifugal forces of
Canadian society. The Crow freight rates had existed very much un-
changed since 1897. Rate increases were virtually taboo because of the
importance of the issue to Western farmers and the inevitable political
fallout which would result from any increases. One of the original
groups that lobbied for increases was the Coal Association of Canada.

By 1980, major western Canadian coal companies had begun to
worry that the rail system had become overcrowded and that the
railways were unlikely to do anything to expand capacity because they
were losing money hauling wheat. In 1981 the Coal Association of
Canada began to lobby for a revision of the Crow rate, and to do this
they had some very impressive talent. The man in charge of the lobby
was Gary Duke, B.C. Resources' Vice President, Government Relations. Duke had an impressive background in government. He had at
one time been executive assistant to former cabinet minister Robert
Andras. He was joined in heading up this campaign by Gerald Joynt,
communications officer for Fording Coal Ltd. of Calgary. Their first
move was to take a "dog and pony" show to Ottawa for meetings with
both government and opposition caucuses. This was just the beginning. What followed was a smooth and well-co-ordinated lobby effort
on behalf of a coalition of lobbies that soon came to embrace the
interests of resource companies and the railways. It was irresistible. By
the time the lobbying opposition realized that there was a problem, it
was too late. The original lobby coalition had, in the words of Stonewall
Jackson, got there "the fu'stest with the mostest."

11

Dialling for Dollars:
Corruption

One of the sad facts of political life is that politicians and civil servants are constantly subject to the temptation of civic corruption. Part of this stems from the fact that there is a lot of money available for the purpose of corrupting politicians. It was Philadelphia mayor Richardson Dilworth who put it best when he said, "For every politician who can be bribed there are at least ten businessmen waiting in line for the privilege of bribing him."[1] Or as an ex-alderman from Quebec City reported, "It is very difficult for an alderman to remain honest because so many businessmen and citizens offer money. Many aldermen enter city hall with the intention of cleaning it up but are caught in the works."[2]

The fact is that politics is business and business people are prepared to do anything to use government to aid them in their business goals. In the beginning of this century, Lincoln Steffens wrote in his book *The Shame of the Cities*, "Politics is business. That's what's the matter with it. That's the matter with everything — art, literature, religion, journalism, law, medicine — they're all business . . ."[3] Nothing really changes. If anything Steffens's words are truer today than ever. Business has just gotten better at the game.

Usually people assume that corruption requires no definition since it is intuitively obvious exactly what is meant. This feeling has not, however, deterred many political scientists and lawyers from attempting such a definition. Rogow and Lasswell have noted that "a system of public or civic order exalts common interest over special interests; violations of the common interest for special advantage are corrupt."[4] James C. Scott in his book *Comparative Political Corruption*, says that corruption is "behaviour which deviates from the formal duties of a public role . . . because of private regarding . . . wealth or status gains; or violates rules against the exercise of certain types of private-regarding influence."[5] There are as many definitions as there are writers on the subject. There is, however, a basic agreement on the idea that corruption is a violation of societal norms concerning the holding of public trust that sees its manifestation in pursuing gain at the public expense. Political corruption can include:

1. Patronage
2 Vote buying
3. Pork barrelling
4. Bribery
5. Graft
6. Conflict of interest
7. Corrupt campaign financing
8. Influence peddling
9. Criminal corruption

The sad fact of life is that all of these techniques operate in the Canadian political scene. All of them are used at one time or other by individuals and groups to influence government or by politicians and government officials to influence and manipulate the people.

Patronage
Patronage has some very distinctive features that set it apart from other forms of political corruption or corrupt forms of influence. Patronage tends to involve large numbers of people since it can only be successful if a large number of people owe jobs, money or favours to the government. It is selective in application and it must be clear to those receiving it from whom it is coming and what is expected in return. There are two sets of people that benefit. The payoff for politicians is power; it ensures their continued rule. The payoff for the recipients is money; they receive jobs and contracts. Patronage comes from elected and appointed members of the government. It is the exclusive tool of the political sphere. It can happen in any political system or level of government, but is most common in electoral systems.

The most remarkable thing about patronage is just how widespread it is. There is literally no federal or provincial government in Canada that does not practice it in some form or other. Opposition parties may damn it, but this is simply cynicism. When their time to rule comes they too will practice it. Apologists explain it away or justify it on the pretext that it makes the system work. It is, according to this view, the grease that lubricates the system. Supposedly, very few citizens would bother taking part in the political system if there wasn't the prospect of these goodies at the end of the political road. This view, then, posits a world where only bribes and promises of enrichment from the public purse can encourage anyone of talent to enter or assist in the political system. This system draws in the very worst of players, the selfish and the opportunistic. There is a good deal of truth to this model in as much as the system of government does at present work this way. This is not the system which is presented to the ordinary public; the politicians and, oddly enough, the media offer up a fairyland of idealism and civic virtue. The difference between the awful reality and the idealized picture produces a terrible cynicism in Canadians.

The saving grace, if there is one, is that usually the corruption goes on quietly and unseen. A very good example of this was the Conservative government in Ontario. After more than forty years in power, this government represented a sure source of patronage appointments for both provincial Tories and their federal colleagues when they were out of power. It was all-pervasive, reaching into every corner of the system.

One of the key techniques the Tories used in controlling the political life of the province involved the 3,500 odd postings controlled by Cabinet ministers. Patronage appointments were made to 370 different agencies, boards and commissions, ranging from Ombudsman and Ontario Hydro Chairman to non-paying positions on boards of art galleries, universities and hospitals which were always attractive because of the prestige and status involved. The positions of Ombudsman and Ontario Hydro Chairman brought with them salaries of $87,225 and $74,635 respectively in 1984.

A friend of mine told me recently that he was asked what appointment he would like in return for past efforts. Apparently, the person with whom he was speaking pulled out a computer printout which listed every appointment, how much it was worth and when it would become available. And it is not just a case of the high paying and high profile positions being touched by patronage; it reaches to the bottom as well. An infamous source of lower level patronage jobs is the Liquor Control Board of Ontario, the famous LCBO. (For the sake of non-Ontarians that is where Ontarians buy their booze.) It has long been known that these jobs, which involve relatively high pay and light work, are best won by political influence. Said Liberal leader David Peterson during the Tory regime, "It reeks . . . How good is it for democracy when a young man walks into my office and says he wants a job at the liquor board but his friend who works there told him he'd have to know an MPP . . . I hear it all the time and I have to tell people I can do nothing to help them because the first thing you have to be is a

Tory."[6] Peterson will doubtless fix this situation now that he is in power. Now the first thing you will have to be is a Liberal.

Jobs were not the only lever the Ontario Tory government used to win friends and influence people. Another technique involved the letting out of contracts. Former Premier Bill Davis almost fell victim to a scandal that involved the awarding of a major contract by Ontario Hydro for the $44 million Ontario Hydro building in downtown Toronto. The job was handed out without going to tender, and the problem was that it went to Canada Square Corporation Ltd., headed by Davis's personal friend, Gerhard Moog. A rival developer, Donald Smith of Ellis-Don Ltd. was quoted as saying that he was told to keep his mouth shut about the deal or he would never get another government job. After the story became known, there was a committee struck to study the matter. While Davis was not found culpable, Ontario Hydro management was raked over the coals.

The use of government contracts as a special way of saying "thank you" was particularly common in the area of advertising, with the big recipients being Foster Advertising Ltd., Camp Associates Advertising Ltd. and Case Associates Advertising Ltd. — all firms with top Tory connections.

Lest I be accused of unfairly being preoccupied with the past sins of the Tories, the Trudeau regime in Ottawa displayed an arrogance and abuse of power that had not been seen at any level since the Duplessis years in Quebec, or at the federal level since the corrupt glory days of the Macdonald regime.

There were features of the Trudeau era that were remarkable in the annals of Canadian influence peddling and corruption. First, there was the amazing speed with which the Trudeau government became degraded and corrupt. What it took the Ontario government forty years plus to achieve, the Trudeau Liberals equalled and surpassed in a mere sixteen. Second, there was the arrogance of the regime's approach to corruption. While the Ontario Tories were able to maintain a fairly clean image and thus keep down voter cynicism by discretion in patronage and pork barrelling, the Liberals gave very little thought to trying to keep their dirty linen hidden. They almost seemed anxious to make it known. Finally, there were the unusually large number of usually fine men and women — previously high-minded, clean and idealistic — who were either corrupted or whose names were touched by scandals or rumours of scandal. Just how corrupt and tainted with patronage the Trudeau government was, we shall never know for certain, but more than anything else, it was the scandal concerning patronage appointments that led to the defeat of the Liberals. The final binge that coincided with Trudeau's resignation was the last straw. In his last month as Prime Minister, he and his cabinet pushed through 225 order-in-council appointments, with almost half the appointments made in the last two weeks. As if this were not enough, Trudeau forced his successor, John Turner, to agree to make some appointments of Liberal MPs that he seems not to have had time for. Of the eighteen that went to their reward, seventeen were sitting Liberal MPs. This was the bone that really caught in the throat of the Canadian taxpayer. Even though Turner was seen as a victim of Trudeau's blackmail, voters nevertheless took out their revenge on him. These appointments were unusually rich. The table on page 262 gives an accounting of the booty that these scoundrels ran off with.

Bryce Mackasey had for a long time been credited with being a watchdog of the interests of the "little guy," and with this orientation he gave very credible showings as head of Canada Post and Minister of Labour. Sadly, his name ended up being associated in the public mind and in the media with influence peddling (even though he was found innocent) and patronage. Mulroney called him "an old whore" on his campaign plane and it was reported across the country. It is doubtful that the label will ever be removed. Eugene Whelan seems to have suffered severe damage to his good name because of his appointment and Yvon Pinard had to endure the humiliation of a Canadian Bar Association public protest over his appointment. Perhaps saddest of all was Mark MacGuigan, a man who had until this time been very much untouched by scandal and who, as an idealist, reformer and associate professor of law had around the beginning of 1964 made the following remark, "In Canada, political morality is almost incredibly low."[7] Twenty years later he was taking part in one of the most sordid affairs in the history of Canadian political patronage. Life takes strange and sometimes sad turns.

These appointments were an indication of just how corrupt the Liberal regime had been. Patronage was a systemic and integral feature of the regime and the way it manipulated and influenced people for the sake of power. A good indication of this was revealed when the Conservatives took office. While the country had anticipated some individual firings of patronage appointees, it was fascinated when the Tories axed two whole agencies, the Canadian Sports Pool Corporation and the Canadian Unity Information Office (CUIO). The Sports Pool was a money loser from the start and was about the only institution that ever lost money trying to pander to a vice. One of its real

16 EX-MPs' SALARIES AND PENSIONS
(TRUDEAU PATRONAGE APPOINTMENTS)

Name	Position	Salary	Approximate Pension	Total
Bryce Mackasey	Ambassador	$82,245*	$34,000 plus $25,000**	$141,245
Mark MacGuigan	Federal Court	$89,100 plus $2,000	$50,000	$141,100
Eugene Whelan	Ambassador	$82,245*	$53,000	$135,245
Bud Cullen	Federal Court	$89,100 Plus $2,000	$35,000	$126,100
Yvon Pinard	Federal Court	$89,100 Plus $2,000	$33,500	$124,500
John Munro	Transport	$68,820*	$53,000	$121,820
Robert Daudlin	County Court	$82,600	$22,500	$105,100
Rod Blaker	Parole Board	$68,805*	$29,000	$97,805
Denis Ethier	Livestock Feed	$68,820*	$28,500	$97,320
Maurice Dupras	Consul-General	$63,805*	$31,000	$94,805
Gerard Laniel	Gentleman Usher	$59,550*	$34,500	$94,050
Paul McRae	CRTC	$68,820*	$25,000	$93,820
Arthur Portelance	Aviation Safety	$59,550*	$31,500	$90,050
Michael Landers	Transport	$68,820*	$19,000	$87,820
Paul Cosgrove	County Court	$82,600	No pension***	$82,600
Rosaire Gendron	Citizenship Judge	$44,855*	$31,000	$75,855

*Where publicly disclosed salaries are a range, salary indicated is the midpoint.
**Mr. Mackasey is reported to receive a pension of about $25,000 since being fired as Chairman of Air Canada.
***Mr. Cosgrove was not in the Commons long enough to collect a pension.

Source: James Rusk, "Mackasey tops patronage income list," *Globe and Mail*, August 4, 1984, p. 5. Reproduced with permission of *The Globe and Mail*, Toronto.

purposes had been to provide jobs for executives with Liberal Party backgrounds. As for the CUIO, the stated reason for its existence had been to dispense information to promote national unity, a conduit for funds and resources to combat the separatist forces in the Quebec referendum battle. Following the defeat of the separatist side, the Office went on to other projects that looked more and more like propaganda for the government. It was behind a great deal of the advertising which appeared in support of repatriation of the constitution, for example. Remember the commercial with the flying geese? The worst was yet to come.

In the last year of the Trudeau regime, cabinet quietly approved a massive increase to the Office's budget (what a surprise just before the election), with some of the big winners in the rush for the funds being MacLaren Advertising ($1-million), Vickers and Benson Advertising Ltd. ($433,550), Ronalds-Reynolds and Co. Ltd. ($373,988) and Goldfarb Consultants Ltd. ($280,000). Both Vickers and Benson and Ronalds-Reynolds were part of Red Leaf Communications, the agency run by Jerry Grafstein that handled the Liberal Party's election advertisements, Goldfarb was the Liberal Party pollster and MacLaren has long had Liberal connections.

Any separatist readers who might be tempted to feel that Quebec independence would isolate and free Québécois from the corrupt practices common at the federal level and in Anglo provinces like Ontario would be mistaken. Alas, the experience of the Parti Québécois indicates that when it comes to patronage and influence peddling, "Québéc est une province comme les autres." The Parti Québécois came upon the political scene like a breath of fresh air, cleaning up many problems and putting an end to abuses which had existed as long as anyone could remember. It soon fell victim to a process of slow degradation of political virtue. In only a few short years it came to be accused of the same forms of abuse of public money and influence that had heretofore plagued politics in the province.

An example of the temptation, and the succumbing to it, came to light in 1981. Actually the story goes back to 1979 when the PQ cabinet authorized the Quebec Housing corporation to give a $381,000 mortgage and a $20,000 grant to La Société de Logement (SDL) for the renovation of a historical building in downtown Montreal for shops, community activities and housing. To help the non-profit group pay back the mortgage, SDL, the Housing Corporation and the Société des Alcools du Québec (the provincial liquor board) agreed to use some of the funds in order to renovate part of the premises for a government liquor store in the building. Among other occupants of the building there was also to be a nightclub which would be named La Grande Passe (The Big Scam). This name was to be prophetic.

So far everything about this project was honourable and steeped in civic virtue. The seamy side now started. SDL hired a company, Transit Inc., to do the work. The owner of this company was Luc Cyr, who was a member of the Housing Corporation. There were a few things about the choice that made it look somewhat suspicious. Among the most damning features were that: Cyr had been involved in planning the project as the head of the Housing Corporation's main repair service; he was a longtime PQ supporter whose political credentials included being a reputed bagman for the referendum campaign in May 1980 and he was appointed to the Housing Corporation on the recommendation of Jean-Roch Boivin, Lévesque's closest political advisor. Everything went along merrily until December 1979, when work was suspended because of the obvious inability of the SDL to pay escalating costs. Three hundred thousand dollars had already been spent. The question was, "Where had it gone?" The provincial auditor found some fasincating answers.

SDL President, Renaud Gendron, provided documents that showed that $23,998 had been paid in salaries to SDL administrators and another $5,773 went as wages to a sister organization, La Société pour le Developement des Arts. And what arts did this organization develop? *Maclean's* magazine followed up this story and received an admission from Gendron that the $5,773 was in fact used to pay the taxes and the liquor licence for the bar mentioned above. Even more interesting was the information which *Maclean's* received which indicated that $50,000 was paid back to Gendron's group by Cyr for demolition work. Now this is an interesting piece of finance if I've ever seen one. The non-profit group hires a housing corporation employee, Cyr, to do work on its premises, and then gets paid by this same person to do demolition work for him — the funds being provided for all of this by his employer. This sort of situation was not unknown to Cyr. He was hired by the Housing Corporation to co-ordinate $8 million in repairs to public buildings in the province. His hiring practices were quite remarkable: he hired his son to act as a buyer, he hired his daughter and he gave a $289,000 contract to his brother-in-law for a project in Rivière Bleue, about 250 km from his home.

Vote Buying

Most people would probably be surprised to see the term vote buying used in connection with Canadian politics. After all, we Canadians are a civilized and highly democratic people. But up until the mid-sixties this practice was quite common. A confidant of mine who was active politically in eastern Ontario in the early sixties, tells me that the usual price of a vote at that time was a case of twelve beer. Supposedly one of the sources of money for this purpose came from wealthy dowagers in one eastern Ontario city. In one election in the early 1960s these same dowagers complained that the cost of a vote had risen to exorbitant levels. It was then two dollars!

During the Duplessis regime in Quebec, in the two to three weeks prior to an election the Union Nationale would "soften up" the electorate with ample quantities of booze. In rural areas of the province UN stalwarts would distribute cases of beer and bottles of whisky, in towns and villages they would organize beer parties and in cities they would go from tavern to tavern buying free rounds of drinks for everyone there. Influential members of the community were often offered government jobs or contracts to come out publicly in favour of the Party, and in many cases these same individuals would be offered a hundred dollars in order to help them better understand the virtues of the government party. More humble individuals were made gifts of hams, shoes, sacks of flour, nylons and other such goods. In one case, during the election of 1956, the families of workers who had been on strike for some time were given enough meat for a week.

While the incidence of these types of election fraud has dropped considerably, it has by no means disappeared completely. It still occurs with some frequency during nomination meetings for candidates for political office. It is not uncommon for people representing someone seeking a nomination in a given riding to offer some gift or inducement for people to take out a (paid for) party membership and agree to vote for their man or woman. Many such instances occurred in the period leading up to the 1984 election, especially in those ridings where the candidate chosen was highly likely to win. It was not just at election nominations either. The meetings held to elect delegates to the PC leadership convention in 1983 saw numerous cases of such incidents. For some reason or other, vote buying went on most frequently in Quebec with both Clark and Mulroney loyalists involved.

The most comical had to be the bus loads of derelicts that came to vote for Mulroney delegates in one Quebec riding. Never had Canadians seen so many members of the disadvantaged joining the party of the better off, in such indecent haste.

New Brunswick's Liberal Justice critic, Frank McKenna, charged in the legislature that in Saint John in civic, provincial and federal elections during the period 1978 to 1983, teams of people were hired to vote on election day under fictitious names or the names of dead or absent people. One person swore an affidavit to the effect that he voted fifty times during the 1983 civic election.

Two Conservative campaign workers were charged with trying to buy votes with liquor and money during a provincial by-election in the constituency of 4th Kings in Prince Edward Island in November 1984. The problem with the charges was that they were laid only a few hours after polls had opened when only about 20 percent of voters had cast their ballots; there was some danger that remaining voters would be influenced by announcements of the charges. This was not the first time that such allegations of vote fraud had been made in this riding. The previous general election had seen an orgy of gravel dumping. Apparently, dozens of private driveways got free gravel or shale on the eve of the election. The RCMP investigated the incident, but the government never released the Mounties' report which stated that charges were not warranted but that the incident had cast "a shadow on the democratic process."

Still, such direct and crude techniques are not all that common anymore. Today's attempts at vote buying take a somewhat subtler approach. No longer do politicians or their flunkies try to buy individual votes; rather, they buy blocks of votes, not with envelopes full of bills but with promises of government recognition and grants once the election has been fought and won. Ethnic groups are the ones most commonly manipulated in this way, probably because they are perceived by politicians to be the most vulnerable groups in society and the most dependent on guidance given by community leaders. The individuals involved in this sort of trade for goodies are those members of the community who are best able to make direct contact with the political mainstream. Originally these leaders traded their communities' votes in exchange for grants and money for the community, but North American materialism and selfishness is beginning to take its toll and these power brokers have "wised up." Instead of asking for rewards for the community, they are now demanding that the rewards be for them personally, in the form of paid appointments to boards of directors and commissions.

Pork Barrelling

One of the more amusing things about pork barrelling is that many people do not recognize it as a form of corruption. For the beneficiaries of government largesse, these goodies are the height of justice personified. Only those who are not lucky enough to receive these gifts are likely to view the practice as corrupt. For them the green-eyed goddess of envy makes them burn with hatred for this obvious inequity. Still, pork barrelling is, objectively speaking, a form of corruption. It, like patronage, is an inducement for voters to vote for the party in power — a corrupt form of influence the government employs to manipulate those ruled for its own advantage — a form of buying voters with their own money. This particular manifestation of corruption is more diffuse than patronage since it does not involve individuals but communities. A new school, a new post office, paved roads, propping up a hopelessly inefficient industry — all of these are examples of "rolling out the [pork] barrel."

The recently departed Trudeau government was a master at this. Every election saw the top come off the barrel and carefully selected constituencies become a land of pork and honey. The election of 1972 was particularly noteworthy. The following goodies were offered to whet voter appetites for the Liberals:

1. Bryce Mackasey announced an $85 million Local Initiatives Program in his riding.
2. Urban Affairs Minister Ron Basford announced the up-coming construction of a $21 million container dock in Vancouver.
3. Two new ferries for service between North Sydney, Nova Scotia and Port aux Basques, Newfoundland. It was probably just a happy coincidence that North Sydney was in the riding of then Privy Council President Allan MacEachen, and that Port Aux Basques was in the riding of the Transport Minister, Don Jamieson.
4. A $10.3 million park at Mont Saint Anne, Quebec in the Liberal riding of Montmorency.
5. A $16 million national historical park in Jean Marchand's riding in Quebec City. Marchand was quoted at the time as saying that there was no harm in announcing good news just before an election.

6. John Turner, then the Finance Minister and MP for Ottawa Carleton, announced a plan to develop 50 acres in downtown Ottawa.
7. MacEachen was able to announce a senior citizens' home in Port Hawkesbury and a $30 million dock for Mulgrave, Nova Scotia; both towns coincidentally falling within the boundaries of his riding.
8. Torontonians were treated to the announcement of the forthcoming construction and development of Harbourfront, the lakefront park enjoyed by so many Toronto and district families during the weekends. That represented a $30 million gift from Liberal incumbents in the Toronto area.
9. Justice Minister Otto Lang announced that advance payments for western grain were being increased by thirty cents a barrel.
10. There was a step-up in the number of contracts for bridges, roads, sewers and so on, emanating from the departments of Transport, Supply and Services and Industry and Regional Development.

The only remarkable thing about this was the incredible arrogance shown. No effort was made to try and gloss over the corrupt quality of these announcements and practices. Quite the contrary. On October 3, 1972, Prime Minister Trudeau told an audience in Shawinigan, Quebec, "In the next week or two, we will have some goodies — candy, as they say in English — to announce for you in the field of leisure."[8] That was one thing about our Pierre. He never used subterfuge or discretion where a slap in the face or kick in the pants would do.

Pork barrelling became standard operating procedure for this government during its time in office. Some of the sums involved were incredible. A number of companies owed their continued existence to it. Such companies have had the happy good fortune of being located in the Montreal and Toronto areas that traditionally returned large numbers of Liberal MPs and cabinet ministers and so had constant and easy access to the public trough whenever they wished.

Four of the biggest boondoggles have to be DeHavilland in Toronto and Petromont and Canadair, in the Montreal area. It is obvious to all that the three are simply black holes for the Canadian treasury that will swallow up any money the government might be prepared to throw at it. So far, that has been a great deal of money indeed. The sensible approach would be to sell off the companies to private industry for whatever you could get in the case of Canadair and DeHavilland with the condition that the purchaser treat the workers with the maximum of consideration. This is in fact what the Mulroney government is proposing to do so reason may finally prevail. Petromont is another case. Here the government does not actually own the company; Union Carbide does. Union Carbide has been threatening to close its east end Montreal plant for some time, due to losses. The result would be the loss of 250 jobs and an enormous loss to businesses and the economy generally in the area. The only government response to date has been to throw away more of the taxpayer's money.

One of the worst tasting morsels to come from the pork barrel must surely be Mirabel, the international airport that almost no one uses, just outside of Montreal. Officially, the line taken was that Dorval, the airport which had handled Montreal's air traffic up to that point, would soon reach capacity and could not easily be expanded, but another theory posits that Mirabel was an enormous boondoggle designed to shore up Quebec's support for the Liberal Party for all time. It is doubtful that there has ever been a scam of these proportions. The federal government expropriated about 89,000 acres and spent almost $500 million to make Mirabel the biggest airport site in the world. Worse than the waste of the money was the expropriation of 3,900 families' land. This ploy may have worked in terms of convincing the voters in the environs of Montreal of the undying love of the Liberal Party for the region, but as of late 1984, Mirabel was an enormous white elephant that handled 1.4 million passengers and 70,000 tonnes of freight a year. That sounds like a lot, except when you realize that Mirabel is operating at only 14 percent of its capacity of 10 million passengers and 500,000 tonnes per year. It looks even worse when you realize that Dorval airport operates at 75 percent capacity and handles 6.5 million passengers and 40,000 tonnes.

Mirabel seems to have inspired unethical behaviour all around. The Canada Lands Corporation, the body set up to develop and handle the lands in the airport zone, has been a source of patronage jobs for the Liberal Party. Former federal cabinet minister Jean-Pierre Goyer went to his political reward as Chairman of the Corporation. The Conservatives did their best to make him feel unwelcome following their landslide victory. He finally took the hint and resigned in October 1984.

In fairness to people in Toronto and Montreal who may feel a little embarrassed about being singled out, it should be pointed out that there have been some rather remarkable cabinet ministers from other provinces who, by their single-handed efforts, opened the public trough to their constituents for elegant dining. East coast Liberal ministers seem to have had great success. On August 17, 1984, it was reported that Halifax Industries Ltd. and its 600 workers had received a little election "goody" in the form of a $10.7 million contract for a refit of the Canadian Coast Guard vessel Narwal. The contract promised to add 125 jobs to the once ailing yard. Part of the new-found health of this company seems to be the result of the efforts of former Energy Minister Regan in Ottawa. The contract announced was just one of three awarded to the company in 1984. One final note — the shipyard was located in Regan's Halifax riding.

Still, Regan was just a hacker compared to the real excellence of "the Laird of Lake Ainslie," Cape Breton's own Allan J. MacEachen. We have already noted the remarkable tendency of projects to land in Allan J.'s riding just prior to or during elections but his real victories were the two heavy water plants built by Atomic Energy Canada Ltd. in Cape Breton Island, the Sydney Steel Plant and DEVCO. Pretty clearly, the heavy water plants on Cape Breton Island make no sense economically. The fact that these plants were built there is a tribute to the political clout of the man. The fact that they have remained operating in spite of the enormous losses racked up each year is almost beyond belief. It is estimated that they cost taxpayers about $100,000 per year to produce a product no one wants. It was MacEachen who was instrumental in getting $100 million to modernize the Sydney Steel Plant in 1981, which is even more interesting when you consider that SYSCO racks up an operating deficit of more than $1 million a week for the Government of Nova Scotia. And finally it was MacEachen who was responsible for getting DEVCO, the Cape Breton Development Corporation off the ground. Ottawa created the crown corporation in 1967 when Dominion Coal and Steel Co. abandoned its coal mines. Up until he left the House of Commons and Cabinet in 1984, it was MacEachen who kept it going through his political contracts.

As we know, toward the end of the Trudeau era, the Liberal Party in the West could have held its general membership meetings in a telephone booth. Indeed, the situation was so bad that Lloyd Axworthy was the only Liberal member west of the Ontario-Manitoba border. His skill at dispensing largesse to his riding has become something of a legend. The West can be proud of their native son in this area. If there were a "Golden Pork Barrel" award, Lloyd's time as a cabinet minister and MP would surely win him the award for his thirteen month reign as transportation czar.

Now Axworthy was not exactly what you might see as a shy or passive sort. He very quickly realized that he was going to have problems with the civil servants in that ministry. This is of course, a very familiar problem for most ministers. Usually, they are defeated by their own mandarins in this battle for control. The mandarins have the power, the information and the experience in the game. They win. The minister becomes a captive — and an impotent one at that — in his or her own ministry. Not Axworthy. When he realized that there was a problem and his civil servants were not interested in doing things his way, he fought back. He hired his friends and former colleagues as consultants to do the work that normally would be done by the bureaucrats. This had a number of benefits. First of all, it resulted in a virtual empire for him, with a tightly-knit group of zealots around him who had no future in government without him. Even better, most of them were either from the West or more particularly from Winnipeg. It was patronage as well. What would help him survive in Ottawa would also help him survive in Winnipeg.

The Axworthy empire was very impressive. Immediately following his appointment to the post of Transport Minister, he began his own lobbying effort. One of his first acts was to initiate a $1.5 million advertising blitz to sell the Crow rates bill to the Canadian people and to tell us what wonderful things the government was doing for (or to) us. This campaign had the added benefit of being a patronage conduit bringing largesse to Axworthy's riding and supporters. The firms and individuals chosen to sell this message just so happened to be close friends or supporters of Axworthy and the Liberal Party. Of course, it wasn't just the Crow. Axworthy found many ways and occasions for rewarding friendship and loyalty. A few examples of the Axworthy gratitude are shown in the table on page 272.

This is by no means the whole story. There were lots of other interesting contracts that were let out. Still, these contracts are even more interesting with a little bit of background. (See table on page 273.)

The really troubling aspect to all of this is that the Mulroney government, which received a good portion of its votes because of its promise to bring about a real change and as a reaction to the patronage and pork barrel tactics of the Liberals, began, once in power, to show many of the same characteristics and attitudes the Liberals had displayed. The white hats very quickly began to become extremely soiled. In Edmonton, new Tory MP Murray Dorin boasted that $777,000 of Canada

THE AXWORTHY PORK BARREL

Diner	Date	Location	Pork Dish Served	Price
Thorne, Stevenson & Kellogg	Aug/84	Winnipeg	For study of railway transportation. From Western Transportation Industrial Development Program	$180,000
V.K. Mason Const. Ltd.	Aug/84	Winnipeg	For construction of National Research Council centre in (surprise!) Winnipeg	$17.9 million
Drew Cringan (a.k.a. D. Cringan Enterprises)	Sept 1/83 to Oct 1/83	Winnipeg	For consulting on Crow Rate issue	$74,000
William Ridgeway	Apr 1 to Sept 30/83	Manitoba	For liaison work and dissemination of information under Western Grain Transportation Initiative	$24,800
Stringham and Grant Tandy Inc.	Nov/83 to Sept/84	Winnipeg	Two contracts for the purchase of space in media	$799,773
Stringham and Grant Tandy Inc.	Mar/83	Winnipeg	Through CUTO conducted a radio and print campaign for VIA Rail youth rail pass	$200,000
Stringham and Grant Tandy Inc.	Apr 1/84	Winnipeg	Transport Dept. contract to promote VIA Rail passes	$245,000
Stringham and Grant Tandy Inc.	1984	Winnipeg	Transport Dept. National safety campaign	$1.5 million
Angus Reid & Assocs.	1983-84	Winnipeg	Conducted five polls	$403,500
Walker & Zimmerman	Mar 1 to July 5/84	Winnipeg	Contract to study rail policy	$33,000
	July 6/84		Contract to study rail policy	$25,000

COINCIDENTAL RELATIONSHIPS

Contract Winner	Background
Drew Cringan	former policy advisor to Axworthy
William Ridgeway	a Liberal candidate in past and unsuccessful provincial leadership candidate
Stringham and Grant Tandy	strong personal ties to Axworthy
Angus Reid & Assocs.	did polling for John Turner during his successful leadership campaign
David Walker of Walker-Zimmerman	has run as a provincial Liberal candidate. He was Axworthy's campaign manager

Works money would be pumped into the riding during the winter immediately following the election, an increase of $677,000 from the amount spent by the Liberals. This is in keeping with Mulroney's claim to reporters that he (Mulroney) had told one story to the electorate on the question of patronage and pork barrelling and another one to party workers. Indeed, Mulroney passed the word on to his Quebec wing that the pork barrelling would soon start in earnest and good Quebec Tories would get their reward. Speaking of the new regime and its approach Edmonton columnist Don Braid said, "The point is that the new Tory rhetoric is the same as the old Liberal blather. They ship us our money, and expect credit for it."[9] Plus ça change, plus c'est la même chose.

Bribery and Graft
While patronage and pork barrelling is viewed with a certain amount of ambivalence, bribery and graft inspire a solid societal consensus. The Canadian public views these activities with such repugnance that even politicians and political bosses are reluctant to touch them. Still, they do go on from time to time and so are worthy of some attention.

Bribery is a crime which carries with it a potentially heavy penalty. Section 108 of the Canadian Criminal Code states that any member of Parliament who "corruptly accepts or obtains, agrees to accept or attempts to obtain any money, valuable consideration, office, place or employment for himself or another person in respect of anything done or omitted or to be done or omitted by him in his official capacity is guilty of an indictable offence and liable to imprisonment for fourteen years."

Graft is an activity related to bribery. In general usage, the term "graft" has become synonymous with "corruption" and "conflict of interest." A more restrictive use of "graft" defines it as an activity where an official requests some form of payment for a service that it was his obligation to provide anyway as part of his job. So in a sense, graft is the reverse of bribery. In bribery it is the petitioner who *offers* money; in the case of graft it is the official who *demands* it. While bribery may be either petty or of a more significant nature, graft often takes on a very broad scope. Graft usually requires some consistency. thus, an under-the-table toll would have to be levied on all licences or contracts offered in a given area. What's fair is fair.

The heftiness of the penalty for bribery is almost certainly responsible for the fact that this act is not all that common at present — at least not in its traditional form of an envelope under the table. Nevertheless, neither bribery nor graft have died out entirely. One area where both seem to have some currency is in the bureaucracy. Curiously enough, Revenue Canada has on at least one occasion been tainted by alleged graft. In one case in 1981 a federal tax auditor was charged with fraud and extortion after a Scarborough, Ontario businessman made a complaint to authorities that he was told that his $33,000 tax arrears would be reduced to $3,500 if he came up with $8,000 in cash. The judiciary is, from time to time, involved as well. In October 1984, a former Crown prosecutor, Gilles Harris, an eight-year veteran of the court of St-Jérôme, Quebec, was sentenced to a year in jail for accepting two bribes from a defence lawyer in connection with his cases. He also was fined $2,000 on two charges of corruption and breach of trust. He admitted at his trial to receiving $1,000 to recommend a sentence of one year for an arsonist and another $1,000 for reducing a charge in a firearms case. The defence lawyer was not charged.

It is interesting to note that almost no politician has been charged and convicted of bribery in the last decade or two. Does this mean that our politicians are innocent of it? I think not. Rather, I think that this recent dearth of charges and convictions has occurred because politicians have become much more careful and because there has been a change in the way that our politicians are bought and sold. For instance, it is far less common for someone to offer a politician an envelope containing money. The more usual technique now involves something resembling either honour among thieves or trading hockey players. It is all a question of future considerations — bribing with power rather than money. The future considerations may take many forms. The politician who has given special help to an individual or company may find to his or her delighted surprise that these same former supplicants respond to his aide's request to buy tickets to a fundraising dinner by buying nine or ten tables worth of tickets. Or, the supplicant's way of saying thanks may be to contribute handsomely to the politician's re-election efforts in the future. It may be money, people to help with canvassing, whatever.

The beautiful thing about this "new bribery" is that it is almost impossible to track or prove. For instance, in the mid-seventies it was charged that there was an unholy coincidence between political contributions to the Liberal Party by Quebec businesses and the award of DREE grants. Jean Marchand, the minister then responsible for this program, denied any connection, saying that considering the large number of businesses his ministry dealt with, it would be impossible to know who was a contributor and who was not. Was he telling the truth? Were his critics wrong? No one can prove it one way or other, at least not to the satisfaction of a court. Marchand himself gave the public some reason to suspect that not all was well with the moral and ethical health of those surrounding Ministers of the Crown. Toward the end of his political career, he seems to have had increasing difficulties in coping. At one point, one of his aides was quoted as having said, "Some days I know he suspects that most of his department is secretly on the payroll of Canadian Pacific Railways." Now, it seems that this was not the case and my repeating such a charge is not to suggest that CP actually engaged in such practices. Rather, it is to suggest that in a general way, where there's smoke there's fire. If Marchand could even conceive of such a thing, it must be that the practice of buying off government officials is not unknown to elected officials.

Conflict of Interest

We have already had a brief look in Chapter 3 at this form of corrupt behaviour. In the discussion it was noted that a conflict of interest allegation involving a former Minister of the Crown, other Ministers and a Deputy Minister (the so-called Gillespie affair) led to a review of conflict of interest guidelines. We reviewed the recommendations of the commission studying the matter and noted that one of the recommendations was for a relaxation of guidelines in one area. This is a classic case of getting rid of a crime by making the activity legal. Nevertheless, that is the way it stands. The thing which is critical in viewing this matter is to recognize that conflict of interest involves a situation where the public servant has a private or personal interest in a matter sufficient that it influences the objective performance of his or her duties. This situation is as common as snow in Canadian winters.

Charges of conflict of interest fly regularly in the House of Commons. Prime Minister John Turner was charged by the Tories with having a conflict of interest involving some of his directorships and once in office, the Tories were accused of conflict of interest by the Liberals. Conflict of interest has become a game that all MPs can play. The trouble is that it seems to be just that, a game. Think of it! What federal politicians have ever been found guilty and punished? Virtually none. Either the charges go nowhere — a silly little accusation made within the safety of parliamentary immunity for the sake of the voters back home — or those charged are found innocent again and again and again. And when there is an investigation of the matter of conflict of interest, as happened with the Gillespie affair, the commission concludes that the cooling off period for Ministers is too long and unfairly affects former ministers' economic futures. Pity the fate of the poor starving former cabinet minister. It would not seem to be overly cynical to suggest that MPs are not enthusiastic about rooting out conflict of interest. One suspects that it is a case of there but for the grace of God go I. I have heard even more cynical people suggest that MPs simply want the rules lax and inadequately enforced because they are awaiting their turn at the trough.

Corrupt Campaign Financing

The problem with this concept is that of determining what financing is corrupt, and what is not. Is it corrupt to promise corporations or wealthy individuals extraordinary influence over government policy and policy implementation? Is it corrupt to imply to businesses that they will have an unusually difficult time getting government contracts or that government departments and regulatory boards will be less willing to hear their problems if they do not contribute to the party in power? Is it corrupt to give more jobs and contracts to those firms and individuals who gave to the winning party's campaign fund? Is it corrupt to let it be known to businesses and law firms that a healthy campaign donation will mean that their calls to cabinet ministers will be returned promptly? If these acts do constitute corruption, then we would have to conclude that a good portion of campaign financing as we presently know it is corrupt.

The simple fact of political life is that what determines what is corrupt and what is not is, by and large, what the public knows and what it is prepared to stomach. To my mind, the two major things which allow most of the currently practised campaign funding techniques to continue are the shielding of the truth from the public and the already considerable cynicism of the public toward politicians and their escapades. This cynicism is not helpful toward finding a solution to the problem.

Influence Peddling

So far I have used the term "influence peddling" in a general sense to mean an extreme form of lobbying, whereby special interests lobby government, often at the expense of a broader public interest or unusually well-placed and powerful individuals and bodies act as intermediaries in the exercise of undue influence. The desired result is the manipulation of the general public or sectors of the wider society or the business community. I have used this term advisedly. It is a harsh term but, I think, an appropriate one since it describes an unusually dirty set of practices and goals. The public and democracy in Canada are the losers in the final analysis.

There is a somewhat more restricted use of this term, however, which describes a situation where a government official uses his or her position and the influence which ascribes to it in return for money or some other valuable consideration. Such a corrupt official might ensure that government policies or actions would be favourable to some individual, company or interest, or he or she might ensure that a company is awarded contracts in a way that was unfair to others or to which it would not otherwise be entitled. This is, of course, just a short list of the possible scams. It is this practice which is covered by the criminal code and various provincial, municipal and federal laws.

As we have seen, influence peddling in this highly restricted legal definition is illegal and carries a very stiff set of penalties. The question I would pose is, why are there so few charges of influence peddling laid? While it is true that Canada is not equivalent in its political corruption to "banana republics," it should be obvious by now that Canada has quite a lot more political corruption than is commonly supposed. Yet very few charges are laid and very few convictions obtained. When there are convictions, the penalties tend to be quite light. Is something amiss?

Even though there have been few convictions, the accusations made and charges laid have proved to be fascinating in as much as they reveal the real nature of politics in Canada. Consider the so-called "Sky Shops Affair." This scandal dragged a number of well-respected peoples' names through the mud before it was over. It involved Senator Louis Giguère, Clarence Campbell, former President of the NHL, Bahamian businessman Gordon Brown and Montreal businessman Louis Lapointe. It was alleged that the business people conspired to give Giguère a $95,000 benefit in return for the Senator using his political influence to help secure the extension of the lease for the Sky Shops duty-free store at Dorval airport. Supposedly, Giguère had been granted a "verbal option" to buy 5,000 Sky Shops shares at $1 per share. A few months after Giguère bought the shares he resold them for $20 per share. In a series of seemingly contradictory verdicts, Giguère was acquitted on all counts, but Campbell was found guilty and fined $25,000. This was by no means the end of Giguère's legal woes. He was charged with three counts of offering his influence as a government official in return for benefits from some business people so as to help Canadian Advertising Agency Ltd. secure contracts with various government bodies. Giguère was acquitted on these charges as well.

Or consider the so-called Mackasey affair. By the time this had ended, it had resulted in the tarnishing of the reputations of a cabinet minister and a former head of the Montreal Board of Trade and some doubts being raised as to the propriety of some of the loan policies of the major banks in Canada. What it came down to was an accusation that Bryce Mackasey benefited from a $400,000 loan in exchange for Mackasey's lobbying on behalf of Les Atelier d'Usinage Hall Ltee., a Montreal machine-tool firm. Witnesses at Mackasey's preliminary hearing told how Mackasey's accountant, Robert Harrison, arranged a loan agreement whereby 109609 Canada Ltd., a numbered company belonging to Mr. Harrison, borrowed $400,000 from the Bank of Montreal to buy Mackasey's stock portfolio valued at about half the amount. The $400,000 was paid to the Bank of Montreal against Mackasey's $625,000 debt to the Bank. Now, this left about $225,000 owing to the Bank. The Bank, it seems, wished to settle the matter and was prepared to take a loss to do it. Part of the problem in doing this was that Mackasey was on the Commons banking committee. The Bank of Montreal reasoned that their taking a loss on Mackasey's loan would look very bad, given his position, and feared suspicions of undue influence. Mackasey resigned in May 1984 for "health reasons," an action that caused a sudden improvement in his financial health — the Bank indicated that it was prepared to declare the matter of Mackasey's indebtedness closed if he would come up with $50,000. It is clear that Mackasey had a guardian angel looking over his shoulder, for grain merchant Robert Strauss, President of Agro Co. of Canada, lent Mackasey the money "as a gesture of friendship."

Mackasey was charged with influence peddling in connection with his lobbying activities on behalf of the machine-tool firm. At the preliminary hearing his lawyer admitted that Mackasey had received a benefit of $200,000 but claimed that this was the result of a pure business transaction and that it had nothing to do with influence peddling. Sessions Court Judge Benjamin Schechter dismissed the charges against Mackasey, saying that it was inconceivable that someone could be put on trial with such flimsy evidence. Then he did something that left the courtroom and media observers confused — he wondered aloud why Mackasey had not been charged with fraud instead. He did not, however, suggest that other charges be laid against him. Mackasey had been cleared, but Harrison and Montreal businessman Jean Bruyere were charged with having tried to bribe him. This situation was strangely reminiscient of the Sky Shops case where the government official was acquitted of being bribed by business people to engage in influence peddling, but the person who had supposedly bribed him was found guilty of just this. Canadian law works in strange ways.

In these two cases of alleged influence peddling, the principals accused were finally acquitted. One of the few series of cases that actually resulted in convictions of the political players are those which involved a kickback scheme in Nova Scotia, the so-called "tollgate affair." The influence peddling charges that resulted from a police investigation were laid against former Nova Scotia Liberal Party fundraisers, Senator Irving Barrows, and retired businessmen, James Simpson and Charles McFadden. Simpson pleaded guilty in May 1982 and was fined $75,000. The other two fought the charge but were ultimately convicted and fined $25,000. The scam in question was fascinating, especially since all three probably just saw their activities as good, old-fashioned Nova Scotia fund raising.

Basically, it came down to a case of companies, mostly liquor companies, having their corporate arms twisted to give to the government party. They were required to pay a proportion of their income to the fundraisers in exchange for the goodwill of the government. Donald McNaughton, the president of Schenley Canada, Inc., testified that he paid McFadden fifty cents for each case of Schenley liquor sold in the province and that he learned from his predecessor, George Kuhn, and from gossip in the industry, that in order to get his labels listed with the provincial liquor commission he must "be in good health from a political contribution point of view." Contractors wishing to bid on government business faced similar demands. For example, Barrow reputedly asked Acres Consulting Services of Toronto to contribute 3 to 5 percent of its fees from government contracts to the Liberal Party. This was no small amount since this would represent about half the company's profits on these jobs. Apparently, these gentlemen had demanded this money between 1970 and 1978. One should not think that just these men or the Liberal government were responsible; there seemed reason to believe that the Conservatives had also been implicated but RCMP investigators said they did not pursue the Tory case because party fundraisers told them that the pertinent documents had been destroyed. Time heals all.

The matter was complicated in the case of Barrow for a number of reasons. One was that he appealed his case, but this was finally settled in September 1984, when the Nova Scotia Supreme Court dismissed all grounds of appeal he put forward. The other complication was his position as Senator and Chairman of the Senate Banking and Commerce Committee. Conservative members of the House of Commons demanded his removal in May 1983 but Prime Minister Trudeau told them that it was the job of the Senate to do this if they wished, not his. This the Senate refused to do. Senator Royce Frith defended this by saying, "If we had refused to support him, people might have thought we were convicting him." Both the business and banking communities rallied to his side in his time of need. Larry Zolf in his book on the Senate has the following to say about this support, "As they saw it, Barrow was guilty of, at worst, a misdemeanor; at best, a playful prank."[10] This attitude toward influence peddling by "the powers that be" may go a long way toward explaining why government seems to be so unenthusiastic about laying charges and aggresively seeking convictions of officials and individuals involved in influence peddling.

A good example of this lack of enthusiasm took place in Ontario in October 1984. In that month the Liberal Opposition leader David Peterson demanded assurances from the Solicitor General, George Taylor, that he would investigate allegations by a Toronto apartment owner that he had paid $500,000 to a trust company to get cabinet approval of his redevelopment plans. In the affidavit which referred to the June 21, 1982 Greymac Mortgage Corporation approval of a second mortgage to Axelrod of $3.6 million, Axelrod had the following things to say: "Mr [Victor] Prousky [then Axelrod's attorney] . . . said that Greymac had assured him that the $500,000 fee would guarantee a rapid cabinet decision . . . He said that the $500,000 "fee" would be used in part to retain public relations consultants to lobby cabinet members, and also that Mr. David Cowper [campaign manager for Ontario Attorney General Roy McMurtry during part of the last provincial election] had become a senior executive of Greymac Trust, that Mr. Cowper was well known in Progressive Conservative circles and would assist in obtaining an early decision from cabinet . . ."[11] Peterson demanded an independent inquiry into the matter. Taylor's reply was that "because it is an affidavit does not mean there is any truth in the material . . . there is nothing to the material, I am sure, but it's under investigation."[12] Concerning the possibility of an independent inquiry, he said, "there is nothing that would warrant an independent investigation."[13] Clearly the Solicitor General had already made up his mind on the matter and was not in the mood for serious examination of the allegations.

Criminal Corruption

It is a strange fact of life that the activities of criminal elements in influencing the political system are almost never mentioned. Is that because they do not exist, because these same criminal elements have been successful in getting to the media and politicians or because neither politicians nor media people see themselves as looking particularly good at the bottom of the lake with concrete shoes? There is some evidence that organized crime has had considerable success in influencing the political system. One major finding that seems to come out of all government studies, no matter what government, is that organized crime cannot exist without the connivance of government officials. One U.S. government study had the following things to say about this relationship: "Today's corruption is less visible and therefore more difficult to detect and assess than the corruption of the Prohibition era. All available data indicate that organized crime flourishes only where it has corrupted local officials."[14] Similar findings have been made by the few Canadian studies on the subject. A Quebec report on organized crime stated, "The unanimous opinion is that it would not be possible for organized crime to entrench itself, develop and prosper without a measure of cooperation on the part of the administration of justice. The principle is bluntly enunciated by stating that there is no organized crime without a measure of corruption."[15]

The simple facts of life are this: the problems of organized crime are very similar to those of big business; they have large sums of money to protect and invest and to achieve both these goals they require conditions similar to those of the typical big business. They need a stable political and social system and politicians and bureaucrats who are sympathetic to their problems. To ensure that selected politicians will be sympathetic, criminal elements use techniques very similar to those employed by business, such as making contributions to selected politicians during election campaigns. It is almost never a case of direct contributions. Rather, these funds will be funneled through lawyers or other well-respected agents. The influence which results will not be directed by the criminals themselves but rather to those who act as their agents. If they know what is best for their health, they will use this influence on behalf of their clients as demanded. For a better understanding of the many ways in which criminal influence is applied and used, read Mario Puzo's *The Godfather*. While the book deals with the U.S., the general situation is virtually the same.

12

The Media: All The Public Opinion You Can Buy

One of the most recent and powerful additions to the influence peddling gang is the media. If we are to believe the pious pronouncements that emanate from both the media and government, we would conclude that the two are involved in a chaste relationship that is completely at arm's length. The media, we are told, is free of government interference and has as its sole task the provision to the citizenry of the objective information it requires to judge the actions of government, business, labour and other social groups and to understand the world about it. The government, we are led to understand, is anxious to avoid any manipulation of the media and is keen to protect and nurture its role as a completely free voice giving expression to the people's will. This is as close to fiction as we are likely to see this side of Winnie the Pooh.

The first thing to realize about the media is that those who make up this estate and those who attempt (often successfully) to manipulate it represent powerful and deeply entrenched interests. With these folks at work, the possibility of a free and unbiased media is about as likely as the snows of Moose Jaw lingering until July. Among others we have the following extremely interested groups using the media for their own fun and profit:

1. Owners
2. Journalists and other media workers
3. Other lobbies
4. Government

All of these groups have just one interest in mind when it comes to the messages put out by the media — themselves.

Owners

The owners and managers of those organizations and companies that make up the media have one major goal in mind — their own personal aggrandizement. One of the key things to remember is that for these people the media are businesses, no more, no less. It just so happens that many media organizations are extremely efficient at making money for their masters. (The CBC and other such government in-spired misbegotten creations are notable exceptions.) There are a hundred different ways they do this: the short-term profit squeeze; the slow, steady growth in earnings per share route that draws out the money from pension plans and insurance companies; the acquisition route and so on.

Each medium has its own peculiar way of making the world enrich its owners, and once you know the key to how the money is made, you know where to look for the influence peddling and lobbying. For instance, once you know that the acquisition of licences from the Cana-dian Radio-Television and Communications Commission (CRTC) is key to the capitalists of the airwaves, you are halfway to understanding where the influencers may be found and how they will ply their trade. It also tells you much more. It tells you how they are vulnerable to pres-suring and manipulation by government and others. It tells you how they will use the media which they own to advance themselves and what self-censorship and censorship from the outside they will employ and permit.

The owners and managers of media companies are by and large uninterested in the messages their employees create and transmit, being more concerned about how it will affect their financial health. Take for instance the question of social and political trends. Over the last ten or fifteen years, the media have been more or less consistently enthusiastic in their coverage of feminism. This movement represents no threat to the owners. It will not hurt profits. Rather, it will probably be good for business. All those new paycheques mean higher consump-tion and that means higher sales of newspapers and higher advertising revenues. Also, many media people see feminism as just a new battle in the war of the sexes, and if there is anything the media understand, it is that sex sells. There is no problem on the race question or abortion or bilingualism. On these issues, the media are by and large quite happy to go to bat for the various interest groups that pressure government for change. It is a cheap form of liberalism, enlightenment and self-righteousness.

The real sticking point comes on economic issues. Here the media end up looking like dinosaurs. Ask yourself the last time you read an article or editorial in a newspaper that damned the profit motive or praised taking from the rich to give to the poor. More importantly, ask yourself the last time you saw coverage that was sympathetic to trade unions. Remember, the media have their own unions and one would not want to encourage members to press management for higher wages. So the owners are happy to praise government for any manner of legislation promoting social change — no matter how radical — as long as it does not hurt business. The message does not matter. Sounds harsh? In 1970, John Bassett successfully appeared before the CRTC with a request to buy CKLW-AM in Windsor, one of the most profitable stations in the country. Its style was brash and often sarcastic; sometimes it came dangerously close to extremely bad taste. Here is an example. One day in 1972 the announcer read the following piece:

> The hitless Tigers can use this guy's talents. The police have a thirty-six-year-old man in custody. Seems he got home about five o'clock this morning from an all-night spree, then ticked-off the little lady, who unleashed a verbal barrage at the man. That apparently was the last straw for him — he picked up his genuine Willy Mays, powerized, lightning-strike, Louisville slugger baseball bat, proceeded to hit a thousand on the woman's head. She's dead. He then turned on the children; they're in serious condition.[1]

Being kind and generous, we might conclude that this would not have been allowed if owner and upright citizen Bassett had known about what was going on in his station. Nothing could be further from the truth. Terry Matte, a reporter for the CBC in Ottawa, sent Bassett a stinging letter telling him of the sarcastic news that was being read over CKLW. Bassett replied,

> I would point out to you that coverage of local news in Detroit is a very different matter than similar coverage in Canada, and I would also point out that, unlike the CBC types, we are on the paying end, not the receiving end of the two hundred forty million dollar subsidy you will get this year, so we do have to be concerned with our competitive position, and CKLW Radio is number one in the Detroit market.
>
> You are quite right that I would never let you get away with that kind of writing at the *Telegram*, but I don't know what that proves as the end result of the *Telegram* indicates, in any event, that we must have been doing something wrong.[2]

The above is not to say that media owners do not have preferences in the political arena. They are, after all, human. Toronto papers, for instance, have a grand tradition of being partisans for one party or the other. The *Telegram* was notorious for its pro-Tory bias, the *Sun* now faults the Tories only for being too left-wing. The *Star*, it seems at times, would recommend the Liberal Party even if its candidates were all chimpanzees. The CBC has long been thought by many to be more or less permanently biased in favour of the Liberal Party's view of Canada. George Grant in his book *Lament for a Nation* claims, speaking of the Diefenbaker government, that, "the Conservatives . . . justifiably felt that the CBC, then as today, gave too much prominence to the Liberal view of Canada."[3] Conrad Winn in his article on mass communication in Canada writes that, "In quiet conversation, some officials of the CBC and of the Canadian Radio-Television Commission, the government regulatory body, may concede that the CBC is timid and uncritical of governments, especially Liberal ones."[4] Would it be too suspicious to suggest that such a bias, if it does exist, might be in part explained by the use of the CBC's Board of Directors as a "happy hunting ground" for long-time Liberal stalwarts over the many years that the Liberal Party was the "government party." There have been charges by some that the CTV network, owned by prominent Tory John Bassett, has a bias in favour of the Conservative Party.

Still, this is a mere peccadillo when compared to the real tough stuff, the lobbying for licences. Owning a television licence in Canada is very much like having a licence to print money. As a result, they are very highly valued and media entrepreneurs will do almost anything to get them. To get them you must persuade the CRTC (previously the Board of Broadcast Governors) to issue you one. What the public sees is business people appearing before hearings and dispassionately presenting their case to the board of commissioners. Clearly it is all above board, right?

Take the fascinating case of how Baton Aldred Rogers won the licence for CFTO, one of the most profitable stations in the country. Throughout the BBG hearings held in 1960, there was a highly political tone. First of all, it is important to note that this was the Diefenbaker era. Diefenbaker, it seems, was so perplexed by what he saw as the pro-Liberal bias of the CBC that he caused private broadcasting licences to be "ladled out to prosperous party supporters."[5] There is no doubt that the Baton Rogers Aldred group fit into the category of "prosperous party supporters." Bassett, one of the principals, was of course a long-time and highly influential Tory close to the centre of power in the party. Joel Aldred, another of the principals, was also heavily connected, having been active in the party since the 1940s. He was also Diefenbaker's closest friend and supporter until Dief's death in 1979. It is true that Aldred made a point of avoiding being seen with Diefenbaker during the licensing period, but the suspicion remained. The other principal, Ted Rogers, was a past president of the Young PCs. John David Eaton, Bassett's financial backer, was an extremely generous contributor to the Conservatives. Eddie Goodman, one of the greatest names in Torydom, was one of the lawyers for the consortium. To balance things, however, there was also the extremely wealthy Paul L. Nathanson, whose lawyer was that all-time great Liberal, Paul Martin. In addition, of the twelve members on the Board of Broadcast Governors panel that heard applications for the licence, nine were well-known Conservatives.

All this is just background. After the consortium was granted the licence, it was alleged that the group had had advance knowledge that they would receive it. This allegation was based on three facts: the group had already purchased twenty acres of land prior to the final decision of the BBG, detailed plans for the station and facilities had already been drawn up prior to the final decision and Bassett was heard on several occasions to say, "We've got it in the bag." Mavor Moore, who was one of the contenders for the licence, claims that Bassett yelled to him, "Mavor, don't worry. I have been promised the licence by John Diefenbaker and George Hees."[6] This could, of course, have been merely a joke or a good-natured outburst. George Hees was, however, asked in a taped interview if there had been any political influence used in awarding the licence and replied, "Let's put it this way, I was very helpful to him in getting him his television licence."[7] The Ottawa bureau chief for the *Telegram* claimed that he acted as a go-between for Bassett and some cabinet ministers during the period and also claimed that Diefenbaker had implied that he had been instrumental in the group's winning the licence.

Earlier I said that most media owners are content to leave the information disseminated to the journalists, producers and announcers. Sure, the CBC management may act as lobbyist for the Liberal Party from time to time, but by and large, broadcast media employees seem to have a fairly free hand. But the newspaper industry seems to have a few publishers who seem to want to guide the opinions of their employees when it comes to what they are to think and what they are to say. Walter Stewart in an article on the *Toronto Star* asserted that the publisher, Beland Honderich, still plays a major role in determining what opinions journalists are permitted to express. He quotes Carl Mollins, formerly Ottawa bureau chief for the *Star*, on the subject of how the process works. Mollins was assigned to write on the problem of rising health costs after a meeting with Honderich and Martin Goodman, former president and publisher. Mollins, after researching the subject, came to the conclusion that there was not a crisis in health costs but that costs were well in line and the provincial government was doing a good job of managing the health care system. He stated this view in a memo to management. Management disagreed and he was called onto the carpet to explain. His conclusion was simple: "I had come up with the wrong answer, that was all. Everyone knows that health costs were out of control, and my job was not to keep knocking the notion but to go out and find out what could be done to bring them down . . . . The newspaper had its position, the one laid down from on high, and my job was to seek out supporting material."[8]

Journalists

The tone of righteous indignation cloaking journalistic exposés of the role of the media bosses takes on a funny and sometimes pathetic quality when you begin to realize the extent to which these would-be champions of the public good do very much the same thing when they get the opportunity. Journalists have their own self-interest and it clouds their work very frequently. They are people just like everyone else, and as such, they are often unable to distinguish between their best interest and the best interest of the country as a whole. Two good examples involve the treatment of women's issues and the question of separatism in Quebec.

There is a consistent bias in favour of feminism in the discussion of the problems of family life and women's issues in the Canadian media. In doing my research for this book I kept copious files on every topic to be covered. My files on women's issues were without doubt the largest. In the period from January to November 1984, I collected 611 clippings from the media on the subject of women's issues and feminism. The closest competitor was multiculturalism with a total of 34 percent. The number of clippings covering other topics dropped sharply thereafter. (The subject with the fewest articles was, not surprisingly, concerned with the views and activities of the Canadian Right. Who says there is a left-wing bias in the Canadian media?) The most interesting thing about the coverage on women's issues and family life was that the vast majority of the articles either were pro-feminist or more or less blindly accepted the feminist agenda and analyses in an uncritical fashion. Of the 611 articles about 400 were about feminism, feminist personalities or feminist issues. The interesting thing about the media coverage was the small percentage of articles that were critical of the feminist perspective. Of these the lion's share dealt with abortion.

Conrad Winn, in his article "Mass Communication," states that media owners see important economic reasons for supporting the women's liberation movement. Speaking of the common pro-feminist bias of owners and journalists, Winn says, "If this thesis is true, it may explain the considerable support provided to the Women's Liberation Movement by the media as a whole. The sympathy of journalists and the tacit co-operation of their employers may explain the enormous media exposure given to the pro-abortion movement even though the Right-to-Life movement has been far more successful at enrolling members and securing signatures."[9] Speaking of this tendency for the media and particularly women in the media to cover stories from just the feminist perspective, Frank Jones, columnist for the *Toronto Star*, puts it this way, "Unless you've lived a few years it's not possible to realize how pervasive one particular set of feminist values has become in the media . . . . The media, in fact, have become the great launching pad for a feminist revolution that takes little count of the views of men and of that large body of women who have serious reservations about the direction their sisters are taking."[10]

Studies have shown that the media represent the major source of information for politicians and others in the government as to what are the issues of the day and the wishes of the people. The result is that the media act as a lobby for the feminist movement in Canada. The opposing view — and it is quite commonly held — has not been expressed, for the only agency which could possibly give it expression has decided in advance that it is illegitimate. You have to be involved in the media to grasp just how powerful this bias in favour of feminism is in terms of the opinions that are given expression. At times it can reach truly ridiculous extremes.

Take publishing as an example. I once acted as an agent for an author who wrote children's books. I approached one of Canada's leading publishers of children's books on her behalf. The book in question was rejected, not because it was of poor quality, but rather because it had a father and mother in it who represented traditional roles. Said the president of the company, "You couldn't find one publisher of children's books in Canada to consider a book, no matter how good it was, if it contained traditional family roles." Even Methuen Publications, the publisher of this book and, I might add, more courageous and fair than most, engages in feminist censorship from time to time. Let me give you examples. My previous book was subjected to what I might describe as feminist exegesis. "Mankind" was changed to "humankind," "man years" became "person years." You get the idea. But that wasn't all. The freelance editor assigned to the manuscript took it upon herself to play with the images as well. For instance, I used a sentence which described my understanding of country life based on my memories of growing up in the country. I talked about gnarled farmers driving tractors, the weathered faces of fishermen and sturdy farm wives baking pies. The farmer and his tractor stayed in. The fishermen (oops, fisherpersons) and dory stayed in. Guess which one went. Apparently, the thought of a woman baking a pie is a major form of violence against women. Next time I use the image it will be sturdy farm wives performing brain surgery and making million dollar deals over their kitchen tables. It happens all the time, at least in the imaginations of yuppie feminists.

Actually there have been some funny moments in this propaganda blitz. My favourite involved a *Globe and Mail* article by Toba Korenblum on women and comedy in Canada.[11] It was a nasty little piece which savaged men (as always) for their sexism in trying to put down women and keep them from their rightful place. Sounds O.K., doesn't it? After all, we read articles like this every day. The catch was that one of the people quoted in the article, comedienne Katie Ford, wrote a letter to the editor two weeks later protesting what she saw as the journalist's intentional misrepresentation of the facts. In her letter she said, "One of the first things that I said to Toba Korenblum when being interviewed was that I didn't feel that being a woman in the mostly male world of stand-up comedy was a relevant issue any more. That was pretty evident, because I was misrepresented in order to allow the boy-aren't-we-oppressed slant that Ms. Korenblum was trying to get across . . . . The article sounded very bitter and angry about how women don't get the work, how audiences still resist them, and how we don't have the recognition of say, a Barbara Hamilton or an Andrea Martin. . . . When I read that men and, more specifically [the Toronto comedy club] Yuk Yuk's owner Mark Breslin, are seen as insensitive and having absolutely no respect for the women comics, I felt that it was too unfair an accusation to slip by."[12]

Well, if this is correct and the media is by and large acting as a lobbyist and propagandist for the feminist movement in Canada, why is it? What is the stake of the journalistic community in this lobbying? As with all things, the answer is that the reasons vary and it depends very much on the personal and selfish needs of each journalist. For women journalists and media people, the situation is quite clear. There is a simple correspondence of the goals of the movement and the goals of many women in the media. Many of the goals — affirmative action, equal pay for work of equal value and so on — would be hard not to support if you were a woman media person. After all, if accepted by the government and if imposed on employers, they must inevitably mean higher pay and faster advancement for the media women who advance them. It's hard to fault people for trying to get bigger paycheques and better offices.

Interestingly, this unanimity of opinion among women is not nearly as strong as it seems. A friend of mine who has worked for decades in both newspapers and in broadcast media informs me that women in the media who do not have a feminist perspective find it necessary to espouse it as "protective colouration." Apparently, the cost of not using the rhetoric is to be frozen out. Still, these non-feminists in the media are probably a minority. The ostensible reasons for the feminist majority are many, including, I might say, the usual ones involving a demand for basic justice and human decency. As we know, however, such stated reasons while eminently reasonable and worthy, often hide deeper, more personal and sometimes a great deal less worthy motivation.

Frank Jones, in his article on the feminist message in the media cited earlier, tackles one which most media women would probably deny and yet which in some cases would apply. Says Jones, "The choice of issue is highly subjective and sometimes, I feel, motivated by bitterness against men. Your standard rape or child molestation exposé, invariably illustrated with highly suspect statistics about prevalence of same, provides, for example, a chance to take a thinly disguised swipe at all men."[13]

The final reason has to do with what I call the "royal road to success" for media women. Journalism and law seem to provide by far the highest number of women for the plum jobs in the "women's issue industry," the status of women's councils, the commissions on various women's issues, the research projects, the various human rights commissions, the lobbies and so on. Consider the following names: Sam Ion, Sally Barnes, Lynne Gordon and Laura Sabia. These four women have two things in common: they are the four women who have been president of the Ontario Status of Women Council, and they are all media people. Lynne Gordon is a broadcaster on the national news network CKO, Sally Barnes was Press Secretary for former Ontario

Premier William Davis, Laura Sabia is a columnist for the *Toronto Sun* and Sam Ion was the working woman's columnist for the *Toronto Sun* and before that a columnist for the *Toronto Star*. Doris Anderson, former head of both the National Action Committee on the Status of Women and the Canadian Advisory Council on the Status of Women, got her start as a journalist. June Callwood is a journalist. The list goes on and on. It is probably unfortunately true that the "Woman's Page," now euphemistically referred to as the Life Section or the Lifestyle Section or the Family Section, has traditionally been and continues to be a low status ghetto; a dead end for women journalists. They want out into the larger world of high pay, high status and exciting assignments. The lesson that many have drawn is that this "beat" with its obsessive preoccupation with the same narrow band of interests can be the stepping stone to bigger things, not in journalism perhaps, but through the "women's issues industry." Government task forces, councils, commissions, even the Senate, with luck, await. The key that makes the breakout possible is dedicated adherence to, and advocacy of feminist causes.

As for the Quebec media, for many years federalist politicians in all parties were critical of what they saw as the bias toward separatism shown by Radio-Canada personnel. Former Prime Minister Pierre Trudeau was particularly critical of this body and launched an investigation which was in fact an attempt to either purge Radio-Canada of its leading apologists for separatism or, barring that, to make the network a mere rump of its former self. Either way he intended to destroy this perceived bias. There also appears to be some empirical evidence to the charge of a consistent radical bias in Radio-Canada. Conrad Winn's statistical study found "a marked bias to the left." He stated, "On the French network, the NDP received almost 70% more exposure than on the English networks, more than twice as much exposure as the Conservatives, and more than 10 times as much exposure as the Créditistes (who were a provincial force at the time of the study). . . . In conclusion, the data collected in this particular study . . . do lend support to the view that the French Language network of the CBC tilts toward the left. Radio-Canada's apparently insufficient coverage of the Conservatives may help to accentuate the bicultural cleavage in the political system by diminishing the salience and therefore the electoral prospects of that party in Quebec."[14]

This left-wing and separatist bias has not been restricted to Radio-Canada, but has rather until recently been a general fact of life among most media people in Quebec. Dominique Clift, a long-time Quebec journalist, asserts that there has long been a more or less complete commitment on the part of most Quebec journalists to the goal of radical social change in Quebec. At times this commitment has been so far-ranging as to make some journalists mere tools of the party in power. Speaking of the period of the "Quiet Revolution" Clift says, "Identification with social progress was so great that a large proportion of the Parliamentary Press Gallery in Quebec City became almost an adjunct of the party in power."[15] This identification of reporters with the forces of social change, first the Liberal Party and later the Parti Québécois, was not totally motivated by a desire for the greater good. "It was also natural for politically-motivated reporters, eager to improve their collective status in Quebec society, to join forces with them." Or later, "This represents the negative side of the kind of heady journalism that is practised in French Quebec. The manner in which deep social commitment becomes a class interest, or the way it becomes inextricably bound up with selfishness and irresponsibility, can sometimes be very disconcerting."[16]

In fairness to the Quebec media, I suspect that it is safe to say that any bias toward some sort of social democracy or separatism in the Quebec media is probably more than balanced out by an equally powerful bias among members of the English Canadian Press in the rest of the country, in favour of federalism and corporate capitalism. I personally despair of the possibility of the English Canadian media ever giving a fair and reasoned portrayal of the problems and aspirations of the French-speaking people of Quebec. Presumably, we will have to continue being told that separatists are evil people bent upon continuing their wicked practices of bringing death and destruction to the country and everyone in it.

Lobby Pressure on the Media

Media owners, writers, journalists, producers, news broadcasters and so on use the media as a lobbying tool, but not all of the pressure and influence comes from within. Much of it comes from other lobby groups seeking to use the media to influence either the government directly or indirectly through the public.

The media are easy to manipulate. You can buy media coverage either by means of advertising or on occasion "gifts," although money does not have to change hands. As we saw earlier, one possible lever is the already developed prejudices and preferences of media owners or journalists. Find the person who is biased in the same way as your group and you are assured of sympathetic coverage. Even this is unnecessary, however. There are many other techniques which can be used no matter who the journalists are or what their biases are. A detailed look at how to manipulate the media is contained in Chapter 13 of this book, "Teach Yourself Influence Peddling."

This success in manipulating the media into popularizing one's messages varies a great deal with the group and its cause. Business groups have been notoriously bad at getting their perspective expressed sympathetically, so they have to use paid advertising. In selling their products, this has been fabulously successful. In selling their point of view success has not come so easily. Likewise, trade unions have been unsuccessful in getting a sympathetic hearing, partly because of their clumsiness and lack of imagination, partly because of the media bias outlined earlier. The groups that have been successful — and very successful at that — have been the social policy groups advocating women's rights, human rights and aid to the Third World. With rather modest resources these groups have gotten a share of media attention and sympathy, and by extension government attention and sympathy, far out of proportion to their numbers.

The mad frenzy of the ideological lobbies to control the media has two major motivations. The first is that he (or she) who controls the media controls the debate on any given issue. The other reason is that lobbying by means of media is about the only technique these lobbies can afford. They do not have large numbers of active supporters as with the trade unions. They do not have lots of money as with business lobbies.

Basically, ideological lobbies have three main lobby targets in mind when they use the media:

1. The government. Politicians and bureaucrats can read and comprehend the written word, are reasonably interested and concerned citizens and do try to keep up with events. They do have feelings and are affected by what they hear, see and read about themselves. All this makes them targets for influence by the media. Some vehicles are, of course, more influential in affecting government policy. The *Globe and Mail*, for instance, is extremely influential. Not only is it read by the vast majority of English-speaking politicians and top civil servants at the national level and used by the government's clipping and file services, but it is also followed closely by other media and often determines what news stories will be carried on television and radio. The newspaper's emergence as a national publication can only

increase this influence. Television too has had, as we all know, enormous influence, especially at the national level. One of the studies done for the Royal Commission on Newspapers, entitled *The Newspaper and Public Affairs*, found that the influence of the media on social policy depends on the respect politicians have for the journalist or media vehicle in question and the influence which politicians thought the piece would have on the public.

2. The Public. The intent here is not to get the public stirred up per se so much as to get the public to pressure the government on behalf of the lobby group in question. This feeds into the second point affecting media influence cited above from the Royal Commission. Politicians and civil servants are often isolated from what the public thinks. The public is often largely unaware of or unconcerned by the events of the day. It can, however, be aroused and its views moulded by lobby groups working through the media. When this happens its influence is very great. The politicians and bureaucrats, unaware as they are of the real ongoing nature of public opinion, have no way of knowing whether these voices from the public are representative or not. All they know is that the voices are loud and the only ones they hear. The result is public policy.

3. The media itself. For really long-term control of the policies of the country and the ideas which people hold you have to get and control the behaviour of the media and journalists on a continuing basis. To do this requires an ongoing struggle to limit the range of opinion the media can express. Fortunately for the would-be lobbyist and advocates of thought-control, there are many ways to achieve this. The best ones are provided for by the government itself. These include legislation and regulations governing the media and broadcasting in the country. These may be interpreted in a very broad fashion if it suits the purposes of government, the courts and the lobbies. The result may be — and has occasionally been — restrictions on the expression of legitimate opinion. This is uncommon though. A more common tactic is to use regulatory bodies to do the censoring. An excellent example is the CRTC which can decree what will and will not be broadcast on the airwaves. Radio and television frequencies are public property and stations use them at the pleasure of the CRTC and hence the government. It is not uncommon for lobbies to challenge the renewal of a licence if the lobbies do not like the views and policies of the station in question.

These techniques may be used individually, but the best lobbies use a combination of these techniques. Again, the groups which have been most successful using the techniques for manipulating government policy by means of the media have been the feminist lobbies. Part of their lobbying activity has been to press for more jobs for women at senior levels, which seems reasonable. There is a more sinister push, though, to ensure that only feminist views of society are portrayed in the media. At first that seems overstated and quite absurd, but consider the stated push to eliminate sexism from the airwaves. What does this really mean? Feminists would say that it means suppression of those views which crush or degrade women. What will be forbidden? In all likelihood it will be any opinions which run counter to those of feminist bureaucrats or timid bureaucratic souls who feel the hot breath of NAC over their shoulders. The result will be a sort of paranoid double-think on the part of journalists, producers, writers and station owners who will be trying desperately to second guess feminist lobbies and government regulators. After all, who wants to lose their licence or job?

The process of getting the media to censor and second guess itself has started already. Some examples:

1. The Advertising Advisory Board, an advertising industry body acting as a clearing house for complaints, tries to "educate" its members to the "proper" way of portraying women and sets up guidelines for members on the portrayal of women. The real effect of such guidelines is, of course, to replace an old set of "sexist" stereotypes of women with a new set of feminist stereotypes of women.

2. The Canadian Association of Broadcasters, representing most private radio and television stations, has established a code of ethics calling for an end to sex stereotyping. New guidelines urge broadcasters to avoid "expressions which relate only to one gender." (Be careful not to fall down a personhole cover!)

3. The CBC, as one might already have guessed, is heavily into the thought-police role. Its policy manual contains this warning: "Ill-advised use of stereotypes tends to reinforce prejudices and constitutes an assault on the dignity of the individual." Not content with making themselves perfect, CBC on-air personalities must make sure everyone else is perfect too. On-air staff have been told "not only (to) present persons as individuals, but also

(to) challenge stereotypes when these may be introduced by other participants."

4. The CTV has created a library on sex-role stereotyping in its Toronto head office and last year held four seminars on improving the image of women.

5. Global TV includes in its production contracts a clause which forbids sexual stereotyping and states that Global intends "not to engage in sex-role stereotyping in TV production in either casting or program content. This contract will be considered in breach if, in the opinion of Global, discrimination or sex-role stereotyping occurs."

6. The CRTC, after a study which exclusively represented feminist views, is now considering new regulations which would severely restrict the manner in which women and family life may be portrayed. Presumably, only feminist views need be considered.

Tens of millions of people are dying of starvation in Africa, the planet faces ecological and nuclear destruction and the Canadian media are obsessed by whether women can be shown on television cooking a meal or changing a diaper. What a country!

Government

So far we have looked at the relationship between the government and the media only in terms of the media lobbying the government both for itself and on behalf of others. This is, of course, something of a simplification since as we know it takes two to tango. The government also lobbies the media and public in its turn using the rather massive resources at its disposal.

The government has many tools for manipulating the media and the public. One is its control over information and who gets stories. The sad fact of the matter is that the old heady days of investigative reporting when reporters relied on their own sources to get their big "scoop" are gone. For a number of reasons, varying from the reluctance of newspaper managements to fund such digging to the occasional lack of knowledge of their byline by reporters, has led to a recent tendency to accept "spoon-feeding" by government. This "spoon-feeding" is good for both government and the newspapers' bottom lines. The newspapers make bigger profits and the government gets the stories either buried or slanted the way it wants. The losers are citizens who don't get the information they have a right to get.

Government finds that it has enormous powers to discipline reporters who embarrass it. All it has to do is to keep them out of the know and to give the background briefings to reporters from other newspapers. Once government decides to blacklist a reporter, he or she might as well start sending resumes and job applications to papers in Albania. A reporter whose government sources have dried up is finished.

Not all of the tools government has at its disposal for disciplining the media are as informal or personal as this. Generally speaking, the government prefers to set limits from the start by means of legislation, regulatory bodies, licencing requirements and guidelines. The advantage of this approach is that the government never seems to be censoring views. Rather, it is just enforcing the laws of the land and bowing to the voice of the people. Those who choose for whatever reasons not to abide by these laws and regulations are punished in typical capitalist fashion — they have their licences taken away and thus lose their ability to make money. This cools the passion for freedom of expression of even the most fanatical democrat.

It a sense these are all passive measures designed to restrain, hinder or distort the work of the media and journalists. There are active features too. These are the techniques employed by the government to get its message out to lobby the public which it claims to represent. This is where advertising comes in.

In the chapter on the multicultural lobbies we saw how the government is able to control opinion expressed in the ethnic press by its decisions as to which papers it will advertise in. Since it is by far the largest (and sometimes the only) advertiser in these newspapers, it has enormous influence over what they have to say about the government and its policies. No support, no money.

This is really just the tip of the iceberg. The real mass of government advertising revenues go into something called advocacy advertising. This concept, which we have already looked at in the chapter on business lobbies, usually consists of advertising designed to justify the unjustifiable. I must admit that there are legitimate uses of government advertising, especially when it has the function of informing citizens of upcoming legislation, hearings, policy changes or the features of legislation just recently passed. What we are talking about here is advertising whose major (and sometimes only) function is propagandizing the government and its policies. Based on the type of governments we have had in recent Canadian history, this does indeed fit into my definition above of "justifying the unjustifiable."

To give you some idea of just how significant government advertising is, all we have to do is to look at the size of the government's ad business, relative to that of other advertisers. The federal government is the largest purchaser of advertising in the country. In 1985, the size of its advertising budget will be somewhere between $50 and $60 million. What is really sickening about this is that it is one of the biggest patronage scams in the federal government. The advertising business goes only to those companies identified with the government in power. It was that way under the Liberals, it is now that way under the Tories. In fact there was something of a furor over the Tories' changing of the guard. It was not because of the dropping of the Liberal companies. That was expected. It was the sleazy way in which the Tories went about allocating this patronage plum. The people chosen to handle this business had not yet even incorporated. This was nothing compared to the allegations made by one of the people who had been selected that they were offered the business on the understanding that they would "kickback" a certain percentage of revenues to the Conservative Party. That did not sit well with a Canadian electorate which had voted out the Liberals because of their corruption and arrogance in power.

In a sense this problem is a relatively new one which stems from the beginning of the Trudeau era and continues to the present as an ever-worsening problem. Every year *Marketing* magazine publishes a list of the top advertisers in Canada. The Canadian government has been the largest since 1976. It is revealing to note that in 1970 it was the twelfth largest buyer of advertising. Federal government expenditures had increased twenty-nine fold between 1964 and 1982 — from less than $2 million to $54 million in just eighteen years.

One of the most glaring examples of the misuse of government advertising funds was that of the Canadian Unity Information Office (CUIO), the body set up exclusively to fight the Quebec referendum. Virtually its entire budget was devoted to funnelling funds through advertising and other vehicles to fight the PQ government's initiative and to organize support for the repatriation of the constitution. It was in a word just a propaganda organ — and the Canadian taxpayer had to foot the bill. Happily, one of the first acts of the Mulroney government was to disband this body. Liberal ad agency executives went to bed hungry for weeks after. But the CUIO was not the only government department which used its ad budget for propaganda purposes. Virtually all of them do now to some extent.

This advocacy advertising has a number of functions. One is to soften the public up for some government initiative, another is to try and drum up public support for some forthcoming measures, yet another is to try and whip up support for unpopular measures once in effect. This one was tried with the energy program of the Liberals in the West. The ad executives responsible for these campaigns would have been well advised to avoid the darkened nighttime streets of Calgary during these campaigns. Finally there is a little trick that the Trudeau government liked to employ in its dying days and which the Mulroney bunch will doubtless employ sooner or later as well. That is to take out ads on behalf of programs that are working, saying virtually nothing more than, "This program is good for you!" In letters ten feet high at the bottom is the phrase "Government of Canada." It is an attempt to remind the taxpayer on which side his or her bread is buttered. Actually this does not surprise me at all that much. Given the dreadful performance of Canadian government programs, it is no surprise that government would want to scream its success to the roof-tops when it finally does something right.

There are, of course, two ways in which you can buy the media you want. One is to buy the services of other companies in the field, as in advocacy advertising. The other way is to buy (or establish) and own the companies themselves. That is very much what the government has done in the case of such bodies as the CBC and National Film Board. We have already looked at the CBC and the signs of a pro-establishment or pro-government bias in the English language service, pro-separatist in the French. So let's look at the NFB.

To my mind the NFB has not changed a bit in its history. It was used in its early day to produce propaganda films for the war effort, but once war was over, the propaganda continued. The worst examples of this propaganda emanate from Studio D, which is devoted to "women's films." I love films. I would go to any film no matter where it came from, when it was produced or what the subject was. There are two exceptions: I hate Soviet films from the Stalinist period and NFB Studio D films. Both have the same moralistic and ideologically ham-fisted quality and sit on the mind like a concrete block.

And look at the films it has produced. *Not a Love Story* portrays men as monsters obsessed with pornography and determined to degrade women (nice and fair). Then there are the two films it produced on abortion (pro, of course!) — *Abortion: Stories from North and South* and *Democracy on Trial: The Morgentaler Affair, 1970-1976.* The latter, which dealt with the sterling life of Dr. Henry Morgentaler, was so unfair that even the CBC, that last bastion of Canada's counter-culture people, found it a propaganda piece and refused to use it for broadcast. Then there was the studio's film *If You Love This Planet*, which was so anti-American that the U.S. government required that it include a statement labelling itself a propaganda movie of a foreign power. I must confess to being extremely sympathetic to the disarmament message of the movie, but even so, I wonder if the cause of peace will be advanced by blinkered vision or a dogmatic presentation of the point of view. There is good news, though, for fans of the studio. Due to pressure from feminist groups, the studio will be immune from the cuts the rest of the artistic community will experience. A victory for truth and justice, I suppose.

PART V

HOW TO GET IN ON THE GRAFT

So far this business has been pretty depressing, hasn't it? Up to now we have looked at the process by which the rich, the powerful or the opportunistic rifle the public till at our expense and distort public policies. Well, never mind. Now I'll show you how you too can get in on the graft, become one of this merry band of buyers and sellers of political influence and become rich and powerful yourself.

13

Teach Yourself Influence Peddling

In preceding chapters we have looked at the various buyers and sellers of influence. Roughly speaking they fall into the following categories:

1. Elite members
2. Professional lobbyists
3. Bagmen (and bagwomen)
4. Party backroom boys and girls
5. Insiders in the system such as politicians, cabinet ministers and upper level civil servants
6. "Friends of the Masses"

These, then, are the career paths open to would-be opportunists and careerists. Each one has its own rewards, entrance requirements and way of playing the game.

Entrance Requirements

Class Position
Let's face it. No matter what the Canadian Constitution or Charter of Rights might say about equality, Canadian society is essentially about inequality. The influence game reflects that inequality. Some career paths like that of the "top dog" are the exclusive preserve of the wealthy and privileged segments of society; the poor need not apply. Oddly enough, having the right class position can determine your success in the other career paths. One thing that should be clear from previous chapters is that experiences and rewards vary enormously in each of the six career paths. For instance, there are bagmen and there are bagmen. If you come from a "nice" background, you will get all of

the "easy-to-collect" contacts. Everything will be conducted in oak-lined boardrooms with friends of the family who knew you when you were a mere munchkin at private school. For those without such "nice" backgrounds and elite connections, the life of the low-level bagman comes to resemble a compromise between a K-TEL television sales pitch and dunning calls from collection agencies. It's tough. It's demeaning. You get all of the cold calls and all of the people who hate your party. It's a tough life.

Some of the other career paths like that of the professional lobbyist do their selecting on class position. Consider the table below:

SOCIOECONOMIC RESOURCES OF DIRECTORS

Resource	Business	Labour	Proportion ranking 'high'[a] Prof-Ed.	Welfare	Instrumental[b]	
	%	%	%	%	%	
SES	76	30	86	81	58	(404)
Income	58	18	38	30	12	(148)
Experience	21	24	15	16	18	(111)
Membership	57	30	60	50	33	(222)
Access	31	13	21	18	16	(98)

[a] 'High' refers to the following conditions: SES, based upon education and occupation, in the two highest levels (I and II) in the Hollingshead index, *Social Class and Mental Illness.* Income: $15,000 or above; Experience: 10 years or more as director; Membership: 3-or-more social groups; Access: direct, personal contact with governmental elites, 'frequently'.
[b] 'Instrumental' groups refers to a residual category, comprising 'non-economic' groups, including religious, social-recreational, ethnic, fraternal-social, etc.

Source: Robert Presthus, *Elite Accommodation in Canadian Politics* (New York: Cambridge University Press, 1973), p. 124. Reproduced by permission.

From this table it is clear that the top positions of the professional lobbying industry are the more or less exclusive preserve of people with high socio-economic status. The only exception is lobbying for the trade union movement. This, of course, meshes completely with our investigation of those lobbies traditionally thought of as "friends of the masses" like the left, the feminists and multiculturalists. The conclusion is simple. If you are from a "nice" background, you have a big future. If you are "ordinary" you are almost certainly going to be consigned to the role of drudge or cannon fodder.

Education

In some ways this is part and parcel of class background. Middle and upper-class families have a much higher percentage of their children in institutions of higher learning than lower-middle or working class families, and in this society a limited education almost always means limited prospects for advancement. There is another feature, though. Having some of your education outside of Canada seems to give you a leg up. Consider some of the powerful influences we have examined.

Somehow a stint at Oxford, Harvard, the Sorbonne or the London School of Economics seems to be seen to have more value than similar study at Canadian universities. Part of this stems from the fact that the cost tends to weed out "the masses" whose only redeeming features are hard work and intelligence. The cost of an education abroad clearly makes a foreign education a status symbol. Part of this is also that permanent scar on the Canadian psyche, the colonial inferiority complex. Whatever the reason, it clearly favours the children of the well-to-do in the influence industry.

A good example of the value of a foreign education is that of those key members of the bureaucratic elite, Bernard and Sylvia Ostry. For those who might not be aware of them, the Ostrys have had two of the most illustrious careers in the bureaucracy in Canadian history. Their climb to success in the 1970s was truly meteoric. Bernard, who had originally been in public affairs in the CBC, found himself happily ensconced as Under Secretary of State. Sylvia went from being Chief Statistician to Deputy Minister of Consumer and Corporate Affairs to head of the Economic Council of Canada. What can explain their success? Surely not their degrees from the University of Manitoba. Of course, they have post graduate degrees and are very bright. But then, so do tens of thousands of other Canadians. The answer lies in their educations abroad. Bernard studied at the London School of Economics, Sylvia studied at Cambridge. Their luck changed for the better when Bernard met Trudeau in London. The Ostrys and Trudeau became long-time friends. Gossip in Ottawa during the Trudeau regime often mentioned this friendship as the real reason for their rapid rise. Doubtless such gossip was filled with envy and malice. At the same time one would have to be a total fool not to suppose that close friendship with the Prime Minister is a help to bureaucrats' career success and influence.

Occupation

Your occupation is important when considering the right influence career path. Some occupations are either direct stepping stones or virtual necessities. Being a lawyer is a great help. As we saw previously, lawyers are some of the major bagmen, backroom boys, lobbyists and party and governmental insiders in Canada today. Journalism is good too. Journalists have found lobbying for feminism and francophone rights provides a quantum leap in career success. If you are an academic or teacher you could do worse than become a militant in the respectable left like the NDP or establishment-oriented feminist lobbies like the National Action Committee. If you are working class, the Trade Union movement is your only hope.

Other Qualifications

I don't suppose I have to say it, but I will anyway. There are some career paths that may be barred to you because of your sex, race, age and ethnic origins. It sounds like discrimination, and it is, but you will get nowhere by protesting. If you are a man you will be barred from lobbying on behalf of feminism. If you are a WASP you are largely out of luck in the realm of multiculturalism. This used to be open — consider Gordon Fairweather and Canon Borden Purcell of the Canadian and Ontario Human Rights Commissions respectively. But the advance of minority rights has brought with it legalized discrimination against majority groups.

Connections

Canadian politics works on connections. It's not what you know, but who you know. These connections may be those of birth, as with the sons of Justice Minister John Crosbie or his nemesis, Liberal MP Sheila Copps, daughter of former Hamilton Mayor Vic Copps; marriage, as with Maureen McTeer or Mila Mulroney; education, as with the Ostrys, or political affiliation, as with Senator Ann Cools. If you have them you thrive and find easy entrance into the upper levels of the "influence industry." If you do not, you are consigned to the lower depths of each area of the industry to be used as cannon fodder or puppets by governments, parties and those in the upper levels.

The incredible thing about connections is that they are common even among the friends of the masses, those individuals who are supposedly opposed to any nepotism and corruption. A good example of the value of connections exists in the NDP. In a June 1985 column in the *Toronto Sun*, Douglas Fisher, former NDP MP, charged that the NDP was rife with nepotism and that he could personally name scores of people with jobs in the party organization who owed their positions totally to family connections. Whether it is true or not, I have personally noted with considerable interest for some time the remarkable way in which a few families seem to corner so many of the key positions in the "friends of the masses" field. At times they are a virtual family business, as with the Lewis family (David, Stephen and Michael).

Choosing Your Career Path

Now you have some idea of what it takes to make the grade in each path. The problem now is for you to choose. To help you in your decision I have prepared a table (see pages 310-11) outlining what each takes to get in and what the potential payoffs and risks are in your new career. Choose well and you too may soon be rolling in heretofore undreamed of wealth, power and acclaim just like those politicians, bureaucrats, lobbyists and other assorted "fat cats" you read about every day. Good luck in your choice.

Getting in on the Graft

Of course, choosing the right career path is only the beginning. Once you have chosen, it is a question of learning the tricks of the trade. After all, how do you take or offer a bribe? How do you get your proper place at the public trough? Who do you ask and what is the etiquette? Be of good cheer. All this shall become clear.

Buying, Begging and Badgering for Influence

There is so much to go after and so many access points and means of approaching the trough that it's hard to know where to start. It's like a child locked up in a candy store. Whether you are a "top dog" at professional lobbying or a "friend of the masses" going the "people power" route, many of the problems are the same — namely, establishing the proper locus of power and figuring out how to persuade the decision makers to act on your behalf. Below are some guidelines for would-be "persuaders."

1. Approach the appropriate people and centre of power. This is particularly important in a country like Canada with a complex federal structure of government. One federal civil servant told me that he was driven crazy by people and groups approaching him on matters that were under the authority of the provincial government. Do your homework in advance. Find out how government works. There is no point in antagonizing your intended target from the very beginning.

   Once you have identified the appropriate level of government, the task is to identify the flow of power and the nature of the decision-making process. This changes, of course, with time, need and the party in power. Under the Trudeau government, for example, the middle and upper level bureaucrats would evaluate the policy options and submit a set of recommendations and proposals to their deputy minister, who would form coalitions with other deputy ministers and, with their support, would then try to sell his minister on taking the lead in advancing the policy proposals. The minister would then take it to the appropriate cabinet committee, which after debate, if it agreed, would sign a cabinet memorandum and send the proposals to the full cabinet for what was almost always rubber stamping. Then the appropriate legislation would be drafted and submitted to parliament.

   The important thing about this process from the lobbyist's point of view was that the closer to the beginning of this chain of actions you could get, the better your chances of being able to influence events. If you got to the civil servants before policy had been decided upon, you had a very good chance of helping to decide what policies they would recommend. The lobbying activity which took place at this stage tended to be of a technical nature with lobbyists providing the civil servants with information they could not easily get elsewhere or perspectives that had not occurred to them. Such input is welcomed with open arms since it helps the civil servants and can serve to lower their risk. The problem is that as you move down the chain, people become more and more committed to policies and your chances of getting them to change their minds is smaller. By the time legislation is drafted and sent to the House, the government is committed and a majority will mean that passage is assured.

Influence Career	Preferred Qualities	Preferred Occupational Background	Potential Payoff	Potential Problems
Top dog	Membership in elite	Any "respectable" one. Sometimes none at all	Money. Direct & easy influence	None
All lobbies but union	High socio-economic status (SES) Smooth, bureaucratic non-confrontational style	Previous experience as upper level civil servant, high level player in party in power, or lawyer	Money, career success	
Union lobbyist	Apparent belief in left & trade union idea	High SES not necessary	Offers potential career for those who would not have entrance into other career paths	Limited career path/career ghettoization. Government usually not inclined toward unions' point of view
High level bagman	Elite background Good contacts High SES	Lawyer Career politician	Money, power, high level patronage (Senate, Order of Canada, board of directors, positions as Governor & Lieu-tenant-Governor	Very occasionally you may be charged with influence peddling
Low level bagman	Work hard Follow orders		Low level patronage	May be used just as "cannon fodder" Sometimes no payoff

				Upon discovery you may be subject to:
Insider	Possess insider information & "flexible" attitude to ethical questions	Elected office or upper level civil servant	Monetary gain from business deals involving government & government decisions Directorships in industry after retirement or electoral defeat	Dismissal from office Being charged under Criminal Code Destruction of good name
High level "Friend of the masses" (feminism, French language rights, multiculturalism)	Female, "visible minority," francophone (outside Quebec; it won't buy you anything in Quebec any more) Righteous indignation Connections by birth, marriage or party affiliation	Academic, media person, lawyer, civil servant, teacher	High level patronage (Senate, Order of Canada; elected office, lieutenant and Governor Generalship, Directorships of Crown corporations, appointment to Human Rights, Royal and Status of Women Commissions, etc.) Media fame Nomination to winnable ridings	Being used as a tool of government
Low-level "Friend of the Masses"	Female, "visible minority," francophone (outside of Quebec)		Low level patronage Nomination to unwinnable ridings	Being used as a tool by government & high-level "friends of the masses"

The election of the Tories in 1984 saw some changes in this process, but the consequences have not as yet fully been appreciated. The most recent refinement of the process has been the addition of chiefs of staff and big staffs to the ministers' offices. There are two major reasons for this development. One represents an attempt to move control from the civil service to the ministerial level. The impetus for such a shift of responsibility had started during the Trudeau regime. We have already seen how the disastrous MacEachen budget (almost exclusively drafted by the civil service) had caused the Liberals to become wary of relying too heavily on the civil service. This government started to move policy initiation from the civil servants to the politicians, especially the PMO and the cabinet ministers and their political staffs. For the Tories there was yet another reason. A "stab in the back" theory has developed among Tories to explain the many problems and early fall of the Clark government. Most PCs are convinced that the civil service sabotaged their efforts at governing because of its supposed pro-Liberal bias. Whether this is correct or not is not as important as the fact that they believe it. They are determined that this will not happen again. In addition to trying to move control to the ministerial level, the intention is that the political staffs will be involved in negotiations between ministries. Clearly, these chiefs of staff will represent new lobbying points of access to lobbyists.

2. Avoid ad hoc lobbying (reacting to specific issues that have arisen on the parliamentary agenda or specific rulings of regulatory bodies). This has until recently been the major lobbying sin of business interests in Ottawa. What they would do is show up to lobby only when some matter arose on the order paper. The usual result was a virtual rout. They did not know to whom they should talk. Usually they went to the wrong people, people who should be the ones with the power but who were not. Also because they were not a more or less permanent presence, they had no network or coalitions of interests to rely upon. There were no friendships with decision makers which could be called upon. Worst of all, by the time they found out that the government was about to do something they disagreed with, it was too late for reasons enumerated above.

Instead of one-shot, ad hoc lobbying efforts, lobbies should develop long-term lobbying strategies and programs whose aims would be to: educate government and the public as to the legitimacy of their cause and their groups' demands, and broaden the base of support for the lobby by developing and broadening their network, setting up alliances and coalitions with other groups for mutual benefit and working with all parties. The opposition parties can help you in the House if your efforts have been unsuccessful to date. In addition, no party stays in power forever. Some day the opposition will be in power and your contacts will be enormously important.

3. Develop contacts and friends in all sectors and levels of government. As we have seen, lobbying access points exist in all parts of the government and you may need some of the less obvious contacts some day.

4. Sell your demands to government on the basis of how these demands plus your support will be a benefit to those to whom you are talking. It may sound harsh, but people in government are primarily concerned with their problems, not yours. Some of the questions those lobbied will have in their minds are: (i) how does this promote my career advancement, (ii) how does this promote my party's chances of re-election, and (iii) how does this facilitate and augment government policy?

5. Use a collaborative style rather than a confrontational style. Show the government that you are part of a coalition that is supporting the government. Small business groups broke this rule during the Trudeau years. The price of this was to be excluded from government consultation. The last five years of the Trudeau regime saw a virtual attack by the federal government on this sector.

6. Avoid the use of rhetoric or histrionics in presentations and other dealings with government. The Canadian Chamber of Commerce has been notably ineffective in Ottawa. A great deal of this has probably been the result of the fact that most of the leaders who deal with government trumpet economic and social positions that Ebenezer Scrooge would have felt comfortable with.

7. Appear to embody the values of the groups and individuals whom you are seeking to influence. You must look like them, talk like them and act like them. This will make you seem likable and unthreatening.

8. Develop and implement a comprehensive lobbying strategy. This will look very much like a military battle plan. It will allow

varied and flexible responses and have fall back provisions. No one wins every battle. When you lose you must retreat to a prepared position to survive, recoup your forces and fight again.

People Power

If you are poor or somehow "beyond the pale," your job is more difficult. But fear not. There are ways to make your dreams come true. The answer lies in what I call the "people power" approach. I call it this because when you lack money, power and connections that the established and establishment groups have, you don't really have much left for a power base except your ideas, convictions and membership. It's people power or nothing.

A pure heart is fine, but when it comes to a grab for influence and power, you are going to need money. Most of the groups which are without powerful sponsorship by government, business or labour interests find this the hardest part of their struggle. The question is, "Where is the money going to come from?" Depending on the purpose to which you plan to put this money, there are sources, one being provincial and federal governments. The problem, of course, is that your group's goals and ideology will have to be more or less in lockstep with those of government. As we saw earlier, the big winners of the federal funding game are groups trying to promote feminism, multiculturalism, disarmament and bilingualism. Government is not fair about this funding in the slightest. If you are supporting traditional family values like REAL Women or right-to-life groups, if you support a strong Western alliance, Quebec separatism, English rights, a "white-only" immigration policy or have a far-left or far-right orientation, you won't get a penny. Life is not fair. Nor is government.

The second problem is that if you do fall into this magic circle of organizations that get funded, the government will try and turn your group into its puppet and mouthpiece. It will fund you on a project and short-term basis so as to keep you dependent and vulnerable to its influence. It will sometimes fund you for a few months just before an election so that the party in power can use it in its election propaganda, but your grant will almost certainly run out just after the election. In many cases funding is not renewed and your project which was claimed as being so important by government members before and during the election will be allowed to die soon after. Scratch one pesky group of malcontents, and no bad public reaction.

Direct government funding is not the only source of funding. There are private sources. For fashionably "progressive" groups, such as those involved in struggles for native rights, environmental issues, various labour struggles and against apartheid and racism, you can draw on the more liberal churches (the United Church, for instance), unions (like CUPE) and so-called public interest groups such as Public Interest Advocacy Centre (PIAC), the Regulated Industries Program (RIP), the Canadian Environmental Law Association (CELA) and the Advocacy Resources Centre for the Handicapped (ARCH). One word of warning about these supposedly independent public advocacy groups! Ask yourself this. Is the government funding real social change through these agencies or is it providing funding for reverse or tame pressure groups?

One of the more popular financing tricks of the trade for various "people power" groups is to set up so-called non-profit charitable organizations, with the advantage being that donations are tax deductible and so are very attractive for people with money to give. Both the pro-life and pro-choice groups in Canada have these so-called charitable groups affiliated with their organizations. Do funds ever get funnelled from the charitable organizations to their lobbying sisters? They claim not, but the temptation must be enormous. One possible use of this sort of ploy is to pay people working on the lobbying activities of the main group by having them supposedly on the payroll of the "charitable group." The effect of this sort of thing is the same as if the money were being given to the lobby organization. Other ways in which this type of structure can be used for the benefit of a lobby are to provide funds for legal actions and to mount an "education" campaign.

The Department of National Revenue, Taxation Information Circular 78-3 which deals with the question of what constitutes a charitable organization, fails to discuss the question of whether funds collected by a charitable organization may be used to fund litigation of a sister organization and thus creates sufficient ambiguity. A publication of the Canadian Advisory Council on the Status of Women advises the following: "Setting up a legal action fund as a charitable organization — donations to which qualify as deduction for donors — may appear to be an attractive option. . ."[1] A good example of an organization that is nominally a charitable organization but which acts in a lobbying capacity at times would be the Planned Parenthood organization. At present the national right to life organization is after PP's scalp as a result of a series of advertisements that had the double purpose of promoting birth control and abortion and soliciting funds to keep on with the good work.

As we have seen, the Right and the "too far left to be fashionable" groups are out of luck when it comes to public funding. After all, government doesn't like to fund the *real* opposition. Anti-feminist groups have a tough time too. The task then is to find an appropriate sponsor. The right-to-life people and REAL Women have the Catholic Church. They deny that this is a factor, of course, but the large amount of advertising from Catholic organizations in their newspapers, plus the fact that some of the columnists are priests, is highly indicative. The Right can count on the rich and some elements in the business community, particularly the "Colonel Blimp" fringe, plus small business; this seems to be part of the support for the National Citizens' coalition. The conservative "think-tank," the Fraser Institute, finds support from the more respectable elements in the big business community. In a real pinch you might consider approaching foreign governments and groups in other countries. There is considerable evidence that the Soviet Union, the United States, the Philippines, Israel and some Arab states as well, have been involved in directly or indirectly aiding lobby groups in Canada. Why not you too? After all, who has as yet offered to act as the puppet of Andorra or Monaco?

And remember, if you don't have much money and don't represent a high proportion of voters, you can still bring pressure to bear on government to get your group's demands heard and satisfied by government by manipulating the media and getting them to pressure government for you. By the time the media gets finished presenting your views as those of a vast majority of the population, the government will beg you to tell them what you want. Here's how you do it:

1. Give the media a good story. The media are forever thirsting for new stories and love novelty and the outrageous. People in the media are under enormous time constraints, with neither the time nor the inclination to go digging or go to a great deal of trouble to find and develop a story. This means that all you have to do to get them to publicize your position is to give them a story that is colourful (maybe humorous) and make sure that everything is there just waiting to be stolen — pictures, background on the organization, its goals, members and history. You might even consider setting up everything in such a way that the media people can plagiarize what you have written. They will never admit it but they do it all the time.

2. Shoot for the editorial and "women's" pages, which are particularly susceptible to human interest stories. Other likely candi-

dates for this sort of story are radio and television interview shows, documentaries and public affairs shows.

3. Try for an editorial in newspapers. These are not widely read by ordinary readers, but are watched closely by politicians and government officials. Thus you are reaching fewer but "better" readers. It is called targetting and represents the difference between using a shotgun and a rifle.

4. Pay special attention to the so-called "special media," such as the ethnic press, church papers and trade papers. Many have a surprisingly large readership. Because they have small budgets, they are often ready to carry ready-made stories with pictures.

5. Solicit wire services. If the story has national significance, it may be picked up and used by a very large number of newspapers across the country.

6. Design your events with news photographs in mind. Make sure you have dramatic backgrounds (like national monuments or beautiful natural settings) or interesting visual details. My favourite illustration of this principle involved a friend who was running for parliament and having trouble getting good coverage from the media for his campaign. The newspapers even misspelled his name. He took advantage of this misspelling to dramatically alter his coverage. He found a woman with the largest breasts he had ever seen, got her to put on a wet T-shirt with his name on the front and had a professional photographer take a number of closeups of her (waist up shots, of course). He sent them to one of the major Toronto papers and discovered the next day that they devoted half of page three to the picture. He burned his name on the consciousness of 500,000 Torontonians that day and assured himself of more sympathetic coverage forever after.

7. Use radio and television wherever possible. For most people this is their only source of information and news. When you make news releases for radio and TV, use short, uncomplicated and colourful sentences. Try to get your organization's name and message on public service announcements. The price is right (free) and it works.

8. When dealing with the print media, pay special attention to getting the journalist responsible to use a catchy headline. In many cases readers only read the headlines, so you only get one kick at the can.

9. If your target is television, stage your event before 3:00 P.M. so that reporters have time to return to the station and process the material in time for the 6:00 P.M. news. Find out in advance what events will be competing with your story that day for media attention. If there are big stories, stage your event another day. Sunday is the very best day to stage events because media people are short of stories for Sunday evening and Monday morning.

10. When approaching the media, call the right person. With television and radio, call specific producers. With newspapers call the reporter who covers your field. To find out who he or she is, you just have to look at a few previous days' papers. Call those people who are likely to be sympathetic to you and your cause.

11. Don't be shy about contacting the media. They need you as much as you need them.

12. When giving news conferences, spoon-feed the media. Give them a written copy of what you are going to say beforehand. It gives them something to follow along with you as you are speaking and it gives them something they can refer to when they get back to the office to write the story. If you have the time, prepare a précis in which the issues are briefly outlined. Provide electrical outlets for radio and television people.

13. Neutralize journalists who are giving you a hard time or attacking you. The Toronto Island residents' lobby used this one effectively. *Toronto Star* columnist Michael Best had attacked it in print. Members of the lobby served him with a writ in the crowded press room above Toronto City Hall Council Chambers in front of all of the other reporters. They ultimately decided not to go through with their legal action against him, but they managed to scare both him and other members of the press. Best stopped writing columns against them.

14. Use letters to the editor. One way of giving the impression of widespread public support is to flood the newspapers with letters from your members without mentioning that they are connected to the same or any other organization. If at all possible, ensure that they use different wording and typewriters with different typefaces so as to give the impression of being unrelated in any way. Better yet use a word processor. This allows you to make dozens of "spontaneous" expressions of the voice of the people in minutes. One of the best ways to ensure that your letters will be

published is to get famous people to write (or at least sign) them. In this way they become newsworthy.

15. Pack the lines of open-line shows. These are not particularly popular in Ontario, but in other parts of the country they are big news. The West is good. So is Quebec.

16. Treat members of the media as if they were human beings, not idiots or objects to be used. Remember that they are human just like you and their treatment of you and your story (if at all) will depend very much on how much they like or dislike you. You'll want repeat business from them so remember the adage, "Leave them laughing!"

17. Proceedings that are unusually boring, like the hearings of regulatory boards, Royal Commissions or enquiries, are often remarkable opportunities for manipulating and seizing media time. Reporters wish that something interesting would happen with a bit of colour just to stay awake, if nothing else. Provide it. Stage a demonstration or skit outside the hearing rooms. Arrange to rent a room right next door to the hearing room and stage an "alternate hearing." If you feel really daring, you might consider trying to disrupt the proceedings of the regular hearings. That will get the media's attention.

Patronage: Getting It

Of course, not all lobbying is for the good of some oppressed group. Sometimes you just get a hankering for some good old-fashioned patronage for you and you alone. Right? Well, there are rules to this just as there are to anything else:

1. You must buy patronage appointments. This does not imply giving your MP an envelope and asking for the chairmanship of the CRTC. It is a little subtler than this, though not much. The simple fact is you must have helped the ruling party in some way — money, people, personal services and so on. The more valuable the help the greater the reward.

   There is an element of luck in all of this of course. Some of the greatest goodies recently have gone to those people who supported Brian Mulroney in his bid for the Conservative leadership. Obviously, picking the leader at the convention is a long shot, but like all long shots, it pays big when your horse comes in. The other bit of luck is that your party has to win. When asked about patronage appointments, Mulroney was quoted as saying that he would consider appointments from the other parties when every living, breathing Tory had received one. There are a large number of living, breathing Tories in line.

There are two services that parties value highest and as a result reward the best. They are raising money and absolute and unquestioning loyalty. We have already discussed the fund raising part of this in detail in preceding sections on bagmen and their contributions to the party system. The matter of loyalty is key as well. There are powerful similarities between how you get ahead in the Canadian political system and how it is done in the Soviet Union. Both depend upon team-work and unquestioning loyalty rather than the outstanding solo contributions of a few inspired individuals. It is not enough to be loyal for now. You must promise to be loyal now and for ever more, no matter what happens and what the party line is or what you are asked to do. Such people can be counted on in the crunch and offer no threat to those at the top.

2. Know exactly what body and what position you would like. This makes it easy for the responsible party officials to act on your request. The easier their job, the more likely you are to get what you want.

3. Understand how the body on which you are seeking a position is funded. Obviously it makes no sense asking a federal cabinet minister for a position on a provincial board or crown corporation. In some cases bodies are funded jointly by many levels of government. For instance, the Ontario Housing Corporation receives funds from the federal, provincial and municipal levels of government, which means you have three different kicks at the can, depending on where your contacts are.

4. Ask. This sounds ridiculous, but some people seem to feel that their good works will be noticed and rewarded without their saying anything. Think of your place of work. Who gets the rewards — the quiet, competent people or the noisy braggarts? This realm is no different. There is no justice in this world, so point out your fine past works and ask for a just reward.

5. Ask the person closest to the decision that you can get. This requires that you do some research as to who dispenses what. The federal cabinet has ministers who have sole responsibility for the dispensing of goodies in their province. Also there are MPs or

cabinet ministers in big metropolitan areas like Toronto or Montreal who are responsible for goodies in their cities. At a much lower level MPs have limited access to patronage in their constituencies.

6. Sell the patronage giver on the benefits to him or her which will flow from rewarding you. Calls to justice or "crying hard-up" will not buy you anything. These goodies are their lifeline to re-election and they must be assured that appointments will aid them if they are to dispense them.

7. Try to get the favour before you have dispensed the service. The appointment of Peter Stollery to the Senate was in part contingent upon helping to get Jim Coutts elected to his seat of Spadina. Coutts kept his part of the bargain. Stollery got his senatorship. Coutts however was appointed and failed to get elected to the seat vacated by Stollery. In this business it's really tough to get a refund.

8. Try to trap or blackmail the patronage dispenser into giving the appointment rather than just making a vague promise. I am not suggesting anything of a criminal nature, just a little arm-twisting to help the giver to decide in your favour. Here is a trick that has been used to great advantage: An acquaintance of mine wanted to get appointed to a certain patronage place on a board of directors. He found the person responsible for giving that particular appointment — an MP whom he had helped in the past. He called the leading member of the MP's riding executive and asked him for advice on how he could get the appointment and whom he should contact (knowing full well who he was). The man told him and suggested the "seeker" call him that weekend. He did call the MP and mentioned that the member of the riding executive had suggested he call. This was clever because now the MP knew that an influential supporter of his was looking over his shoulder. The MP promised him the appointment. The "seeker" then called back the key influencer on the riding executive to tell him that the MP had agreed to appoint him. The result of this was that the executive member called the MP to congratulate him on his good judgment and the MP was stuck. He could not go back on his word without looking bad in the eyes of one of his key supporters.

9. Don't trust in the word of those responsible for those positions. If they will cheat the taxpayers by filling up these posts with political hacks who are often completely incompetent, they will surely

cheat you and break their word if it suits their purposes. A good example of this was the case of former Kitchener Ontario Mayor Morley Rosenberg, who claimed he was offered a judicial appointment by the Tory government if he ran for the Tories in the 1981 election and lost. He did not get the judicial appointment. Rosenberg then gave a copy of a letter he sent to the premier on the subject which seemed to support his claim. The PCs managed to weather the storm and Rosenberg ended up happy too. He recanted his charges and now has an appointment on the Ontario Municipal Board at $60,000 a year. The secret then, is to have some evidence with which to embarrass the government if it reneges on its promises.

10. Get into a position where you either control a bloc of votes or can credibly bluff that you do control a bloc of votes. This ploy has been used very successfully in those playing the multicultural, women's and French language influence games. Once you have a constituency among the electorate, make certain that there are always problems and unresolved issues. If the complaints of your constituency are ever completely satisfied, your supporters will no longer need you and you will lose your leverage.

Selling and Using Influence: the Insiders' Game
So far we have just looked at how outsiders attempt to buy influence or use their resources and contacts in such a way as to manipulate the government to get what they want. That is only half of the fun. The insiders get to play too, not only for personal enrichment, but to increase their own power and influence.

Manipulating the Electoral System
The major preoccupation of politicians is re-election. After all, if you are not in office, there is no possibility of keeping all of those goodies which you value so much. Some of the major techniques which you can use to ensure that you and your party will remain in power are:

1. Make extensive use of patronage and pork barrelling. This is a good one. There is a strong relationship between the amount of goodies dispensed and electoral success. So use your position as a cabinet minister or influential MP to ensure that lots of public works programs and other project funds go to your riding, then be careful that only those companies, individuals and groups that

support you, your party and your government's policies get these funds. It is important that it is clear to everyone in your riding that people in the riding understand that only those supporting you will be helped; the object in all of this is to make as many people and groups dependent on you as possible. The welfare of all in your riding is not the goal. Also, use your position to place as many people as possible in well-paying government jobs. For those who are very worthwhile, you might consider using the technique of one former cabinet minister which was to expand his ministry enormously and hire lots of people who were personally loyal to him in those positions. Once again only supporters get jobs. Employ lots of people in your personal ministerial staff. Such people will be personally loyal to you and have a powerful stake in your personal political welfare. They are ready-made workers for you if you should choose to run for party leader and are more trustworthy than civil servants anyway. And finally, make deals with those who control blocs of votes or who seem to be vocal and well respected leaders of restive groups, especially women and ethnic groups. Suitable enticements are research contracts, funding for newspapers and magazines, bestowing legitimacy on these individuals' groups instead of their competitors and helping them to consolidate their hold over their own constituencies.

2. Manipulate interest groups. Left to their own devices, these groups are dangerous since they are unpredictable in their demands, tactics and support. The task is to win their leadership over, control their activities and demands and get them to lobby their own members to support you, your government and its policies. So (i) get them dependent on government funding, (ii) determine which groups will survive and which will not by dispensing funds and legitimacy to only a portion of the groups out there, (iii) give consistent and reliable funding to those groups that you wish to encourage and unreliable and short-term and non-renewable funding to those of which you do not approve, but would make you look bad in the media if you made no effort to support them at all, and (iv) co-opt the leaders of those movements that represent the greatest danger to you if left to their own devices by giving them lucrative government research contracts to study and advise government on issues concerning their interest groups' concerns.

3. Manipulate the media. Make the most of your political and elite contacts to get the odd damaging story spiked. A telephone call to the publisher should do it. It has in the past. The use of threats or legal action against reporters and publishers can help to cool the investigative ardour of print journalists. To pacify especially inquisitive journalists, use the official sources ploy, giving access to information and interviews to everyone except the offending newspaper and reporter. Another great technique might be to give a difficult reporter information which might lead him or her to write something that they could not prove or which was not true. Goodbye credibility!

One technique that presently shows great promise is the use of stronger anti-hate laws, more vigorous human rights commissions and the inclusion of clauses in the broadcast act and CRTC guidelines forbidding a specific portrayal of groups in a certain way. You probably will never have to use this against the standard media, but just having it there will cause editors and program directors to go through the most tortured self-examination and introspection to avoid contravening the law and CRTC guidelines.

Rules for Influence Peddlers, Grafters, Bribe-takers and Others

So far we have been quite general in discussing how insiders can manipulate the system. That discussion has really only been concerned with holding power and manipulating others. The question then is what is the payoff? When do you get the fruits of your labours? How do you use your insider position to enrich yourself? Below are some of the rules that past insiders have used successfully to go for the gold:

1. Don't take part in graft, which is to say, do not solicit bribes. This is, among other things, very low class. If you are not important enough for business people to come to you on their own initiative, then you might as well forget it. Besides, by demanding bribes you are increasing your chances of being detected. Sooner or later you are going to run into that honest individual who will resent your overture and inform the authorities or the media and thus force authorities into acting. Better to wait coyly until the offers start coming in. One advantage of this approach is that the bribe givers are most unlikely to be morally outraged when you accept and go public. Also, they happen to be guilty of an illegal

act themselves in trying to bribe you and so have a vested interest in keeping the transaction quiet.

2. Do not take a bribe when the transaction can be traced. This pretty much rules out cheques, credit cards, stock and bonds and so on which leave an audit trail and can be traced back to you. Accepting gifts of tangible assets like houses and cars while you are still in office is also forbidden for the same reasons. Cash could be acceptable since it is harder to trace, but there are problems here, too. One is that there is a stigma in this country which attaches to bribes involving envelopes of money, probably the result of the heavily puritan and Catholic origins of Canadian society. Another is the possibility of leaving an inadvertent audit trail. For one thing, the company that offers the "gift" may be silly enough to label the expense in their books as exactly what it is. Take the case of the Toronto-based Fidinam (Ontario) Limited in 1971. It donated $50,000 to the Ontario Progressive Party one month after the Ontario cabinet approved a contract between the company and the Worker's Compensation Board (WCB), specifying that the WCB would lend Fidinam $15 million for the company's Upper Canada Place development and that the WCB would take a twenty-year lease for space in the building at $1.4 million a year. The Swiss parent company queried the entry in the Ontario company's books and the secretary-treasurer tele-graphed back that the cheque was "a political donation related to UCP (Fidinam's Upper Canada Place development)/WCB." This telegram was subsequently published in the *Globe and Mail*. Finally the president of Fidinam (Ontario) declared publicly that the money was a political donation but had nothing to do with the cabinet decision concerning the Worker's Compensation Board. I cite this incident to show would-be "flexible" officials that gifts of any kind, if given while you are in office, carry a danger with them. There are many silly and thoughtless employees in private industry and they could suddenly ruin your life by disclosing what has gone on.

3. So, do not, if at all possible, accept "gifts" from people or com-panies for which you have done or will do favours while you are still in office. Be patient. Wait until you are no longer in public life. The trick in this strategy of delaying payback is that you have to be certain that the bribe giver will pay when you are out of office. There are a number of ways in which you can make certain

that the other half of this transaction will come through with their part of the goodies. One way is to only do this type of deal with companies and individuals with a tradition and reputation of paying off. You won't find this information in books of course, but your network should be able to provide you with this information. In a limited way there is honour among some thieves. After all, if they burn you, you can blacken their name and make sure that they never make another corrupt deal at a high level again. Another way would be to get some dirt on the company that has never before surfaced. In this way, if they cheat you, you can leak this information to a friend in the media, the police or attorney general's office and make them sorry they ever met you.

4. Do not put anything on paper or tape. In ordinary business transactions, things are put on paper so that if anything goes wrong you can seek redress in the courts. It is obviously out of the question that you will take the other party to court if they do not pay off. The only thing that a record of your meetings can do is hurt you.

5. That leads to the question of how the negotiations should be conducted. Never talk on the telephone (assuming you do not have a scrambler). Avoid your home, their office or some place chosen by them. Your own office or government buildings may not be safe either. The danger is that of being bugged — by the other side, by political opponents, by political rivals and enemies in your own party, by the police (assuming that this might be a "sting"), by a foreign intelligence agency or by any number of people. Avoid talking in cars, including your own. These can be bugged too. Prefer public places like parks, coffee shops that you have chosen at the last minute and so on. There is of course the danger of body packs, but there are devices you can buy which will detect their presence. It all depends on your level of trust — or conversely, paranoia.

6. Try for directorships of corporations or plum jobs following your leaving political life. You will still be plugged in to power since the company will use you as a very high-level lobbyist on their behalf. This means that you will still be wandering the halls of power. The company or interest for which you are labouring will give you substantial resources with which to work. Those now in power will be glad to talk to you and do business with you so you will still have power, just of a different kind. You will now

be buying influence instead of selling it. It will probably seem very similar. In addition you will be paid well by your employer and will be rewarded for past services on his behalf. By this time, any charges by the media or opposition critics will just roll off your back.

7. Try for a place in the Senate. This is the happy hunting ground for insider lobbyists. Here you will be on the public payroll and be able to lobby for your favourite interests at the same time. The best location for the senator-lobbyist is definitely on the Senate Committee on Banking, Trade and Commerce.

8. Line up your supporters in advance just in case. This means sympathetic journalists, top individuals in all parties and member of the judiciary, if you can manage it. Obviously, you are not going to tell them why you are suddenly so nice and picking up all the cheques at the press club and the parliamentary dining room; just let it be a matter of your being an all-round nice guy or gal. Think of it as fire insurance. No one wants to have to go through a fire or even think about it, but it is nice to have the policy if it happens.

9. Those at the municipal level have found the land game a source of real profit. Many municipal politicians have used their insider information to profit from rezoning applications before the city, and even those who have been exposed seem to have suffered no ill-effects. Usually they were never charged or even censured. When they were, most were found not guilty and the results of being found guilty were not all that dire anyway. Even voters seem to be easy on politicians like this. Clearly the risks are not that great. The payoffs, however, can be enormous.

PART VI

THE MORASS AND HOW
TO GET OUT OF IT

All right, enough cynicism! So far we have seen how various lobbies and individuals are using their influence and connections to get the various levels of government to operate on their behalf. Sometimes that results in government actions which are beneficial to the country as a whole, but often it has little regard for the greater public good; there are even many occasions in which these actions are actually contrary to the common good. This section will deal with some of the dangers that this system of influence buying and selling presents for Canadian democracy and with some ways out of the morass.

14

The Death of Democracy?

In the chapter on the real world of politics we noted some trends upon which virtually all political observers concur. These changes involve:

1. A major decline in the importance of MPs and the legislature in Canadian politics.
2. A decline in the importance of the individual in the thinking of government. Rather, a premium is now placed on the input from organized groups in society, with the more highly organized and more bureaucratic the more likely to be listened to by government. Doubtless this has something to do with the increasing complexity of society and the size of government institutions. Government is at present just too big and too remote from its citizens to be able to deal directly with individual citizens and their needs as it did in the past.
3. The increasing influence of organized interest groups in the policy-making process.

Of this there is very little disagreement. It is the interpretation of these events that causes experts to diverge in their views.

The dominant view in government is that of the pluralist or participatory democracy viewpoint. It draws on John Kenneth Galbraith's view that the increasing influence and activity of interest groups represents the ultimate in democracy and is in fact an extension of democracy since it gives everyone a chance to be heard and gives a voice to those who would not be heard as individuals. In this view, government funding of such groups is good because the system takes a lot of money to be effective. Without this funding only the rich would have the resources for exerting political influence. The pluralist view posits a world where every interest has a fair chance of being heard. To paraphrase Mao, "A thousand flowers bloom. A thousand schools contend." From all of this blooming of varying views and political contention, the government is then able to hear all and then work out a consensus which will satisfy most people and provide stability and political legitimacy to the rule of those in power.

Another view is that of the Marxist critique which asserts that any image of the state as a neutral arbiter is simply a comforting illusion concocted by a cynical few in power to deceive the great mass of the population into misunderstanding the real and exploitative way in which power is used to maintain rule by a few. In this view, interest groups serve not only to express viewpoints but also to act as vehicles for social control.

Yet another view is the overload school of thought, which condemns excess demand for public services and the excessive growth of the public sector with their concomitant economic and political rigidities. For these people the solution lies in the reduction of expectations and "smaller" government.

There is a moral critique as well. The pluralist world of competing interest groups has been recently condemned by Daniel Bell, the noted American political philosopher, as spelling the end of *civitas* — civic virtue and responsibility which seeks the public good rather than some narrow self-interest at the expense of others. Bell's argument is reminiscent of the chaotic state of nature described by the seventeenth-century British political philosopher Hobbes who spoke of "the war of all against all."

All of these critiques contain elements of truth, but when they are added together, the result is a major threat to Canadian democracy and personal freedom.

Unequal Resources

One of the major underpinnings of the pluralist or participatory democratic model being used by virtually all governments in Canada is the assumption that all interest groups have an equal opportunity to express themselves and that after all the interests have been heard, government is then able to make an optimal decision. But not all groups are equal. Everything in this book indicates that some groups have vastly superior and greater resources than others. The class backgrounds of lobbyists, the money available and the legitimacy which the government and elite give to these groups determines if they will be heard and how successful they will be in pressing their demands. Many voices among the Canadian people never get heard. In spite of all the rhetoric from government as to its openness to all points of view, it is clear that it is a claim which is far from truth. Large bureaucratic organizations with offices in capital cities get heard; organizations with lots of money for lobbying, publicity campaigns, high-priced lawyers and other experts get heard; those with the right political and social connections get heard; those with the same goals and world-view as the government get heard; so do the rich, and those from the same social background as the members of the social, bureaucratic, political economic and ideological elites. The rest, which is in essence "we the people," do not get a real hearing.

Most of what passes for seeking the input of the people is appearance, a sham. This idea that the most powerful in society are constantly getting their way at the expense of the population as a whole is supported by the best and brightest observers of the political scene and interest group behaviour in Canada. Perhaps the best scholarly study of pressure groups in Canada is that of Robert Presthus. In his book *Elite Accommodation in Canadian Politics*, he states, "Another aspect of effectiveness is the common view that the "really effective" lobbying in Canadian politics is done, as an Ottawa director (of an interest group) put it, "by individuals of stature who are representative of capital and who are more influential than the orthodox organizations of private enterprise.' "[1] This we have seen is true not only of business interests competing for government largesse but all other groups in society.

Much Influencing Goes on in Secret

Very little that is written or spoken about lobbying in Canada describes the total picture of how influence is brought to bear. It is true that there are groups that function as they are supposed to and faithfully portray their members' wishes to government. Sometimes government even decides on the relative merits of each group's case. More often, when the stakes are high, the real lobbying and influencing goes on behind our backs. Secret conversations between long-time friends and allies go on in private and the powerful and rich are successful because of their wealth, power and contacts. Returning for a second to that Ottawa lobby director quoted by Presthus, "Prestigeful groups, he insisted, are not always effective as interest groups, but rather through 'personal friendships and connections with ministers and top civil-servants.' This observation is sometimes accompanied, as it was in this case, by the judgment that such behaviour is often covert and hence impossible to document systematically."[2] This is an assertion which has been supported by much of this book. Probably this situation is inevitable as long as election to high office requires the spending of large amounts of money and the endorsement of very prestigious figures. Nothing comes from nothing. If politicians wish election and re-election they must seek the support of the rich and powerful. To get this support the parties must promise to return the favour once in power.

The Present System of Influence Supports the Status Quo

Part of this tendency to support the present social, political and economic distribution of "goodies" is a result of the continuity of class and social background in all of the Canadian elites and in all of the successful interest groups. They have the same needs and goals despite appearances to the contrary on occasion. One would expect this with the pro-establishment groups like business or the leaderships of the political parties, but what is surprising is that the makeup of the leaderships of the so-called anti-establishment groups like the NDP or the feminist groups are remarkably similar to those of the pro-establishment and elite groups. After all, the Lewis dynasty of the NDP is far from struggling. Stephen Lewis, UN ambassador and former Ontario NDP leader and his wife, feminist leader Michelle Landsberg, send their children to one of the most exclusive private schools, and the present leader in the province, Bob Rae, is from a prestigious mandarin family and received a private school education abroad. Just how threatening are such people to the existing system?

Government Growth and Manipulation

As we have seen, government tends to fund those groups which already sing the same song as the party in power or which show that they can be used in the future to broadcast and generate enthusiasm for the government's message. Also we saw that the government often funds groups in such a way as to destroy those that it does not like or to make the interest groups that are just too useful or hardy to destroy increasingly dependent on government funds and thus government itself. Once they are fully dependent on government, they can be totally controlled and will do and say whatever the government wishes them to say. Perhaps even worse are the reverse pressure groups which are actually created by government to pressure it in the way that government wishes to go in the first place. As we saw these are quite common. Finally we saw that the leaders of independent interest groups change through constant contact with the government. After a time they come to resemble government officials more than they do their own members. Worse yet, their organizations come to be less democratic and less open to ideas from individual members back home. There is a slow but sure trend toward bureaucratization and centralized control from the head office. When this happens, the members' interests are sacrificed to those of the groups' leaders or government.

More demands from interest group spokespeople mean more government services and funds to meet those needs. More services mean more people and money for ministries and departments. More people and bigger budgets mean greater power for top civil servants. More power means faster and and better promotional opportunities for civil servants. Sometimes when interest groups are not effective enough in making their demands to the bureaucracy, the bureaucracy may help them out with funding and good advice. Where groups do not exist, the bureaucracy may create and fund new organizations. After all, it is in their best interest that they be lobbied effectively. The result of this is an enormous growth in government and the resources that are consumed by the public sector, often in very poor or inefficient ways. As we all know, this is not a time when resources can be consumed in a wasteful manner. There are too many needy people who should get first call on these scarce resources.

System Overload

Related to the forced growth of interest groups to meet the desire of government departments for growth is the question of system overload. The essence of system overload is that there are now so many different groups in society making demands on government that government is simply no longer able to cope with all the groups. The trouble is that people have been encouraged to make demands of government and have been told that it is their right to demand and get anything they want. When they do not get their demands met, they feel angry and the victims of injustice. Had they not been so encouraged in the past, they might well not have had such unrealistically high expectations in the first place and so would never have become alienated. The result of a large number of unfulfilled demands must inevitably be social discontent and unrest. Setting up segments of the population like this is a serious disservice to the people and is destructive of public peace.

Selfishness

One of the most terrifying aspects of the growth of interest groups in Canadian society is the apparent fostering of private selfishness at the expense of some sense of civic virtue, good citizenship or whatever else you would like to call it. We have all been regaled on the evening news or in the press by spokespeople for some interest or other who proclaim loudly that they do not care what the problems of government or other groups are. They want what they want and to hell with everyone else. The problem is that no society can survive such an attitude. As most people have noticed, the social fabric in Canada has developed quite a few tears for just this reason. A further problem is that there is simply no way of governing any country which has no sense of a larger national interest.

Constant Conflict

If interest group leaders get and keep their power as a result of their ability to represent and fight for the group which they represent in the face of problems and conflict, there is a danger that these same leaders may try to create or perpetuate problems. In short, leaders of groups have a vested interest in preventing the resolution of the problems of their members.

Take the question of racism. Now it is true that racism is an unacceptable practice and a terrible evil that takes away the humanity of both oppressor and victim. At the same time, there seems to be some possibility that there are large number of people — interest group leaders, members of Human Rights Commissions, civil servants in departments concerned with the problems of race relations — that have enormous motivation never to see improvement. When the problem is perceived to go away, these people will suffer. They will lose their jobs and the status and power that go with their position. The recent discovery of the concept of "systematic discrimination" may be an example. Recent studies have indicated that the incidence of overt acts of racial discrimination and violence have dropped dramatically, but just as overt discrimination has fallen off, interest groups leaders, academics, members of human rights commissions and royal commissions have developed the concept of an unintended and subtle form of racial discrimination that only they seem to be able to identify. This, we are told, is probably even worse than the form which has been defeated. It does not seem overly cynical to suppose that this is the best news that these people have heard in years. Their jobs have been saved by the bell. My prediction is that when affirmative action programs have been instituted and the natural process of assimilation and acculturation have dealt with this form of discrimination the same people will suddenly discover some even more subtle form of injustice. We can be certain of a future constant stream of crises in race relations for the foreseeable future, each one more subtle and harder to identify than the one before.

Corruption

There is a pleasant myth in Canadian politics that corruption is virtually non-existent. As we have seen again and again, corruption has existed as a serious problem throughout history and continues to be a major problem. Because of the way in which elections work and the things which politicians have to do to stay in power, it seems unlikely that we are going to see an end to the wide-scale patronage and pork barrelling which is rampant in Canada at all levels. These practices may not, by and large, be illegal but they are certainly immoral and dishonest. They cheat the people of jobs and resources that are theirs by right. It is a form of fraud, and one of the most terrible results is the creation of a horrible cynicism among citizens. Joe Clark, one politician widely known for his past honesty (some might say naivete) remarked of the 1984 election that he had never seen so much cynicism in his political career and that he would probably not run the next time if the situation had not improved. Given the initial moves of the Mulroney government in the patronage and pork barrel fields, Joe had better start taking computer programming courses.

There is "hard core" political corruption in Canada — intentional conflict of interest, influence peddling, graft and bribery. There is criminal influence of government. The thing that makes me furious is that government refuses to charge those that it knows are guilty, and when they are charged, the courts let them off. At the same time the judges and courts convict shoplifters and other petty criminals and throw the key away. As the German folk expression goes, "They hang the little thieves. The big ones they let go."

How you view the above depends on two things: whether you are profiting from the existing system and whether you have a strong stomach. If you profit from the existing system, you doubtless think that all of the above is rubbish. The same goes for the folks not easily driven to nausea. For the rest of us — the vast majority of Canadians — this can only add up to one thing. Democracy is in serious trouble in Canada.

15

What Is To Be Done?

Here are some ideas that, if followed, could go a long way toward correcting the present injustices and inequities:

1. *Obey and enforce existing laws.* There are laws on the books that if enforced would go a long way toward curbing the corrupt practices that occur in the political arena and in the operation of government. Politicians who are found in contravention of guidelines or legislation should be removed from office and prosecuted to the full extent of the law. Politicians and government officials caught engaging in influence peddling should be investigated by law enforcement agencies so as to provide evidence that would permit successful prosecution. A sincere effort should be made by authorities to obtain prosecutions. No more half-hearted efforts or laying charges under the wrong sections of the law.

When government officials and politicians are found guilty they should be punished severely. It is ridiculous that there is a mild and weakly enforced law for people in power or the rich and another which is severely applied to those convicted of non-political offenses (like robbery, fraud, tax evasion and so on). The law must not only be fair but must be seen to be fair. The same goes for other crimes like bribery, graft, election fraud and acceding to influence from criminal elements.

2. *Strengthen existing laws.* Present laws, particularly those dealing with influence peddling and conflict of interest, are inadequate. Some of the inability to prosecute or take action against those involved in very flagrant forms of conflict of interest results from ambiguities in the various laws dealing with the activity. Furthermore, instead of the relaxation of conflict of interest rules or "cooling off" periods for government officials as suggested in the whitewash report submitted by Messrs. Sharp and Starr, rules should be made more strict. When politicians and those in high office wink or thumb their noses at the law, it results in a general decline in public respect for law. People

reason that if the "big shots" can get away with obvious scams then why not them? Why not indeed?

3. Stop widespread patronage and pork-barrelling activities by political parties. The activities of the political parties in financing their activities make a mockery of anyone's concept of honesty and fair play. Filling jobs with incompetents whose only assets are their political loyalty and large contributions to party coffers hamstrings the effectiveness of the crown corporations, boards and commissions on which they serve. Worse yet, it creates a cynicism toward politics among the general population that ensures that honest and high-minded citizens will stay away from seeking political office, leaving the field to scoundrels and rogues.

Other ways must be found for financing and fighting election campaigns apart from contests which are won by those who spend the most money and then owe the most political favours to the rich and powerful in our society.

4. Government should stop manipulating interest groups. Let the voice of the people and the needs of various sections of the population be heard clearly without trying to force them into acting as mouthpieces or puppets for government. Let all be heard, not just those who support government policy, or who come from similar class or social backgrounds as upper level bureaucrats and politicians.

5. Government should stop playing games with the funding of interest groups. The government should fund all groups or none. At present it uses funding as a way of ensuring that only some groups will be heard and funds groups it dislikes (when it does) in such a way as to ensure that once an election is over they will die from lack of money. Apparently, this is the case with grass-roots women's organizations that have the misfortune of being a little too radical for government's taste or take a different line on social policy and goals.

If the government were to decide to fund all groups so as to allow a full and balanced picture of what our society is *really* about it might consider adding the following to its list of clients:

   a. grass-roots women's organizations.
   b. non-feminist or anti-feminist organizations.
   c. radical feminist organizations.
   d. groups opposing multiculturalism.

Radical group extreme od jb wow (handwritten annotation)

e. those groups who oppose the present bilingualism policy, not only English language groups but also Quebec separatist groups. Both these sets of groups have perspectives shared by large segments of the Canadian population.

f. groups on the left or right who are more radical than government finds fashionable. These groups have their truths too.

My own preference is for a major reining in of government funding for interest groups. The only result of the present funding of interest groups is manipulation and a further strengthening of the status quo by mobilizing support for the government and official policies.

6. *Government should stop engaging in propaganda campaigns.* The present government should follow up on its elimination of the Canadian Unity Information Office to make a thorough housecleaning of its media and advertising. It should cut back on its advocacy advertising budget. It is ridiculous that the federal and provincial governments should be some of the largest advertisers in the country. Let them stand on their records instead of trying to manipulate the public. It should restrict the activities of the CBC, the NFB and other organs to providing balanced information rather than a soapbox for their employees' peculiar hobby horses and pet peeves. Obvious first steps would be to insist that Radio Canada provide the occasional pro-federalist program and that the NFB Studio D do films that are not potboilers for feminism. An interesting project for them might be to do a pro-Joe Borowski film to accompany their film on Dr. Morgentaler.

7. *No more secret deals.* One of the things that we have observed is that very frequently there are friendly telephone calls by "individuals of stature." Let us all have an equal chance to put our case before government. Let decisions be made on the basis of merit, not on the basis of birth or connections.

8. *Let labour be heard as well as business interests.* One thing that is crystal clear is that the representatives of labour and working class interests do not get heard. Part of this is because of the composition of government or the debts that are owed to rich contributors. Another part of this is that labour lobbyists do not look, sound or act like the lawyer-politicians and bureaucrats who run this country. All the more reason to hear what they have to say. It might be a nice change for members of the government to hear views that are a bit different from

what they and their sycophants claim to hold. Besides, labour leaders are probably more representative of large chunks of the population than are the politicians.

9. Parliament should pass a law requiring lobbyists to register and declare for whom and what they are working. This is not to say that there is anything wrong with lobbies and lobbyists. In some ways they are helpful and functional. They provide the government and bureaucracy with valuable information, often of a technical nature that is critical and which cannot be obtained elsewhere. Let's just clarify and regularize the situation. This is part of the earlier recommendation of no secret deals. Let's find out who is working for whom, on what. Then everyone has a better chance of a fair shake.

10. Eliminate the Senate. It is obscene that taxpayers should have to pay for the upkeep of lobbyists for society's fat cats. They are busy, but not on our behalf. Their work in emasculating the Combines Investigation Bill and restricting competition in banking in the past is a black mark on an already black record. Add its role as a patronage plum for the most notorious bagmen and party hacks in the country, and it is clear that every dollar spent on the upkeep of the Senate and Senators is a dollar spent to promote special interest and public despair.

What is *really* going on in the Canadian political system is not a pretty picture. It is not pleasant to read about. Still, that is the way it is and we might as well know the truth. By now some, especially those interest groups whose oxes were gored, are probably furious. As the saying goes, the truth hurts. But the activities of these same groups are hurting millions of Canadians every day, and the pain of these millions of Canadians counts for more than the hurt feelings of selfish lobbyists, corrupt politicians and bloated Senators.

Apart from criticizing the existing system of graft and undue influence, I have tried to promote a few simple ideas: that politicians and civil servants should act in an honest and public-spirited manner; that interest groups should have an equal chance of presenting their cases to government; that government should allocate resources on the basis of the merits of each case, the needs of the Canadian people and a wider national interest; that government should not allocate resources because the supplicants possess money and power solely because of some accident of birth or because they bought the politicians through huge political contributions; that laws concerning political and administrative behaviour should be fair and enforced without fear or favour; that the trend to devaluing the individual and emphasizing groups should be reversed and that government's purpose should be to promote the welfare of the nation and its citizens, not to enrich and empower a selfish and power-hungry few.

That is what I expect of government. That is what I suspect every honest Canadian expects. That's not too much to ask, is it?

NOTES

Chapter 2

1. A. Leblond De Brumath, *Bishop Laval* in the Makers of Canada series (Toronto: Morang & Co., Limited, 1906), p. 113.
2. *Documents Relating to the Colonial History of the State of New York,* quoted in Gustavus Myers, *A History of Canadian Wealth* (Toronto: James Lewis & Samuel Publishers, 1972), p. 13.
3. *Ibid.,* p. 6.
4. George Bryce, *The Remarkable History of the Hudson's Bay Company . . .* (Toronto: William Briggs, 1910), p. 15.
5. J. C. Langelier, *List of Lands Granted by the Crown in the Province of Quebec, 1763 to 1890,* quoted in Myers, *A History of Canadian Wealth,* p. 65.
6. *Ibid.*
7. *Ibid.,* p. 66.
8. Public Archives of Canada, Annual Report 1899, Note D. — Political State of Upper Canada in 1806, No. 26 — Judge Thorpe to Sir George Shee (Canadian Archives, Series Q, Vol. 305, p. 189), p. 57.
9. *Ibid.*
10. John George Lambton, 1st Earl of Durham, 1792-1840, *Report on the Affairs of British North America from the Earl of Durham* (Montreal, 1839), p. 56.
11. *Ibid.,* p. 85.
12. Report on Canadian Archives 1892, Note C, "Ecclesiastical Affairs in Lower Canada," p. 17.
13. Myers, *A History of Canadian Wealth,* p. 75.
14. Adam Shortt, *Lord Sydenham* in the Makers of Canada series, p. 251.
15. Letter No. 13 to G. W. Cass Esq. (Montreal, July 1, 1872) from Hugh Allan. *Ibid.,* p. 212.
16. Journals of the House of Commons of Canada, 2nd Session, Second Parliament, 1873, Appendix (No. 1), p. 144.
17. Larry Zolf, "In defence of political patronage," *Toronto Star,* August 19, 1984, p. F4.
18. Quoted in Herbert F. Quinn, "Quebec: Corruption Under Duplessis," in *Political Corruption in Canada: Cases, Causes and Cures,* ed. Kenneth M. Gibbons and Donald C. Rowat (Toronto: McClelland & Stewart, 1976) p. 71.

Chapter 3

1. James Gillies and Jean Pigott, "Participation in the Legislative Process," *Canadian Public Administration*, Vol. 25, No. 2 (Summer 1982), p. 260.
2. Robert Stevens, "Lobbyists a Big Cog in Ottawa Economy," *Ottawa Journal*, May 8, 1980, p. 29.
3. Canada, House of Commons, Bill C-22, "An Act to Register Lobbyists" (Ottawa: Fourth Session, Thirtieth Parliament, October 30, 1978).
4. Bill Gillies, "The issue is political honesty and not freedom of speech," *Toronto Star*, July 14, 1984.
5. Aubrey Golden, "Pandora's box opened on election spending?" *Globe and Mail*, July 17, 1984, p. 7.
6. Jackie Smith, "Trudeau's fighter eyeing role as MP," *Toronto Star*, March 29, 1984, p. D1.
7. *Ibid.*
8. *Ibid.*
9. Hon. Michael Starr and Hon. Mitchell Sharp, *Ethical Conduct in the Public Sector: Report of the Task Force on Conflict of Interest* (Ottawa, Supply and Services Canada, 1984).
10. Henry Jacek, "John Munro and the Hamilton East Liberals: Anatomy of a Modern Political Machine," in *Their Town: The Mafia, the Media and the Party Machine*, ed. Bill Freeman and Marsha Hewitt (Toronto: James Lorimer & Company, 1979), p. 65.
11. Thomas Walkom, "'Of course there's patronage' in appointments, Munro says," *Globe and Mail*, July 2, 1974, p. 1.
12. Maggie Siggins, *Bassett* (Toronto: James Lorimer & Company, 1979), p. 131.
13. Starr and Sharp, *Ethical Conduct in the Public Sector*, pp. 34–49.

Chapter 4

1. Quoted in Alan Phillips, "Graft in Civic Office," in *Political Corruption in Canada: Cases, Causes and Cures*, ed. Kenneth M. Gibbons and Donald C. Rowat (Toronto: McClelland and Stewart, 1976), p. 94.
2. *Ibid.*
3. Donald Higgins, "Progressive City Politics and the Citizen Movement: A Status Report," *City Magazine Annual, 1981* (Toronto), pp. 87-88.
4. J. E. Rea, "Parties and Power: Analysis of the Winnipeg City Council 1919–1975," Appendix IV to the *Tareska Report*, Winnipeg, 1976.
5. Matthew J. Kiernan and David C. Walker, "Winnipeg" in *City Politics in Canada*, ed. Warren Magnusson and Andrew Sancton (Toronto: University of Toronto Press, 1983), p. 235.
6. Elizabeth Amer, *Yes We Can! How to Organize Citizen Action* (Ottawa: Synergistics Consulting Limited, 1983), p. 79.

7. Beverly Bowen, "Bureaucrats dine high on hog," *Globe and Mail*, October 26, 1984, p. 1.
8. Susan A. Fish, "Winning the Battle and Losing the War in the Fight to Improve Municipal Policy Making" in *Politics and Government of Urban Canada*, ed. Lionel D. Feldman and Michael D. Goldrick (Toronto: Methuen, 1976), pp. 181–83.

Chapter 5

1. Jean Buy Lague, "One Step Forward, Two (Three?) Steps Back!" in *The City and Radical Social Change*, ed. Dimitrios Roussopoulos (Montreal: Black Rose Books, 1982), p. 176.
2. R. Kendall, "Encounter," *London Free Press*, May 20, 1984.
3. Minutes of the CUSO Annual General Meeting, December 5 and 6, 1981.
4. "Tomorrow: Only a Day Away," *CUSO Forum*, Spring/Summer 1981.

Chapter 6

1. Ian Pearson, "Citizen Brown: Has the Embattled Middle Class Picked Colin Brown to Voice Its Fears?" in *The City and Radical Social Change*, ed. Dimitrios Roussopoulos (Montreal: Black Rose Books, 1982), p. 10.
2. Michael Wilson, Excerpts from a speech at the founding meeting of the Toronto East European PC Association, quoted in *Decision '84* (election leaflet published by PC Canada Fund), p. 1.
3. Val Sears, "Canadians of far right plot their revolution," *Toronto Star*, December 11, 1984, p. A10.
4. Michael McAteer, "U.S. 'Holy Terror' not likely here observers say." *Toronto Star*, March 17, 1984.
5. Sears, "Canadians of far right plot. . . ."
6. "Citizens' coalition a threat to democracy, MP says," *Toronto Star*, December 19, 1984, p. A10.

Chapter 7

1. Margaret Frenette, Letter to the Editor, *Canadian Forum*, August/September 1984, p. 5.
2. Michael McAteer, "Carter attacks report on women," *Toronto Star*, October 25, 1984, p. A1.
3. *Ibid.*
4. *Ibid.*
5. Jackie Smith, "MPs ignore feminism at own peril," *Toronto Star*, March 12, 1984, p. B3.

6. Frank Jones, "3 million women don't have one voice," *Toronto Star*, April 10, 1984, p. A13.
7. *Ibid.*
8. Smith, "MPs ignore feminism . . . ," p. B1.
9. "REAL Women of Canada refused grant," *Campaign Life News*, January 1985.

Chapter 8

1. Larry Zolf, "The cultural and political explosion of Jewish talent in the Trudeau era," *Toronto Star*, October 14, 1984, p. 9.
2. Richard Dildy, "*Toronto Sun* — moral disaster," *Contrast*, July 13, 1984, p. 8.
3. Joan Breckenridge, "Jewish group, paper reach accord over alleged anti-Semitic articles," *Globe and Mail*, July 18, 1984, p. M5.
4. Joe Serge, "Canada's like a pizza, says ethnic council chief," *Toronto Star*, February 7, 1977, p. A6.
5. David Vienneau, "PM must apologize to Italians, MP says," *Toronto Star*, December 15, 1984, p. A4.
6. *Ibid.*
7. "Sharp promises top jobs to Italians," *Toronto Star*, February 25, 1974, p. 9.
8. Joe Serge, "Loyalty, cash at stake as rivals woo Italians," *Toronto Star*, April 7, 1979, p. C4.
9. Joe Serge, "New Italian president aims to improve group's image," *Toronto Star*, August 1, 1983, p. A9.
10. "Metro council denounces CBC series," *Globe and Mail*, April 11, 1979, p. 5.
11. Dick Chapman, "CBC flayed for anti-Arab bias," *Toronto Sun*, April 8, 1984, p. 55.
12. *Ibid.*
13. "Anti-Semitism must still be fought, cleric says," *Toronto Star*, December 13, 1984.
14. James Rusk, "Invitation to PLO creates a furor," *Globe and Mail*, April 4, 1984, p. 1.
15. Robert Matas, "Heritage language program meets the expectations of backers, foes," *Globe and Mail*, February 15, 1984, p. 4.
16. *Ibid.*
17. *Ibid.*
18. *Ibid.*
19. Ross Howard, "Ethnic publishers fear favouritism in federal advertising," *Toronto Star*, February 22, 1984, p. A13.
20. *Ibid.*

21. Trish Crawford, "Rae says politicking behind lower grants to immigrant groups," *Toronto Star*, February 28, 1984, p. A18.
22. Joe Serge, "Italian Canadians form federation," *Toronto Star*, February 21, 1974, p. B3.
23. Laureano Leone, "National Congress of Italian Canadians" in "Briefs on Multiculturalism in the Next Five Years" (Unpublished paper presented to Third Canadian Conference on Multiculturalism, Ministry of State, Multiculturalism, 1979).

Chapter 9

1. Dalton Camp, "How bilingual bigots almost felled federalism," *Toronto Star*, November 14, 1979, p. A18.
2. Robert Matas, "Francophones fear financing threatens French high schools," *Globe and Mail*, December 6, 1984, p. M4.
3. Lynn Herzeg, "The New Face of English Quebec," *Canadian Forum*, August/September 1984, p. 10.
4. *Ibid.*
5. Robert McKensie, "Not afraid of violence, anglo maverick says," *Toronto Star*, April 18, 1979, p. 10.
6. Dan Smith, "NDP avoids party split over language question," *Toronto Star*, Feburary 20, 1984, p. A8.
7. "Fired over French, worker complains," *Globe and Mail*, November 17, 1984, p. 11.
8. "'Manitoba will pay,' Hatfield warns," *Toronto Star*, March 2, 1984, p. A13.
9. Kathryn Clark, "N.B. language hearings criticized as stalling tactic," *Globe and Mail*, September 19, 1984, p. 4.
10. Michael Harris, "Language pot close to boil," *Globe and Mail*, December 21, 1984, p. 8.
11. *Ibid.*
12. Michael Harris, "N.B. language proposals kindle fear," *Globe and Mail*, December 19, 1984, p. 13.
13. Robert Matas, "Bilingualism is resented by French, study says," *Globe and Mail*, January 5, 1982, p. 5.
14. "Northern natives caught off guard by French plan," *Toronto Star*, March 20, 1984, p. A8.
15. Ross Laver, "Sports funds threatened over bilingualism," *Globe and Mail*, February 18, 1984, p. 1.

Chapter 10

1. John Brehl, "Tape states Munro 'started whole thing' harbor trial told," *Toronto Star*, May 31, 1975, p. 1.
2. Olivia Ward, "Running for office can be costly, businessmen say," *Toronto Star*, August 6, 1984.
3. Robert Bothwell and William Kilbourn, *C. D. Howe: A Biography* (Toronto: McClelland and Stewart, 1979), p. 262.
4. Charlotte Gray, "Friendly Persuasion: A New type of Lobbyist Is Speaking to Ottawa on Behalf of the Private Sector — and Ottawa is Listening," *Saturday Night*, March 1983, p. 14.
5. Ian Middleton, "Thomas d'Aquino: The Voice of Business in the Halls of Power," *Canadian Business*, March 1983, p. 17.
6. Gray, "Friendly Persuasion," p. 14.
7. John M. Godfrey, quoted in James Gillies, *Where Business Fails* (Montreal: Institute for Research on Public Policy, 1981), p. 68.
8. Robert Presthus, *Elite Accommodation in Canadian Politics* (New York: Cambridge University Press, 1973), p. 168.
9. Fred Thompson and W. T. Stanbury, *The Political Economy of Interest Groups in the Legislative Process in Canada* (Montreal: Institute for Research on Public Policy, 1979), p. 36.
10. *Ibid.*
11. *Ibid.*, p. 3.
12. Colin Campbell, *The Canadian Senate: A Lobby from Within* (Toronto: Macmillan, 1978).
13. *Ibid.*, p. 12.
14. *Ibid.*, p. 14.
15. *Ibid.*, p. 19.
16. Quoted in Duncan McDowell, ed., *Advocacy Advertising: Propaganda or Democratic Right?* (Ottawa: Conference Board of Canada, 1982), p. 64.
17. *Ibid.*, p. 68.
18. "Ottawa said to give IBM an unfair advantage," *Toronto Star*, June 22, 1984.

Chapter 11

1. Quoted in Alan Phillips, "Graft in Civic Office," in *Political Corruption in Canada: Causes, Cases and Cures*, ed. Kenneth M. Gibbons and Donald C. Rowat (Toronto: McClelland and Stewart, 1976), p. 103.
2. *Ibid.*
3. *Ibid.*
4. A.A. Rogow and H.D. Lasswell, "The Definition of Corruption," in *Political Corruption: Readings in Comparative Analysis*, ed. Arnold J. Heidenheimer (New York: Transaction Books, 1970), p. 54.

5. Quoted in James C. Scott, *Comparative Political Corruption* (Englewood Cliffs, N.J.: Prentice-Hall, 1972).

6. *Ibid.*

7. Peter Bruton et al., "Graft Never Hurt a Politician At the Polls," in *Political Corruption in Canada*, ed. Gibbons and Rowat, p. 225.

8. Quoted in Walter Stewart, *Divide and Con: Canadian Politics at Work* (Toronto: New Press, 1973), p. 159.

9. Don Braid, "Tories are made-over Liberals," *Toronto Star*, October 2, 1984.

10. Larry Zolf, *Survival of the Fattest: An Irrelevant View of the State* (Toronto: Key Porter Books, 1984), p. 69.

11. Alan Christie and Rick Haliechuk, "Taylor dismisses influence-buying claim by landlord," *Toronto Star*, October 24, 1984.

12. *Ibid.*

13. *Ibid.*

14. *The Federal Effort Against Organized Crime.* Hearings held before a subcommittee of the committee on government administration, Part I. (Washington, D.C., 1967). Quoted in Bill Freeman, "The Hamilton Mob and the Politics of Organized Crime," in *Their Town*, ed. Freeman and Hewitt, p. 86.

15. *Crime, Justice and Society* (Report of the Commission of Inquiry into the Administration of Justice on Criminal and Penal Matters in Quebec), Vol. 3 (Quebec: Government of Quebec), p. 20.

Chapter 12

1. Maggie Siggins, *Bassett* (Toronto: James Lorimer and Company, 1979), p. 227.

2. *Ibid.*

3. George Grant, *Lament for a Nation* (Toronto: McClelland and Stewart, 1965), p. 19.

4. Conrad Winn, "Mass Communication," in *Political Parties in Canada*, ed. Conrad Winn and John McMenemy (Toronto: McGraw-Hill Ryerson, 1976), p. 134.

5. Grant, *Lament for a Nation*, p. 19.

6. Siggins, *Bassett*, p. 200.

7. *Ibid.*

8. Walter Stewart, "The Crazy Rat Syndrome," in *Canadian Newspapers: The Inside Story*, ed. Walter Stewart, (Edmonton: Hurtig, 1980), p. 121.

9. Winn, "Mass Communication," p. 132.

10. Frank Jones, "Day after day . . . the media is the feminist message," *Toronto Star*, November 5, 1984, p. A13.

11. Toba Korenblum, "Minefield loaded with laughs," *Globe and Mail*, November 15, 1984.

12. Katie Ford, "Women and Comedy" (Letter to the editor), *Globe and Mail*, December 1, 1984, p. 7.

13. Jones, "Day after day. . . ."

14. Winn, "Mass Communication," p. 137.

15. Dominique Clift, "French Journalism in Quebec: Solidarity on a Pedestal," in *Canadian Newspapers*, ed. Stewart, p. 214.

16. *Ibid.*, p. 218.

Chapter 14

1. Robert Presthus, *Elite Accommodation in Canadian Politics* (New York: Cambridge University Press, 1973), p. 175.

2. *Ibid.*